£8.95

INSTRUCTIONS
to
YOUNG SPORTSMEN

Sketched by J. Childe. Engraved by H. Adlard. & Published by Longman & C°. 1830.

INSTRUCTIONS

TO

YOUNG SPORTSMEN

IN

ALL THAT RELATES TO

GUNS AND SHOOTING.

BY

LT COL. P. HAWKER.

THE FIELD
LIBRARY

SEVENTH EDITION,

CORRECTED, ENLARGED, AND IMPROVED:

WITH EXPLANATORY PLATES AND WOOD CUTS.

Southampton
Ashford Press Publishing
1986

Published by **Ashford Press Publishing** 1986
1 Church Road, Shedfield, Hampshire. SO3 2HW

First published 1833 (Longman, Rees, Orme, Brown, Green and Longman)
Reprinted 1971 (The Richmond Publishing Company)
Reprinted 1986 (Ashford Press Publishing)

British Library Cataloguing in Publication Data

Hawker, P.
Instructions to young sportsmen in all that relates to guns and shooting. – 7th ed., corr., enl. and improved – (The Field Library)
1. Shooting
I. Title II. Series
799.2'13 GV1153

ISBN 0-907069-36-3

Printed and bound in Great Britain.

TO

HIS MOST EXCELLENT MAJESTY

WILLIAM THE FOURTH

THIS ATTEMPT

TO INSTRUCT THE RISING GENERATION IN AN ART FOR WHICH WE HAVE LONG BEEN THE FIRST NATION IN THE WORLD, AND AN EXERCISE ACKNOWLEDGED AS BEING CALCULATED TO INVIGORATE US FOR THE SERVICE OF OUR KING AND COUNTRY,

IS

WITH GRACIOUS PERMISSION

MOST RESPECTFULLY DEDICATED

BY

HIS MAJESTY'S EVER DUTIFUL SERVANT

AND

LOYAL SUBJECT

PETER HAWKER.

PREFACE.

THE original edition, which led to the publication of the following pages, was hastily written, at the particular request of some sporting friends of the Author, who had recourse to the press, in order to present each of them with a legible copy. A few supplementary impressions also were provided, for the amusement and instruction of the inexperienced sportsman, to whom, alone, he still presumes to offer so humble a production.

To prevent enlarging this work to an expensive publication, all needless embellishments have been studiously avoided. By thus omitting ornamental plates on the worn-out subjects of common shooting, useless anecdotes, and other extraneous matter, there is a saving of time to many, who would be better employed than in reading superfluous volumes, on a mere subject of recreation; as well as of expense to those who could not conveniently afford to purchase them.

Every thing here asserted has been the result of many years' trial and experience; and, therefore, all reference to other publications has been as much declined, as have statements from *report;* and it has been attempted to dilate *most,* on what has been the *least* explained by other authors.

So much, indeed, has been published, by more able writers, on *field sports* of every description, that little remains to be said on the subject. The pursuit of game is already too well known to require much instruction. The author has, therefore, thought it far better, instead of treating too copiously on that head, to give *particular directions* for (what *gentlemen least understand*) GETTING ACCESS TO WILD BIRDS OF EVERY DESCRIPTION.

With regard also to *guns,* and the various other subjects that form the remainder of the book, he has taken up his pen with the determination of neither borrowing, without proper acknowledgment, from other works, nor trusting to any thing from the experiments of other persons.

From having thus declined all assistance, and wholly confined himself to the limits of his own humble experience, he will have to apologize perhaps for some errors, and no doubt for many deficiencies. But even this, it is hoped, will make the work less objectionable than swelling its dimensions to an unreasonable size, by relating incidents that possibly never occurred, or commencing a system of piracy on other authors, which nothing should induce him to do, after the very flattering manner in which his former editions have been received by the Reviewers and the Public.

He now offers to their notice the seventh edition of this work, which has, of late, been in many parts materially altered and enlarged. The improvements here added have been the result of still further experience; and, therefore, may be considered, in some degree, as finishing lessons to those young sportsmen, who have before done him the honour to attend to his earlier instructions.

The original matter, however, on which no improvement happened to present itself, will, of course, remain as before, for the benefit of younger pupils in shooting. But every thing, which was written previously to the year 1816 that could be improved, up to the present year, has been introduced on a different, and, he trusts, a more perfect system.

All the new directions, which this work contains, have been first experimentally tried, and taken down, from time to time, in a pocket book; then detailed, as soon after as possible, in the most specific manner; and, before they were entered among these pages, abridged to about a tenth part of their original bulk, through consideration for the patience of the reader.

Some apology may, perhaps, be requisite for the abrupt style which this very abridgment occasions, as well as for the author having been so generally obliged to write in the first person. Dictatorial, however, as may appear the one, and egotistical as may be thought the other, yet it is presumed, that his colloquial style may not be objected to, when all circumstances are considered, by those persons who are most able to criticise, and who are invariably the most liberal judges.

Some apology too may be necessary for neglect of that ceremony, which the public have a right to expect from every author. But, while occupied in forming this work, it must candidly be confessed, that the writer could not divest himself of feeling rather as one conversing, without reserve, among his brother sportsmen, than as an author, whose work was going before a public tribunal.

The summit of his ambition, therefore, will be, to give some little additional knowledge to those for whom the work is intended; and his earnest hopes are, that these his further, and probably his last, efforts on the subject, will meet with that indulgence, which he has experienced on all former occasions.

⁎ As there will appear in this book some recipes which might fail, if the articles required for them should not be of the best quality, it has been thought necessary to give the names of a few tradesmen, whom the author has reason to hope may be depended on.

In a work of *this* kind, it requires more ingenuity than the writer can boast of, to avoid entirely those inimical appendages to reading —notes and parentheses. The frequent use of Italics, also, he is aware has an ugly appearance. But, nevertheless, they have before answered his object, which is to impress as strongly as possible on the memory of his young readers, those directions which require to be read with particular attention.

Painted by A. E. Chalon R.A. Engraved by H. Allard.

London. Published by Longman & C.o 1830.

LIST OF PLATES, &c.

CONTENTS.

* In writing on this subject, I have applied the word "*carronade;*" and, *if improperly,* it was, no doubt, through my "land-lubber"-like misunderstanding of naval friends, to whom I submitted the invention. For ships' *swivels,* the mode of easing the recoil, I think, may be adapted as here shown; but for *carronades,* it would, I presume, require a somewhat different construction.

GAME LAWS.

NEW GAME ACT.

OLD GAME LAWS NOT REPEALED.

GUNS AND GUNMAKERS.

THE great demand for this work having exhausted the third and fourth editions in so short a space of time, I was resolved that the printer's devil and I should have absolution from sporting subjects for at least a year or two, and therefore inflicted on my publishers a treble dose of copies; or, seriously speaking, I gave a very large impression of the fifth edition. About three years and a half had elapsed since that was in the press; and in this little time what a complete revolution took place in the sporting world! or at all events among the gunmakers!!—Joe Manton, the life and soul of the trade, obliged to dispose of all his valuable machinery, and sell off every thing in Hanover-square; then rallied at Marylebone Park-house, where all was again soon wreck and confusion; and the best workmen in the world left wandering about like a disbanded army!—Poor old Asell, the father of the working-trade, died in Marylebone hospital—his son started off as a regimental armourer—John Hussey, the flash borer of the age, obliged to fly, with his lathe, from the Philistines, and get a crust for his family where he could—the prince of lock-finishers, Penn, driven to do by-jobs for temporary subsistence,—and others condescending to go and work for masters who knew not half so much as themselves!

So much for the establishment of the only man whom any first-rate judge of work could consider as qualified for a leader, or king, among the gunmakers! Such was the *esprit de corps* among his men, that they rallied round him till the very last, rather than serve under any artist in whose abilities they had less confidence.

[It may perhaps be thought bad taste to speak about common journeymen. But I like to do justice to the *subs* as well as to the commander.]

The sixth edition (consisting of 1500 copies) being now sold off, I am this moment unexpectedly called on for a seventh: but here there is little to add on the subject of gunmakers; except that poor old Egg is dead, and succeeded by his son John. Instead, however, of his "cutting up fat," as was expected, he died like a man of genius; or, in other words, with his balance on the shady side of the book!—The gunmakers, in short, remain, as I left them in 1830—like the frogs without a king; and, as before, complaining bitterly about the dulness of trade. But for this they have to thank their introduction of the detonating system, by which they got caught themselves in the very trap that was laid for their customers. When *flint*-guns were the order of the day, few sporting gentlemen of distinction ever thought of using any thing but the gun of a first-rate maker, for the simple reason that—on the *goodness of the work* depended the *quickness in firing*, and consequently the *filling of the bag*. But, *now-a-days*, every common fellow in a market town can detonate an old musket, and make it shoot as quick as can be wished; insomuch that all scientific calculations in shooting, *at moderate distances,* are now so simplified that we, every day, meet with jackanapes-apprentice-boys who can shoot flying, and knock down their eight birds out of ten. Formerly shooting required *art and nerve*—now, for tolerable shooting (at all events for the use of *one* barrel) *nerve alone* is sufficient. Formerly a first-rate gun was a *sine quâ non;* now, the most that we can call it is a *desideratum;* since all guns are now made to fire with nearly equal velocity. Still, however, fortunately for the leading gunmakers, there are yet left many requisites which induce good sportsmen, though a much smaller number than formerly, to go to the heads of the trade: viz. 1. soundness and perfect safety in guns; 2. the barrels being correctly put together for accurate shooting; 3. the elevation being mathematically true, and *raised strictly in proportion to the length of barrel;* and 4. the stock being properly cast off to the eye, and well fitted to the *hand and* shoulder. I say nothing of the balance, because any good carpenter, with some lead and a centre-bit, can regulate this to the shooter's fancy.

Who is now to be called the leading gunmaker I hardly know, and there are so many competitors for the title, that it would be an unthankful office to name any one in particular. Mr. Manton and Son, in partnership with Mr. Hudson, carry on the old-established house, at No. 6, Dover-street, in the best possible manner. Mr. Purdey has, at this moment, perhaps the first business in London, and no man better deserves it. I once asked Joe Manton whom he considered the best maker in town (of course excepting himself); and his answer was, "Purdey gets up the best work, next to mine." This was when Purdey occupied a small shop in Princes-street.

Lancaster, who has raised many gunmakers to the head of the trade by allowing them to put their names to what was his work in all the essential part of barrels, has some time since started for himself. This I advised him to do if ever Joe retired; and I anticipate that he will, sooner or later, be entitled to the name of leader, vice Joseph Manton. I recommended to him, for an assistant, Mr. Long, who was formerly a master at Andover, and who has a head little inferior to that of Joseph himself. Mr. Wilkinson, jun., an artist of great mechanical talent, has bid adieu to the smoke of the city, and started, with his father, in great force at the west end, where he appears to have every thing in the first style. Mr. Nock, Mr. Moore, Mr. Smith, and it would be endless to say how many others, are now quite *au fait* in the detonating system of gunmaking.—Also Mr. William Moore, who was an old hand at Joe's, and knew, to a hair, how to fit a man's shoulder with a gun. I have often stood over him when he was a journeyman, and no man better pleased me with a job. Depend on it he will do well, and get to the top of the tree; though, like a wise fellow, he starts carefully at first, by feeling his way at a small place, instead of jumping into a "swell" residence, and from that into gaol; as many people, both in and out of trade, are now-a-days so frequently doing. "Billy Moore" is a right-hand man with the "knobs," or crack pigeon-shooters, and their patronage is a host in itself towards a good lift in business. Though I have said this of Moore, I never dealt with him, because, for my own part, I prefer Lancaster's guns to any others in London.

[Since the sixth edition, Moore's business has increased more, in proportion, than that of any other maker in town. This proves that I have not been a false prophet.]

Westley Richards is quite the star of Birmingham, with more business than ever; and his Bond-street agent, Uncle Bishop, is now perhaps the first man in London to serve all gentlemen who want a good gun at a few hours' notice. Buying a ready-made gun at a respectable shop, is cheaper and better than going to an inferior maker, by reason that, instead of waiting six months for one, which, after all, you might not be pleased with, you may here at once suit yourself, and, *sometimes*, full as well as if you had spared no expense. You should, however, first try and examine it, as the gunmakers themselves, as well as the broken-down gentry, are frequently obliged to have a little commerce with pawnbrokers.

Parsons, of Salisbury, stands as high as ever in the west of England, and many of the country makers are giving great satisfaction. So much for the detonating system. What a change from the time of Joe when he lived in Davies-street! In *those days* we had but *one* gunmaker—now they are "*all*—ALL" gunmakers!!!

Within these very few years the detonators have been much improved in shooting, in consequence of their being bored differently from flint-guns. *They now detain the shot longer in the barrel, in order that the powder may have time to kindle*, which is done to such a degree as to occasion an increase of recoil, and a liability to become "leaded" with much firing. Many waddings have been invented to counteract this, and I shall hereafter speak of them in another part of the book, as they have their merits; but still none of them will make a detonater, of *equal weight with*, shoot quite so strong and regular as a flint-gun. Though, like the rest of the sporting world, I have long been kidnapped into the constant use of detonaters, still I have no reason to alter the opinion I gave in 1822; and, were my time to come over again, I might probably be content with the flint; though I have of course, as every one does, shot more accurately, and missed fewer quick shots, with the detonater. But, to return more generally to the subject of all guns, let me observe, as before, in answer to those who deprecate the idea of giving a good price for a gun, that the workmen employed by the first makers require wages *and indulgence*, in proportion to their skill in the respective branches of the business; and it thereby becomes necessary to charge for the guns accordingly.

Many wiseacres abuse all the heads of the trade, and swear that they can *always ensure having the best of guns, at a quarter the price, from Birmingham!* This may be, provided a person has such good judgment, or interest there, as to get *picked workmen* for the *whole process* of his order; but, in *general*, the immense business carried on at this place is for the *wholesale line*, and only requires to be *in the rough;* from which circumstance the workmen are not so much in the *habit of finishing* as those employed daily for *that purpose.* Moreover, if there is a first-rate and enterprising workman, he hears of the high wages, and contrives to get off to London. I should, however, except those who work for Westley Richards.

But, as far as the judgment of some people goes, it

would certainly be a wanton extravagance to give more than fifteen pounds for a double, or eight for a single gun. I allude to those who, on being shown a superior one, would view it like a fossil or a picture; and, on being requested to "feel how fine the lock is," thrust their forefingers as far as they can into the guard, sticking up their thumbs as if going to be dressed for a wound, and often finish their inspection, by breaking one of your locks, and abusing the man who made them.

N. B. When I had before written thus far, I met Joe Manton, and he announced to me that he had set up again, at Burwood Place in the Edgeware Road, and was coming out with a *new patent,* that would "take the shine out of every thing hitherto invented, and show what fools all the gunmakers have been!!" But, as this remained to be proved, and as Joe would have had to recruit his fine army of workmen again before his promise could be carried into execution, I of course did not alter what I had then written on guns and gunmakers. Joe *did* make the attempt; but failed. Now, however, his son John is come home from India, and report says that he will set up in business, in which his father will be acting manager. But at this moment (I mean while I am now writing on the first sheet) Joe is actively employed in some clever inventions for government.

BARRELS.

I shall now proceed to the particulars of what a gun should be, and begin with the barrels.

The usual method of trying a barrel is to *fire at a single sheet of paper*, and pronounce, at once, that the one which puts in the *most* shot is *the best,* without considering any other circumstance.

Such a mistake is excusable in those, who merely take up a gun for exercise, or, at times, when they cannot hunt; but, that a person, who wishes to excel in shooting, and even a London gunmaker, should fall into the same error, argues as much against the judgment of the one, as the qualification for his business of the other.

In throwing shot from a barrel, closeness and strength cannot be combined beyond a certain proportion of each; and as, in either extreme, the one is incompatible with the other, the desideratum is for a gun to partake as much as possible of both advantages.

For example: how is the barrel made to throw shot *very* close? By a too long continued relief forward, without a proportional opening behind: this (from a want of that impetus, or friction, which the shot receive while passing through the *cylindrical* part of the caliber) makes the gun shoot so slow, that the sportsman often fires *behind* his game; and, of course, so *weak,* though well directed, that, instead of his birds *dying in the air,* they are brought down in a slovenly manner, and half of them escape being bagged, although their *skins* may *be filled with shot* enough to make a *brilliant display at a single sheet of paper.*

Many are apt to suppose, that, if a bird, killed by a long shot, has been struck with four or five pellets, their gun will always be *certain* of doing execution at the same distance, if properly directed. But so far is this from being the case, that it may proceed from the barrel throwing the grains in *patches,* and therefore being liable to let even fair shots escape through an interval.

Indeed, the effect of this mode of boring might be equally well produced by wetting the shot, or loading with very little powder, and elevating so as for nearly all the shot to *drop into* the mark (a common trick, when an old hand wishes to sell a gun to a cockney, or win the Christmas prize at an alehouse by shooting at a mark). But enough of imperfections; and now for what a barrel ought to be——

With the common-sized guns, which are now made for the sports of the field, the usual mode of boring is, to leave a *cylinder* for about *three-fourths* of the barrel (always taking care, in a FLINT-*gun*, but *not* in a *detonater*, to preserve *a little tightness* or *contraction just where the shot first moves*), and let the remaining part of the caliber be *gradually relieved to the muzzle.* For instance, suppose a barrel to be two feet eight inches long, we would say (beginning at the breech end) about six inches tight (if for a *flint*); twenty-one inches a cylinder; and the remaining five inches relieved to the muzzle. All this must be done with the most delicate possible gradation, and in so small a degree, that even some gunmakers can scarcely discover it. How natural then is it, that many sporting authors should be so far deceived, as to fancy the best guns are bored a true cylinder to the very muzzle, and, therefore, argue in its favour! This relief has the effect of making the gun shoot as close as it can do, compatibly with the strength and quickness required: which should, however, be increased as much as possible by the best-constructed breechings. But, with the new alteration, for short *detonaters*, a mere cylinder, or nearly so, with a few inches' relief forward, is now found to answer best;

and therefore we require more weight of metal, in order to ease the recoil of a charge that is longer detained in the barrel. Thus the detonating system simplifies the boring to the whole trade, as well as the art of killing to the shooter. With longer and heavier guns, we may take still further advantage, and have a little opening behind. All this relief must be given in a very *trifling degree;* because, should the barrel be too much opened in any part, it would admit of the powder escaping between the wadding and the sides of the caliber, by which the shooting of the gun would be rendered weak. For this reason, I should object to having a hole through the wadding that covers the *powder*, which many do to prevent, as they think, the confined air from resisting the ramrod; which it rarely does until after you have put in the *second* wadding.

A barrel with *flaws* has the same *disadvantage* of not *keeping the powder air-tight* from the shot. If, however, a barrel is *very short*, you are almost obliged to *reverse* the mode of boring in order to get strength by friction; consequently it *recoils*, and never answers so well.

For a *duck*-gun, or piece of any *considerable length*, the barrel should be bored so as to feel *more* and more *tight* on ramming *down* the wadding, particularly on coming just above where the shot lies; and with a very little opening, from where the shot lies, down to the breeching. This you will perceive, by a relief to the ramrod, just before the wadding reaches the *powder*. If, however, the gun is very long, you may then, of course, have the barrel further opened behind, in proportion to the length; and, thereby, give more force to the powder, which will enable you, with propriety, to extend the relief forward, and, by that means, get close shooting combined with strength. *This is the reason why long barrels may be made to shoot further than short ones.* Thus the shot has friction by being forced through the cylinder, and is then gradually relieved all the way *in going out;* and this more in proportion again as the shot leaves the muzzle. In a word, the shot should receive all the force of the powder while *tight in the barrel,* and then, as before observed, *go easier and easier all the way out of it.* This mode of boring is the best calculated for large wild-fowl guns, because the first friction makes them shoot *strong* (by means of giving due time to burn the powder), and yet with as much *ease,* as any caliber that can be made to answer that purpose.

In answer to many absurd arguments in favour of short guns, and observations about "lateral pressure," I shall here subjoin a schedule, in order to show how were bored the five best guns I ever saw fired, exemplifying how far they were from being bored a perfect cylinder, and therefore proving the absurdity of those arguments which are all grounded upon this mistake. Were a gun-barrel bored a true cylinder from end to end, it might shoot nearly, or quite, as well if two feet long as one of greater length, because a superfluity of what may be strictly called lateral pressure would do more harm than good, by checking, instead of assisting, the force of the charge. But to these two feet of cylinder let me add some more caliber, and that to consist of proper opening and relief, and then shoot the guns for a wager, and see how those new-discovery gentlemen would come off who have been holding forth to the public such nonsense in favour of short guns.

Cannons are bored a cylinder, because they are

generally used for firing *ball*, and therefore may be short: but how have they always thrown loose *shot?* Why, most miserably, till General Shrapnell invented his admirable shells that keep the charge together for a second explosion, which takes place a little before the shot has reached the object. It is one thing to speak of things plausibly, another to state them correctly.

In the following schedule I have taken three of the largest-sized guns, *because* a little sporting-gun is on so small a scale, that although the relief may be *felt* in a moment by passing a proper guage through the caliber, yet the barrel is so diminutive, that it would be difficult to measure, and *specify*, the exact *depth* of this relief.

N. B. If any gunmaker had candidly informed me as to his mode of boring barrels, I should have felt myself bound in honour never to divulge, much less to publish, the secret. But as the little knowledge I possess has been acquired by my own discovery, and proved by experiments to be correct, it becomes my own property; and as such therefore I have no further hesitation in presenting it to my readers.

A SINGLE SWIVEL-GUN.

Barrel made by Fullerd: average of bore, an inch and ½: weight of barrel 62lbs.

	Feet.	Inches.
Cylinder . . .	2	8
Relief . . .	4	1
Opened behind . .	0	6½
Total (exclusive of plug)	7	3½

Depth of cut.—Relieved to the 20th of an inch: opened behind to the 24th of an inch.

MY NEW DOUBLE SWIVEL-GUN (weight 193lbs.).

Barrels by Fullerd.

	Feet.	Inches.
Cylinder . .	2	9
Relief . . .	4	2
Opened behind . .	1	3
Total (exclusive of plugs)	8	2

DEPTH OF CUT.—The bore, in cylinder, an inch and $\frac{1}{2}$ *all but* a 32d: relief forward an inch and $\frac{1}{2}$ *and* a 32d (a 16th difference), and cut rather less deep behind than at the muzzle.

A SINGLE STANCHION-GUN.

Barrel 69lbs. (made in Birmingham.)

	Feet.	Inches.
Cylinder . . .	2	7
Relief . . .	4	4
Opened behind . .	0	10
Total . . .	7	9

DEPTH OF CUT.

Cylinder	inch and $\frac{1}{4}$	barely.
Relief		and a 16th.
Opened behind		and a 32d.

A SINGLE GUN.

(Musket bore and the average weight of a musket.)

	Feet.	Inches.
Cylinder . . .	1	$10\frac{1}{2}$
Relief . . .	1	0
Opened behind . .	0	$7\frac{1}{2}$
Total . . .	3	6

A COMMON FOURTEEN GAUGE DOUBLE GUN.

(Weight altogether $8\frac{1}{2}$lbs.: barrels by Lancaster.)

	Feet.	Inches.
Cylinder . .	1	9
Relief . . .	0	5
TIGHT *behind* . .	0	6
Total . . .	2	8

Q. Why is the common sporting-gun *tight* behind, when the other guns are *opened* behind?

A. Because a sporting-gun requires to be fired so many times in a day, that we must adopt an inferior mode of getting friction, in order to prevent the barrel from becoming *leaded;* and therefore to make it shoot, *through the whole day,* nearly as well as when clean, and without recoil to the shoulder. Again, a sporting-gun must, of necessity, be short, for the convenience of covert, and snap-shooting; and therefore the length that would properly suit that relief which must follow an opening behind (in order to prevent recoil, and preserve close shooting) would be generally objected to as an inconvenience.

[Here I allude only to flint-guns; as a detonater *must,* in a great degree, be *debarred* from this *advantage;* because, if too tight behind, without any subsequent check, *the powder would be blown away so quick as not to be half kindled.* This is the new discovery in boring for detonaters, which I before alluded to, and which has probably saved them from being wholly abandoned.]

Q. Suppose, then, you were to have your fourteen gauge barrels two feet ten inches, how would you dispose of the extra length?

A. I would have seven inches of relief instead of five, by which my shot would be thrown equally strong, and decidedly closer.

[On this proportion I ordered a gun for a friend, who writes to inform me that he has hitherto beat every gun he shot against. It is but justice to say that the maker was Mr. Westley Richards, who is considered, by many of our best sportsmen, as "*Joe Manton the second;*" and I should say deservedly so, from what I have *lately* seen of him and his work. Mr. Richards is really a scientific man; instead of having more tongue than brains, like many of our gunmaking charlatans. His barrels are as good as any in the world, being made of pure Holland stubs, and twisted in a manner best suited for service and for safety. Within these last two years Mr. Richards has run some of the best London makers so hard that they begin to wish him and his prime minister Bishop in—"another and a better world!"]

Gunmakers, who know their business, form their calibers more or less, according to circumstances, on the plans already stated; except those of *rifles*, and guns for firing *ball*, which must be regularly *tighter* all the way *out*, as with these we have no reason to fear the *want of strength*, or the risk of a *recoil*, and the only object is to keep the ball in the *straightest possible direction*, and regulate the barrel to the most accurate line of aim. This should be done by having the gun of the *utmost length* that can be used, and steadied by *immense substance* and *weight of metal*.

While speaking of rifles, I must not omit to mention two of the finest pieces of mechanism of the present age—Mr. Purdey's *double* rifles, and Mr. Lancaster's new-invented machine for rifling barrels. But to say what is here due to these excellent artists might lead me into a detail that would exceed my intended limits.

The *farther* the sight at the *breech is placed* from *that near the muzzle,* the more *accurate,* of course, *must be the line of aim;* and the *heavier the gun,* the more likely you will be to *preserve it in firing.*

With regard to having a barrel *too* far opened forward, when left with mere cylinder behind, and the various tricks that are played to ease the explosion, for the sole purpose of throwing the shot as close as possible, it will be needless to trespass on the reader's patience.

Though a barrel, bored as before mentioned, will not shoot quite so close as it might be made to do, yet, taking every thing into consideration, it has the tenfold advantage of *doing justice to a good shot,* and even *assisting a bad one,* by the irresistible force given, *not only* to the *body of the charge,* but also to the *pellets, which fly wide of the mark.* Let the sportsman, therefore, rest assured, that a gun, which will shoot sufficiently close a surface to ensure two or three shot (of No. 7, at forty yards) taking the body of a bird, and, at the same time, distribute them in a *regular manner,* is better than a *very* close shooting gun. It was formerly the custom to make barrels, although so small as fourteen, sixteen, or even two-and-twenty in the gauge, of three or four feet in length; and now, since it has been ascertained that two feet six inches will shoot equally well, at the short distance of a gunmaker's confined premises, many have gone *too much* to the *other extreme,* and cut them to two feet four inches, and less. The disadvantage of this is, that even the best shots are more liable to miss; for, although we allow, that a short gun, at a short distance, will kill as well as a long one, yet the latter gives you *a more accurate aim*, and considerably *lessens the recoil*, by which you shoot to a *greater nicety*, and with *more steadiness*. To avoid all extremes, I should recommend small barrels, never less than *two feet eight*, nor more than *three feet* in length. My readers will observe that my remarks here have been altered since publishing my earlier editions. Mr. Joseph Manton, who knows, at all events, as much as, if not more than, any man in Europe about a gun, assured me, after innumerable experiments, he has proved that two feet eight for a twenty-two gauge barrel is the best proportion for a sporting-gun. Take therefore a *fourteen* gauge barrel, and see whether or not I am right for recommending one of two feet ten inches, and three feet, where it can be used without inconvenience! But mind one grand point—*have plenty of metal near the breech-end;* not only for strong shooting, but for good elevation. Let all barrels be tapered like a bulrush: no hollowing out, as this ruins their shooting.

It may be thought a bold assertion, but I have every reason to believe that we have all, to this very day, been completely in the dark about the length of guns. Mr. Daniel (speaking of a duck-gun) said that a barrel, three feet eight inches, is "as capable, or more so, of throwing shot sharp and distant, as a barrel two feet longer." In my second edition (deceived in the same manner that all the gunmakers have been, by not having made their trials on a sufficiently large scale) I gave it as an opinion, that except the aim being better, and the recoil less, a long gun had no advantage over a short one. On the contrary, I have now proved that a short gun has no chance with a long one, in *keeping the shot well together* at *long* distances.

The experiment must not be tried with little pop-guns that are used for pigeons and partridges, but by guns on a gigantic scale, by which we can make every observation in the clearest possible manner, with the same advantage that an astronomer, with his large telescope, has over the naked eye, or diminutive glass, in discovering a planet.

I had once made up my mind, that a barrel, of whatever size it might be, would kill the farthest if made forty-eight times the diameter of the intended caliber, and entered in the MSS. for my third edition some observations to that effect. But had they gone to the press, I should have been open to the criticism of every good experimentalist: for I have since discovered, that the *larger the gun, the longer it must be in proportion;* because the further the shot has to travel, the greater the resistance of the atmosphere. In addition to my own experiments I am indebted for the perusal of several observations (which corroborate my opinion on them) to that excellent engineer, General Shrapnell, of the Royal Artillery. I shall, therefore, say no more by way of argument, but lay before my readers one of the clearest proofs, selected from the number I have made:—

TRIAL, taking the average of several shots, at twenty sheets of thickest brown paper, at a target, placed in the middle of a sheet of water, in order that all by-standers may see fair play, as to correct shooting:—

Distance, 90 yards:—shot BB.

A best finished London duck-gun: weight of the barrel, 59lbs.: bore, $1\frac{1}{2}$ inch: length, 5 feet 8 inches.

No. of grains in 1st sheet.	Ditto through 12th sheet.	Ditto through 20th sheet.
26	10	8

A Birmingham gun : weight of barrel, 69lbs. : bore, $1\frac{1}{4}$ inch : length 7 feet 9 inches.

1st sheet.	12th sheet.	20th sheet.
50	35	22

I then sent my gun to the late Mr. Durs Egg, desiring him to get the same barrel forged, by Fullerd, one foot ten inches longer, making it seven feet six inches; and by means of unavoidably being obliged to reduce the metal after joining it, the barrel, when sent home, was scarcely 3lbs. heavier than before. I then shot the gun about twenty rounds, and the average was

1st sheet.	12th sheet.	20th sheet.
46	30	20

by which it evidently appeared to me, that if the metal is disposed of in length, it has the advantage over a short thick gun.

From having 10lbs. more weight of metal, however, the Birmingham gun still had rather the advantage, because it carried seventeen ounces pleasanter than the other carried fifteen.

Substance *and length*, therefore, are what we want in as great a degree as can be used without inconvenience.

For instance: Fire a fourteen gauge sporting-gun, two feet eight inches, or forty-four diameters, at a gunmaker's iron door, against one of three feet, and there will probably be no difference. But go out in an open field, and particularly on a windy day, with the two feet eight inch barrel, and try it at sixty yards, and after the shot have gone about two-thirds of the distance, they will begin to open in oblique directions, where the three feet barrel keeps the shot together. For instance: Take a funnel (or a paper cut triangularly like one) four inches in diameter: pin up a sheet of brown paper, and stand at three or four yards from it. Then look along either edge of the funnel, and you will see how very wide a cylinder thus relieved carries the outer parts of its circle beyond the paper. Then take a funnel of the same diameter *eight* inches deep, and you will see how much more of the funnel is filled with the paper.

Now, as guns must be relieved in order to shoot well, I take all this in the extreme, the more clearly to demonstrate why length has the advantage at long distances. But, on the other hand, go almost close to the paper, the short funnel will lay the whole of its circle within it; and the long one can do no more, and, therefore, at *this* distance you give no trial. So it is with barrels that are tried in a gunmaker's yard, and at the *usual distances*. Moreover, the *extreme* friction that is absolutely required to send a charge strong has the effect of scattering and recoiling so much in a *short* barrel, that a certain sacrifice of power must be made. But in a long barrel, which admits of greatly increasing the relief, the shot are kept without any sudden check so long together, after this violent concussion, that we are enabled to combine both strength and closeness in the most powerful degree; and this, together with less recoil, and a better aim. We have, therefore, been half a century making, as it were, the tour of the world in guns, and at last come home again to discover, that, in regard to the length of barrels, we were not so near the mark as our grandfathers!

Mr. Durs Egg, in opposition to the whole trade, and

all the sportsmen, weathered the storm, and always maintained the same opinion. We all laughed at him, but, before he died, it was his turn to laugh at us, as he could, with justice, say that on this point he knew more than all of us put together!

Be cautious, therefore, of shortening an old barrel that shoots well; and recollect, also, that, if much of the length is taken off, you alter the relief.

As a gun, which is *top-heavy*, is inimical to *quick shooting*, the usual plan, unless the barrels are very short, is to make them "light forward;" that is, thin towards the muzzle. This I conceive to be bad; as a barrel, which is everywhere tolerably stout, is not so liable to expansion, and, consequently, will *shoot stronger*, and *last many more years*, than one which is rendered so by being in any part too thin. A gun, thus substantial, can always be made to mount well, by being properly balanced with *lead under the heel-plate*, which will be far more convenient and neat in appearance than a huge piece of wood for the but, and will thus admit of the stock being made light and elegant.

In choosing the size of a caliber, it may be considered, that a fourteen gauge is at all events the best for a bungler, and, on the whole, the most destructive gun. But, with a very accurate shot, the size is not of so much consequence for killing *game*, as the necessary substance to prevent the recoil of a large bore cannot be brought to bear so quick as a somewhat lighter gun; and, therefore, what is gained by weight of metal might be lost in time.

The original and celebrated London barrel-maker was Mr. W. Fullerd, who married; *retired from business;* and (perhaps, *consequently,* I may add) *died,* since we last went to press. He is succeeded by his brother Thomas, who was always equal to him in every respect, and who some of the gunmakers would persuade you is about to follow his example. But, knowing them of old, I made a point of ascertaining the truth, *from himself,* before this sheet was corrected for the printer. The story proves, as I expected, to be all a fudge. So far is Tom Fullerd from giving up the business, in which he stands at the head of the list, that he is now about to erect a steam engine for its increase, and improvement. This is, at all events, desirable information for all who may want *large* guns, for the forging and safety of which there is not his equal in Europe.—What was the object in extinguishing Tom and his forge? I'll tell you—If a sportsman gave an order for a gun beyond the usual size, for India, for the Cape, or for wildfowl shooting, the barrel would be ordered from Birmingham, at about one-third of the price, by which the gunmaker (alias the master, or "salesman") would save the other two-thirds in his outlay!—This is all very well for *small* barrels, which are now made to *perfection* in Birmingham; but, for the others, which are *not,* it is but fair, when there is no restriction of price, to employ those who are best able to manufacture them.

Mr. Lancaster no longer serves the trade in barrels, now that he is established as a gunmaker. But Henry Godsall, who worked nine years for him and eight for Joe Manton, has just established himself, as barrel filer and finisher, at 86, Oxford Street, where he showed me some of his improvements for making more perfect the screws of breechings, and putting well together the barrels of double guns. On *his* plan, however badly the barrels may be filed outside, they *must* be mathematically true in the position of their cylinders.

But to return to Mr Lancaster—he receives his barrels in the rough, from Birmingham; and then uses a self-acting machine for turning the outsides of them from end to end, and producing, mathematically true, the proper shape and curve from the muzzle to the breeching. This apparatus has cost him immense pains and expense, and is, no question, the best invention that has ever been adopted; as regular shooting must, in a great degree, depend on the regular thickness and regular tapering of the barrel. While only known as a barrel-finisher, Mr. Lancaster was in the habit of "ribbing," "breeching," and putting together the barrels; then "boring" them "for shooting;" and, in short, completing them for the field, all but the browning and engraving.

There are very few gunmakers who are well versed in putting their barrels together. For instance, barrels of 2 feet 10, require to be somewhat differently set from those of 2 feet 8, and also require more elevation. The recoil of all double guns makes each barrel swerve outwards in firing; and, in order to counteract this, each barrel must be set rather inwards, insomuch that, if the gun was fixed in a vice, the left barrel ought to shoot a little too much to the right, and *vice versâ*. Then take the gun out of the vice, and fire each barrel from the shoulder, and the swerve or kick would just bring the centre of the shot into the bull's eye. There is not one maker in fifty who knows much about this; but the masters get out of many difficulties by deputing Tom Fullerd, or some other clever fellow, to do all the essentials for them; otherwise, what would their guns be worth?

DAMASCUS BARRELS.

Most sportsmen are aware, that a twisted barrel is formed by horse nails, or other tough iron, being beat out to a long bar, and then twisted round a kind of anvil, much in the same manner as leather is put round the handle of a whip-crop. The Damascus is a mixture of iron and steel, and has its grain directly crossways when beat out; so that the bar of Damascus, when twisted, forms a continuation of small grains running *longitudinally*, which must be more liable to open, if not to burst, than a continued round of solid well-beat iron. It may be compared to a piece of wood cut across, instead of with, the grain. All this may be easily demonstrated, by putting some acid to eat away the iron. I should not have ventured to pronounce my feeble judgment on a point of this kind, was it not that I am of the same opinion as Mr. Joseph Manton, and some other first-rate gunmakers.

I shall now conclude under the head of "Barrels," with a copy, verbatim, from a part of my journal when last at Birmingham.

"Saw the process of making Damascus barrels, the mixture of iron and steel for which is beat out in long bars, and then, previously to being wound round the anvil, twisted by a kind of turning-lathe (similar to wringing cloths when wet), and then beat flat again. Although these are by far the dearest barrels that are made, yet the price of one in Birmingham is very trifling: viz.

	£.	s.	d.
Forging	1	10	0
Boring and grinding . .	0	5	0
Filing and patent breech . .	0	11	0
Proof	0	1	6
	2	7	6

" The stub barrels, which are generally used for best guns, cost about sixteen shillings each.

" Went to the proof-house, and was present at the proving of an immense number of barrels. The proof, as ordered by act of parliament, is to one ounce ball, thirteen drams and a half of best cartridge powder, with a very stiff wadding of paper on each; and so on, more or less, according to whatever ball will tightly fit the caliber. It has been observed to me here, that the London gunmakers do not go the cheapest way to work, as they commonly employ the tradesmen of the town, instead of the master workmen, who actually do the business, and consequently, they have to pay an extra price, beyond prime cost, for the article with which their country agent supplies them. Their reason, however, may be much to their credit: a wish to secure the best barrels. Were I a gunmaker, however, I should prefer keeping at Birmingham a first-rate foreman, or agent of my own, who could pick and choose, and supply me direct from the factories."

Formerly the Birmingham proof-masters would *prove* a barrel *in the rough*, when it might stand very well: but, after being filed and finished, it became so reduced, as frequently to fly all to pieces with the common charge. Now, however, they *refuse* to prove a barrel *till after this reduction of the metal has been completed, and consequently the Birmingham barrels are much more to be depended on than they were.* Formerly the rogues got all the rubbish proved at Birmingham, and sent the good barrels for the London proof-mark; but now both proofs are alike. This is a sad blow to the London trade. In reply to a letter of inquiry that I lately sent to Mr. Westley Richards, he says, "The barrels at our proof-house are proved singly or together, as the parties desire. I prove mine singly, as this is a greater trial to a barrel."

Westley Richards told me, in 1828, that, for a small barrel, you should go to the Birmingham forgers; but that, for a *large one, Fullerd could beat them. Joe Manton also made the same observation.* This was just the reverse of what I *then* supposed.

All shooting articles in Birmingham are usually sold, or to use the term of trade "put in," by the dozen, at a mere nothing in comparison with the retail price. Many of the gunmakers are here supplied with all kinds of turnscrews, brushes, tools, &c. Here are sold also fishing-rods, reels, and almost every thing that can be required in the sporting way, at about one-fifth of the price that you pay in London.

ELEVATION.

As a proof of my original argument in favour of Joe Manton's elevation, my readers need only observe how universal it has now become with almost every gunmaker in, and even out of, the kingdom. It would therefore be a waste of time to reprint my former arguments in support of it, particularly as I may substitute, in place of them, something new on the subject.

By further discoveries, I have pretty well proved that all of us sportsmen, the whole trade, and even Joe himself, have been somewhat in the dark about the *precise degree for this* elevation; and this is perhaps the reason why many quacks have fancied that short guns will kill the furthest. They talk nonsense; but still the short guns have often *shown off best* in the field. Why is it? because the gunmakers regulate their elevations to shoot well *to* the bull's eye; whereas they ought to shoot *above* the bull's eye; and THE LONGER THE GUN, THE HIGHER MUST BE THE ELEVATION! Let this be placarded as a golden rule for every sportsman and every gunmaker in the kingdom. Let me state a proof of this:—I ordered a gun some time ago, fourteen gauge and two feet *ten* barrels, and selected Charles Lancaster as indisputably one of the best makers (I should give offence perhaps if I said the *best maker*) now in London. This gun shot beautifully; but no better than my 2 feet 8 barrels! "Now then, sir," said many in the trade, "won't you be convinced that your extra two inches are superfluous?" At first I began to, what is vulgarly called, "draw in my horns;" but I soon discovered what was the matter. A 2 feet 10 gun, with the rib no more elevated than a 2 feet 8 gun, invariably puts the body of the charge under the mark at all distances beyond about 35 yards. I therefore had this gun botched up, for mere experiment, with more elevation: and *then* there was not a detonater in my possession that stood any chance with it. This was merely giving *enough* elevation, supposing the object to be within *point-blank range*, and *stationary*, or going *straight on.* But, when we consider that all objects above 40 yards are so far *beyond* point-blank range, that, if the gun is not kept well up, the shot will fall from its own gravity; that a long snap-shot is always at a *rising*, and not at a straight-forward-going bird; and that if a good shot misses through being nervous, it is almost always *because his left hand drops as he flinches;* we should rarely err by somewhat *over*-elevating our guns. I never perhaps should have proved this, but from experiments with large coast-guns, which, as I before observed, like large telescopes, bring things to light; and, by means of being fired sometimes on water as smooth as a looking-glass, give a *decided evidence* of all the effects that are produced in gunnery. With regard to *elevation in proportion to length,* my friend General Shrapnell will tell you what has here been said; and so will the Baron de Berenger, who showed me a very clever scale on elevations, and therefore it would not be fair in me to publish one; as, by so doing, I should more or less have to copy the sketches of the baron. Enough of this dry subject; so now let the gunmakers, and many sportsmen, recollect that up to the latest period there has still been something for them to learn! How contemptible therefore is it for any man to fancy himself or his works perfection! Now I dare say the gunmakers will tell you they knew all this before! *If so, then, why have they not profited by it?*

N.B. To try not only the elevation, but *more particularly the putting together of your barrels, and the casting off of your stock,* fire at a stump, or any other object, in SMOOTH WATER; because you may fill a quire of paper with shot, without the body of the charge going precisely to the centre. But water will demonstrate every thing if you are attended by competent persons to take observation.

If the body of the charge goes to *the same wrong point several times in succession*, you may conclude that there is something about the gun not quite right. But you may shoot at paper, away from water, for seven years, and not be able to find this out so well. Give me *quires of paper* to try the *strength and closeness*, but a *stump*, or *cork, in still water*, to try the *accurate shooting* of a gun. It need scarcely be observed that there should not be a breath of wind when you do this. The water should be like a mirror. No better time than one of those fine butterfly-days that usually follow a night's pinching *white frost;* and which, by the way, are almost always the prelude to miserably wet weather.

I have, by the foregoing plan, found out many a gunmaker's blunders; and I am therefore *serving* all who *know their trade* by publishing it, because it may be the means of proving first-rate from inferior work in the most essential parts of gunmaking.

THE SIGHT

Is little used, except for *beginners*, and *slow poking shots*, who *daudle* their guns after a bird for ten or fifteen yards; and, therefore, *the less it is the better:* one scarcely bigger than a pin's head will be more out of the way if not wanted; and for those who require it, the smaller it is the more readily it will help them to the centre. But you may preach this doctrine till you are hoarse, and yet some of the gunmakers will still persist in putting sights three times as large as they ought to be. Others, however, are, *at last*, beginning to find out the advantage of what I have so long recommended!

THE RAMROD,

Which has a worm, on the same principle as the *solid corkscrew*, is the best to take hold of all kinds of wadding, and admits of a brass cap as well as any. The one made like a screw, after a little wear, is of scarcely any more use than the end of a stick, and the *common worm* is apt to flatten and become troublesome.

Many young sportsmen have been puzzled by shot falling into the barrel when the ramrod was there; but if, instead of trying to pull it out by force, they would turn the gun upside down, and press the ramrod into the barrel, the shot would immediately become disengaged, and fall out.

Some of the old school, who still keep to the use of paper, have been obliged to leave the field from having wedged in the ramrod, through a neglect to disengage it in time from this sort of wadding. In such a case, I conceive, that putting oil, or something wet, into the barrel, and softening the paper, by using a little friction with the ramrod, would, most probably, disengage it; and, by holding the gun with the muzzle downwards, after the paper had sufficiently absorbed the moisture, the shooter would have less risk of wetting his powder.

DIRECTIONS FOR TRYING BARRELS.

A MAN *may be taken in* with a *horse*, or a *dog*, but *never with a gun*, after being simply told *how* to try it.

Having taken out the breeching, and ascertained that *the barrel is free from flaws*, or unsound places, let him fire about a dozen or twenty shots at *a quire* of *the thickest brown* paper, by which he will know, to a certainty, both the *strength* and *closeness* with which the shot is driven; and he should remember, that the *strongest* and *most regular shooting* gun is *the best*, provided it does not throw the shot so thin as for a bird to escape between them.

The same quire of paper might do for all, if *one fresh sheet* is put *in front* of, and another *behind* it, every time the gun is fired.

[Another, somewhat inferior, though a quicker and cheaper, way of trying barrels is to borrow an *iron plate*, and *whitewash* it every shot. By doing this you save the expense of, and time required for nailing up, paper; and can form a *tolerable* idea of the *strength*, by observing the impression of the lead; as the *stronger* the gun shoots, the flatter the pellets are beat, and the *larger*, of course, therefore will the *dark spots* appear on the white surface.]

Before concluding on the examination of barrels, it may be proper to observe, that a barrel may be pretty good and perfectly safe, and yet not able to bear the scientific inspection of a first-rate maker or judge. That is, to hold the barrel up to the window, and gradually raise it till the shade, from above the window, runs along its surface, by which inspection you will easily discover the most trifling want of finish. For instance, examine a barrel of Mr. Lancaster, in this manner, and the shade will run along it like the even surface on a flow of smooth water. But take a barrel of an inferior finisher, and you will perceive the iron all in bumps, as if that flow of water was agitated by wind. To the many, however, who fancy themselves good judges of a gun, the one might appear as perfect as the other; and so indeed it would, to every person who examined it in the ordinary way. To inspect the *inside* of a barrel, raise it in like manner, and if the stream of shade, as it were, flows true and steady, the boring may be considered straight, and free from any palpable defect.

THE STOCK,

To be neat in appearance, should be cut away, as close as strength and safety will admit of, and well tapered off at the locks. The but may be *rather full.* A *cheek-piece,* however, is not only as frightful as its *usual companion,* the *scroll-guard,* but is sometimes apt to give the very blow it is intended to save. If, however, a sportsman prefers having something to steady his hand, Lancaster will show him a plan of mine for a *moveable pistol-gripe,* that can be put to any stock, and taken off at pleasure. This proves to answer well; but I dislike all the others, both for use and appearance.

The stocks of single guns are generally tipped, or capped, with horn; but some makers have discarded this, through fear of its being *split* by the *recoil,* and either leave a clumsy continuation of the wood, or tip the stock with a gingerbread-looking piece of silver; whereas, if they would only *leave a space* about the thickness of a shilling *between* the *end* of the *rib* and the *horn*, the recoil, however great, could have no influence on that part.

The *length*, *bend*, and *casting off* of a stock, must, of course, be *fitted to* the shooter, who should have his measure for them as carefully entered on a gunmaker's books, as that for a suit of clothes on those of his tailor. He has then only to direct, that his guns may be *well balanced;* to do which, the maker will put lead, in proportion to their weight; so that, on holding each of them flat on the left hand, with the end of the lock opposite the little finger, he will find a sufficient equilibrium to make the gun *rest perfectly steady* ON *the hand.*

I have proved, that this degree of balance answers best, as a but too much loaded is apt to hang on the right hand in bringing it up, and *vice versâ*, on the left, with a gun which is top-heavy.

N.B. The lower down the but the lead is let in, the steadier the gun will keep to the shoulder; as it then acts like ballast to a rolling vessel.

All stocks should have a good *fall in the handle*, and not be, as some are, nearly horizontal in that part. This has nothing to do with the general bend or mounting of the stock, but is merely to keep the hand to the natural position, instead of having, as it were, the handle wrenched from the fingers, while grasping it. This is the only point on which we are beat by those execrable gingerbread guns, which some of the foreigners have the effrontery to compare with ours.

If a stock, in every respect, suits you as to coming up to the eye, &c. &c., the way to have one precisely like it is to leave with your gunmaker a thin piece of board, made to fit with the greatest accuracy to the profile of the bend, all the way from the upper part of the but to the breeching. By *later* experience, I should say even *farther still*. Let the profile extend at least a foot *beyond* the breeching. Why? because you may have two stocks as much alike as if cast in the same mould all the way to the breeching, and yet the *barrels*, by being *sunk deeper in the wood*, may point so much downwards as to give the line of aim *more bend;* or, on the other hand, by *not being let in so deep*, they would *mount straighter* than the profile. But if you continue the profile for a foot along the gun, you will then be pretty sure of keeping precisely to the bend you want. By being made to fit into this, your new stock *must* be like the old one. But if you trust to a set of memorandums that are often mistaken, or, in the hurry of business, not half attended to, you may have as many new stocks as would almost amount to the price of a gun, before you would get two precisely alike.

A stock that is deep, and comes out well at the toe, or bottom of the heel-plate, is the most steady when pitched on the object.

I lately had a hack gun for boat-work, with which I could scarcely touch a feather, because the barrels *dipped* so much in mounting that the muzzle never came up to the mark. I made a carpenter saw off the end of the but, and then put on a piece of wood which came well out at the toe; then shot (without a heel-plate) and killed every thing in good style.

Many a journey to town would be saved to a sportsman if all these trifles were properly attended to by the makers.

For those who take a pride in the appearance of their stocks, and select handsome pieces of wood, I know of nothing better, to keep them polished, than a *little* linseed oil, and *plenty* of, what is vulgarly called, *elbow-grease;* unless sportsmen choose to take the additional trouble of adopting the following recipe; which I shall here give, under the idea, that, if considered too troublesome to apply to *gunstocks*, it may still be found worth inserting, from its excellence in giving a *dark* polish to *tables*, or any kind of *furniture*.

RECIPE FOR KEEPING THE POLISH ON GUNSTOCKS.

Cold drawn linseed oil . . .	1 quart.
Gum arabic (dissolved in warm water) .	½ ounce.
Alkanet root	2 ounces.
Rose pink	½ ounce.
Vinegar	½ pint.

Boil these together, and put them in an earthen pan to stand for a day or two, after which the mixture will be fit for use.

To apply it, rub a small quantity on the wood: let it lie on all night, and rub it off clean in the morning. With a few such dressings, you will bring out a superior polish.

If a stock, which, in other respects, suits you, is, in a trifling degree, too straight or too much bent, the maker could rectify it by means of *boiling it in hot water*, instead of persuading you to have a new one.

BREECHING.

A gun-breeching, till of late years, was simply a plug, screwed into the end of the barrel, so as to reach to the touchhole.

The first improvement was to bore a hole down the centre of this plug, and bring the touchhole to it in a right angle, thereby having the communication *directly through* both the male and female screws. How far this may be *safe*, I leave to the more experienced to judge; but it certainly shoots so well, that I never could find any solid breeching to beat it, until Mr. Joseph Manton brought out his, which, like the rest of his work, has been *abused* and *imitated* by most of his filing fraternity!

To treat on the various kinds of solid breechings, that have been made since the *original invention of Mr. Nock*, would be wasting time, and consuming a volume, when we can at once warrant, that there are none superior to the one above-mentioned.

For example, a breeching on Mr. Manton's construction places the touchhole *literally to* the chamber, and thereby not only cuts off all superfluous angles, which impede quick firing, and collect dirt, but the narrowness of this chamber admits of the outside metal being *filed away*, with the *most perfect safety*, and *lets in* the lock so far, that the pan is brought close to the charge of powder, by which means the discharge of the gun becomes as instantaneous as possible. All this, however, may be more clearly demonstrated by a reference to the sections of all the different gun breechings, of which there are now published so many engravings, and in comparing which the other *decided advantages* of this improvement are fully manifested.

Should it be suggested, that the narrowness of this tube renders it difficult to be cleaned, let it be remembered, that the rod, when it goes to the bottom of the breech, forces the air through the centre tube with such violence, that neither oil nor damp can be left behind; and, in the event of any dirt falling in, there is a probe, which you screw on the ramrod: and this little appendage is, or should be, attached to your flint-case.

It may be well, however, to observe, that many of the gunmakers, who now adopt this breeching, commit a sad fault, by making the centre tube *too* small; they are led into this error by knowing, that the *narrower the tube* the *stronger the gun will fire*, and are satisfied with the result of a *few shots*. But were they to take their guns out for a *whole day's work*, they would find, that, by thus attempting to improve on a *ne plus ultra*, they had rendered their breechings liable to *repeated flashes in the pan*, as well as more *difficult to see through* (for ascertaining that all is clean and safe), when held to the light.

Let me now conclude my observations on the foregoing gun breechings by recapitulating on each, in reference to the following wood-cuts.

Letters of Reference, which apply to all the following Sketches.

A—Calibres.
B—Male screws as they go into them.
C—Chambers which fill with powder.
D—Screws for getting at and countersinking touchholes.
E—Touchholes.
F—Solid iron, which, in Mr. M.'s breeching, admits of being cut away.

N.B. My attempt to give a clear conception of each breeching, in one sketch, makes it necessary to deviate, in some degree, from perspective, which would not fully admit of showing every part.

No. 1.
Common Plug.

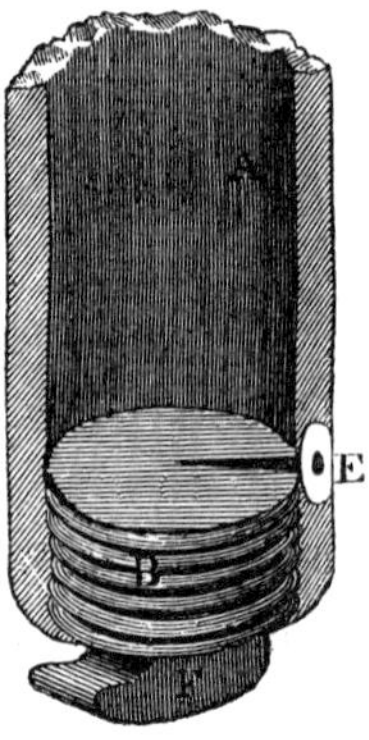

No. 2.
Chamber Plug.

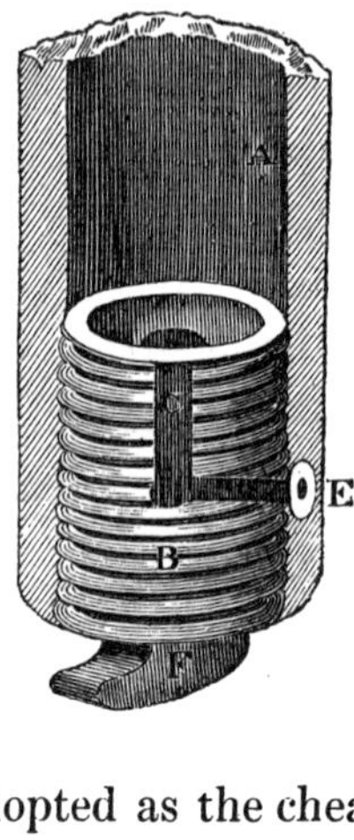

The *common plug*, No. 1, is adopted as the cheapest and best calculated breeching for rough usage, dirt, and neglect; and is, for this reason, generally put to all fire-arms that are merely used for personal protection, the service of the army, &c. Some make the common plug, with a little notch at the end, which is filed, to hold a greater depth of powder at the touchhole; others think that this collects the dirt, and leave the surface quite plain. I have heard many sportsmen say, "After all, give me the old common plug; it fires as well as any, and can never be stopped up." But, on taking out their breechings, their "old *common* plug" has proved to be the *chamber* plug, which is precisely the same to all *outward* appearance.—See the Sketch.

The *chamber plug*, No. 2, has the advantage, not only of the common, but most of the *patent* breechings, by means of the small perforation leading to a concave, or cup, at the top; where the powder is suddenly ignited from the centre. But, as the touchhole goes through the threads of the female screw in the barrel, it must be met by a hole nearly as large as the tube itself, which comes from the tube in a right angle, through the male screw or plug. This perforation is apt to wear, and sometimes to get damp from the oil which is used for screwing in the breech-plug. It is also liable to become corroded, and, therefore, *sometimes difficult to be taken out.* Excepting for these defects, the chamber plug is much to be recommended; and having recourse to it is almost the only way that an old gun can be improved with that economy, which should be observed in all expenditures on a worthless foundation.

No. 3.
H. Nock's
Original Patent Breeching.

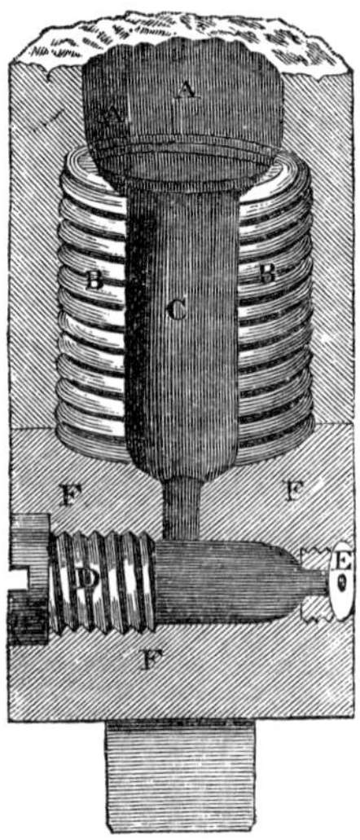

The solid breeching of the late Mr. Nock, No. 3, is a discovery of great merit; and, as we have to thank him for this *foundation* to all our improvements, it would be an injustice to his memory not to give him every credit for the original invention. The objection, however, to the solid breeching, as first made (when compared with the improvements that have since been adopted), is, that it shoots too weak, from the powder in the chamber *not being in a sufficiently narrow compass to ignite suddenly and forcibly in the centre*; and too slow, in consequence of the *great length*, which there is through the whole *communication*, from the touchhole upwards; add to which the superfluous *angles*, and the difficulty of probing the antechamber. Mr. Grierson's patent came the nearest of any to the original. His plan was to cut off the angle by shortening the antechamber and bringing it to the other chamber in an oblique direction. There was certainly a degree of ingenuity in his improvement; but yet there remained the objection of the centre hole, or chamber, not being so narrow as to ignite the body of the charge so suddenly, in the centre, as in the breeching of Mr. Joseph Manton.

NO. 4. MR. JOSEPH MANTON'S BREECHING.

A left hand Breeching.

J. M.'s ditto for double gun.
G the hole which he used to cut for a water-drain.

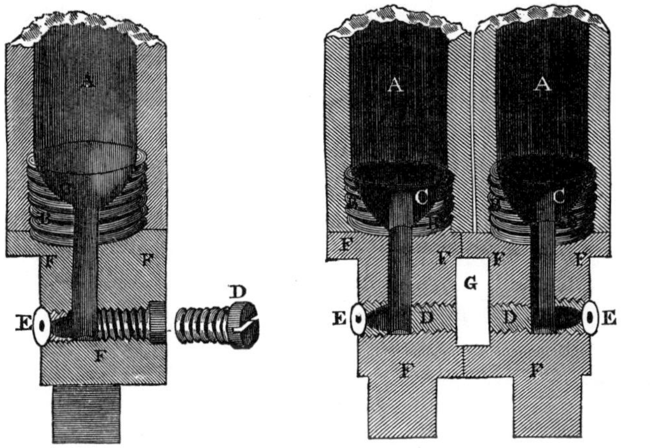

As a *proof*, that this is by far the *best* of any, I need only observe, that it is now adopted by almost every gunmaker in the trade. [*For its adaptation to percussion guns I shall give some new sketches under the more modern head of " detonating system."*]

The first three breechings may be put, as they here stand, to a common lock; but, with those of Mr. Joseph Manton, the *lock* must be *constructed on purpose*, unless you have an antechamber long enough for the touchhole to reach to the pan without filing away any of the metal. I should prefer *this* to having any *other sort* of breeching (provided the barrel was worth something better than a chamber plug), as I have *proved*, that it answers remarkably well. It then becomes like the chamber plug, shoots about as well, and will be safer and much more durable.

IMPLEMENTS FOR FLINT-GUNS.

*** As I may be called " out of date" if I now show forth my pages too conspicuously on what relates only to the flint-gun, I shall present all on that subject in the smallest possible compass. I had before done this to the best of my abilities, and therefore I can only reduce it more now by having recourse to smaller print.

Touchhole.—Nothing contributes more to *filling the bag* than the disposal of this apparently trifling concern; insomuch, that an old musket, with a touchhole put in by a clever mechanic, would beat a gun, with all the new improvements, if this *important* part of it were left to the *job of a bungler*.

Touchholes of *platina* are considered the *best*, as those of steel are apt to collect rust, and one of gold is more liable to blow out, and, therefore, will not admit of being made so thin; consequently (from requiring to be *thick*), does not *shoot so sharp*; for the *thinner* it is, the *quicker will be* the *firing of the gun*.

The touchhole should be *countersunk*; and, to get at it for this purpose, the solid breechings have a screw directly opposite, which (although in those of Mr. Manton scarcely visible) is easily taken out and put in again.—*Vide Sketches*.

Lock.—Any comment on the perfection to which this part of a gun is now brought would be quite redundant. Notwithstanding, however, that almost every country maker can turn out a tolerably well-filed lock, yet few, *even in town*, have the knack of making the springs to go so *pleasant to the touch*, and (if I may use the expression) feel *so oily*, as those made by the two Mr. Mantons, the late

Mr. D. Egg, Mr. Nock, Mr. Smith, Mr. Purdey, Mr. Lancaster, and some *few* others. I mean, that many, even of the *best finished locks,* have an *unpleasant harshness,* which is not only *disagreeable to feel;* but, by reason, *not so ready to action.*

The plate of a lock should be so far substantial as to be insured from *bending,* which, *if it occurred,* would be the means of *injuring all its movements.*

Although, for large breechings, a long plate is required, yet it is not necessary to put such very *clumsy locks* as we sometimes see, on even highly finished wildfowl guns.

As remarked at the time when I wrote my former editions, many attempts were then in vogue for making the locks water-proof, and all of them equally ridiculous. That they might avert a few drops from an immediate entrance to the pan, there could be no doubt, and they might keep the powder dry somewhat longer than locks with the hammers on the common construction; but, that they could so completely resist the *effect of a damp atmosphere on the nitre,* as always to keep their priming dry throughout a rainy day, *I denied;* although it might be very easy, by way of *showing off* the lock *in a shop,* to *pour water* over it *without wetting* the powder. For quick firing in a *damp atmosphere,* the best of all the flint-locks I have yet tried is one of Mr. D. Egg's, on the hammer of which he puts an oval of platina and, into that, dovetails a sharp edge of the pan. This, with coarse powder and a lock-cover, I have used on salt water, for several winters, and it scarcely ever failed, while the detonaters (at least those with *caps*) were repeatedly missing fire! This happens to be a self-primer, and the only one that I have ever yet seen that does not go slow. Two other kinds of self-primers were brought out by two great makers, and, as a third observed, if "you owe a man a grudge, advise him to have one of them."

Since the short time ago when the foregoing observations were made, it appears that almost every gunmaker has been studying to complete some water-proof lock or other, at the expense of sacrificing quick shooting, and many other advantages, that are of more consequence than a guard against rain. For, after all, what is the object to be gained? If you shoot in the rain, neither partridges nor snipes will, in general, lie well; and if you shoot in covert, your dogs are soon cowed by the wet, and the sport is any thing but pleasure; and if you go after wildfowl, you cannot choose a worse time for your sport or your health than in wet weather.

I formerly observed, that if a man was so destitute of resources within himself as to be miserable unless he was shooting, he had only to provide himself with one of Mr. Forsyth's fulminating locks, which certainly defied the weather *longer than any others* at that time invented; though, perhaps, from the effect of the atmosphere on the oxygen, *they* might not be proof against a continual pour of rain. The invention is certainly of infinite merit, and has, of late years, been so much improved on, that scarcely any thing is now thought of but detonating guns. I have, in consequence, been making trials in every way that appeared necessary, in order to be able to give a few directions solely dictated by the result of experiment.

After dismissing every thing concerning the flint-lock, which I find must ever predominate for one kind of fire-arms—very large single wildfowl-guns—I shall treat exclusively on "detonaters."

SPRINGS.—If the mainspring be too strong, in proportion to that of the hammer, the cock is often broken for want of resistance; and, if the hammer or feather-spring be too stiff, or should *shut down with too much force*, it becomes difficult to throw it, even with a strong mainspring. Here, till some years ago, most of the gun-makers were *in the dark;* as nothing *was* more admired in a lock, than the hammer shutting down with great velocity. This is not only, for the reason already mentioned, a sad *fault;* but the hammer by thus coming down escapes, in a certain degree, from the influence of the spring; and, consequently, loses its pressure on the pan; by which the priming is not so closely covered, and the *hammer* is apt *to react,* instead of *obeying* the mainspring. In a word, let your *hammer shut down dull,* and *fly back smart.* The mainspring, to be well regulated, should *at first* pull up very hard, and then draw progressively easier: because it requires an accession of force after it has recovered the first sudden escape from the scear-spring, otherwise it will go slow with a flint, and be liable either to cause a snap, or allow the cock to be blown back, with a detonater.

COCKS AND HAMMERS.—If the sportsman has no objection to its clumsy appearance, I should be inclined to recommend the solid cock which *falls on its end,* instead of being *stopped in the middle* by the lock-plate. It will therefore admit of *mainsprings as strong* as you please; and, by this means, add considerably to quickness in firing. But if you have very stong mainsprings, with the *common* cock, the resistance from the hammer-spring, *to prevent its breaking, must* be so great, that you would soon wear out your hammers, by being obliged to use an immoderate quantity of new flints. With this another part of the lock also is safer, because the solid cock is received on a firm support annexed to the pan; while the one on the other construction suddenly catches the lock-plate, and is therefore liable to jar, and *break* either the *tumbler itself*, or the *pin* of the *tumbler*. A solid cock has many other advantages, from its durability and strength: it is proof against all awkward hands, and particularly desirable on guns which are liable to meet with rough usage in a boat.

The reason why some gunmakers object to it is, that it is not so easily regulated to strike higher or lower with new hammers as the other. *New hammers!* for which most of them have had some patent or fancy of their own; and with this they took care to accommodate you on every favourable opportunity. Add to this, the solid cock is not apt to break like the other, and is therefore *not so good for trade.* With due submission, however, to the superior judgment of those in the business, I must beg to observe, that I have always found an *old hammer new steeled* to fire *better* than a new hammer; insomuch, that I have had *new* hammers *new steeled* before I ever used them; and surely an old hammer, if sound, must go pleasanter than a new one, which has scarcely been used enough to get rid of its harshness. The reason why *new facing does best* is this:—in making new hammers, the steel is welded and incorporated with the iron; the process of which requires so *much heat*, that it *softens* and *reduces* the quality of the *steel;* whereas, by putting only new *faces*, this evil is avoided, and the steel may be kept in the *best possible temper*. Gunmakers *know this* perfectly well; but whatever may be their abuse of one another, to customers in their shops, yet they have the sense to agree on one point, namely, to keep among themselves this, and other little *secrets* belonging to the trade.

On the other hand, I shall now recommend something to their *advantage;* which is, that every sportsman be at first equipped with *extra hammers* and *extra springs* to his gun; so that, by being provided with a *spring cramp*, and shown how to use it, he may be able to remedy an accident with his own hands, which might otherwise oblige him, from the midst of good shooting to send away his fowling piece, to be left at the mercy of a gunmaker's punctuality, or endangered by the unrelenting hands and tools of an awkward country blacksmith. Hammers, like crockery-ware, are *none the worse for age,* though *liable to be broken.*

There are two ways of putting a hammer in motion ; one with a wheel in the feather-spring, and the other with a *bridge there,* over which a *wheel in the hammer* is made to run. We may give to both of these trivial concerns their separate merits ; the former, that of being the *neatest,* and the latter, the *least likely to react,* and leave the choice of them to the gunmaker.

Mr. D. Egg and Mr. Manton usually made the first mentioned ; and Mr. Joseph Manton the other. With this he was enabled to have a long neck, which, immediately on being put in motion, *raises* the *hammer so high,* that it *cannot prevent any of the sparks from falling into the pan.* No locks, however, could go pleasanter than those made by Mr. John Manton and Mr. D. Egg, which proves, that the difference between the two modes of construction is very immaterial.

It may be as well to make a few observations on another point ; *viz.* the improvement of passing a current of *air through the priming without suffering* the *powder to escape ;* by which it is *kept dry,* and *not liable to cake* and stick to the bottom of the hammer. This has been completely effected, both by Messrs. Manton and Mr. D. Egg ; but, as credit for the original invention is due to Mr. Joseph Manton, I shall chiefly confine my description to the hammer for which he got the patent. The object attained by this is, that when you ram down the wadding, the *air passes through* the small perforation at the lip of the hammer, and goes out through a groove in the bottom of the pan : yet this hole in the lip is so small as *not to admit* the *powder.* This, although *apparently* a trifling alteration from what had been before adopted, is a very great advantage, and the *first* attempt that ever had the *desired effect.* That some air, in *all* locks, *must* pass, it stands to reason ; but, if the *powder also* passes, it must be recollected, that, in coming *from the chamber* of breechings on Mr. Joseph Manton's construction, it *leaves a vacuum ;* whereas, with this improvement, the chamber is always *kept so full* of dry powder, that not a grain can be lost, or even out of its place, and thus there is produced a *sudden and instantaneous fire.* The forcible passing of this current of air also effectually *dries the powder in the touchhole.*

N.B. Whatever new hammers may have since been brought out,

for new fashion, or, in other words, for the good of trade, yet, after all, I find that this hammer is decidedly the best, and produces by far the quickest ignition.—1832!

In this improvement of a gun-lock, Mr. John Manton so far imitated his brother, that a trial, which took place in the court of Common Pleas, was chiefly relating to his alleged infringement on the patent. He there, however, gained his cause by producing some hammers with perforated lips; as well as on the other point (concerning the elevation), by bringing forward an old double gun, which it has been generally understood was in the possession of the late Lord Berkeley. It appears, however, that in this statement there was some mistake, as the gun in question was made for, and expressly to the order of, the late Evelyn Medows, Esq., by Mr. John Manton, when foreman at Twig's; and it was from this gentleman that he borrowed the gun, which he produced in court, in order to show that that for which his brother had obtained a patent was not an original invention. (I was favoured with this statement by Mr. Medows himself.) But, query, if Mr. Joseph Manton had not made the discovery, that this elevation, and this hammer might, with a trifling alteration, be adopted as the greatest improvements, would the one at this moment have been *universally known?* Or, might not the other have been for ever *buried in the filings of Birmingham?* Or, would not both (to use a lawyer's expression) have become *obsolete from non usage?*

If a hammer is too hard, the flint will make scarcely any impression on it; and, if too soft, it soon becomes dented, like lead; but when in good temper, the impression is *moderate,* and the *sparks,* before they are extinguished, *pause in the pan* and occasion a *whizzing noise.*

You will seldom get a London maker to temper, or even face a hammer, if he can persuade you to have a new one; and it is as common a trick to construct hammers so that the flints may *soon cut them to pieces,* as it is to set a fellow to work with unmerciful relays of *scouring paper,* to help *to wear out the barrels,* under the old plea, that *the trade must live.*

Pan.—If the pan is not placed considerably below the touchhole (that is, with its edge *just under* the touchhole), the gun will always fire slow, because instead of catching the first flash, which invariably *rises,* the charge is not ignited till the priming *has burnt down* to below the touchhole, and consequently the discharge is prolonged into two motions. If a pan is placed too high, therefore, the remedy is, to put a very little depth of priming.

If, on the other hand, the pan is placed *too* low, the gun will of course be liable to flash, instead of going off.

TRIGGER.

Let the triggers of all your guns be made to go nearly alike; for, if one requires *too hard* a pull, it is a sad *check to shooting*; and, if it goes *too easy*, you are liable to the *accident of firing the gun* before it is fairly brought to the shoulder. Any tolerable mechanic may rectify these extremes, by filing, more or less, the part *where the scear catches the tumbler*. The most accurate way to regulate the pull of a trigger, as well as that of a cock, is by a small stilliard, which will draw out and regulate those of twenty guns to the same focus.

The triggers are now kept well in their places, by the constant pressure of little springs, and you must therefore push them back before you can let in your locks.

In cleaning locks, the best places to put a *little* oil are,

1st. (For a *flint*-gun). In front of the pan, immediately under the neck of the hammer, from whence the oil will find its way through to the wheel and spring.

2d. (For ALL GUNS). On the pivot nail, or centre of the tumbler, on which the whole of *the works* move:

3d. On the lockplate, under the works, where a feather may be inserted:

4th. Where the scear catches the tumbler.

TO TAKE A LOCK TO PIECES.

In the event of breaking or weakening a spring, and therefore having to replace it with an extra one; or, in case the works of a lock should have become damaged by rust and neglect, every sportsman should be provided with a little *spring-cramp*, which may be carried with his gun-case, and with which he may himself take his locks to pieces, with as much safety as the first workman in London. I have, therefore, here given specific directions, regularly numbered, by ***having which before him*** he will, I trust, find it almost impossible to mistake, either in taking his locks to pieces, or putting them together.

TO TAKE OFF THE [HAMMER AND] SPRINGS.

N. B. *In cramping springs, be sure never to confine them closer than is absolutely necessary, otherwise you will soon weaken and spoil them.*

MAINSPRING.

To take off:—

1. Put lock to full cock.
2. Cramp the mainspring.
3. Let down the cock, and the mainspring will drop off.

To put it on again:—

(Let cock be left down.)

1. Hook the end of the mainspring on the swivel, or chain.
2. Move it up, and into its position on the lock-plate.
3. Unscrew the cramp, and the mainspring will be replaced for action.

[HAMMER.

To take off:—

1. Shut down the hammer.

2. Keep gradually cramping the spring, till by shaking the lock in your hand, you can just hear the hammer rattle, from being loose.
3. Take out the screw from behind, and the hammer will fall out.

To put it on :—

1. Put the hammer in its place again.
2. Turn in the screw.
3. Set the spring at liberty.

To take the hammer *spring* out, you must first take away the hammer, and also the mainspring, to *get at* the screw behind. The hammer-spring must be then confined till taken out, and put on again to receive the hammer.]

TO DISSECT THE SMALL WORKS OF A LOCK.

(In doing which be careful not to *mix* your small screws.)

Having *previously* taken off your mainspring,

1. Unscrew, and take out, the scear. This must be done by half cocking, and then pressing the fore-part of the lock against your left breast, by putting the ball of the thumb against the back part of the cock; and, with this, *pushing the cock forward*, while you *squeeze* together *the scear* and scear-spring, *with the fore-finger* and thumb, for the facility of taking out the scear-screw.
2. Undo the two screws, and take off the bridle.
3. Unscrew and take out the scear-*spring*.
4. Unscrew and take off the cock, which will come from the tumbler by being gently tapped inwards, with the handle of your turnscrew.
5. Take out the tumbler.

TO PUT THEM TOGETHER AGAIN.

1. Put in the tumbler, and screw on the cock.
2. Screw on the scear-spring.
3. Set on the bridle with the two upper screws.

4. Put in the scear; to open a clear passage for the screw of which, you must observe the same pressure of the fore-finger and thumb on the scear and scear-spring, and the pushing of the cock forward, as before described for *taking off* the scear.

The reason for this pressure being required, to put in the scear, is, to get the hole in the scear opposite the hole in the bridle, so as to admit the scear-screw to pass freely. What most frequently puzzles people, who are not used to mechanics, is, that they neglect to *keep pressing the cock forward,* and by that means the scear is constantly *slipping* out of the tumbler, and they are plagued to get the holes in a line, to which they would immediately be brought by the *pressing forward of the cock* and the *pressing inward of the scear.*

(Having finished so far)

Let down *the cock,* to put on the mainspring, as before directed, and your lock will have every thing in its place.

Observe well, that except the pressure required to put in the scear, which is the only part in the least difficult, there should be *no force* whatever used with the works of a gunlock.

With *detonating* guns, however, we have but half the trouble, and the only extra dissection that may be required for those which are now most usually made is, to screw out the nipple or pivot with a small wrench or key.

In doing all this, or indeed any thing to a gun, it is advisable to put on an old pair of gloves, as the warmth of the skin is apt to produce rust, and the hand, with the glove on, has a better purchase for taking out the scear.

As a key to the foregoing directions, the following is an alphabetical list of the proper names for the principal parts of a gun, which may not be universally known among sportsmen.

ALPHABETICAL LIST OF NAMES

OF THE

PRINCIPAL PARTS OF A GUN.

BOLTS. Pieces of steel, which push through the loops to fasten barrel into stock.

BRIDLE. Polished piece of steel, which caps the tumbler, is then put on with two screws, and afterwards receives the scear-screw.

CAP. Tip of stock ; or covering for worm of ramrod.

CASTING OFF. Inclining outwards of the but, so as to bring the line of aim inwards, and more ready to meet the eye.

CHAIN, or SWIVEL. A little catch, suspended from the neck of the tumbler, to receive the end of the main-spring.

CHAMBER. Centre or principal tube in breeching. The *Ante-chamber* is the smaller tube, leading from this to the touchhole.

COCK-SCREW. That which screws in the flint.

COVER. The piece of iron which holds, by a spring, the copper *primer* in detonaters.

CUP. Concave at the top of improved breechings.

ESCUTCHEONS. Pieces of silver, to prevent bolts from wearing stock; and also the shield on which the crest and cipher are usually engraved.

FACING (of hammer). Part which, by coming in contact with flint, strikes fire.

FALSE-BREECHING. Part where the ends of the breechings hook in, before the barrels can be laid in the stock.

FALSE-BREECH-SCREW. That which passes through the stock into the trigger-plate, and screws them together.

FENCE. Part between cock and pan, on which is received the solid cock.

GUARD. Bow which defends the triggers.

HAMMER-SPRING. On which hammer is moved.

HAMMER-BRIDLE. Part which the tail of hammer works in.

HEEL-PLATE. Plate with which the but is tipped.

JAWS. Lips of the cock, which hold the flint.

LOCK-PLATE. Plate to which all the lock is formed.

LOOPS. Eyes to barrel, which receive the bolts that fasten it into stock.

MAIN-SPRING. That by which tumbler is worked with cock.

NIPPLE (or Pivot). Protuberance on which strikes the cock of a detonating gun, which is ignited by copper *caps*.

NIPPLE-WRENCH. Pocket-machine, to take out the nipple, if required.

PIPES. Bands to receive ramrod.

RIB. Piece, or strip, on which slides the ramrod.

SCROLL-GUARD. An extra bow, continued from the guard, to steady the hand.

SCEAR. Part which catches the tumbler, for half or whole cock, and which, being pushed up by trigger, lets off the gun.

SCEAR-SPRING. The spring, which presses the scear against, and holds it in, the notches of tumbler, for either the half or whole cock.

SIDE-NAIL. Screw which fastens on the locks.

SIGHT. Little bit of gold or silver, to bring up to the object, when taking a deliberate aim.

SPRING-CRAMP. A small instrument for dissecting locks.

STRIKER. The *moveable* head to the *best sort* of cock, which strikes a copper cap.

TAIL. The arch, shoulder, or neck of a hammer.

TOP-PIECE. Groove, or elevation, along which is directed the line of aim.

TRIGGER-PLATE. Plate in which the triggers work.

TRIGGER-SPRINGS. Small springs, to keep triggers constantly pressing close to scear. (Invented and always used by Mr. Joseph Manton.)

TUMBLER. The moveable centre-piece of a lock, which falls with, and is subservient to the cock.

TUMBLER-SCREW. The little screw which fastens on the cock.

VENT-HOLE. A small hole at the side of the breeching, in a detonater, to let out the gas, and lessen the recoil.

WORM. Screw, at the end of ramrod, for drawing out the wadding.

*** When you find a lock rub, or bind, be sure and see that it does not do so in consequence of some little screw or other having worked loose, before you attempt easing the part of the stock where the friction takes place.

DIRECTIONS FOR CLEANING GUNS,

AND

PRECAUTIONS AGAINST THEIR HANGING FIRE.

Let your barrels be first washed perfectly clean with *cold*, and then *fill each of them* with *hot* water; which, by the time it has nearly run out at the touchholes, will accelerate their being wiped dry, as much as though boiling water had been used; and, before they have completely discharged the water, stop the muzzles and touchholes; and, after shaking it up and down in the barrels, turn it out at the muzzles, by which means you will effectually stir up and expel any extraneous matter, that may have lodged in the bottom of the chambers. To ascertain this, hold them with the touchholes towards the window, and (with the breechings which I have recommended) you will, by looking into each muzzle, plainly perceive the light in the chamber, appearing like *one dot* surrounded by *two* (and sometimes *three*) *rings*.

I have recommended washing guns with *cold* water, from having found that it always more readily removes the foulness occasioned by the powder, which, from sudden heat, is apt, at first, to dry and adhere more closely to the caliber: whereas, with cold water, it remains in a moist state, and immediately mixes.

In cleaning barrels, a little *fine sand* or brickdust will remove *the lead*. If *hot* water should be *required* for *this purpose*, the gun may be scoured with it, *after* having been *washed with cold*.

Some have their guns, occasionally, only dry wiped, which is not so well, as the introduction of the cleaning-rod drives the dirt into the chamber, from whence it becomes difficult to remove it without water.

The tow proper for cleaning guns is that fine sort, which is called *surgeons' tow*, and *sold by the chemists:* but, for cleaning *barrels*, the *breechings of which cannot* be readily *seen through, and particularly those of* DETONATING *guns*, I should recommend using nothing but *cloth*, which answers nearly or quite as well, and by which means you are not liable to the *serious* accident that might happen from having tow left in the chamber; and this you cannot always guard against in guns which have not the inverted breeching.

Cloth is also more *portable for travelling*, as the same pieces of it may, by being washed, serve for several times.

Some of our moderns recommend a sponge! fitted to the end of the cleaning-rod. Let us have a receipt to kill birds without shot, and this will do vastly well; but unfortunately guns, after being fired, become *leaded*, and then of what avail is a *sponge?*

We are told, that a barrel should be cleaned after having been fired about twenty rounds; but, as it is not *every manor* that will *now* afford *so many shots in a day*, it becomes a query, how often we may venture to put away a gun which has been used. I think, that if eight or ten shots have been fired from each barrel, it will be best to have the gun washed on returning from the field; and, if not, the way to prevent it hanging fire (if kept loaded) is simply to prick the touchhole, put fresh prime, and give the but a few smart strokes with the hand: or, with a detonater, to prick the hole of the nipple, and lodge therein a few grains of powder, before you put on the cap, which, by the way, should never be left on, when the gun is put by for any length of time. Should the gun have been in the damp, or loaded some time, the *more certain way* is to fire it off; then put in a fresh charge of powder, *while the barrels are warm,* and *afterwards* take off your locks, and wipe them, as well as the outside of the breechings and touchholes, which may be warranted free again, by being probed with the clipped end of a stiff feather: and *all* this done in *less time* than it *requires to explain it.*

When you put away your gun empty, you, of course, always *let down the springs of the locks;* and, as their being kept long at the half-cock tends so much to *weaken* them, it would even be advisable for those who keep their guns *loaded* to do the same. A piece of tow should be put in the pan (or on the nipple, if a detonater) to prevent damp, and the ramrod left in, as a caution to those who might otherwise take up the gun. It is highly improper, however, under any circumstances, and particularly where there are children in a house, ever to leave fire-arms about charged, unless secured out of reach, or by lock and key.

A little cleaning ought to be occasionally had recourse to in the field. Were the pans of a flint-gun *wiped* and the *feather inserted* in the touchholes after every shot, your gun would scarcely ever be known to hang fire, unless this precaution had been *counteracted* by your forgetting to load it while warm, or some other circumstance; and I see nothing to justify your neglect in this, except the incessant rising of birds, in which case you may be permitted to await a leisure opportunity. Nothing is more absurd, *if a gun has been washed,* than dirtying it, long before there is any occasion for so doing, by what is called squibbing, which answers the purpose only of alarming women and poultry, putting your cattle into a gallop, and your kennel full cry; and, in short, making a general disturbance among your domestic animals!—very excusable in a boy, who would desire no better fun!

If a gun, after your having *probed* the touchhole, should ever flash in the pan, you had better draw the shot; and, in firing off the powder, hold the gun *sideways* (that is, with the touchhole uppermost). I have seen shooters plagued for half an hour with their guns, which have *gone off immediately* on being held in *this* manner.

The proper, safest, and most certain way of ascertaining that your gun be perfectly clean, is to hold it to the light, and look through it (as before recommended); and to prove that neither oil nor damp be left behind, put your charge of powder into the barrel, and, before you add the wadding, *see* that the few grains, which you can shake into the pan, are quite dry; and *if so,* prime, and finish loading; but observe, that in trying this with Mr. Joseph Manton's original patent hammers (which are the best he ever invented), you must, for the *moment,* leave the *pans open,* or *no powder will pass.*

If a stupid fellow wedges dry tow into your gun, with the cleaning-rod, pour boiling water on it, and the rod may then be turned round and drawn out. I remember this occurred with a large punt-gun, at which I caught four men hauling away most unmercifully, but to no effect. I luckily came by and saved the destruction of the cleaning-rod, if not the injury of the barrel, by suggesting this simple contrivance.

These little remedies, I am aware, must be insipid to the reader; but, *when wanted,* often prove worth double the price of a book; so that I have never failed to pencil down, and afterwards insert here, all that I thought had the least chance of being original to the average of sportsmen.

GRAVITATING STOPS.

An insurance from accidents, with a double gun, is completely effected by Mr. Joseph Manton's *gravitating stops,* which *act of themselves,* to remedy the serious danger of loading with a barrel cocked; and, with these stops, you may, by holding the gun downwards, carry both barrels cocked, through a hedge-row, with little or no danger, if *any circumstance* could *justify* such determined preparation.

The gravitating stops, I should not omit to mention, require to be kept *very clean,* as, with rust or dirt under them, they will not fall so readily, and thereby prevent the gun from going off. This I name as a *caution* to a *slovenly shooter,* and *not* as an *imperfection in the plan.* It is much to be regretted that these gravitating stops have gone out of fashion, when they have been the means of preventing many serious accidents to young sportsmen. *I should still decidedly recommend them to all beginners in the use of a double gun.* How Joe can reconcile himself to putting them forth as indispensable, and then become the first to discard them, is to be accounted for no other way, than because they were, of necessity, superseded to admit of a clap-trap-looking thing, called "the cover," which receives and holds copper *primers.*

The primer-guns *should* be contrived without this ugly appendage; and I have reason to think they *will,* before we have completed this edition.

DETONATING SYSTEM.

Now that every gunmaker and almost every sportsman is so infatuated with the detonating, or percussion, system, I can easily imagine that the whole of this edition, which relates to the flint, will by many be considered an obsolete subject, and therefore an useless insertion. I fancy that I see a fashionable sportsman opening this little work, catching his eye on the word "flint," "pan," or "hammer," throwing down the book, walking out of the shop, and exclaiming, "a hundred years out of date!" little aware, however, that, for these last twelve years, I have made, perhaps, more trials of detonaters than any gunmaker in the kingdom; and were I to print every schedule that was carefully noted down at the time of trial, I might compile a work, which would be formed of pages, more, in appearance, like a book of arithmetic, than a work of sentences. I shall therefore not trouble my readers with a dry detail of evidence, but merely insert one of the schedules, with a copy of an impartial opinion which I sent to Mr. Joseph Manton in 1822; as every subsequent trial, up to the present time, has only served more strongly to confirm that opinion.

Were I inclined, however, to make any further observation, it would be to say, that on further and more general trial, I find, so far from not having done justice to the percussion principle, I have, like all other modern shooters, been rather *over*-rating its merits than otherwise: for the more shots I fire, the more I am persuaded that the *flint*-gun shoots the *strongest into the bird*, and by far the *easiest against the shoulder.*

It seems a paradox that a percussion-gun should fire *quicker*, and yet *not stronger* than a flint-gun; but, most assuredly, this is the case. It may perhaps, in some measure, be accounted for thus: the gas flies instantaneously through the whole charge of powder, and puts it in motion with such rapidity, that one half of the powder is not ignited till the other half and the shot have made some progress up the barrel, and, consequently, there takes place (owing, perhaps, to the vacuum which is thus occasioned) a violent concussion or reaction, which, so far from giving strength to the shot, is rather inimical to projectile force, though it causes a severe strain on the barrel, and therefore shakes every other part of the gun. For this reason I find, that instead of almost *equal measure* of powder and shot *(the sure proportion for strong and good shooting)*, a *detonater*, in one's own defence, had better be loaded with *three quarters* in *measure* of powder, to four quarters of shot; and that *long barrels, which are opened behind, and nip the charge, in the cylinder, till more of the powder is burnt, do more justice to the percussion system than the others.* I had ample proof of this by an experiment with a musket of three feet six inches, and a double gun of two feet eight inches. The musket, when made into a detonater, shot very near, if not quite, as well as when a flint-gun; but the double gun did not shoot so well, afterwards, by at least one-fourth! which evidently shows that *quickness and strength* are *not always combined.* For instance: load one gun with large-grained powder, and another with very fine canister-powder. We are quite sure that the latter will fire the *quickest;* but I would back the other to fire the *strongest* if of equally good quality, because the larger powder has the more projectile force. Again, fire a small detonater and a swivel-gun, ay, a twelve-pounder if you please, at a mark only thirty yards off, and see if the little gun does not shoot up to that *distance* as *quick* as, or quicker than, the others! And yet would it not be ridiculous to compare them for *strength?*

Mr. D. Egg made to me a droll, though a good comparison, on the ignition of detonating guns: he said, "If I were to kick a fellow out of my shop, would he go off so strong on his legs as if I allowed him to *walk* out?"

I am not fond of quoting, but nevertheless I must copy a few lines on the percussion principle by Ezekiel Baker, one of the very few master-gunmakers in London who understand *barrels.* I never saw Mr. Baker, though I have read a few extracts from his work, which prove that he has the ability to discover, and the honesty to publish the *real state* of the case. He says, "By the detonating, or percussion principle, the whole of* the powder is fired instantaneously; but the very quickness with which the powder is burned, in my opinion, lessens its general effect, and I am satisfied more execution

* "*The whole of!*" These are the only three words that I have the least doubt of throughout Mr. Baker's observation: as this question, I conceive, depends on what quantity of powder you put into the gun.

will be done at an equal distance with the charge from the common flint. Indeed, I have proved this by many experiments from the same barrel. In rain, or snow, the percussion-lock will act, from its detonating power, more correctly than the common flint-lock; and this, by sportsmen, is considered its greatest, and, I must confess, it appears to me, its only advantage." This, *and I* should *add* (as I observed in 1822) the "wonderful accuracy it gives in so readily obeying the eye:" and (as I observed in 1824) "having scarcely any flash from the lock of the first barrel to intercept the sight of the second."

Another observation should be made: A well-known gunmaker (not Joe Manton), in presence of a well-known sportsman, offered to bet me fifty guineas that a detonater of equal size, &c. would beat a flint-gun. I immediately took up the bet, told his clerk to book it, and offered to double it if he chose. He then fought off, and would not stand to what he proposed. Soon after the sportsman left the shop, and the gunmaker then said to me, "You are quite right; but if you had not taken me up I should have got an order for a brace of detonating guns!" Let this be a lesson, then, to gunmakers, not to be so ready in offering wagers to gentlemen. This was before the late improvements in barrels and the new mode of boring were adopted; for *then* every gunmaker *knew* that he was *deceiving* his customers when he asserted that a detonater would shoot even *equal* to a flint-gun.

In short, it does not require a succession of arguments and anecdotes to prove, that if guns on one principle are sooner shook to pieces, and worn out, than guns on another, it is the interest of the trade not only to universally adopt them, but to employ people, who will write any thing for so much a sheet, to overrate them to the credulous, through the medium of some publication or other. Let the reader, however, put down all that I have said, or that others, in argument against me, may say, as nothing; and only take a walk to some field with a few flint-guns and detonaters, of equal sizes, and fairly try them at two or three quires of paper, and then let his opinion be guided by *facts* instead of *words*.

In the mean time, I will proceed to repeat the same trials that I gave in the earlier editions.

" TRIAL on the 8th of November, 1822, of a 17lbs. Joseph Manton duck-gun, at fifty yards, loaded with four ounces of B. B. shot, and rather more than an equal measure of fine cylinder-powder, at a sheet of pasteboard, and twelve sheets of thick brown paper, which presented a target of 28 by 22 inches in size.

" WITH FLINT-LOCK.

	In the first sheet.	Through the pasteboard and the twelfth sheet.
" Round 1	54	54
2	45	41
3	38	37
Total	137	132

" WITH DETONATING LOCK.

	In the first sheet.	Through the pasteboard and the twelfth sheet.
" Round 1	36	34
2	43	40
3	30	30
Total	109	104

"Majority in favour of the flint in the aggregate of three rounds.

	In the first sheet.	Through the pasteboard and the twelfth sheet.
"With flint-lock	137	132
Detonating lock	109	104
Majority	28	28

"One round, as above, with No. 1 shot:

"WITH DETONATING LOCK.

In the first sheet.	Through all.
75	64

"A round from one of the best fourteen gauge double detonaters in the kingdom, made by Mr. Joseph Manton, with No. 1 shot, as above (with wadding cut by his *new dented punch* on *both powder and shot)*; in order to show, that even the very best small guns will not throw *large shot* like duck-guns:

In the first sheet.	Through all.
35	30

"A second round from the same barrel (loaded with wadding cut by a *common punch* on the *powder*, and wadding cut by a *dented* punch on the *shot)*:

In the first sheet.	Through all.
40	36

"From the result of very many experiments, Col. Hawker is of opinion, that for neat shooting in the field, or covert, and also for killing single shots at wild-fowl, rapidly flying, and particularly by night, there is not a question in favour of the detonater, as its trifling inferiority to the flint is tenfold repaid by the wonderful accuracy it gives in so readily obeying the eye. But, in firing a heavy charge among a large flock of birds, the flint has the decided advantage ; and, moreover, the sudden, and additional, recoil of a detonater, with the full charge of a duck-gun, is apt, if the shooter be not careful, to strike the hand back, and give him a severe blow on the nose.

"A detonater that *does not* light at the *side*, however, is, he thinks, quite" (I should *now*, by further experience, rather say "*almost*") "equal in power to the flint ; but one that *does*, he should be induced, at a rough calculation, to consider one-fifth inferior ; consequently he prefers the guns with breechings made expressly for caps, to those fired with tubes, or any other primers, at a *side* touchhole ; and if this plan was adopted, perhaps the flint might be altogether dispensed with even in *duck*-guns : besides, this invention is more simple, more water-proof, and admits of the gravitating stops. A *detonating gun*, to be sufficiently independent of the muriatic *acid* which is *produced* by the *de*composition, or *detonation* of the fulminating powder, should have *no springs, or moveable bodies outside the lock-plate*, that are dependent on cleanliness ; and, in short, a detonating gun can never be so near perfection as when it has *no springs whatever, except the main-spring and scear-spring*, which, on the principle last mentioned, being well protected inside of the lock-plate, and free from the smoke that is apt to be driven, *even there*, by *all side* communications, no part of the machinery is here dependent in its action on being kept clean from the foulness and rust which is always occasioned by the oxygen gas." (As a more effectual remedy against this, the "back-action" locks are now getting somewhat in vogue. Joe says he discarded them long ago. They may do very well for a hack-gun; but they so disfigure and inconvenience the handle of the stock, that I never desire to see them on any gun of mine, except on a coast "cripple-stopper." But Mr. Bishop has shown me some new locks of Westley Richards that are equally well protected, and far neater in appearance)

"The superiority of the foregoing plan may, perhaps, in a great measure, be accounted for thus:—*every* gun that fires at the *side*, *positively must* have some of its *advantage in shooting sacrificed* to a *good-sized touch-hole*, *or* it will be for ever *liable to miss fire.* A gun that fires near the bottom of the breech, by the hole in a nipple or pivot, has that hole, *however large it may be*, closed up, with the cock, or striker, *by the very blow that puts the charge in action;* and consequently no powder can escape, there being no hole then left open, except the very little gas-hole, which lets out the detonating flame."

SUBSEQUENT TRIAL, on the 18th of November (with No. 7 shot), of a fourteen gauge gun (barrels by Lancaster), with flints, and afterwards with cocks and hammers put on, with which was used the detonating powder:—

	FLINTS.				DETONATERS.			
	RIGHT BARREL.		LEFT BARREL.		RIGHT BARREL.		LEFT BARREL.	
	In 1st sheet.	Through 12th Do.	In 1st sheet.	Through 12th Do.	In 1st sheet.	Through 12th Do.	In 1st sheet.	Through 12th Do.
Round 1	81	49	110	62	89	31	91	42
2	121	61	122	54	69	40	116	47
3	143	63	98	40	80	29	102	49
Total	345	173	330	156	238	100	309	138
Majority in favour of the Flint					107	73	21	18

A round was then fired from each barrel of a *larger* and *heavier detonating* gun of Mr. Joseph Manton's (barrels by Lancaster, and of the same gauge), made expressly to fire with caps, at the *bottom of the breech instead of* through a *side* touch hole:—

RIGHT BARREL.		LEFT BARREL.	
In.	Through.	In.	Through.
120 . . .	75	157 . . .	78

Which seems, as far as cursory observation will prove, to confirm the opinion given after the trial on the 8th instant.

This gun, however, which, from superior weight of metal, had the advantage in the foregoing trial, was afterwards shot against a flint-gun of equal weight; and then the *flint-gun* had the advantage, not only both in strength and closeness, but also in regularity of shooting.

The foregoing trials will show the very great uncertainty of even the best guns at all times throwing the shot alike, and therefore prove the absurdity of talking about people who " never miss," which every one must often do, who shoots beyond thirty-five or forty yards; and consequently this trumpery kind of reputation is only to be maintained by picking and choosing every shot, and therefore losing a third, or perhaps the half, of those birds, which might, otherwise, be put in the bag.

We will now treat on every principal part of the detonating system, in the same order as the flint; and, of course, as briefly as possible.

GUN.

To fire with detonating powder, the gun requires to be much stronger than that used for a flint; it must be heavier to stand the recoil; of a large-sized caliber, in order not to have the powder too narrowly confined, which is absolutely dangerous; and *the London gun-makers will find out sooner or later* that the barrel should rather be 2 feet 10, than 2 feet 8, or the dispro-portionate length of 2 feet 4, or 2 feet 6; unless abso-lutely required to be short, for the convenience of shooting in covert. The breeching should be made on purpose; and I therefore fully acquit the gunmaker of any wish to impose on his customers, when he hesitates to alter the average of flint-guns. A good heavy four-teen gauge gun may be altered by means of a new breeching, or (as a very inferior *make-shift*) with a roller screwed into the touch-hole; for either of which you must of course alter your lock-plate, so that it can no more be used with a flint. The way, however, to use both flint and detonater on the same lock is very simple, but so apt to break the hammer-bridle, that out of six locks which I had altered, five of them were spoiled by this means. *Were the hammer-bridle forged very strong*, I have no doubt it would answer perfectly well; so that if you wished to use either flint or de-tonater, a new lock-plate must be forged on purpose. The hammers which I had put on in town were for ever missing fire; those by Mr. Parsons of Salisbury, by the trifling alteration that I suggested, of placing the nipple as near as possible to the touchhole, and lining the pan all through with platina, fired about eight hundred shots with only about three misses fire, and were decidedly the most certain of any detonating guns, or hammers, I had ever used; till at last, like all the rest, off flew one of the hammers. I am ready to admit, that a nipple on the *centre of a hammer* is *less likely to strain the hammer-bridle;* but then the communication, by placing it there, is so much longer, that the discharge of the gun can never be depended on. I had my hammers done in this way at first, and when on salt water, the gun, on an average, missed fire every eight or ten shots; and, in field-shooting, about once in twenty shots. Several sportsmen, however, have assured me, that their guns have gone well for a whole season, after being altered in this way. Far be it from me to doubt their word; but still it is my duty to the public to speak of this, and every thing else, not as I have *heard of*, but as I have *found* it. I afterwards had a double gun "*detonated*" to my order (with new breechings, &c.) by Mr. Parsons. I then tried sixty shots with it, and part of the time in showers of rain. It did not miss fire once; and it is but justice to observe too, that the alteration is done in as workman-like a manner as if it had been turned out of hand at nearly double the price in London. I have occasionally used this gun ever since,—and no work can stand better, or do more credit to any tradesman, than this job does to Mr. Parsons of Salisbury.

A new patent self-priming detonater was completed by Mr. Joseph Manton, previously to his failure in Hanover-square; and, what with doing, undoing, new tools, &c., cost him perhaps not less than £200. He brought it to show me, and I told him it would never answer; and, as some proof that I was right, I need only state, that this gun was bought at the sale for a mere nothing (Lancaster told me £14), and then I believe was discarded by the purchaser. It is but seldom, however, that Joe has invented any thing without success; and as to his workmanship, as I always said, was I merely to observe that Mr. Joseph Manton's guns are so far before those of the gunmakers in general, that those who cannot see this are like indifferent judges of a picture, who, for want of profound science, would be as well pleased with the gaudy painting of some young artist as with the picture of a fine old master, I should appear like a hireling of this maker. But I only beg of whoever differs with me in opinion, when he next sees any other first-rate gunmaker or mechanic in town or country, to say to him, "Now tell me, on your honour as a tradesman, whose guns, NEXT TO YOUR OWN," [*mind this*] "are the best and most scientifically made?" and if they do not say (or think) "Mr. Joseph Manton's," I will resign all claim to judgment of a gun, or to the kind patronage with which my work has been honoured. In short, let any one look (not with the naked eye, but with a *magnifying glass*) at the work in every part of Mr. Joseph Manton's guns, and at those of most other makers, and he will discover about the same difference that there is between one of Leader's or Houlditch's town-built coaches, and that gothic vehicle which among our moderns is yclept a "*Jarvy.*"

But let every man make every part of a gun himself, and then, I believe, the late Mr. D. Egg would in his younger days have had the laugh against them all. This, however, is no more required than that an architect should handle well a hammer or a trowel; and a great part of those mechanics who set up and work for themselves consists of those who, from having been journeymen in only one department of gunmaking, are probably but superficially acquainted with even the theory of the other.

THE BARREL

Should be fourteen gauge, to let the powder burn easy; and (as before observed) *at least* two feet eight inches; and if two feet ten inches, or even three feet, so much the better; in order not only to keep the shot together at long distances, but to prevent the gas from driving out the powder before it is thoroughly ignited. It has been argued to me (by the way) that many people have cut long barrels shorter, and found that they afterwards killed even better! Very likely: and for why? —because the barrels were *improperly bored for a long caliber*, and therefore, the length, from this circumstance, became mere lumber, if not an obstruction, instead of being the greatest possible assistance.

THE BREECHING

Is cupped similar to that for a flint, though of course with a shorter chamber; and by all means should be forged in one solid piece. Joe Manton's breeching has hitherto proved by far the best for detonating guns; and I will therefore give the modern sections of it. But I will leave them till we treat of the *caps* and *primers*, in order to *point out, in a good place, the different modes of ignition.*

In the mean time, while under this head, let us introduce another new, or at all events newly adapted, breeching.

Mr. Wilkinson's Breeching.

To show the necessity of retarding the powder, in detonating guns, in order that it may be all ignited, I will only beg the favour of any one, who may doubt this, to call on Mr. Wilkinson, in Pallmall, and look at an ingeniously contrived machine that he has invented for the purpose of *proving* it. By this experiment you will *see the detonating flame pass through a whole charge of even fine powder*, the greater part of which he will afterwards pour out on a sheet of paper, and thus prove to you that it has not exploded. This has induced him to invent what he calls a "*counter-parabolic*" breeching; or, as high-flown language on subjects of this kind savours too much of the cock-loft style, suppose, by way of variety, we go to the other extreme and say "*Jack-boot*" breeching. *Vide Sketch**.

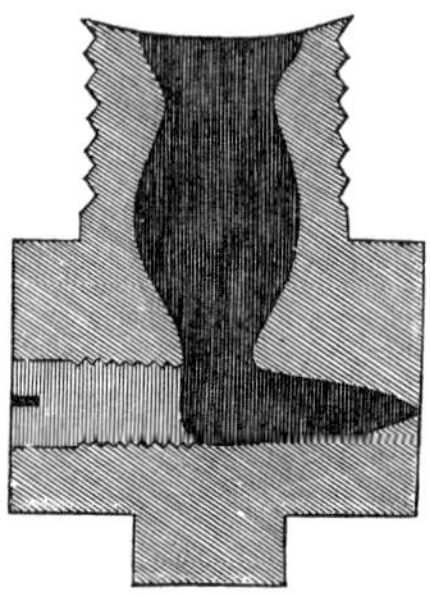

This breeching, as will be seen by the annexed representation of it, has a chamber somewhat like that

* Mr. W. now means to call it his "Elliptical" breeching.

of Mr. Wilkinson's relation, the celebrated old Henry Nock, except being *contracted towards the top*. He has published a well-written pamphlet, in order to state and explain its advantage, in strength, over other breechings. But further experience will best show whether or not this is more difficult to clean, or gives a more severe blow to the shoulder; and whether this, or opening the barrels behind, is the best mode of gaining strength by retardation. Perhaps Mr. W. will give the barrels an increased weight of metal, in order to avoid the risk of additional recoil, as the best means of getting his breeching into repute. The other gun-makers say, "This is as old as the hills!" Well, and what of that?—was it ever tried with *detonaters* before? Whenever people abuse any thing, be sure that they have no sinister motive in so doing before you attend to them.

VENT-HOLE.

A detonater without a vent-hole, though perhaps it may shoot a little stronger, is very liable to corrode, and recoils most cruelly. The best vent-hole, to my fancy, is a fixed one of platina, similar to a touchhole; as *vent-screws*, I find, are liable to rust in; and, unless lined with platina, are either soon choked up with rust and dirt, or blown too large by repeated shooting.

THE NIPPLE, OR PIVOT,

Is best plain or polished; the caps, if made well, will always keep on; but when the pivot is made like a screw, it collects rust, always looks bad, and gives additional trouble in cleaning. The hole in the nipple must not be too small, and well increased in size downwards, or this deadly poison to all fire-arms (the oxygen gas) will choke up the communication with rust, and repeated missing fire will be the consequence. A very strong main-spring will counteract all the bad effects of a large hole, by firmly closing it with the cock, in striking the very blow, as I before observed, that puts the charge in motion. The nipple (the only article that need be made to separate from the breeching) must, of course, have a square base, so as to be removable at pleasure, by means of a little wrench.

There are various opinions as to placing the nipple or pivot. The favourite plan appears to be that of having it perpendicular, for the convenience of putting on the copper caps. For my own part, however, I prefer it sloping, because, in the event of the copper flying, the eye is not then parallel with the circle of splinters, should one of them, by accident, escape from the concave head of the cock or striker.

THE COCK, OR STRIKER,

Should cover the nipple with a deep concave head, so that scarcely any of the copper can escape, or a man may lose his eye. Several accidents have happened through the neglect of this. If, however, the concave head of the cock is too small in diameter, or strikes the least on one side, so as to cause any friction against the side of the cap, the gun will most probably miss fire.

Another important observation should be made under

this head: people try copper-cap guns in a *shop*, and fancy they are safe if the copper does not fly about. *This* is *no trial at all;* because the way that accidents happen is through the *recoil of the gun* forcing the cock from the nipple, and then all security is at an end. Try this by having a heavily loaded gun with a weak main-spring, and the cock will fly up so far as to catch at the half, if not the full, bent, unless you happen to have a nipple-hole so small that it would be for ever missing fire. To obviate this, be sure that your main-springs are strong, and have their greatest force on the *first pull;* and, as a still further security, you might have an extra shield or fence round the cock *. By far the best striker is the moveable one that Joe Manton always used, and with which I never heard of an accident; because, with this, the cock may be set mathematically true, on the nipple, before the striker is added. But now the trade have no better guide than the mere sweep of a pair of compasses; and "serve you out" with a frightful-looking thing called the "dolphin"-cock. Why is this? because any tolerable workman can make half a dozen of the one, while it requires a first-rate mechanic, with as much time and expense, to complete a pair of the others!

SAFETY-COCK.

I had, last year, a narrow escape from losing my eye, although with a gunmaker's expensive copper cap of double thickness. I was firing an almost perpendicular shot (from the left lock, which is, of course, by far the most dangerous) with a "dolphin-"cock; and received

* The succeeding article will show that this is not only desirable, but absolutely necessary.

the *wound* from nothing but the *gas* or *flame;* while the cap itself remained as perfect as when first put on the nipple. I therefore contrived a shield, and sent to Lancaster every cap-lock in my possession, in order to have new cocks, or strikers, on this plan. But, to cut the matter short, I 'll now conclude with a sketch of it; as I then enable every one to make it, and may thereby save many serious accidents.

Applied
To common " Dolphin." To superior Striker-Cock.

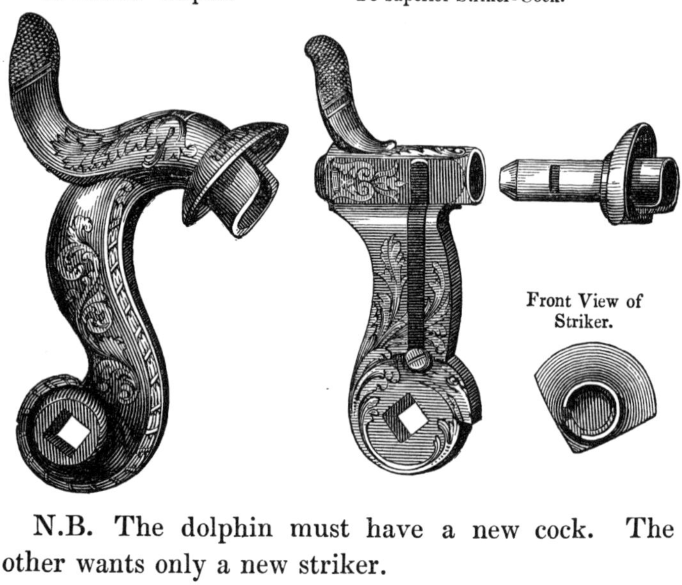

N.B. The dolphin must have a new cock. The other wants only a new striker.

No one, as yet, understands this job so well as Lancaster.

COPPER CAPS.

The copper cap is now in general use for detonaters, and it gives me satisfaction to see it; because, from the first, I always pronounced it to be the best mode of priming, and even in opposition to Joe Manton himself. I do not mean to say that I was the inventor of it—very probably not: but this I must beg leave to state:—when Joe first brought out his detonaters, in Davies-street (those which were discarded from giving so much trouble), he made me the most perfect gun I ever saw; and, doubting whether such another could be got, I set my wits to work in order to simplify the invention. At last the plan of a perforated nipple, and the detonating powder in the crown of a small cap, occurred to me. I made a drawing of it, which I took to Joe. After having this explained, he said he would show me something in a few weeks' time; when, lo and behold! there was a rough gun altered precisely on my own plan! His factotum, poor old Asell, assured me that the whole job was done from my drawing. Thus Joe, who led the fashion for all the world, sent out a few copper-cap guns, and I know with some degree of reluctance. The trade, finding that he had then deviated from his own patent, adopted this plan; and it proved to answer so well, that we now see it in general circulation. So much, and no more, have I to say about the wished-for discovery of the copper-cap inventor. But if Mr. this and Mr. that have any fancy to claim the invention, they may safely fire their ammunition into all the periodicals they please, as I shall not indulge them with any paper-war on the subject.

The innumerable accidents that have occurred with copper caps have been occasioned by three causes: 1st, bad workmanship, in not bringing the blow of the striker to act equally on all parts of the nipple; 2dly, *want* of a *proper fence* to *protect the eye;* and, 3dly, a want of sufficient strength in the *first lifting of* the main-spring. I need scarcely add, too, that having the caps of bad quality has perhaps doubled the number of accidents. For instance, French caps, being now to be had for about two francs a thousand, are frequently imported to England, and sold at an immense profit; and, although these may do very well with *weak French* powder, yet they are so unfit to be trusted with *our* powder, that the loss of many sportsmen's eyes has been the consequence. I know one gunmaker who recommended them for no other purpose than to ruin the copper-*cap* guns, and thereby improve the trade for *primers.*

N. B. If the hole of your nipple should become choked up with copper, as is frequently the case, *put on another cap and let it off, before you load the gun;* and nine times out of ten the force of the fulminating powder will clear the hole. But if this is done, it should be with *anti*-corrosive caps; as the other preparation, *unless mixed with powder*, materially injures the iron. This being so quick a remedy, we may always try it before we have recourse to the nipple-wrench. Let us now inspect the breechings before we go on to copper primers.

Copper-Cap Breeching. — Copper-Primer Breeching. — Outside View of a Copper-Primer Breeching.

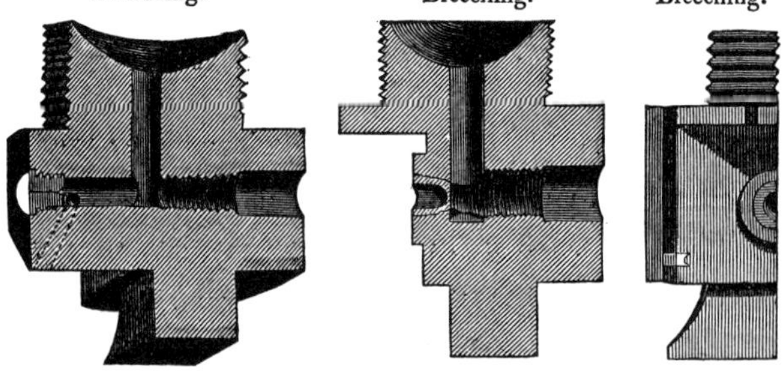

The two dotted lines point out the hole into which the gas from the *cap* is driven.

N.B. Now turn the book: and, by looking at these sections with the page lengthwise, you will perceive that they are *not* left-hand breechings, as they appear to be in the above position. But each one is the *upper* half of a *right*-hand breeching, cut through the centre, as you would divide the body of a lobster.

CAP-CHARGERS.

An invention of French origin; though Mr. Sykes has made them for some years. Mr. Brownjohn of Basingstoke has improved them so much, that they are now generally patronised by our Hampshire sportsmen; and those which he sent me answered extremely well, after a few amendments that I suggested. They are sold by Mr. Beatly of Basingstoke.

My friend, Captain Ward, has also contrived a very good cap-charger, one of which he was kind enough to send me, and it answers perfectly well. The chief novelty in his is a dial-plate, by which you can see how many rounds you have, without taking off the cover. This charger, I believe, is sold by Burnett of Southampton.

Greenfield has also his invention, which I like as well as any; because, to prime on *his* plan, you have only to pull the machine off at right angles, instead of raising it up, and thereby frequently loosening the cap.

A round charger is decidedly preferable to a long one; not only from being pleasanter to carry, and to handle, but from the facility of placing it between the cock and the nipple, where the long one, in many guns, takes up so much room that you are obliged to put your lock to the full cock before you can prime.

With regard to the merits of the cap-chargers, there is but little difficulty in forming an opinion.—When you have *two* barrels to load, there is one motion less to go through, than if you had to dip twice in your pocket: they enable you to prime with gloves on, which is a great comfort, in cold weather; and they are at all times desirable for clumsy-handed shooters. But to load *one* barrel in warm weather, I could be *sooner* ready *without* the charger; because the *time that it takes to put the charger back in the pocket* might be occupied in knocking down a snap shot.—I say nothing about suspending such things to the button or shot-belt, because they are there a great annoyance, and particularly in covert.

COPPER PRIMERS; OR TUBES.

These were decidedly invented by Joe Manton; and give the quickest of all communications. [*Vide* Breechings.] But with a copper *primer* you have the inconvenience of pushing the little tube against the resistance of a spring, every time you load, and the extra trouble of keeping clean the machinery on your lock-plate, not to say a word of its ugly appearance. Although the copper primer may be perfectly safe to the shooter himself, yet wo betide the eye of his companion if the tube happens to escape and fly off sidewise! It must be admitted, however, that for battûs and other *incessant* firing, the copper primer is not so liable to "choke up" as the copper-cap gun. This primer is the *only percussion recipe* that will give a short communication, and therefore certain ignition, to *large duck-guns:* moreover, it is by far the best for *salt* water; as you can wax the primers, and make them water-proof. [The *anti*-corrosive powder should *never* be used for copper *primers.*]

TUBE-CHARGER.

This is the invention of J. Greenfield, who lives at No. 14, Molyneux-street, Bryanstone-square, and who was not only one of Joe's very best workmen, but his cabinet counsellor in all matters of difficulty. No man in London has invented more little articles, *for other people to get the credit of*, than Greenfield. I cannot describe the use of his charger better than from his own statement, which is as follows :—

" The object of this invention is to" prime " guns with expedition and certainty, which experience has proved to be a matter attended with much difficulty and inconvenience by the mode hitherto practised, of supplying the charge with the fingers. Nor is this the only advantage to be obtained by the use of this instrument; as by its means, a much shorter tube may be applied, which will in a very considerable degree prevent the outward flash, and lessen the report occasioned by its explosion, and thus effectually remedy the evil so generally complained of by gentlemen who have been in the habit of using the tube guns."

WESTLEY RICHARDS'S NEW STEEL-PRIMER.

Of all the inventions that have been brought out since the flourishing days of Joseph, this, in my humble opinion, is decidedly the best. I have tried it repeatedly, and never yet knew it fail; and my son shot with it for a whole season, and never had one miss fire. I shall therefore give an engraving of it; as well as a copy of Mr. Richards's specification.

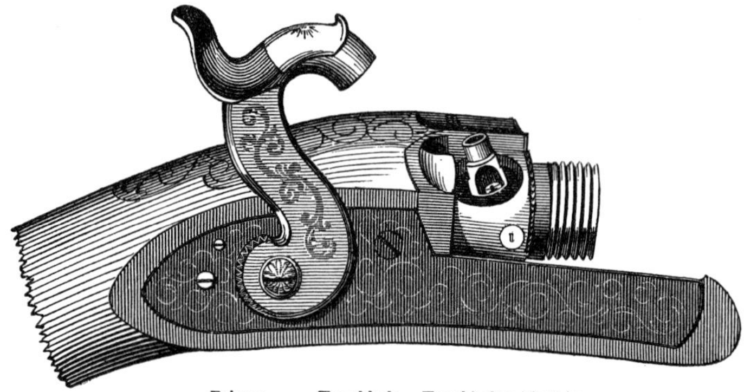

Primer. Touchhole. Touchhole with Primer.

" The quantity of percussion powder requisite for the steel primers is very small, consequently the flame and noise made by them is much less than from the copper cap; when the gun is discharged, it is not so distressing to the ear and head. Many sportsmen will find this a great advantage.

" The impossibility of unexploded material, or copper, annoying the face and eyes, an inconvenience that often happens from the use of light French, or badly manufactured, caps.

" The communication to the charge is considerably shortened, which affords a more complete and quicker ignition of the powder in the breech. The touchhole can never be stopped up from copper, as the cone of the copper cap frequently is.

" The primers are of a large size, and very ready to handle in cold weather: the gun therefore is primed with great facility. They may be removed from the touchhole instantly, which is a perfect security against accident, should the gun be entrusted to any person to carry, or be brought into the house loaded.

" The steel primers are waterproof in wet weather *. They must be pressed well home.

" All copper cap guns can have the patent touchholes applied to them, *without interfering with the copper cap system.* The touch-

* Provided they are waxed, or varnished.—*Author.*

hole and the primer, or the cone for the copper cap, may be *used in the same breech.*

"The greatest possible care and attention will be paid in the application of the patent touchholes to the guns of other makers."

THE SIDE-NAIL

Should be made of the *best tempered spring steel,* and *stouter* than that for a flint-gun.

All side-nails, whether for flint or detonaters, should go through both locks in a double gun, and have a notch at each end, so that, if they break, they may be screwed out, and replaced by an extra one in the field.

THE DISSECTION

Is much more simple; and your locks remain on the stock while in the case, so that you have only to put in your barrels *(remembering that you must draw up the cocks first),* and your gun is ready for the field.

CLEANING.

Similar to a flint-gun, and rather less to do: but you must leave every thing, as well as the inside of the barrels, kept a *very little* damp with sweet oil, or your gun will rust fifty times worse than with common powder.

It should be observed, however, that when the oxygen *mixes with gunpowder,* in its explosion, it becomes less injurious to the iron; consequently the cocks and breechings receive even more damage from this composition than do the insides of the barrels.

Now for a little petty larceny;—book-making—paper and paste work;—an easy way of doing business:—

DIRECTIONS,

That Lancaster has printed, proper to be observed by gentlemen using detonating guns.

1. Load with the cocks down, which prevents the powder from being forced out of the pegs that receive the copper caps.

2. Prime the last thing; otherwise, in ramming down the wadding, the powder will be driven into the caps, and become so firmly compressed as to destroy their effect.

3. Should the caps be put on by mistake, prior to loading, force them off with the turnscrew, and replace them with new ones.

4. Keep the caps dry. If exposed to the fire for a few minutes when required for use, they will never fail. Take care that no oil or grease gets to them.

5. Always clean those parts of the barrels and locks that the detonating powder acts upon with a wet rag; then rub them dry, and leave them in oil, to prevent rust. The pegs should not be taken out too often.

6. Before you take out the barrels, bring the locks to half cock. The locks do not require to be taken off every time the gun is used: once a fortnight is quite sufficient. Put a little fine oil to the parts where there is friction: but if the gun has been used on a wet day, the locks should be taken off to be cleaned and oiled immediately.

N.B. Detonating locks should not be snapt either with or without the copper caps, but in the act of shooting. When the gun is loaded, the flash from the detonating powder never enters the inside of the barrel, but if snapt upon the caps when the gun is unloaded, it drives the detonating gas into the barrels, which creates rust; and if done without the caps the works are liable to be injured, by reason of the cocks meeting no resistance in their fall, as in flint-locks.

The pegs should by no means be used after the holes are worn large by repeated firing, as it will weaken the force of the gun, and damage the lock.

Directions for cleaning Guns.

1. Place the breech end of the barrels about three inches deep in a bucket with cold water; then, after wetting the sponge, cloth, or

tow, introduce the rod into the barrels, and work it well; then apply the wire brush attached to the cleaning-rod with some clean hot water, which will take out all the lead in the operation. This should be invariably attended to, as it is well known washing only will not remove the lead.

2. Wipe the rod and outside of the barrels dry, and set the latter upright, muzzle downwards, for two minutes, to drain, after which rub them out perfectly dry.

3. Wipe the barrels out clean, then pass an oiled rag down the inside, and rub over the outside; leave them a little oily, which will prevent rust.

The use of cloth is preferred, as not subjecting gentlemen to the serious accidents that have happened from leaving tow in the chamber.

Brass, being in its nature softer than iron, allows of the brush being used without the possibility of injury to the barrels.

"So much for" Lancaster—and all very right; except that I prefer a little fine sand or brickdust to the wire brush.

> "A man convinced against his will
> Is of the same opinion still."

LOADING.

As I before observed, you are obliged, in your own defence, to load a detonater lighter than a flint-gun; and as it goes quicker (though not stronger, as the gun-makers would wish to make you believe), and for other reasons before given, you may use a fourth less powder than with a flint-gun. Many sportsmen feel quite positive that a detonater shoots *much stronger* than a flint. This, I have no doubt, is because it does not allow them time to flinch, and therefore they *fire the body of the charge so much more accurately* with a detonater, that they kill cleaner and at greater distances.

The *safest* way to load a detonater is to put the caps on *last*, taking care to leave down the cocks; or the powder, unless of large grain, would, on ramming the wadding, be forced through the hole in the nipple. [But let me observe, *en passant*, that I think the use of large-grained powder ridiculous, at all events in small copper-*cap* guns, because you are never sure that it will fill a dirty chamber, much less arrive near the hole of the nipple.] If you put away your gun loaded, always take off the caps, not only for safety, but because the locks must either be left straining at half cock, or if let down and suffered to remain all night, the odds are that the powder would be jammed into a sort of damp paste, and both barrels would miss fire. But if you take fresh caps, and prick both the vent-holes, and the nipple-holes, your gun will generally fire with its usual rapidity.

Detonating powder I *have found* very liable to miss fire after being long in contact with any salt or damp, such as a strong pressure on the elastic fluid of gunpowder; being all night in a punt in the sea air; the spray that comes over a boat in sailing, &c.

In a word, although detonating powder may be *put in water*, and *then fired off*, yet it frequently *misses fire* after being *long in the damp*—and particularly when shooting on *salt* water. I am inclined to account for it by the following comparison :—Take a piece of biscuit, or (what would answer the proof much better) crisp gingerbread; dip it in water for a short time, and it will nevertheless remain hard enough to crack before it will bend. But, on the other hand, if you lay it in a damp cellar all night, it will not be found crisp in the morning. So it is with detonating powder; by *long-*

continued damp it loses its crispness, and then, of course, will no longer crack, or, in other words, fire by percussion.

One of the recipes for making detonating powder is:

One ounce of oxymuriate of potash,
One-eighth of an ounce of superfine charcoal,
One-sixteenth of an ounce of sulphur,
Mixed with gum-arabic water, and then dried. It should be mixed up in wood, for fear of accident.

Another, and, I am told, a far better proportion, is:

Five of oxymuriate;
Two of sulphur; and
One of charcoal.

I merely give the recipe, in case a sportsman should be in a place where he cannot buy the composition, as I presume, that no one in his senses would run the risk of being blown up, in order to make, perhaps indifferently, what he could so cheaply purchase in perfection. But why should I dwell for a moment on this *now?* when there is scarcely a shop in any country town but can serve you with caps which are, at all events, equal to home-made ones.

The foregoing directions are, I trust, sufficient; and I have confined them to the most simple, and, therefore, as yet, the best detonating system: which, in the trifling matter of caps, patches, &c. may be suited to the shooter's fancy; but, as to all those intricate magazines, moveable bodies, and other complicated machinery, I leave their merits, and the directions about them, to the dissertation of some very learned mechanic, as their advantage and utility are far beyond my comprehension.

ANTI-CORROSIVE PERCUSSION POWDER.

In August, 1824, I gave the following statement relative to this powder:

"Since the first part of this work was printed off, a letter has been received from Mr. Joyce, chemist, 11, Old Compton-street, Soho, commenting, as he is fully justified in doing, on the injury done to fire-arms by the oxymuriate of potash; and enclosing a specification of a new 'ANTI-*corrosive*' percussion powder. The author, however, is extremely tenacious of misleading his readers, by recommending any article that has not been thoroughly tried; and, therefore, all he can as yet say is, that he has fired 24 copper caps with this new powder, after dipping each cap, for some time, in water, and not one of them missed fire; nor was there any acid produced by the decomposition.

"Were Mr. Joyce's invention good for the gun trade, it would soon find its way to the public; and, if defective, he might expect every assistance for its improvement. But as, on the contrary, it is rather the reverse, he may probably meet with obstacles to getting it fairly circulated for trial; and, for this very reason, the author is induced to mention it. He hopes, therefore, that some other sporting-writer, who may be going to press after the ensuing season, will have time to review, and further inform the public as to the merits or demerits of this invention."

Little was I aware, at the time of writing this, that the third edition would be out of print in a few months, and that it would fall to my lot to give the next report of this powder.

I before said, "as this new system is the life and soul of trade, let us hope that the gunmakers will exert their chemical powers to render this 'devil's powder' (as Mr. D. Egg used to call it) less poisonous to fire-arms."

It appears, however, that the gunmakers knew better. But Mr. Joyce has proved a sad enemy to the fraternity who fatten on the destruction of iron, by establishing a manufactory of this anti-corrosive percussion powder, in which he does away entirely with the oxymuriate.

It may be hardly fair to say publicly what the composition is (*because Mr. Joyce candidly told me*, though I believe it is pretty well known); and although it was long ago adopted by Mr. Goode Wright of Hereford (according to a statement which, as an utter stranger, I was favoured with by this gentleman), yet Mr. Joyce has had so many obstacles to overcome before he could bring it to perfection, that we must, at all events, give him a great deal of credit. In short, it is of no consequence to me as the writer, and much less to the public as readers, how much credit is to be given to one of these gentlemen or to the other; so let them fight it out themselves, and, in the mean time, leave me to go on with my work. For I have as much dislike to superfluous writing, as to interfering with the contests of others. Enough of this—now again to the point about the powder.—When Mr. Joyce first brought it forward, his agent in Birmingham had served him with caps of *brittle cannon-metal*, instead of the *best worked copper*. The consequence was, that many sportsmen, and I among the number, were severely cut, and had nearly lost an eye, owing to the quality of the *cap*, *not* the *powder*. This was of course a glorious victory for all Mr. Joyce's oxygen-opponents, and the fault was *unjustly* laid on the *composition*. I can only say, however, by subsequent experience, that *since Mr. Joyce has used nothing but good copper*, all the caps that I had of him have gone as well as any in the kingdom, and his percussion powder does not injure the guns any thing like so much as the other. Let him, therefore, be *very careful, in future, to get supplied with* GOOD COPPER, of a good substance, and I may safely venture to recommend his "Anti-corrosive percussion powder." He is *now* sure to be well served, as he employs Greenfield.

P.S. 1830. Mr. Joyce, having since paid great attention to this, has now completely established his powder all over the world ; and is therefore no longer in need of any one to plead his cause. A large new manufactory is now established by him at No. 55, Bartholomew Close, West Smithfield; and so extensive is this business, that the chemical establishment in Compton-street has been resigned to Mr. Potter, who is Mr. Joyce's retail dealer in, and therefore the best agent for gentlemen to apply to if they want, copper caps. There is now a great deal of imposition going on in the copper-cap line; and I feel it my duty to mention it, in order to put gentlemen on their guard.

Mr. Joyce's manufactory, which I formerly spoke of, was burnt down, by which he lost about £5000, as he was refused insurance. But, in my last edition, I was just in time to announce his intention of rebuilding it. Now all is complete again, and his concern, I am happy to say, is in a more flourishing state than ever.

SHOOTING,

Difference in, between a Flint and a Detonater.

Here we come to a part of the subject, the very title of which, in the present day, would soon clear off an edition of a pamphlet: and it therefore becomes a matter of surprise that the book manufacturers have not been more on the alert in reaping a harvest from it; as this fashionable theme, if well diluted with anecdotes and specifications, might be spun into a good-sized volume. All that is really wanted, however, is the essence of the subject, and therefore I shall make my humble attempt to give it.

As a detonater goes so very much quicker than a flint, it becomes necessary, in firing one, to avoid shooting *too* forward; and I should, therefore, revert to my former hints for young men learning to shoot, and say, *observe precisely all that I before said under the head of shooting*, but IF YOU HAVE A DETONATER make only HALF the allowance; that is, where you would fire SIX inches before a bird with a flint, fire only THREE INCHES with a DETONATER; AND SO ON. If a sportsman has been all his life an indifferent shot, which he may be, either through never having acquired the knack of firing sufficiently forward; flinching as he pulls the trigger; dropping his hand before the gun is fairly discharged; or many other such circumstances: I most strongly advise him to lose not a moment in getting a detonater, because I have known many instances, where a man had been a very bad shot all his life, through defects which the use of a detonater might so effectually remedy, that by taking up one he might, almost immediately, become a tolerable, if not a very good shot. For one, however, who has always shot well with a flint, it becomes somewhat difficult to give advice. On first taking up the detonater, he will, by habit, fire well forward at all his game, and, very probably, have the mortification to miss such shots, as he was before in the habit of killing. (Of this I was an eye-witness when out with one of the most certain shots in England.) He will soon, however (to use a sailor's expression), "know the trim" of his gun ; and, taking all things into consideration, most probably shoot still more accurately with a detonater than he had been used to do with a flint, by reason of its *very great readiness in obeying the pull of the trigger, before the eye or hand has time to vary ;* its equal rapidity in foul or damp weather ; and having scarcely any flash from the lock of the first barrel to intercept the sight of the second. He must, however, compound for a greater recoil to the shoulder ; and, on the whole, I should say, to missing fire rather oftener than with a good flint, *provided he is out in fine still weather.* We may, therefore, on the whole, taking all things into consideration, say, that *at first* a detonater may make a *good shot* an *indifferent shot,* and *both first and last* an *indifferent shot* a *good shot,* and therefore we may be rather inclined to give the balance in its favour. But, to coincide with all the panegyrics that are written, by keen young sportsmen who happen, perhaps, to have been shooting extremely well, and despatch their bulletins on the spur of the moment, would be to overrate the detonater, and to underrate the flint, and therefore not giving a fair and disinterested opinion.

Why it becomes a question whether a good shot ought to fly to a detonater or not is this:—After he has been using one for a season, or even a few weeks' shooting, he will, on taking up his flint-gun again, find that it goes comparatively so slow, after the other, that it will appear to hang fire; and, very probably, so puzzle and disconcert him, that perhaps his best and favourite gun is either packed up for the pawnbroker, or stripped of its flint-appendages, and metamorphosed into a detonater. And the whole armoury, if he has many guns, is considered as mere lumber, unless altered, or exchanged for guns on the detonating system. He therefore takes to fulminating powder, like a wife, "for better for worse," and this is one of the chief reasons why the percussion plan has so rapidly superseded the flint. Did both go equally quick, I am inclined to think the flint would have held the majority. If a sportsman, who has no money to throw away, has been *accommodated* with the loan of a detonater, the only way for him to *back out* of it, is to *modulate* as it were into his flint-gun again, by using the slowest old musket he can lay hands on, and then taking, *after that*, his best flint-gun.

Before dismissing this subject, I must just name one circumstance:—While I was using nothing but detonating guns for four seasons, it was the remark of my man, that he never had the pleasure to see me make such long shots as I was once in the habit of doing; and I, ready to lay all the fault on myself, or rather to a premature attack of that anno domini complaint which must befall the best of us, felt that I dare not blame a system which my superiors had so universally adopted. I took up a flint-gun. This was worse and worse; as its comparative slowness made me miss even fair shots. The next year, however, having been prevented, by illness, from taking a gun in hand till just before the end of the season, the sensation of firing a flint and a detonater became as it were *de novo.* I accordingly took out a *flint*-gun, and *down came the long shots,* as in former days!—I name this as a simple fact. Let others argue the point as they please. So I shall now conclude the subject by reducing the matter to a very few words. Can you shoot well with a flint-gun? Yes! Then "leave well enough alone!" Can *you?* No! Then, by all means, go and get a detonater!

I have now, I hope and trust, fairly and disinterestedly stated all that is necessary, both for and against the detonating system, which, at no small expense, I have tried by every kind of experiment, in order to be able to give my opinion to the public independent, instead of with the assistance, of gunmakers. But, before I close the subject, let me not appear inconsistent:—I still maintain that the detonater has not the power of the flint-gun, and yet I admit that, by a different mode of boring, the percussion-guns are now wonderfully improved: insomuch as to be almost equal in strength to the flint-guns. Nay, I will say even more:—give them an increased weight of metal, which to many is a trouble to carry; retard the charge, and thus increase the recoil; and then I admit, with the very great improvement that has lately been made in barrels, they will no doubt *even beat* those flint-guns which were manufactured a few years ago; but, without all this, they would be found as inferior as ever to flint-guns.

GUN-CASES.

THE wonderful improvements and increase of light coaches have of late rendered travelling sportsmen more independent of the mails, or to use the modern term, "*paper-carts*;" so that we are no longer at the mercy of guards and coachmen for taking a gun-case on a journey. But, in the few instances where it may be found inconvenient, the shooter may carry his gun in a sail-cloth, and over that an oil-skin case: or, as a safer plan, have a short piece of wood, just to *fill up* the *hollow* of his stock, made flat at the top, and with *loops* to receive the *bolts* at the bottom. Let the parts where his locks fit in have pieces of wood fitted into them also; and the locks may be put in his portmanteau. The stock, thus secured and covered over, may then be safely put in the coach-seat, and he may either lay the barrel with it, or carry it in his hand; or sling both, in a bit of canvas, under the inside of the roof. But, with copper-*cap* percussion-guns, all this trouble, about the *locks*, may be avoided; as they are more simple, and therefore less liable to accidents.

POWDER.

All our trouble with guns would be ill bestowed, if we neglected a due attention to the care and choice of this article.

Gunpowder, when good, is made of ingredients perfectly pure, properly mixed, and judiciously proportioned.

The *principal ingredient, saltpetre,* should be entirely divested of *marine salt,* as that is a great obstacle to the production of good powder, of which there is, in all saltpetre, a certain, and often a considerable quantity; and, in proportion as it is more or less freed from *that impurity*, so the powder will be more or less liable to imbibe damp air, and become proportionally moist and weak. But when it is *perfectly freed* from marine salt, the powder will suffer but little diminution of its strength from being carelessly kept, or even openly exposed to a moist atmosphere, as what it might, by this means, have lost, would be presently restored by drying it.

Your powder should always be properly *dried;* in order to do which, make *two* or *three* plates very hot, before the fire, and *(first taking care to wipe them well, lest any particle of cinder should adhere to them)* keep constantly shifting the powder from the one to the other, without allowing it to remain sufficiently long on either, to cool the plate. The powder will then be more effectually aired, and more expeditiously dried, than by the more common means of using *one* plate, which the powder, by lying on it, soon makes cold, and therefore the plate requires to be two or three times heated. (This is another little discovery since the earlier editions.) Nothing preserves the strength of powder better than, after being dried, to put it into canisters, securely *corked* from the air. Mr. Butts latterly did so, by my advice. Beware of going any where near the fire to dry powder on plates. Recollect how far a hot cinder will sometimes fly, and therefore, to be on the sure side, run with your hot plates out of the room, and go where there is no fire. As a still safer plan too, I might name the use of a common pewter *water-plate*, or dish; by having recourse to which there can be *no* risk of accident; except that, through awkwardness, the powder might be *wetted*, instead of being *dried*. *This* way of drying is much on the same principle as that which is now in general use in powder works; viz. by means of steam passing through pipes, or other receptacles, by transfusion of heat through those pipes, or cases, from which the air of the drying-room is heated to as great a degree as is requisite for the purpose of drying the powder.

Good powder burns *red in the pan*, will keep its strength for two years (or more, if made with due care and attention to the principles before mentioned), and may be had from most of the mills.

As I formerly observed, Pigou and Andrews's has

the name of being the best, and is unquestionably most excellent; but I have never found any to please me quite so well as the *cylinder powder*, which was originally prepared by Mr. Butts, of Hounslow, whose more important concerns, in manufacturing for government, had for many years (luckily for his rivals) prevented him, in some degree, from showing forth in the sporting world. In my former editions, I stated that the government contracts, though probably not at an end with Mr. Butts, would soon be considerably lessened; and we should, therefore, have reason to hope, that there would not exist that difficulty, which there was then, in procuring this extraordinary good powder. My predictions have since been verified; and Mr. Butts, after highly distinguishing himself in the sporting world, retired with the ample fortune which he deserved; and, I regret to add, died in November, 1824. His successors are Messrs. Curtis and Mr. Harvey, from whom I continue to receive the cylinder powder, if possible, better than ever. Their mills are on Hounslow Heath; their gunpowder office is No. 74, Lombard-street.

Mr. Lawrence, of Battle, Mr. Burton *, and several others, have now brought their sporting-powder to the greatest perfection.

With regard to the strength and other good qualities of gunpowder, I shall, instead of saying any thing

* I one day used some very good powder of Mr. Burton's (office, 69, Old Broad-street). But he does not sell less, at a time, than 28lbs. Taken in this way, the price of it is 2*s*. 2*d*. per lb., and 3*d*. more, for each pound, if you have it in canisters. There are other powder-merchants who supply *sportsmen* in like manner.

farther, recommend the *epreuvette* (or *powder-proof*), whereby we can always be *certain* of finding out the best; provided that this machine is properly made, properly used, and nicely cleaned after every fire. I should observe, however, that the *little* trifling things called *powder-proofs* or *powder-tryers*, which sell for three or four shillings, are as likely to mislead as to inform the person using them.

The proper " epreuvette" is very correctly made; the wheel on which the gradations are marked is large, and the spring strong; consequently the resistance to the force of the powder is considerable. *The stronger it is, the better;* for without the *resistance is* strong, a *correct* proof cannot be obtained; because, if *not sufficiently strong to detain the powder in the chamber* long enough for *all* the particles to ignite, many of them (especially in powder of good firm grain) will *fly* off *unburnt*, and, of course, a *part only* of the charge would be proved.

The part, attached to the wheel of the epreuvette, which shuts the mouth of the chamber, should be so nicely adjusted, that on looking closely at the parts, when in contact, no light can be seen between them; for, if *any light*, there is of course so much *vacancy*, and consequently so much *windage;* and, *in proportion* to the *windage*, the proof will be *lower;* and, therefore, *incorrect*.

Three fires, at least, should always be made in proving, and the *average* taken as the mean amount; for variations frequently happen in fires immediately following each other, although made with considerable attention. Care should be taken, after every fire, to clean the chamber nicely, or otherwise the *foulness* left by the preceding discharge *would lessen the space*, by which the succeeding charge would become proportionally less.

The best powder for copper-*cap* guns is the "*fine cylinder;*" because with *them* the large-grained powder is so liable to miss fire. But with copper *primers* we may venture on that of larger grain; and particularly in damp weather or on salt water. But by experiments, in 1829, I find that the size in grain of the powder should be as duly proportioned to that of the gun, and the long distances for which it is required, as the wadding must be to the size of the caliber.

As I stated to Messrs. Curtis and Mr. Harvey, I have invariably observed that small-grained powder fails to answer in large guns; particularly on salt water, and in damp weather. It always shoots weak, beyond fifty or sixty yards, and is very liable to hang fire. If a punt-gun is loaded with fine powder, and brought in at night, the chances are that it would hang fire in the morning. But, with coarse *cannon*-powder, I have known a gun that has been loaded a fortnight go off as well as possible, by merely being probed and fresh primed. I may perhaps be asked by some green gunner (such a one, for instance, as would ask a man with a punt, a dog, and mud-boards, how he got the birds after killing them?!) "Why not fire off the gun and reload it?" To this the answer would be, that the discharge of *only the powder* would, most probably, clear a small pond, or even harbour, of every bird that was in it; and therefore be liable to spoil a grand shot. *Un*glazed powder is the strongest and quickest. Why they glaze powder at all I am at a loss to know, unless it is to tickle the fancy of the dandies.

I one day tried a coast-gun with fine powder—it shot miserably; then with large-grained powder (such as Joe used for detonaters)—it shot but so so*; and then with *unglazed cannon-powder*, and it shot *admirably*. Here is the thing proved at once! I therefore requested Messrs. Curtis and Mr. Harvey to make me a sample of superior powder, unglazed, and of that sized grain. This I have tried for the three last winters, and, although the severe weather, by cutting off all communication, obliged me to *keep the gun* and punt *constantly afloat* for *several weeks*, I had not one miss-fire. Of all the powder used, I never had any so good as this; and, in order to know what to ask for, I proposed that it should be called my "sea-gun" powder. [But, remember this is only for large punt-guns, that carry about two ounces of it.]

Messrs. Curtis and Mr. Harvey now serve only the trade, which is perhaps no more than just: but I confess I regret this; because, whatever powder came direct from them was of superior excellence; whereas a retail dealer may receive his powder good, and then completely spoil it by damp, or too long keeping. *I* will be answerable only for gentlemen at the fountain-head; so let *them* be answerable for their retail dealers. It may be right, however, to say that the gunmakers are by far the best deputy powder-merchants, and take great pains in the management of

* I once stated *this* to be the *best* of all; but I have since had to apologise for an error, which I was led into by the bad quality of the cannon-powder against which I tried it.

their powder; because on that the killing of *their guns* must depend; and therefore we must readily forgive any innocent little bit of "*bam*" as to putting their own names to it, &c. This is all fair; and it is really a charity to let them earn a trifle, now that they have been half-ruined by getting caught in their own trap—the detonating guns; and then sadly troubled with the "shorts," from gentlemen finding it impossible to "cash up," owing to the failure of their farming tenants.

SHOT.

MANY select their shot *in proportion to the size of the bird*, when it ought to depend *more* on that of the *caliber;* for it is not so much the *magnitude of the pellet*, as the *force with which it is driven*, that *does the execution*.

For instance, a common-sized gun (well breeched, and properly bored) will shoot No. 7 better than any other shot; and although a deviation, according to circumstances, may be *sometimes* necessary, yet I am confident, that had you, for a whole season, no other sized shot in your possession, you would (*taking every thing*, from mallard and hare to quail and Jack-snipe) find that you had shot with more universal success, killed more game, and brought down your birds in a handsomer style, than you had ever done, while whimsically following other plans.

For my own part, I should scarcely ever, *with a small gun*, use any other shot, except for killing snipes in February and March, when other birds *should not be fired at*. In this case, unless I had a very close-shooting gun, I should use No. 8, the difference between which and 7 is more than that of any other two numbers, from 1 upwards. All sizes above 3, or 2 at largest, I shall bring under the head of duck-guns, with which only they will lie *compact in the caliber;* though, if I went out solely for the purpose of shooting *wildfowl* with a small gun, then I should of course prefer No. 3 to No. 7.

No. 9 is rather too small, and the *use of dust shot absurd,* except for *small* birds; as, at any *distance,* snipes will *fly away* with it, if *shot in the body;* and, to *break a bone with it,* the bird must be very close: add to which, its disadvantage in windy weather, and the impossibility of manufacturing it so well as the regular numbered shot.

The reason why small shot answers best is, that it *lies more compact* in the barrel; and, consequently, receives more effectually the force of the powder than large shot, which can only have this advantage in a proportionably large caliber. Thus it is, that *a grain of small shot, from a small gun,* will kill far better, *in proportion,* than *one of large;* and, with it, you have not only the chances multiplied in favour of taking a vital part, but the same advantage of penetrating feathers, that a *pin* would have *(with a moderate pressure on it)* over a *nail;* and it shoots so *regular* a surface, that a bird, at forty yards, could very seldom* get away; whereas the large shot, from the objection before named, will often fly so wide and *irregular* that

* I say, *very seldom,* instead of *never,* by reason, that the best gun in England, tried (although regularly cleaned) two hundred times at sheets of paper, the size of birds, may once, or more, *not put a single grain in,* although *properly loaded* and *well directed.*

the game will *escape between* the void *spaces* of the circle.

It must, however, be admitted, that, with No. 3 or 4, a few more *accidental* shots, at immense distances, may be made, than with No. 7; but then let it be recollected, that, for the sake of killing one bird now and then at seventy yards, we are not only *wounding* many others, by being tempted to fire large grains at such distances, but sacrificing the almost *certainty* of killing fair shots, for the *mere chance* of making long ones; as well as *uselessly dirtying* and *wearing* our guns.

Now, as I have recommended small shot, many persons may say, "Suppose we go out in November, we may then possibly get twenty shots in a morning, provided we choose to take our chance at fifty or sixty yards, and perhaps during the whole day may not have one opportunity of firing our guns within thirty yards; do you mean to argue, that, in this case, small shot is best?" In answer, I should say, "If you go out with the prospect of getting shots only at long distances, or through thick wood, you certainly may succeed better with No. 2, or 3, than 7; but if you wish to avoid occasionally *missing the fairest shots*, although with the *most accurate aim*, you will, for this purpose, lay aside your double gun, and take the largest single gun that you can possibly manage, as you may then use No. 1, 2, or 3 shot, without any risk of throwing it in patches."

All those who prefer No. 4, or 3, in common-sized guns, contend, that as large shot will kill at a long distance, it *must kill* at a short one. *Kill* it may *when it hits;* but is it always so sure of hitting? And, if it does take a bird, is not a vital part more likely to escape from three or four straggling pellets, than from ten or a dozen grains, which are *regularly* distributed in the same space? Why does large shot in too small a caliber fly not only thinner, but in a *wider circle?* Because the larger the grains, the more, by rotary motion, they rebound away from each other.

The annexed schedule is about the usual weight of shot.

SCHEDULE OF SHOT,

According to labelled samples, which were sent me from Messrs. Walker, Maltby, and Co., Patent Shot Tower, Lambeth. The firm is now Messrs. Walker, Parker, and Co., as Mr. Maltby is established in the shot-business by himself, at the new round tower on the other side of the bridge.

MOULD SHOT.

		No. of pellets to 1 oz.
LG	. . . .	$5\frac{1}{2}$
MG	. . (hardly)	9
SG	. . . .	11
SSG	. . . .	15*
SSSG	. . . .	17

* Best made, and by far the most useful of all mould shot.

PATENT DROP SHOT.

AA	40
A*	50
BB	58
B	75
1	82
2	112
3	135
4	177
5	218
6	280
7	341
8	600
9	984
10	1726

The *pleasure* of using and counting the *dust* shot, I leave to those who recommend it!

The shot of different manufacturers varies much in size: for example, an ounce of No. 7, from Messrs. Walker and Parker, amounts to 341 pellets; and the same weight, from Mr. Beaumont (late Preston), 398 ditto, &c.: and in some places the numbers are *reversed.*

Many sportsmen recommend the use of unglazed

* In the general use of a common duck-gun, at *flight,* where the coast is much *disturbed,* I have found this to be the best shot for wildfowl, as they most commonly present *ten* long shots for *one* fair one, and are so apt to *fly* after being mortally wounded. But for the proper night-shooting afloat, with a 70lb. barrel, that will burn 2 oz. of powder, No. 1, in the long run, is worth all the other sizes put together.

Both AA and A are made at, and sent from, Newcastle, Messrs. Walker's London tower not being sufficiently high for the rounding of so large a grain.

shot; others wet their shot with sweet oil. I had tried both these plans, but not finding sufficient advantage in either to justify my recommending them, I passed the matter as one of little importance. I have since however, in 1832, discovered that with UN*glazed* shot a gun will keep clean much longer than with shot which is glazed; or, in other words, uselessly dirtied by being polished off, for mere show, with black lead. I named this to Mr. Walker's *factotum*, the other day, and he quite agreed with me that we could dirty our guns fast enough without putting an useless material to soil them. It would therefore be a saving to the manufacturer, and an acquisition to the shooter, if this process was entirely dispensed with.

NEW PATENT SHOT.

Mr. Joseph Manton, some years ago, obtained a patent for a great improvement in shot, which simply consists in mixing a little *quicksilver* with the lead. By means of this process the shot is rendered harder and heavier, and wholly divested of the *arsenic*, which was one of the chief objections to the original patent shot.

The advantages thus derived are, that shot of a small size, which lies the most compact, and therefore always answers best, in the calibers of small guns, has, from its additional weight, the same force as shot of rather a larger size; and the game, after being killed with this shot, will keep much longer. Moreover, by the foregoing process, the shot becomes as clean as silver to handle, or carry loose in the pocket; and its friction, when firing, leads the calibers little or nothing in comparison to the old shot.

An advantage, too, above all the others, I should not omit to mention, is, that in this shot the surface of every pellet is precisely alike, owing to a different process of manufacturing; which could never be the case with shot that had arsenic in its composition.

This must, of course, tend to make the charge lie with more precision in the barrel, and consequently be more evenly dispersed in and round the object.

*** Before this article first went to press, I made a point of procuring, for examination, a sample of the new shot, and then of going down to Messrs. Walker and Co.'s manufactory expressly to ascertain all particulars as to its advantages: consequently I did not begin writing on the subject from the mere ipse dixit of Mr. Manton. I then used this shot for the only fortnight that I took up a gun the season after it first came out; and, as I never shot better, or made more long shots, since detonaters have been the order of the day, I have every reason to speak well of it. The number of shots tried I do not remember; but I have a memorandum of killing 207 head of game in six days (though a part of each day was devoted to some extraordinary sport in trout fishing, owing to damp *windy weather*). I may therefore venture to say that I have given this shot a pretty fair trial. It appears however that, perhaps owing to the extra price, there is now but little demand for this shot; and indeed the new system of saturating the edges of the wadding, with a mercurial preparation, serves as a substitute for many of its advantages.

ELEY'S PATENT SHOT-CARTRIDGES.

I have taken as much trouble about these cartridges as if I had been a partner in the concern; because I found the invention to be one of great merit. But, for want of these cartridges being brought to perfection before they were served to the public, there arose many prejudices which it may now be a work of time to overcome. It would be an absolute waste of paper to publish the experiments I have made, and the correspondence I have had, with Mr. Jenour the inventor, and Mr. Eley the purchaser of the patent; because all that the public can wish for is to hear, from some disinterested person, who has thoroughly investigated the subject, the merits or demerits of the invention.—In 1827, Mr. Jenour waited on me, as an entire stranger, relative to publishing a pamphlet entitled "An Essay," &c. &c. on the "*Spiral Cartridge*;" an invention for which he received a premium from the Society of Arts, but which he had made too public to admit with safety of his taking out a patent. He however felt anxious to bring the invention into notice; and Mr. Davison (whose death, since the last edition, I have sincerely to regret), most kindly, on my introducing him, undertook the printing of his pamphlet. To be brief,—this led to his inventing a better, because more simple, kind of cartridge; and this he wisely kept as a secret, till he could meet with some one who had the wherewithal to speculate in a patent. Messrs. Eley became the purchasers; but latterly the concern remained with Mr. Charles Eley alone. To describe the many blunders that were made, first by putting sand, and then tallow-grease, with the shot (against which I wrote letter after letter of remonstrance), would be needless; but suffice it to say that, by the time the cartridges were brought so far to perfection as to be *worth their weight in gold, for certain purposes*, the circulation of the *im*perfect ones had given them an almost irretrievable blow; and here ended the grand establishment in Charlotte-street. Mr. Eley then retired to Waltham Cross, and employed a Mr. Fairman as agent, at a little shop in Fitzroy Market; till, at last, Mr. Purdey, the gunmaker, took to the concern, and purchased for £100 what had the year before been refused £10,000 for! This Purdey told me himself; and I would take his word as soon as that of any man in London. This was a masterly manœuvre of Purdey; because it enables him to cope with Lancaster, and every other first-rate barrel-borer in doing execution at enormous distances. He must however be content with a fair living profit, and regulate his price accordingly; as almost any one could make these cartridges, to use the modern vulgar tongue, "on the sly." But I beg pardon; I am intruding on my readers too much of the *history*, instead of the *quality*, of the patent cartridge. Let me then direct my observations to the more *useful* part of the subject. The rock on which Mr. Eley's patent at first became wrecked was this:—he made his wire a great deal too stiff, and his meshes too small; and the consequence was, that every now and then, the cartridge either flew, like a ball, in one solid body, or left so much of the charge in one end of the cage as to have an effect equally dangerous; and nearly as uncertain for correct shooting. But at last he became convinced of what I repeatedly stated to him, and sent me some cartridges that I tried all last season; and, for long distances, they surpassed any thing I could possibly have expected. They killed birds quite dead at distances that it would have been folly to fire at with a common charge; and when applied to *wildfowl* guns, they *proved, as I always predicted*, the *most useful invention in existence*. He made some with mould shot, which were a decided failure. But those with patent shot, and particularly the small shot, were fired through the season without once "balling." But I found it necessary to *take aim lower with the patent cartridge;* because it keeps rising in the same ratio with the cylinder of the gun; instead of falling, from its gravity, to the point-blank object. In shot for LONG SHOTS, either in a wild *open* country, or shooting *by day* at wildfowl, I cannot say too much in favour of the cartridge in its present improved state. But for *general shooting*, and particularly *close shots*, it is *totally out of the question:* it increases tenfold the difficulty of killing the object *when very near*, and spoils the birds when hit; and is of course dangerous for covert or battû shooting. Let me therefore conclude with recommending my sporting friends not to adopt the cartridge for general shooting; but only to make use of it on particular occasions.

FLINTS.

NONE are better than the *most transparent* of the common black flints. Great quantities (considered as good as any) come from Lord Cadogan's estate, at Brandon. They should be put in with the *flat* side *upwards,* stand *well clear of the hammer,* and yet be *long* enough to *throw* it. Screw them in *with leather;* as *lead strains the cock,* and *cloth* is dangerous, from being *liable to catch fire.* If very particular about the *neat appearance* of your gun, get a *punch* for *stamping* the *leathers,* and change them as often as you put new flints.

To make a flint strike *lower,* you have only to *reverse* the usual way of putting it in; but, if you want it to strike *higher,* you must either put a *very thick leather,* or screw the flint in with a bit of *something under* it. This temporary way of regulating a lock, so as to *make the hammer fall,* is worth knowing, as it often saves vexation and loss of time.

WADDING.

PAPER *not being stiff enough,* hat *dirty,* card *too thin,* and leather apt to soften with the heat of the barrel, the common, and, perhaps, the best *punched* wadding is *pasteboard.* The *larger* the bore, the *thicker* should be the *wadding.*

All this attention, however, is only required in covering the *powder;* as *(except in double guns,* where the *charge* of one barrel has to *encounter the explosion* of the *other)* it would be better to wad the *shot* with common card, or even paper, knowing that much resistance on *that* does more harm than good.

Common cartridges are bad, as they do not keep the powder sufficiently air-tight, like the proper wadding; add to which, they sometimes fly unbroken, and can never be depended on. I should therefore make use of them only when I wanted to load in a great hurry. I have a friend, however, an old sportsman, who would, for many years, never even hear of any other mode of loading. He was at last persuaded, by a gentleman in Dorsetshire, as good a shot, and as good a judge of a gun, as any man living, to try some experiments, which he readily agreed to do, from a confidence of making good his argument in favour of cartridges. What the particulars of this trial were, I do not exactly remember;

but I know that my friend has *never used a cartridge since.*

Nothing is better to punch your wadding on than a round block, sawed out of some close-grained kind of wood; such as beech, chestnut, lime, sycamore, &c. lead is improper, as it wears out the punch.

Be careful not to let your wadding get damp, or, in drying, it may shrink so much as to become too small for the caliber of your gun.

If you have a punch which is *too large*, and you have consequently trouble in forcing down the wadding, just *bite it* a little *edgeways*, and you will contract it so as to load in a quarter of the time, without the risk of either leaving a vacuum, or breaking your ramrod. This, of course, I only name as an alternative, till you can change your punch. If, on the other hand, the punch is but a mere trifle *too small*, it may be enlarged by being *rubbed on a whetstone;* to do which, place it flat, as you would on the pasteboard; and, unless you grind it too much, there will still remain a sufficient edge, owing to the gritty substance in its composition.

If you have separate wadding in two pockets, and have that which covers the shot pierced with a small hole (or, what is *better*, cut with Mr. Joseph Manton's dented punch), you will load as quick again. I detest all frivolous trouble, but you will here find great advantage in the saving of time. The pasteboard which covers the *powder* should (as before observed) be kept air-tight from the shot. This, indeed, seldom troubles you, as the air that passes, more or less, through all locks, will admit the first wadding to go down pretty freely; but, after this and the shot are in the barrel, the resistance, if the wadding fits tight, as it ought to do, is then so great as to be unpleasant to the hand, and inimical to expedition.

Both pockets must be in reach of the same hand, as there would be no time saved if you had to shift hands with the ramrod.

When using different waddings, have them of different colours, to avoid mixing them.

NEW PREPARED WADDING, FOR PERCUSSION-GUNS.

Since I had last the honour to address my readers on the subject of *wadding*, as complete a revolution has taken place in *that* as in guns. Instead of sending sportsmen sheets of pasteboard and a punch, it is now the order of the day to serve them with bags of, what is called, "*patent* wadding." But who really has a patent for the article, or who has not, I never took the pains to ascertain; though it may be known immediately, by application at the Patent-Office. The artist who first started this new concern is Mr. Wilkinson. He brought out his "*elastic concave wadding*," accompanied by a treatise on it, with explanatory drawings. At first, he made it a great deal too thick; and I begged of him to reduce it to one-third the size of the caliber; since his doing which, it has shot remarkably well. This, being made of *felt*, is the only wadding, EXCEPT OAKUM, that I have ever found to answer well in duck-guns.

Mr. Purdey, and Mr. Lancaster, then brought out waddings, cut by a dented punch, and anointed, round the edge, with a chemical preparation (mercurial ointment will do) that has the effect, not only of cleaning the gun, but, in a great degree, of removing that increase of lead which is *now* occasioned by *retarding the charge*, in order to make a detonater shoot equal to a flint-gun. I received a sample of this wadding from Mr. Lancaster, and it answered most beautifully; because, with this, the gun kept clean, and shot equally well through the whole day; and *nothing could be more pleasant to load with.* Mr. Eley sent me a sample of cork wadding; but with this the gun sooner became leaded. Then down came a batch of wadding, with a request that I would try it, from Mr. Joyce. I then underwent the operation of blazing away for a whole morning, at quires of paper, with these waddings, against Joe Manton's best pasteboard. (Nothing but a wish to give correct information, in a work that has been so kindly received, would have induced me to submit to this insufferable "bore.") While the guns were clean, the difference, among them all, was so trifling as scarcely to be worth naming; and indeed Joe's pasteboard was rather the best. But the guns which were loaded with cork and pasteboard soon began to "lead;" while those with the "patent" wadding kept clean, and free from being, what Tom Fullerd calls, "choked up." There is not a question, therefore, as to their merit. But it is somewhat singular that, after all this exertion of their brains, our artists never served us with *one* kind of wadding for the *powder*, and *another* for the *shot*; because, if there is any way of making a gun shoot stronger into the bird, and easier against the shoulder, than another, it is this. For, I must repeat, that the wadding which covers the *powder* should be *thick* and *air-tight;* while that which covers the *shot* should be *thin*, and *with vent.* This and a few trifling improvements in wadding, I was anxious to see put in practice; as I have *had my* day, and therefore wished to serve others, if I could. I then resolved to explain this to some new *wadding-merchant;* and, as the gunmakers have enough to do, if they mind their *guns*, I thought no one more proper to select than Mr. Joyce, as the quality of his waddings has proved *most admirable;* and he is a practical chemist, who looks a little to the *esprit de corps*, as well as to the *£. s. d.* This wadding is now out, and every day increasing in circulation over the kingdom, which is the best possible proof of its efficacy. Mr. Joyce, I see, has made the shot-wadding with a *hole* in the *centre;* though my wish was to have it *triangularly dented* round the *edge.*

Some of the wadding-merchants object to the trouble of serving two sorts: when this is the case, let me recommend young sportsmen to wad their *shot* with *thin* pasteboard, cut by a *dented* punch. For the *powder*, however, they should use one kind or other of these anointed waddings; or their guns will soon get "leaded," and become as dry as the very subject I have been writing on.

LOADING.

*** THE following directions were originally written for, and, therefore, relate only to, *flint*-guns. In *percussion*-guns the powder must be reduced about one-fourth, as I before observed under the head of "Detonating System."

Much as may be said on this *important head*, I shall attempt to explain it by one simple example: for instance, to load a single gun of six, or double gun of seven, eight, or nine pounds' weight, take a steel charger, which holds precisely an ounce and a half of shot; fill it brim full of powder, from which first prime, and then put the remainder into the barrel: to this add the same measure *bumper* full of shot, and then regulate the tops of your flasks and belts accordingly.

Some little difference of charge will, of course, be required between a twenty-two and a fourteen gauge; and, in this, we may be guided by the shoulder, observing, at the same time, the *proportion* of each here recommended: but, *unless* the gun is very *heavy*, a gauge of *fourteen* will *recoil more* than one of *twenty-two*; so that, after all, the above charge might do equally well for both.

For those who have scales at hand, another way will be to ascertain this by *weight*: for instance, to the guns above mentioned put one drachm and a half of powder, *exclusive of the priming*, to an ounce and a half of shot. The proportion for a twelve pounds gun to be *doubled;* eighteen pounds *trebled;* twenty-four pounds *quadrupled*, &c. with one trifling deviation; viz. the larger the gun the *less* should be the proportion of *shot*, as the larger and longer the caliber the more powder may be damaged in going down it.

Much more *may be fired*, but not always *with ease to the shoulder.* (The powder I have measured by *apothecaries'* weight, the *shot* by *avoirdupois.*)

The same proportion will hold good from a *lady's gun* to the *firearms of a punt shooter*, though it may, in a trifling degree, be altered, as barrels shoot thin or close.

Although I have mentioned being guided by weight as *one* way of regulating a charge, yet this is not the *most correct* means to be used, with regard to the *powder*, for the following reason, which is not generally known:—As sportsmen charge by *measure*, the gunpowder-makers endeavour to include, in the *space* to be filled, as much *weight* as possible; and in so doing, include as much projectile force as the composition is capable of; it is, therefore, evidently better to be guided in the *powder* by *measure.* All the powder made for the king's service is exposed to the air of the magazine, with the door open all day, for three weeks, before it undergoes a second proof, to ascertain whether it will imbibe moisture, and *increase in weight*, which if it does beyond a certain small allowance, it is *rejected.*

Gunmakers will obstinately dispute this method of loading; and for why? Because they try their guns in confined places, use larger shot than No. 7, and look chiefly to the *closeness* of their shooting. But we should remember, that if a gun is *overloaded* with *shot*, a great part of it, at any *distance*, *drops short* of the object; and the *remainder* has *not so much strength* left, as if *that only* had received the *full force* of the powder.—Try this *on the water*.—I do not, however, say, but, at even a little distance, *some shot* must strike *(not fall) short*, if a bird is swimming. These are the grains, which, in spreading, would take the *under part* of any thing placed perpendicular. It should also be observed, that with a *small charge* of shot you are not so liable to fire *behind* an object crossing, or *under* a bird which is rising, by reason that the *less* the weight of shot is in proportion to the charge of powder, the *shorter* time it requires to travel through the air.

POWDER FLASK.

If you expostulate with an old wildfowl *gunner* on the danger of his *piece*, he may retaliate on that of your spring powder flask ; while he (with a cow's horn, stopped at one end with a piece of oakum, and at the other with a bit of *ood*) can fill his *backey-pipe*, and load with more safety than *you gemmen!* 'Tis very true! Many serious accidents have happened from sportsmen not having had the precaution to *detach their charge* before they put it into the barrel, which *may* have a fatal spark remaining! A spring powder horn should have a cap to it, from which you can load, and by means of which you keep all dead leaves, and other dirt, that may fall in the pocket, from crumbling into the *top* of it.

Having pushed back the spring, to fill the top or charger, let it *gradually close* again on the thumb, instead of allowing it to fly back and *snap*. I mention this in consequence of an accident, which happened to one, who, in doing the latter, had his hand dreadfully mangled by the explosion of a flask, which it is supposed was occasioned by the adhesion of a piece of flint.

The late Mr. Egg and Mr. Sykes have each invented powder flasks, in which, if a charge is blown up, all communication is so effectually prevented, that no farther damage can be done. I have *seen* the one of Mr. Egg repeatedly *tried by himself.* To do this, he dropped a red hot nail into the barrel, which, of course, instantly *fired the measure put into it.* He then unscrewed the top, and *showed me the remainder of the powder in the horn,* having only guarded his right hand by a shield of pasteboard, to avoid being burnt by the charge from the barrel.

The principle of it is so secure as to render it impossible for the powder in the flask to ignite, while in the act of loading, by the passage being completely cut off, from the lever being placed on the top of a strong plate instead of underneath. It also prevents the flash out of the barrel from injuring the hand, as the charger is fixed in an octant position, with a vent to let out the flame.

The springs of these powder flasks must be kept very clean and free, or, like many other ingenious patents, they will fall victims to the abuse of slovenly sportsmen. Mr. Egg said, he "begged leave to caution gentlemen of a trumpery Sheffield flask (sold in the shops), with an upright charger, not being calculated to answer the purpose intended, though it was an infringement on his patent." I have now used also the flask of Mr. Sykes, since it has been improved. It appears to be perfectly safe; and nothing can be more convenient: and, what is desirable in these hard times, this flask is not an expensive one.

Another *caution* relative to powder horns in the *field:*—If you should have fired one barrel, and, while in the act of reloading it, other game should be sprung, *beware* of firing the other barrel until you have *either put the flask in your pocket*, or *thrown it on the ground.*

I could name several, who, through a neglect of doing this, have been severely wounded by blowing up their flasks; and among them, two excellent shots of my acquaintance.

With regard to a powder horn in the *house,* common sense will, it is to be hoped, teach us to take care of it; and, with a moment's reflection, convince us of the danger and absurdity of frying powder in the flask, on the hob of a chimney, during the whole time of a meal, or other preparations, before starting for the field.

SHOT BELT.

In my humble opinion, there is, after all inventions, no method of loading better than the *common* shot belt; but it so often falls into awkward hands, and *steel chargers* are such a pretty little item for a gunmaker's bill, that it is almost considered too vulgar an appendage for a gentleman. Let it be observed, however, that a *shot belt* is *light*, and no incumbrance *when empty*; does not *fill the pockets*; is *not liable to be lost*; and, *if properly managed*, is, on the whole, *as quick* a mode of loading as any that can be adopted. For instance: First, if you have fired both barrels, and should take out a charger left full only on *one* side, some little time is lost in using another. Second, if you load with gloves on, the hand is apt to catch in the pocket, from which steel chargers are not so easily taken as a powder flask (or, if they were, they would be liable to be lost). Third, if you do not take a supply for the whole day, they must be replenished; and this office generally falls to the lot of some marker, or servant, who, being perhaps a clumsy handed fellow, on a fidgety horse, wastes a considerable time as well as a great quantity of your shot.

Frivolous as it may appear to mention so trifling a subject, I shall endeavour to describe the manner by which a shot belt may be managed so neatly, that it may be used for a whole month without your losing half a charge.

While pressing the spring with the forefinger and thumb, draw the top just out; then take a fresh hold *over handed*, so as for the first finger and thumb to steady the hand by pressing the muzzle of the belt, and the second finger to be just within the ridge of the top, and by closing the second finger a little, the top will be sufficiently drawn out. The instant you have taken this fresh hold, lean the body, with a little jerk, to the right, and the shot will fill the top, of which your second finger will have such a command, that none will be spilt.

Before you put the first measure into the barrel, lean a little to the left, or the shot will pour out of the belt; and in loading your second barrel, you must observe the same motion of the body to the right and left. In doing all this, the left hand should never be taken from the gun. Be sure always to keep the *spring inwards*, and have your shot-top made rather *longest* in the part which *comes under* while filling it.

When we have acquired the knack of this, nothing can be more *quickly done*, long and *tedious* as it may appear in *explanation*.

Always have the tops of your shot belt made to fit nicely into the muzzle of your gun, by which means, in the process of drawing your charge, you can empty your shot into them without losing a grain.

DRESS OF A SHOOTER.

THE study of dress, in every thing further than always to appear like a gentleman, or strictly in the character of what a man professes (except to the age of two or three and twenty, when it is as natural for a young man to study dress as for a child to play with toys), might possibly, with many persons, give rise to a reflection on a man's understanding, or a suspicion that he was a "knowing hand," who made a business of adorning his person, in order to get on the weak side of weak people. I therefore, lest the book should fall into the hands of some philosopher, feel a hesitation in introducing any subject so frivolous, except for the object of suggesting what contributes to *comfort*, for the perusal of some citizen, who makes his first start as a shooter. We all know that a jean, nankeen, or any kind of thin jacket, is the pleasantest wear for September, one of fustian for October, and one of velveteen for the winter; and that, for a man, who, at all times, uses but one kind of jacket, fustian would be about the medium. That called "*baragan*"-fustian is by far the *best and most durable*. After having tried almost every thing that is commonly used, and some of the wretched articles that are puffed by advertisement, I have found nothing better for a light summer jacket than what is made at Manchester by the name of *satteen, jeanet*, or *florentine*, which is printed on each side, in imitation of cloth. This stuff far surpasses the others for lightness, comfort, durability, and every thing that can be required for warm weather; but, as there is no particular interest in making it (rather the reverse), it is not every where very easily procured; so that your tailor would probably be obliged to order it, in doing which he cannot choose it of too good a quality.

With regard to the other part of the dress, but few persons appear to know what is really comfortable, and I may, therefore, appear singular for considering as most *uncomfortable*, that which is commonly, and was till of late years, universally worn: I mean *shoes* and gaiters. To say nothing of being tormented with two or three dozen of buttons every morning, and having your ankles and knees in a state of confinement through a hard day's exercise, it need only be observed, that, if you step in the least puddle, you are wet; if you tread in moist ground, your shoe is pulled down at heel; and you are often liable to be annoyed by your shoes untying, and thorns and bits of stick, &c., getting into them, or between the buttons of your gaiters. How much more comfortable, then, is the dress here recommended! With lambswool stockings and flannel drawers, put on a pair of *overall-boots*, and then draw over them a pair of *trousers*, which may be made either of fustian or leather, and so *strongly defended inside the knees*, that no thorn can penetrate. Thus you are equipped without trouble or loss of time; you have your muscles perfectly at liberty for hard exercise, and are free from every annoyance; not to say a word on the advantage and safety you have in the stirrup, if on horseback, or on the infallibility of this remedy against the annoyance of harvest-bugs in September. Since this was first published, I see that what is here advised has become very much in fashion. I have not, however, the vanity to suppose that it was from my recommendation, but because people now begin to find out the comfort of it.

For those who *prefer gaiters*, the best way to wear *them* is with *half boots*, that *lace* close above the ankle, and which require them no longer than just to reach that part.

A shooting waistcoat of the same stuff as the jacket is always desirable and economical. It saves an increase of baggage in travelling, and may be made long to cover the loins, with pockets expressly to your own fancy. I have found, however, that one of dark-gray cloth, with mother-of-pearl or bone buttons, is the most comfortable (unless the weather be too warm for it), and will last so as to look well longer than any other. A small sidepocket above the left breast is handy for wadding, which may be got at with the forefinger and thumb, without taking off your glove; and as (by the way) keeping the hands warm in frosty weather is a matter of necessity in shooting, I shall recommend a little bit of copper wire fastened either to the lower button, or the shot belt, which is *always ready* as a *gunpicker;* never rusts; will not injure the platina of a touchhole; and, if you fall, will bend, instead of running into you. This, if bent to a right angle, does very well too as a probe for the nipples of detonaters.

A dissertation on a shooting-jacket would be absurd, farther than to recommend, that, if you wish to have what is commonly called a *harepocket*, it be *lined with oilskin*, by which you may sponge off the blood, instead of having, as many do, a jacket, that would serve as a drag for a pack of harriers, by way of a nosegay for ladies at a breakfast table. But I have now totally discarded *black*, or *dark-green*, velveteen jackets, for *open partridge* shooting. They may please the "kiddies," but they frighten the birds. In the fourth week of September, 1829, an old sportsman laughed at the idea of this. But, at last, he changed his black hat, and black-velvet jacket, with a servant of mine, who followed him, for a light fustian and a straw hat: he then became so convinced of his getting nearer to wild stubble-birds, as to swear he "would never mount another dandy-velvet!" Again, when driving a covert, place an old rusty-looking gamekeeper in one station, where hares and rabbits are driven towards him, and the black-velvet exotic in another, and see to which they will approach the nearest; barring, of course, the mask of yew-tree, fir, or holly-bush. When too cold for a straw hat, use a white *radical*-beaver, or one of the new *felt* hats, or, what is better, a drab-coloured cap. When advising all this, remember I am only prescribing for the advanced part of the season; because in the *early part of* September, while the *stubbles* are *thick* and the *birds tame*, a man might sally forth even in a regimental uniform and not get a shot the less.

APPARATUS.

It may not be amiss to remind the *beginner* what articles he should *know that he has with him* before starting for the field (exclusive of having an oilskin gun-cover in case of rain): *viz.* powder flask, shot, wadding, a knife, and a flint-case, with a gunpicker and turnscrew, which, as well as a little chamber-probe, are usually attached to this case. We will say nothing about a game-bag, as a man, who requires to be told all this, is very unlikely to kill more than may be contained in his pockets.

In case he should forget some of these things, I only beg the favour of him to learn one poor line of blank verse, which will be easier remembered than one quarter of what has been here said in prose:—

Take powder, shot, gun, wadding, flints, and knife,

or, if with detonater,

———————————— caps, and case.

SHOOTING.

*** I SHALL leave the following directions as they originally stood, for flint-guns; repeating my observation that, with *detonaters*, the young sportsman has only to make *half* the allowance at crossing objects, &c.

Let every one, who begins shooting, take warning from the many serious misfortunes, that have, alas! too often occurred, and start with the *determination* of *never suffering a gun, at any time, to be held for a moment*, or even *carried*, so as to be *likely to come in the direction of either man or beast*. One, who strictly abides by this *golden rule*, would be less liable to accidents, even if he *went from his door* with *both barrels cocked*, than he, who neglected it for a few frivolous maxims.

Although we are not all blessed with such nerves, as to aspire to being first-rate shots, yet I have no doubt but almost every man *may be taught to shoot* tolerably well; and, indeed, the art has of late been so much improved, that although but little more than half a century ago one who *shot flying* was viewed with *wonder*, we now frequently meet with schoolboys, who can bring down their game with the greatest dexterity.

Most men, who can, in a slow, bungling manner, kill more birds than they miss, or *now and then shoot brilliantly*, have the name of being "excellent shots;" and, as this character has an *opening for scandal*, the *world* is too *happy to indulge them* with a *circulation* of it, while others, who have *real skill*, are *laughing in their sleeves*, and have *real sense* to conceal it.

But (to be brief, which is here my study) allow me to suggest an humble attempt for the instruction of *the complete novice*. First, let him take a gun that he can manage, and be shown how to put it to his shoulder, with the *breech and sight on a level*, and make himself master of *bringing them up* to a *wafer*.

Then, [with a wooden or bone driver, instead of a flint, or any thing to protect his lock from the concussion of iron versus iron, if a detonater] let him practise at this mark; and, when he thinks he can draw his trigger *without flinching*, he may present the gun to your *right eye*, by which you will *see*, at once, if he is master of his *first lesson*. In doing this he must remember, that the moment the gun is brought up to the centre of the object, the trigger should be pulled, as the *first* sight is always unquestionably the best.

Then send him out to practise *at a card with powder*, till he has got steady, and afterwards load his gun, *occasionally*, with *shot;* but never let *the time* of your making this addition be *known to him*, and the idea of it being, *perhaps*, *impossible* to strike his object, will remove all anxiety, and he will soon become perfectly collected.

The intermediate lesson of a few shots, at small birds, may be given; but *this plan throughout* must be adopted *at game*, and continued, in the *first* instance, till the pupil has quite divested himself of all tremor at the springing of a covey, and observed, in the *last*, till most of his charges of shot have proved fatal to the birds. If he begins with *both eyes open*, he will save himself the trouble of learning to shoot so afterwards. An *aim thus*, from the *right shoulder*, comes to the *same point* as one taken with the *left eye shut*, and it is the most ready method of *shooting quick*.

Be careful to remind him (as a *beginner*) to *keep his gun moving*, as follows:—*before* an object, *crossing*; full *high* for a bird *rising* up, or flying away *very low*; and between the ears of hares and rabbits, running *straight away*; all this, of course, in proportion to the distance; and if we *consider the velocity*, with which a bird flies, we shall rarely err, by firing, when at forty yards, *at least* five or six inches *before* it. (As the barrels of double guns usually shoot a *little inwards* at long distances, there is so far a preference in favour of the *right* barrel for an object crossing to the *left*, and *vice versâ*, that if we were beating along the side of a hedge, it would be best to keep the barrel next to it in a state of preparation.) Till the pupil is *au fait* in all this, he will find great assistance from the sight, which he should have precisely *on* the *intended point*, when he fires. He will thus, by degrees, attain the art of killing his game *in good style*, which is to *fix his eyes on the object*, and fire *the moment he has brought up the gun*. He may then, ultimately, acquire the knack of killing *snap shots*, and bring down a November bird *the moment it tops the stubble*, or a rabbit *popping* in a furze-brake, with more certainty than he was once used to shoot a young grouse in August, or a partridge in September.

Many *begin* with very quick shooting, and kill admirably well; but are often apt not to let their birds fly *before they put up their guns*, and therefore dreadfully mangle them, and, I have observed, are not such *every day shots* as those, who attain their rapid execution on a slow and good principle.

Others *potter* on, in the *old way*, all their lives, and offer to *shoot with any man in England*, because they can *cock an eye*, and kill *twenty slow shots running!* Such *adagio* sportsmen take care never to *fire random shots*, as *they call all, that are the least intercepted*, or *confined to time;* but usually point, and then *take down* their guns—a practice, that is seldom admissible. Such is my opinion of a slow poking shot, that I would rather see a man miss in good, than kill in bad, style. For instance, if I saw one man spring a covey of birds close to his feet, and keep aiming at one till the covey had flown thirty or forty yards, and even bring down his bird dead, and another man miss both barrels, within the same distance, I should say perhaps the latter, if in good nerve, may be a good shot, but I was quite sure that the former never could be one, because he was an hundred years behindhand in the art of using a gun. I know many old pokers who would feel sore at this assertion; but this I cannot help:—it is my humble opinion, and therefore I have a right to give it.

There are few of my young readers, I dare say, that have not, at some time or other, met with a man, who, wishing to show off his shooting, has never fired but when he was pretty sure of killing, and whose pride was to be able to boast after dinner, that he had bagged so many birds without having missed a shot the whole morning. But before we give this person credit for the name to which he aspires, let us ask him whether, in so doing, he brought home as much game as he ought to do? or whether, in order to bag a dozen head of game without missing, he has not refused at least twenty shots, in covert, &c., and, taking all chances, about eight or ten of which ought to have been killed? It is generally the mistaken idea of those who are no judges of shooting, that if a man kills a certain number of times without missing, he is to be put down as a first-rate shot; and that another person, because he has been seen to miss, is to be considered as his inferior.

For example, the one man goes out and springs birds enough to fire fifty times, within forty yards, and perhaps, being a *reputation* shooter, only twenty of these shots happen to suit his fancy. He never fires a second barrel unless the birds rise one at a time, or a covey happens to spring from under his feet; and, in short, he kills his twenty birds in twenty shots. The other man takes the whole of the fifty shots, many of which may be very difficult ones, and under extreme disadvantages: he kills thirty-five, and misses fifteen. A fair sportsman and really good judge, I conceive, would not hesitate to say, that the latter has claim to be considered the better shot of the two.

We will then bring a first-rate shot into the field, and he shall kill forty-five out of the fifty (never failing of course to work both his barrels on every fair occasion): he will then have missed five times; and would any old sportsman judge so unfairly as to place *before him* the *never-miss gentleman* with his twenty trap shots running?

For my part, I should not, even if he missed an open shot or two within five yards of his nose; because such a circumstance might arise from his being nervous, or an accident, when the other, if put to the difficulties that he had been doing, would acquit himself no better than an old woman.

If such a person, therefore, has a pride about him, and wishes to be thought a great shot, let him throw aside his double barrel; and, under the plea of having only one charge to depend on, he may come off with great éclat among the average of shooters.

With regard to the *distance*, which constitutes *a fair shot*, there is no speaking precisely; but, as far as such things can be *brought to paper*, and *guns to an average*, I should say, that, provided a gun is held straight, a bird should scarcely ever escape at *forty yards;* and that *that* is the *outside* of *point-blank* range, although, at *fifty yards*, the chances are *three to one in favour of killing*, with a *good aim;* but as a gun *never shoots twice alike*, a bird, at *this* distance, may *sometimes* be struck with *three or four shot*, and, at *others*, may *escape through an interval*, though the piece be never so well directed. But, if a pellet should take a bird in a *vital part*, or *the wing*, at *seventy* or even *eighty yards*, it would probably come down, though the odds (at such distances) are, of course, against your hitting it at all. Birds *flying straight away*, or *coming to you*, require a *much harder blow*, than those *crossing* or *flying directly over your head;* by reason that, in the *first* instance, they are partly *shielded by the rump*, and, in the *second*, the *feathers* are apt, at long distances, to *glance the shot.*

Under these circumstances, a man MUST *either* PICK his SHOTS *or occasionally* MISS, though his gun *be every time held straight*. I may venture to say, there is no sportsman living who has not been known to miss the *fairest shots;* and there are very few but *now and then in a season* will shoot badly for a *whole day*. It stands to reason when the *most skilful* may become, for a time, *unnerved* for shooting, by *ill health, oppression of mind, one night's debauch,* or any thing that will operate on the *temper or nerves.*

One, who vexes himself about missing a fair shot, is the less likely to support himself at all times as a first-rate performer, because that vexation alone might be the very means of his missing other shots, and therefore he could not be so much depended on as another man, who bore the disappointment with good-humour. When a good shot misses, from being nervous, it generally occurs through his *left hand dropping* as he pulls the trigger; and, if it happens that his gun should miss fire, he will immediately detect this, by seeing that the muzzle has fallen below the line of aim. The best way to remedy this is to make a firm resolution to *fire full high,* and *firmly grasp the stock* for a *few shots;* and, as soon as a few birds have fallen handsomely, he will, most likely, recover his nerves and his shooting. I have luckily felt just enough of this annoyance to enable me to prescribe a little remedy for it; as I well know the unpleasant feelings of a shooting sportsman when deprived of his usual skill:—he becomes, like one with gout, love, or sea-sickness,—cruelly tormented, and laughed at into the bargain.

When two persons are shooting together, there cannot be a more simple way of avoiding confusion than for each man, when a covey rises, to select the outer birds on his own side. Let all birds that cross belong exclusively to that shooter for whose side their heads are pointed; and let all single birds, that may rise and go away fair for either person, be *taken alternately,* and *left entirely for the two barrels of the shooter to whom they belong.* By this means there is no " *wiping of noses!*" as they call it; no "*blazing a volley into the brown of 'em!*" or, in other words, no jealousy; no unfair work; and two sportsmen may thus shoot coolly together with good nerves and in good friendship, instead of with jealousy and greediness, which not only destroys all pleasure, but soon lessens their good shooting, if not their good fellowship. I adopted these regulations for three seasons, with one of the best shots that ever went into a field; and our diversion, by this means, invariably went on so pleasantly, that we shot with additional confidence when in each other's company. The gentleman alluded to was my lamented friend, the late John Ponton, Esq., of Udders House, Dorset.

Taking the average of shooting companions, however (except to beat a double hedge-row, or divide what could not be seen on both sides), I should pardon any old sportsman for saying that he would rather have their room than their company.

From one, who professes himself an adept with a *double gun,* it is expected, that he will kill a bird with each barrel, almost every time the covey rises within fair distance; unless impeded by the *smoke of his first barrel* or other *obstacles,* which he should *endeavour to avoid.* The usual method is to take down the gun, and present it afresh, after the first shot; but as I have seen fourteen successive double shots killed the *other way,* I shall venture to recommend it, as being more expeditious. It is, never to take the gun *from the shoulder,* till *both barrels are fired;* by which means so little time is taken between the two shots, that the *first, as well as* the *second* bird, may be suffered to fly to a proper distance; and let those, who are *not to be trusted* with *both* barrels cocked, get the *gravitating stops*, or use *a single gun*.

Since publishing the first edition of this work, I have seen, on the plan here recommended, *fifteen* double shots at partridges fairly killed in succession, provided I may be allowed to include one of the number which towered and fell at so great a distance that it was never bagged. It is, of course, *not* meant to include among these *doublets* such birds as were *sprung* by the *report* of *one barrel*, and *killed with the other*. Shots of this kind certainly intervened, as well as single ones at different sorts of game. The number altogether, killed by the same person, in about five days, amounted to sixty head, without one miss.

As a further proof of the quickness with which two barrels may be correctly fired, *provided the gun is kept to the shoulder*, I shall mention an instance.—John Ford, gamekeeper to the Earl of Portsmouth, and a man about *six feet six! laid his gun on the ground*, of course with both barrels cocked; and, after *throwing* off two penny-pieces *himself*, he *took up his gun*, and hit them both, most handsomely, before either fell to the ground. He requested me to try, with his gun, if I could do the same. At first I failed, for want of being, what we used to call at Eton, a good "*shy*;" but, after Ford had given me a few lessons in the throwing department, I did it the first time (though, perhaps, more by luck than skill), putting five shot in one, and six in the other; which led me to conclude that, by *practice*, this might be reduced to about the same degree of certainty as other quick double shots. As to a man with his gun in his hand, throwing up, and hitting, two penny-pieces, or halfpence, it is no more than what many good shots can do, by the mere knack of *catching the first just after the turn*, and *presenting well under the second:* but the other performance is really a difficulty. Let some of the pigeon-shooters try this, by way of a "spree," and they will save a deal of innocent blood, and find they have enough to do. Most people will say, "This is not like shooting *birds.*"—True; but I say this,—it distinguishes, to speak musically, the *prestissimo* from the *allegro* in *handling a double gun;* and this is one of the points by which we may judge as to the brilliant or *first-rate* style of shooting. But Ford is a capital game-shot *also;* and, as for his talent as a dove-butcher, a pair of old blues have no chance with him; though he is unknown to all the celebrated artists of the trap. (His gun was made by Willmot of Andover, successor to Long, and *élève* of Parsons; and never, since the days of Joe, have I seen one that pleased me better in the mounting. Since the last edition, Willmot has gone off on "*spec.*" to Van Diemen's Land, where I hope my recommendation, though not I, may follow him.)

Many sportsmen of the old school would be quite irritated if laughed at for their extreme caution in never allowing their gun to be cocked till *after the bird had risen;* but if they will show me one among them that can cock a gun, and bring down a snap shot with as little loss of time as one who had nothing to do but to present and fire, and particularly in making *double* shots, I will resign all pretensions to argument on the subject. This system may have done very well half a century ago, when they might almost have "put salt on the birds' tails," and when the art of neatly using the second barrel was wholly unknown; or even now, among the tame birds in the preserved turnip-fields of Norfolk and Suffolk, where they may pick both their shots, or keep the second barrel for the chance of springing another bird. But those who shoot on this system, in a wild country, would stand a poor chance in competition with one who went up to his game with both barrels cocked, at a time when the birds were wary, and when the loss of an instant made the difference of ten yards in the distance. Then only is it that the difference is to be seen between a first and second-rate shot; and, consequently, that those who pride themselves on skill, instead of easy slaughter, have the opportunity of distinguishing themselves. The argument, therefore, as to not cocking a gun, can only be heard on the question of *safety*. And here again I must confess I have my doubts as to their correctness. We will put a cool and steady old sportsman out of the question: but suppose an eager young man, who is unaccustomed to shooting, walks up to his dog with his gun half-cocked; the moment the birds rise he is in such a state of agitation, that in attempting to draw back the cock of his gun, with a trembling hand, he lets it slip before the scear has caught the tumbler. Off goes the gun! and the best fortune that can be expected is the happy escape of a favourite dog, or the life of his fellow-shooter. While, on the other hand, if he goes up with his gun cocked, *and his companion or follower sees that he advances with the muzzle in a safe and elevated position*, the worst that can happen is, that he may fire it by accident, in a direction that may be as likely, or more so, to kill a bird than when he aimed at it, or, at all events, in one that could endanger neither man nor dog. With regard to presenting a gun, the hand, when near the guard, is in the safest, and when grasping the stock in the firmest position. Here let the shooter please himself.

Avoid squaring your elbows when you present a gun; it gives you an unsteady position, and has the same outlandish appearance as the squared elbows of our half-strangled exquisites who drive about the streets. Nothing can be neatly or gracefully done that is not done with ease; and a man may as well say that he can sit with the same comfort in the stocks as on a sofa, as that he can, in reality or appearance, be as easy with his elbows forced outwards, as when in their natural position.

If we consider for a moment, then, we shall perceive, that in doing most things, squared elbows have not only an unskilful, but an ungraceful appearance.

When a man is no further versed in shooting than just to have become quite expert at bringing down his bird, I conceive that he has only learnt about one-third of his art as a shooting sportsman. Knowing where to place himself for shots; how to spring his game to advantage; what days and weather to choose for the different kinds of sport, constitute at least the other two-thirds, till he is master of which he may often get beat in filling the bag by a very inferior *marksman* to himself. Again, admit him to have learnt every thing in the ordinary way, then comes wildfowl shooting; the requisites for understanding which are so totally different, that there are many of the greatest field sportsmen in the kingdom, who know no more about it than children.

FINISHING LESSONS IN SHOOTING.

I shall now add a few little hints, that may possibly be of service to many of my readers who have had some practice in shooting, but who, I trust, will not be offended at my offering a few *finishing* lessons, under an idea that something, in general, may be learnt even from the most inferior person, and because that, after I had shot for more than twenty years, not a season, no, not even a month or a week elapsed without my discovering that I had been previously ignorant of some trifle or other. If, therefore, a person feels himself above hearing an opinion in this, as well as in every other art, he decidedly gives the greatest and most positive proof of his own deficiency and narrowness of conception. Safely, however, may it be said, that in field sports, as well as in other pursuits, there are thousands who fancy that no one can show them any thing, when they have literally not learnt above a twentieth part of their art; and such people are always best left alone; as, like blighted fruit, they have a bastard colour of maturity, that must for ever debar their coming to perfection.

With apologies for this digression, let me now endeavour to recollect what hints I can, that are not universally known.

In killing snap shots fix your eyes, and immediately pitch your gun and fire, as it were, along, or rather over, the *backs* of the birds. Recollect they are generally *rising*, and not flying forward, *when you take them very quick;* and that as the birds required to be so taken are usually at a distance, an elevation, at all events, can do no harm. If you cannot acquire the knack of doing this, your snap-shot birds, being struck in the breast, will go off, and tower before they drop.

If you have a double gun, always contrive as much as possible to get cross shots (which you will most likely do by walking across, or heading your dog, instead of going, like a bungler, directly from him to the game), or otherwise your second-barrel birds, by flying straight away up wind, down wind, or, in short, in the smoke, may sometimes defy the best shot in Europe. Recollect further, that, as birds fly across you, they not only become clear of the smoke, but give you more time, and present to your charge a more vital part. Be assured there is a great deal of *generalship* (if I may use the expression) as well as *marksmanship* in showing off a brilliant day's shooting. But, when a man, over his bottle, talks to his company of killing to a certainty double shots in whatever situation you choose to spring the game, within forty yards, " hear him," as Lord Chesterfield says, " with patience, and at least seeming attention;" although you might feel disposed to confer on him the order of the long bow, or put him on your list for a knight's companion of the golden hatchet. Recollect, however, it is but liberal to allow those persons who have most frequently the mortification to do but little, the comfort of astonishing the credulous by talking a great deal.

In firing at random distances, where birds are crossing you at the distance of sixty or seventy yards, the average of good shots generally present not more than half a foot before them. But it should be recollected, that after the shot has been driven through the air to the point-blank distance, it travels so *much slower*, that the allowance must be *greatly* increased; and that although a few inches may be sufficient to fire before a fair cross shot, yet at sixty or seventy yards I should fire at least *two or three feet* before the bird, *if it went with any velocity.* Yes, even with a *detonater* I should do so, at *this distance!* Let any one of my young readers, who shoots fairly, try this against one that adopts the ordinary system, and see who will make the greatest number of long shots. While attending to this, however, he must take care not to present too low, but pitch his gun well up, or, if any thing, full high for the mark.

In shooting by guess at rabbits, or any thing in covert, fire at least a foot or two before the object, because, *on losing sight of it,* your hand will *imperceptibly obey the eye* in coming to a sort of check, by which you will invariably shoot a long way behind it.

In walking up to your dogs, in turnips or high stubble, when birds are wild, lift your legs high; and by thus making less noise, you will get twice as near to your game. In an open country, where the stubble is thin, advance as quick as possible, tread light, and crouch your body as low as you can. Why does a pointer sometimes get within ten yards, when the birds fly up from the shooter at above 100? Because a dog is so low the birds cannot see him, and rapidly advances on them without making a noise. The sceptic may fancy this an " old woman's story"—but, for all that, he'll get beat by the man who attends to it.

If a dog stands at a high hedge, go yourself on the opposite side, and let your servant be sent where the dog stands. When he hears you arrive opposite, let him call to you; and when you are ready for him to beat the hedge, give a *whistle*, because a bird, being less alarmed at a whistle than a man's voice, will most likely come out on your side. Some people heigh the dogs in. This, I need not tell a *sportsman*, is the way to spoil them, and to prevent them from being stanch on such occasions. It sometimes happens, that there is a close twisted hedge on the opposite side, so that the birds, in order to extricate themselves, must face the dog; and it is for want of cunning to do this that young birds are so often caught in hedges, to the great delight of ammunition-savers and pot-hunters. In the latter case, keep with your dogs, and send round your man to poke the hedge with a stick.

If your object is to get a great deal of game on the same beat, *provided you have it to yourself*, do not go out above three days in a week. By so doing you will kill at least twice as much as by following the birds without intermission. Many people, who wish to secure all the partridges they can during the month of September, make a point of shooting every day, and are quite disconcerted if they lose even half a day's sport. All this is natural enough in keen young sportsmen, and very well, *provided* they have fresh dogs and *fresh ground to beat*, but under other circumstances they would stand no chance with a man who went out three times a week; because his birds, having intervening days to be left quiet, would lie so much better, that he, *towards the end of the month*, would continue to fill his bag, while another would have so driven and harassed his coveys, that he would scarcely be able to get a fair single, much less a double shot. (I name this, and indeed all I have asserted, not as a mere opinion, but as the result of decided proofs, that I have witnessed no small number of times.)

In boisterous weather, contrive, as much as you can, to sport on the windward part of your beat, or you will drive the birds away from your own property to where they may fall a prey to other shooters, or be driven into the heart of another manor by some knowing game-keeper. Many old sportsmen will not beat their ground at all in windy weather. This I hold to be bad, for birds run a great deal when it blows hard; and, by such means, often *run* out of bounds. When birds are young and tame, a windy day is generally the ruin of good sport; but when they are strong and wild, the most boisterous weather is frequently the best for one who shoots quick and well, as the birds cannot hear so far, and will often lie the closer, for the sake of shelter.

For one who happens to be deprived of his only dog at the critical time of the shooting, or when there is no scent, on a dry sultry day, there is many a worse plan for killing birds than to get two boys to drag the ground with a rope, from ten to twenty yards long, kept down with a weight or stone at each end. This plan first struck me from the immense number of birds that have been sprung by the land-measurers, after harvest, at a time when the best of sportsmen have left behind them a great deal of game. If there is one shooter, he should keep in the middle, a little behind the rope, and the boys should be well drilled to drop like dogs when the game rises. But if two shooters, then one may be on each flank, and the rope may have a longer sweep.

For a person who has regular business to attend, and therefore can only go out for a few hours in the day, I should, in *September*, always recommend him to dine at one o'clock, and shoot in the afternoon (the grand time for filling the bag). His nerves are then sure to be in a pretty good state for shooting, and his head perhaps would then be less disposed for application. When he returns, let him take with his refreshment *tea* or *coffee*, instead of other beverage, after which he will feel himself cool, clear-headed, and again fit for business, instead of being disposed to throw himself into an arm-chair and snore away the evening in concert with his dog. Do not let him think that by thus advising I wish to deprive him of his *nightcap*, or he may at once condemn me and my book for ever! No! if he likes grog, or other liquor, he may finish the evening with a *bucketful*, only let business be first done, and put out of the way.

For gentlemen who require a delicate hand in drawing, mechanism, surgical operations, music, &c. &c., I should advise them always to shoot in gloves, and the moment they return from the field to wash their hands in very warm water, using with it a more than usual quantity of soap; or their hands, by constant shooting, will, for a time, become so coarse and hard as to spoil and unfit them, in some degree, for that nicety which may be required in their more valuable occupations. Many people cannot, or rather fancy that they cannot shoot in gloves, and consequently their hands become as coarse as those of a gamekeeper, which, utterly as I abhor *dandyism*, I must yet observe is not quite in unison with the appearance of a perfect gentleman. I shall, therefore, recommend to them dark kid gloves, which will stand a month's shooting much better than might be supposed; and if they fit nicely to the fingers, are so thin as not to be the least incumbrance between the triggers. Of these and other gloves, the best and strongest that I can any where procure are sold by Mr. Painter, No. 27, Fleet-street.

If a person is extremely nervous from hearing the report of his gun, or from the noise of the rising game, let him prime his ears with cotton, and his inside with tincture of bark and sal volatile.

It sometimes happens that a covey of birds is always to be found, but never to be got at; and are always seen going over one hedge, as soon as you arrive at the other. In this case let the shooter, if distressed for a brace of birds, place himself behind the hedge they fly over, and send a person round to drive the birds to him. He will then probably get a double shot, and very likely disperse the covey.

When birds are so wild that they will not lie, you often see them running across a barren field; in which case keep out of sight, if you can, and make a little noise, in order to drive them to the opposite hedge, but do not show yourself, or they will, perhaps, fly up, and be afterwards so much on the alert as not to be got at without great manœuvring.

When birds run (but are not visible on the ground, and the dogs keep drawing across a whole field), as they will do, most particularly in a dry easterly wind, they are almost sure to get up at a long distance. My recipe on this occasion is to have a man on horseback, and make him take an immense circle, and after he thinks he has arrived well a-head of the birds, to gallop up and down in a transverse direction, by which means, between the two enemies, the covey are often induced to squat down close in their own defence; or, what is even better, to *disperse* before they take flight. In beating a narrow strip of turnips, with two shooters, when birds are wild and run, let one of them enter the croft about 80 yards in front of the other, and walk on in *echellon*, as the man in advance will then have the wild ones coming to him, and his partner the tame ones, if some of the birds happen to lie well.

If you have a piece of turnips very near a small covert, into which you wish birds to be driven for good shooting, at a time when the birds have become wild, be careful what you are about in windy weather; because birds, when shot at, will of course fly much farther than if quietly sprung, and particularly if borne away by the wind. It will often happen, therefore, that by your refusing two or three shots on such an occasion, you will get twenty or thirty shots after the birds (which from running among the turnips frequently become dispersed) are dropped all over the covert; whereas if this covert is not very large, they might probably have flown beyond it had you discharged a gun. Many eager sportsmen, however, would be loath to trust to such a lottery, and argue, that "a bird in hand is worth two in the bush;" but such I have proved to be the case; and this, as well as every other part that relates to shooting, has been pencilled down in the field, with a *query* as to its future confirmation; and if it has stood repeated tests, entered in MS. for this work.

If birds are so very wild that all fair and quiet shooting fails, they are *still*, ninety-nine times in a hundred, *to be got*, if absolutely wanted, to win a wager; for a sick person; or any very particular purpose. But the process for *this* is *any thing but* steady sporting, and can only be well followed in an open country. It is simply to establish a picket of mounted markers, with directions to give a signal when the birds drop; on receiving which you must gallop to the one who has watched the birds down, and instantly gallop with him to within about eighty yards of the spot. Then spring from your horse, and walk briskly to the birds, without a dog, taking care to advance, if possible, in a direction that may drive them to the best of your other markers. Many a brace of birds have I seen bagged this way, before an old dog could canter up fast enough, even to be in at the death, much less to run the risk of spoiling your shot for want of scent. Another recipe, for wild birds, and for which we have to thank a gentleman in Norfolk, where it is least wanted, is to fly a *paper kite*, regularly painted like a bird of prey, at about thirty yards above the ground, and with a very long string, so as for the man who flies, and walks on with it, to be at a distance; while the shooter and his dog approach behind the kite. I tried this one day, and it answered; otherwise I should not have named it.

In calm weather, after September, never go bellowing out "P—o—n—t—o", "T—o—h—o," &c. (like a boy hooting at birds on corn.) Your keeper will do this, at another time, if the dog requires it, and be pleased with his own noise. But rather take your chance of the second dog's seeing the point in time; or you may probably do much more harm than the very dog that you are rating. If, however, the dog is going down wind, the case alters; but even then I should rather try the expedient of a menacing attitude, seconded by a clod of dirt, or a turnip, to using my voice on such an occasion. (Of course I mean if I *wanted birds*, otherwise a good sportsman ought always to lose a shot, rather than neglect his dogs.)

If you *really want game*, when the scent is bad, and see precisely where a covey has dropped, let your dogs be taken up, and go first without them; and if the birds get up singly, never think of picking them up, but make the best of your time in loading and firing. Should you, however, want your dogs, have them one at a time, by making a signal, or whistling to your man who holds them; but do not speak, lest, by so doing, you might spring the covey.

If you have a small beat, rather give leave to one of the best shots in England, who is content to shoot twice a week, than to an idle bungler, who is lounging out with a gun every day; because the one, although he kills game himself, does not prevent you from doing the same, while the other, by harassing the birds, day after day, without intermission, will make them wild, and very probably drive them into another country.

The foregoing are a few hints that I had hitherto kept to myself; but as now (thanks neither to age nor imprudence, but to accidental circumstances) I have no longer eyes or nerves for pretensions to the name of a shot, the greatest pleasure that can possibly remain for me is to resign the little I have learnt for the benefit of young sportsmen. The rising generation of shooters might otherwise be left, as I was for many years, to find out all these little matters, which not one man in a thousand (admitting that he knows them) likes to impart to another; and yet which are so necessary to be known, before even the best shots among them would be able to cope with a crafty old sportsman.

PARTRIDGE SHOOTING.

Most young sportsmen, and many old ones, fancy that nothing great can be done on the first day, without they go out as soon as they can see to distinguish a bird from a dog. This may possibly be necessary for those who start from a *town,* where two or three unfortunate coveys are to be contended for by half the lawyers, doctors, schoolmasters, sporting parsons, and tradesmen in the place ; but under other circumstances, this is the very *worst* method that can be adopted.

In the first place, the birds being at this time on the feed, will very seldom lie well. By your *springing them from the run,* the covey are pretty sure *to take wing altogether;* and being *once disturbed in this state,* it becomes, afterwards, much *more difficult to disperse them,* than if they had been *left quiet till the dew had dried on the stubble.* Secondly, you throw off with long shots instead of fair ones; which, to say the least of it, is not a favourable beginning either for yourself or dogs. Thirdly, for one who may have no relay of pointers or setters, it should be recollected, how much better bestowed would be the work, which he takes out of them while *slaving to little purpose* in the *dew of the morning,* if he reserved it for the *afternoon.* This, from about three till six, is the time of day (in the early part of the season), that *all the best shots are to be got.* The birds are *then scattered,* and driven to the low grounds and meadows: where, with steady dogs, they may be found one or two at a time, and kicked up as fast as you can load and fire.

The most partridges that I had seen bagged in a day

by one person *(when this work was first printed)*, in a country *not* preserved, were twenty-three brace, in killing which I remember, that although he *began* in the very best quarter, and every thing *favoured*, as well as it possibly could do, his *starting at daylight*, yet he only got *three shots before nine o'clock*.

Although he had *four relays of dogs*, he felt confident that he should have killed at least *seven brace more*, if he had left the coveys *undisturbed* till about *half past seven or eight*.

The person who performed this, and the double shooting before alluded to, went out in a subsequent year at nine o'clock, surrounded by other shooting parties, who had been hard at work since the break of day. He had this season a far inferior breed of birds, and he had only one, and that a very old dog. He took refreshment, and rested from twelve till two; shot again till six, and then went home to dinner, having killed fifty partridges and a hare, with only missing two very long shots, though he invariably used both his barrels whenever the coveys rose within gunshot. To this one dog he bagged in all, at different times, in a wild country, 3163 head of game. In 1827, when the breed of birds was good, the same person shot with only *one dog* (except a short trial of a young one that did more harm than good, but with several markers), and, in eight hours, he bagged fifty-one brace of partridges (besides three brace lost) and a hare; and then he did not "throw off" till nine o'clock. This is perhaps the best day on record, for a *wild country* and *one dog*.

Much game as I have seen killed in a September day, I do not recollect one solitary instance of any thing *extraordinary* being done *very early* in the *morning*.

Many people tell me about killing ten and even twenty brace before breakfast; but I never yet had the fortune to *see* the chance for such a performance; because the dew is seldom off before eight or nine o'clock. It would be bad manners to doubt their word; so I will conclude that they mean before some *dejeuné à la fourchette* at 12; or perhaps *before their breakfast on the following day.* With regard to where and how we are to beat for game, &c. &c. it would now be unnecessary to inform even a schoolboy; and, indeed, *others* having mentioned all particulars, is a sufficient reason for *my* not imposing on the reader's patience with what he will have seen before, and what, to describe, would lead me into the very subject of other sporting-authors. Suffice it therefore to say, that the great object is, *first* to have good *markers** judiciously *placed*, and *then* to disperse the birds; the best way to do which is to head your dogs, by taking an extensive *circle.* The second is, to make no more noise than what cannot absolutely be avoided, by doing as *much by signal* and whistling, and as little by *hallooing* as possible. Thirdly, go first on *hills to find*, and drive down from them, the birds, and then in *vales* to *kill* them. Fourthly, when distressed for partridges, in a scarce country at the end of the season, take a horse, and gallop from one *turnip-field* to another, instead of regularly slaving after inaccessible coveys. After a storm, *as soon as the ground is dry,*

* Always be sure to tell a young marker that he must *carry his eye well forward* when a covey of birds begin to skim in their flight, and consider, that as they may continue doing so for a field or two, he cannot safely say that he *has marked them down,* till he has *seen them* stop and *flap their wings,* which all game must do, before they can alight on the ground.

or the next day, birds will lie in a calm; and, after a calm, they will lie in windy weather. Birds are frequently as much on the listen as on the watch; and this is why, towards the end of the season, we sometimes do best in boisterous weather.

Many an excellent shot has come home with an empty bag, under the following circumstances. He has gone out in a cold raw day, and found that the birds were scarce and wild, and that even in turnips they would not lie. But had he then tried one kind of land, to which almost every man, as well as his dog, has a dislike—the *fallows*, he might possibly have got some good double shots; because the birds, finding it a misery to run here, particularly if he walked across the fallows, will sometimes lie till they are sprung the fairest possible shots.

Let me conclude, under this head, with a few observations as to taking *horses* into the field. If birds are wild, a sportsman, who goes out with his man, and has no other attendant, will bring in more game if he contrives to mount that man, *or rather a light boy*, behind him; because, the moment the dog stands, he can then dismount (by throwing his right leg over the horse's neck), and leave the man in full possession of the Rosinante, instead of being encumbered with a led horse, which frequently precludes the possibility of his galloping on to mark a covey, or follow up a towering bird. Moreover, it requires no conjurer to discover, that two horses make more noise than one; and all *noise, after the first few weeks*, is the *ruin* of *sport*. The gentleman with his stud would say,—Why not have three horses? This, I admit, is a more dignified way of taking the field, than the subaltern turn-out of the Johnny Trot behind; but then we have the clatter of three horses, with the chatter of two servants' tongues, an increase of noise that would set the birds on the run; and it would be as vain to attempt the suppression of the one as the other. In short, I would back the double-mounted gent. against the great squire and his stud. Two on a horse, and the "cad" to be *helmsman*, is an excellent way of giving the shooter the liberty of his hands, the moment a covey springs unexpectedly. Recollect too, in wood, about five feet high, a mounted man can shoot where one on his legs cannot see; and again, if a hare runs straight away, she may be killed ten yards further, if you are well above her, and catch her head and pole clear of her high rump. All these little *et ceteras* are what we may call the finish: as to ordinary sporting, in the present day, we may as well tell a man how to eat his dinner. Double-mounted markers are always ready to act in any country. I took the hint from the French cavalry, who had frequently riflemen mounted up behind them, for the purpose of what, as a foxhunter, I should call "drawing the covers." Mounted markers have a droll appearance; so let us choose a respectable group of them for a new frontispiece, as our old one is getting rather stale. But, as going out with a banditti of this kind appears like any thing but fair sporting, it is highly necessary that I should explain why it was done. The country which it became necessary to scour, *in one's own defence*, was in an absolute state of siege with contending shooters; insomuch that, unless you killed the birds down, within the first ten days, you could scarcely make up a basket for a friend. Directly the birds got wild, and began to run, they were cleared off by wholesale, with a new mode of snaring, in places too far from home to be conveniently defended from poachers. Now, however, this country is preserved and in peace; and therefore (after exhibiting a few of the characters, taken by Mr. Childe on the spot, and among them our old rat-catcher*, who is up to every thing, from a foxhunt down to the killing of all kinds of "*warmunt*," and even the taking of a "*wapses*'†" nest) we will disband the army; and, for the future, conduct the partridge shooting on the peace-establishment.

GROUSE SHOOTING.

The foregoing observations relative to partridges may be nearly as well applied to grouse shooting, when we recollect that Lord Strathmore's keeper, *in killing forty-three brace* of muir-game *before two o'clock* in the *afternoon*, had only bagged *three birds* at *eight* in the *morning*. [This, however, is nothing in comparison to the recent performances of Lord Kennedy, and many others of our first-rate shots.]

The chief difficulty to be guarded against in this delightful sport is the manœuvre of the old cock, who runs cackling forward, in order to lead you away from the brood. Old sportsmen and old dogs, however, should be too well aware of this stale trick to pay any farther attention to him, than to destroy him, if possible, on his first appearance. A dog, who has been used to this sport, will sometimes *head him*, and be too cunning for him; or at all events will not suffer him to prevent the sportsman from getting a good shot at the rest of the pack.

To *find* muir-game at the beginning of the season,

* To find him, look on the donkey.

† Wasps'.

take as many pointers or setters as you can get to hunt steadily together. To *kill* them, when *found and marked down*, take up all but *one stanch dog*.

For shooting grouse, select a fine sunshiny day, from *about eight till five in August or September*, and from about *eleven till three* at the *later* periods of the season, as they are then extremely wild, and will only lie tolerably during the few hours which are favoured by a warm sun. Unless the weather is very fine, you will *see them running* and getting up five hundred yards before you. In this case, let one person take an immense circle, so as to head them, while the other remains behind, to press them forward when he is ready; and above all things you should, for killing them at *this* time of the year, use either No. 1, 2, or 3, shot, in the *largest single gun* that you can possibly manage; or, what is better, a good stout double gun, loaded with Eley's cartridges. Grouse take a harder blow than partridges, and do not fly quite so regular and steady.

Scotland is the best place for this sport, as the *heather* there being much *higher*, they will *lie closer* than in Yorkshire and the other moors of England: add to which, the sport there has, in many parts, the pleasing addition of blackcock and ptarmigan shooting. Such, however, is the misery of the Highland public houses, and particularly to our perfumed young men of fashion, that I have generally observed nine out of ten of them, however good may have been their sport, come home cursing and swearing most bitterly about their *wooden berths*, *peat fires*, and *oatmeal cakes*.

I have had very good grouse shooting close to the inn at Arden Caple, in Dunbartonshire, although in the depth of winter, when interspersed with woodcocks and wildfowl. But these birds *then* lose their fine flavour, and become somewhat similar in *taste* to a *dry red-legged* partridge. The Highland shepherds poach them in the snow, by means of decoying them to an ambush with an imitation of their call, and then raking them with a large gun.

To send grouse any distance, put some pepper to the parts where they have been shot, as well as into their mouths, and then pack them, carefully separated from each other, and kept as air-tight as possible, in boxes of *hops*.

SHOOTING PHEASANTS,

&c. &c.

WITH A FEW DIRECTIONS TO THE INEXPERIENCED FOR RECOVERING THEIR OWN GAME, IF UNHANDSOMELY DRIVEN FROM THEM, SHOOTING IN COVERT, &c. &c.

For shooting *pheasants* it often becomes necessary to start very early in the morning, as *they* are apt to lie during the day in high covert, where it is almost impossible to shoot them till the leaf has fallen from the trees. We can never be at a loss in knowing where to go for pheasants, as we have only to send some one the previous evening, for the last hour before sunset, to watch the different barley or oat stubbles of a woodland country, and on these will be regularly displayed the whole contents of the neighbouring coverts. It then remains to be chosen, which woods are the best calculated to shoot in; and, when we begin beating them, it must be remembered to draw the springs, so as to intercept the birds from the old wood. If the coverts are wet, the hedge-rows will be an excellent beginning, provided we here also attend well to *getting between the birds and their places of security.* If pheasants, when feeding, are approached by a *man*, they generally *run* into covert; but if they see a *dog*, they are apt to *fly* up.

If a person holds land, over which keepers have a reservation, and therefore *drive it* in the morning to spoil his sport, he should sprinkle it well with barley and white pease, for which the pheasants would most likely come back again in the evening, and he has then only to *begin beating with his back to the extreme point of his liberty*, and the birds, being cut off in their retreat, will either *fly to him* or *lie very close.* If the wind should blow strong *from* the preserves, or if the foxhounds should happen to run through them, he would then, by this means, be still more sure of having retaliation on those who had been taking pains to defeat him in the fair and lawful amusement of sporting on his own ground.

This plan, however, would be followed with little success, if the person adopting it should take out a cry of *noisy spaniels*, or a set of *wild pointers*. He should recollect, that, in order to intercept the birds, he may be obliged to work down the wind, and it therefore becomes necessary that he should have only *one steady old pointer*, or *setter*, who will keep within gunshot, and quarter his ground with cunning and caution, so as to work round every stem of underwood, instead of hastily ranging forward; and, above all, be well broke, either to *fall to the gun*, or *lie down when he has brought a bird.*

There are very few old sportsmen but what are aware that this is by far the most sure method of killing pheasants, or any other game, where they are tolerably plentiful, in covert; and although to explore and beat several hundred acres of coppice, it becomes necessary to have a *party* with *spaniels*, yet, on such expeditions, we rarely hear of *any one* getting much game to his own share, except some sly old fellow, who has shirked from his companions to the *end of the wood*, where the pheasants, and particularly the *cock* birds, on hearing the approach of a rabble, *are all running*, like a retreating army, and perhaps flying in his face faster than he can load and fire.

For one alone to get shots in a thick underwood, a brace or two of very *well-broke* spaniels would, of course, be the best. But were I obliged to stake a considerable bet *(taking one beat with another*, where game was *plentiful)*, I should back, against the sportsman using them, one who took out a very high-couraged old pointer, that would keep near him, and would, on being told, break his point to dash in, and put the pheasants to flight *before they could run out of shot.* This office may be also performed by a Newfoundland dog; but, as *first getting* a *point* would direct the shooter *where* to *place himself* for a *fair shot*, the Newfoundland dog would always do best *kept close to his heels*, and only made use of to assist in this; and particularly for *bringing the game;* as we rarely see a pointer, however expert in fetching his birds, that can *follow* and *find* the *wounded* ones half so well as the real St. John's *Newfoundland* dog.

It will, of course, be recollected, that the pointer kept for *this* purpose should never be taken with regular-broke dogs. He will, however, before the season for pheasant shooting, be as *well worth his keep* as *spaniels*, by the service he will render his master (single handed) among potatoes and bean-fields; the beating in which (and particularly if there are land-rails, or *red-legged* partridges) is by no means a good practice for thorough-broke pointers or setters.

It often happens that the boundary of a liberty ends with a broad hedgerow, which may be *too high to shoot in*, and may have *land* on the *other side belonging to some one* who is *not on terms* with the owner, and for whose property all his game fly out on the *wrong side* of this little covert. He has then only to sow *sunflower-seeds*, and plant *Jerusalem artichokes* for the *pheasants;* and *Swedish turnips, Dutch clover*, or *parsley*, for the *hares*, on his own side, and cut down a space *broad enough to shoot*, on the *enemy's* side, *in* the hedgerow, which will soon induce him to compromise on equitable terms: because, should his competitor even do the same, he will most probably still have his share; and, if not, he will get away a great part of *his* game.

If the hedgerow is hollow at the bottom, he should send some one to the end of it, as many of the *old hares* would probably *run forward* rather than *cross him*, or *take away from home*.

If a rival shooter (some stranger) races to get before you, push him hard for a long time, always letting him have rather the advantage, and then *give him the double* without his seeing you. Having done this, go quietly round (supposing you have been beating up wind); and, on reaching the place where you began, work closely and steadily the whole of the ground or covert that you have both been racing over, and you will be sure to kill more game than him, who is beating and shooting in haste, through fear of your getting up to him; and (if the wind should rise) driving the *dispersed*, and, consequently, *closest-lying* birds to your beat, as fast as he finds them.

When staying in a *town*, take care not to let every one know where you shoot, by pompously riding through it with a display of guns and dogs; but either send on the latter in the dark, or take them closely shut up in your dog-cart. If driving, cover your shooting-dress with a box coat: if on horseback, ride out of the town on some road diametrically *opposite* to where your sport lies, and then double back again on other roads, or by crossing the country. If you return by daylight, enter the town again by this means, or at all events in the most quiet and private manner, otherwise you will soon have your beat (if on a neutral place) worked by every townsman, who can muster a dog and gun.

If there is one month worse than another for the amusement of shooting, I should be apt to consider that it is *November*. The warmer weather of September and October is then gone by, and the birds become wild and cunning. The fall of the leaf, with the sports of rabbit, woodcock, snipe, and wildfowl shooting, are not in general to be fully enjoyed till December and January; so that, in the event of a sportsman finding it necessary to leave the country during the shooting-season, on any business, the precise time for which might be at his own option, I should advise him to choose this, the middle month, for laying aside his gun.

COCK SHOOTING.

The pursuit of woodcocks, with good spaniels, may be termed the *fox-hunting of shooting!*

A real good sportsman feels more gratified by killing a woodcock, or even a few snipes, than *bags full of game*, that have been reared on his own or neighbour's estate; and one who does not, may be considered a *pot-hunter*. In a country where cocks are *scarce*, be sure to put a *marker in a tree*, before you attempt to flush one a second time; and when you have *marked down* a cock, remember how very apt he is to *run*, instead of *rising* from the spot in which you may have seen him drop. If a cock flies away, and continues to rise wild, go safely beyond where he may have last dropped, and then back again to beat for him (leaving some one to make a noise on the side where you had before advanced on him), and he will then most likely either lie close, or fly towards you. If this will not do, take your station quietly to windward (as cocks generally fly against the wind), give a whistle when you are ready, and let the other person then draw on, and flush him. His cry of "Mark!" will assist in frightening and driving the cock forward, and be a signal for your preparation.

No more on cock shooting, as directions enough about it have been given by other authors.

SNIPE SHOOTING.

The pursuit of snipes is declined by many, who plead their inability to kill them; than which nothing may be easier acquired, by a pretty good shot. Snipe shooting is like fly fishing: you should not fix a day for it, but when you have warm windy weather, saddle your horse and gallop to the stream with all possible despatch. Should there have been much rain, allow the wind to dry the rushes a little before you begin to beat the best ground, or the snipes may not lie well. Although these birds frequent wet places, yet the *very spot* on which they sit requires to be *dry to their breasts*, in order to make them *sit close;* or, in other words, lie well.

If they spring from nearly under your feet, remain *perfectly unconcerned*, till they have *done twisting*, and then *bring up your gun and fire;* but, if you *present it in haste*, they so tease and flurry, that you become nervous, and, from a *sort of panic*, *cannot bring the gun up* to a proper aim. If, on the other hand, they rise at a *moderate* distance, *down with them before they begin their evolutions.* When they cross, be sure to fire *well forward*, and (if you possibly can) *select*, as I before said, a *windy day* for this amusement; as snipes then usually *lie better*, and, on being sprung, *hang against* the wind, and become a good mark.

In springing snipes, always contrive to get *to windward* of them, by which you will be more likely to prevent their moving, and seldom fail to get a cross shot; in taking which a young sportsman is not so liable to be confused by their twisting.

To kill snipes, *first* go *silently down wind* to *walk up the wilder ones;* afterwards let go an old pointer *up wind* to find those which may have lain so close as to allow you to pass: and before you spring them, take care to make a circle, and head your dog. Look always for snipes in places which are *not frozen*. I have always found, that the worst time to shoot snipes is in a *white frost*, as these birds then generally take to the uplands, or get into some rivulet, in small whisps, or flocks, and spring up all together, instead of being well dispersed, and thereby affording a number of shots, as they do in boisterous weather. But, *after* a *frost* has *brought the snipes into the country*, you are pretty sure of *good sport* on the *first open windy day* that follows it. Stick to these birds when once you find them, as they may all disappear in one night.

Before I conclude under the head of "snipe shooting," I am induced to insert a letter that I wrote to Mr. Martin, wherein I had occasion to introduce this subject. I hope my readers will pardon me for copying the letter at full length; as, although in other parts wholly irrelevant to the present subject, yet it all, more or less, may concern young sportsmen. They may, however, say, and with reason, what can *snipe shooting* have to do with *fly fishing?* With their indulgence, then, I will tell them:—Most young sportsmen, probably some old ones, are not aware, that no two sports may be better combined than snipe shooting and trout fishing! The snipes are never better than in February and March, and at this time the trout are often pretty good, and of course much easier caught by a young angler than when in high season, as they have then scarcely tasted a gnat, and will rise at any thing. A dark and mild dry day, with a good breeze from the south and west, is the most favourable time for *both* of these sports, which may also be combined at the fall of the year, when the trout, and particularly the large ones, often remain in high season.

Mr. Martin, it appears, has published my letter in his second edition, from which I copy it verbatim, and wherein he does me the honour to say—

" Major P. Hawker, who is an entire stranger to me, further than as the well-known author of that much-admired work, entitled ' Instructions to Young Sportsmen,' has done me the favour to transmit the following letter:—

" Longparish House, October 11th, 1818.

" Sir,

" On my return to this place, I was favoured with a copy of the ' *Sportsman's Calendar*,' which you have done me the honour to send; and which, no less for its utility than for the remembrance of your attention, shall have a place in my library.

" I can, without flattery, assure you, that I am well pleased with the work, because you have comprised, in a small compass, all the necessary information; and, instead of prosing on the various subjects, and taking up the trade of *book-making*, by the detail of useless anecdotes, that are perhaps nothing more extraordinary than have occurred to every old sportsman, or have been handed, for ages, from one book to another, you have judiciously inserted that which is most useful on other points. In short, you have given, in the way of directions, recipes, &c., all that can be required for a good sportsman; and then, very properly, devoted the remainder of your little volume to the purpose of becoming an universal, though portable, calendar.

" As I see you have thought a few of my instructions worthy of notice, permit me to observe, that there are two points on which I dissent from you in opinion:—

" 1st. About cocking the gun after the bird rises:—I have so many times nearly had one of my dogs killed by young shooters letting the cock escape from the thumb before the *scear* had caught the *tumbler* (through eagerness to fire), that I have, by subsequent experience, found less danger in allowing them to cock their gun when the dog stands, making it my first object to see that their guns are always carried in a safe direction. No man can kill *double hots brilliantly in December*, if he takes down his gun to cock the second barrel; and, as for *danger*, Mr. Joseph Manton's gravitating stops, which may be put to any gun, will preclude the possibility of an accident, even admitting that you are so unfit to be trusted with a double gun as to load one barrel without uncocking the other.

"2dly. With regard to *Snipes*: It is only when they *lie well* that you can allow them to finish their twisting; the greater part of them require to be taken extremely quick, and the knack of doing *this* constitutes the *crack snipe-shot*, who will kill a dozen of those birds where a slow *poking* marksman of the old school can only fire his gun a few times.

"Having been thus far so rude as to criticise your work on the subject of *shooting*, allow me to make the *amende honorable* by giving you a useful hint on trout *fishing*; viz. For small rivers the *yellow dun*, as made by Chevalier, is, in the long run, worth all the other flies put together; and I can safely assert, that my sport has never been so good as when fishing through the whole season with this fly at the end, and a small *red palmer* for a *bob**. A great deal, however, depends on *throwing well*, so that the gut should drop on the water before any part of the line, which is seldom the case when our *soi-disant* anglers fish with their whole bodies; and, instead of throwing gracefully from the wrist, which ought to be done equally well with either the left or the right hand, they labour like a person threshing, and keep bowing like a candidate to his constituents at an election. What is the consequence of thus flogging the water? they frighten away the large fish, and catch only the small ones.

"With many apologies for the scarcely legible manner in which the greatest haste and an accumulation of unanswered letters oblige me to write,

"I have the honour to remain,

"Sir,

"Your obedient humble servant,

"P. HAWKER.

"P.S. One who can throw a fly well *across* the wind has a great advantage in catching the large fish, as in this case the line, before it falls, becomes for a moment suspended over the water, and therefore drops lighter than when thrown directly with the wind."

* It would be ridiculous to lay down this as a rule for every county. I only speak of the small rivers that I happen to have

TROUT FISHING, &c.

As this letter has led us into trout fishing, it may really be worth while (before I proceed to the alphabet of birds) to make a few remarks on this favourite pursuit, for the information of the young sportsman; because, although much has been, yet a little more may be said on the subject, as every art must daily improve in a new school.

A few hints, however, are quite enough on that which is foreign to our title. Almost every one is now-a-days a "*piscator.*" The *Fanatico*, about Easter, goes off as busy as the cockney on his *n*unter, when bound to Epping. He generally takes a great many things, and kills a few fish. The old angler takes a few things, and kills a great many fish. Some dark, warm, windy, drizzly days, early or late in the season, and particularly when a fine breeze blows from off the banks of a river, where no one has begun fishing, the trout are so easily taken, that a basket full is but little proof of skill. One might then almost train a monkey to catch a trout*. But, at other times, and particu-

fished for many years, in Hampshire and part of Dorsetshire, concerning which I can therefore speak from experience.

* It is not generally known, that at the very early part of the season, and before the trout are worth dressing, they will sometimes rise in almost any wind *(except just before rain)*, and even with a bright sun. A friend and I caught twenty brace in an hour and three quarters, on the 24th of March, in a severely cold wind, and on a sunshiny day. But, *after the season had advanced,* we might as well have thrown our flies on the grass, as attempted flogging the water at such an unfavourable time.

larly when fish are well fed, is the time to see who is, and who is not, an angler.

About ninety in a hundred fancy themselves anglers. About one in a hundred *is* an angler. About ten in a hundred throw the hatchet better than a fly. Here we take the average. Now for a few very common faults. One who lets his fly lie too long in the water, after dropping it, is a better killer of time than of fish. He who tries to land a large fish against weeds and stream, when he can take him down, or allows a fish so much line as to be able to rub his nose against the bottom, may be considered as one in need of a *fishing-master.* Enough, however, of defects. I will now, therefore, take in hand the best fly rod I have (which was made by the late Mr. Higginbotham*), and a set of tackle, as made to my order, by Chevalier (No. 12, Bell Yard, Temple Bar), with a pen and ink before me. Though I should first premise, that I only speak of fishing in a *trout stream.* I have no right to go further, because a man cannot be answerable for what he publishes, unless all his statements and representations are faithfully *written on the spot,* and *with the materials before him.* The directions for a *two-handed* fly rod *(for trout in a small river),* I leave to those who can see the use of it; for my own part, I can see none, except to drop the *natural* may-fly with, or to facilitate the art to those

* Mr. Higginbotham was, to my fancy, the best fly rod maker in the kingdom. His successor was Mr. Clark, who retired from the business, which is now carried on in the best possible manner, by Messrs. Willingham, 91, Strand. Chevalier's *forte* is a trolling-rod, flies, and tackle. In naming these makers of fishing tackle, it would be improper not to say, however, that Ustonson, Holmes, Bowness, and many others, are also excellent performers.

who have not learned it in the best manner. Now, then, to the point.

ROD.—About twelve feet three inches long, and about fourteen ounces in weight. It must not be top-heavy, nor it must not have too much play in the lower part, but the play should be just in proportion to the gradual tapering; by which there will be very little spring till after about the third foot of its length. A rod too pliable below is as bad a fault as being too stiff; and, from being too small there, is, of course, more liable to be top-heavy, which nine rods in ten are. The consequence is, they tire the hand, and do not drop the fly so neatly. I have seen some Irish rods (I think of Mr. Martin Kelly's, Dublin), which, if they had not been too pliant, would have been worth any money.

REEL.—Put on your reel with a *plate*, and *wax-end*, fifteen inches from the bottom; and handle your rod close below it, keeping the *reel uppermost*, as the line then lies *on*, instead of *under*, your rod, and is, therefore, *less likely to strain the top* between the rings. The closer the rings are put together on the top, the less chance, of course, you have of straining or breaking it between them. Use either the multiplying or the new *click* reel, *without a stop;* and, by not confining it with the hand while throwing, you are sure never to break your rod or line, by happening to raise it suddenly, at the moment you have hooked a large fish or a weed. Let your reel be full large in proportion to the quantity of line, or it will not always go pleasantly with it in winding up.

GUT *and* FLIES.—Use about eight feet of gut, and the addition of that on the tail fly will bring the whole *foot-line* to about three yards. Put on your *bob* fly a few inches below the middle; or, if in a very *weedy* river, within little more than a yard of the other; lest, while playing a fish with the bob, your tail fly may get caught in a weed. More gut than is here prescribed will be found an incumbrance when you want to get a fish up tight: insomuch, that, of the two, I would rather have a little less than more of it.

A small fly-book may, of course, be taken; and I should recommend it on my plan, which is of *Russia*-leather, in order to repel the moth. This no one will do better for you than Chevalier. A common *beaver hat* is the best thing to *hook*, and *keep* flies on; and, if you have not two rods by the river side, always keep a gut length and flies ready to put on, round your hat, in order to avoid the waste of time and torment which you would have, if you had much entangled your line.

The beauty of fishing is to do the business quick (though not in a hurry), because this sport is every moment dependent on the weather. Walton says, "before using, soak what lengths you have in *water* for *half an hour*." In the new school, I should rather say, draw what lengths you want through *Indian rubber* for *half a quarter of a minute*. Let a gut length or two (ready fitted up with flies), and also a few spare tail flies, be thus prepared to go on in an instant, and put round your hat. For flies (as Barker observes for his night angling) take *white* for *darkness; red* in *medio;* and *black* for *lightness*. The yellow dun and red palmer, which has a black head, partake a little of all; and therefore, with the addition of a white moth for dark *nights*, the angler may, in what few rivers I have ever fished, do vastly well. No doubt, however, that an occasional variety of flies might answer a little better, and particularly if these had been too much hacknied by other people. But, in the long run, I have never found sufficient advantage from variety to be troubled with taking more than two or three kinds of flies. As to carrying, as many do, a huge book of flies, nearly as large as a family bible, for common trout streams—it is like a beginner in drawing, who uses twenty cakes of colour or more, where a quarter the number, if properly managed, would answer the same purpose. The "*piscator*," however, has a right to take what he pleases. He may go to the river side with a book of this sort, or even twelve pounds of lead in his pocket; they will both, perhaps, be equally necessary. But who has a right to find fault? If he is determined to go well laden to the river—why let him. With regard to *hooks*, I have always found the Irish ones far superior to ours. The best, I believe, are bought in Limerick.

Now I have given the outline as to tackle, I will proceed as to *throwing; not in my chair*, with a pen and ink; but with a pencil and a book, *on* the *banks of the river*.

* * * * *

THROWING A FLY.—I am just returned from the river (and, by the way, not badly repaid for my trouble), and, as near as I could there bring the matter to paper, shall now say as follows:—

In throwing a fly, raise the arm well up, without labouring with your body. Send the fly both backwards and forwards by a sudden *spring of the wrist.* Do not draw the fly too near, or you lose your purchase for sending it back, and therefore require an extra sweep in the air, before you can get it into play again.

If, after sending it back, you make the counterspring *a moment too soon*, you will *whip off your tail fly*, and if *a moment too late*, your *line will fall in a slovenly manner*. The knack of catching *this* time is, therefore, the whole art of throwing well. The motion should be just sufficiently circular to avoid this; but if too circular, the spring receives too much check, and the gut will then most probably not drop before the silk line. In a word, allow the line no more than just time to unfold, before you repeat the spring of the wrist. *This must* be done, or you will *hear* a *crack*, and *find* that you have *whipped off* your tail fly. For this reason, I should recommend beginners to learn, at first, with only a bob; or they will soon empty their own, or their friend's fishing book; and, at all events, to begin learning with a moderate length of line.

I have observed, that those young men who have supple wrists, and the power to whip off flies, ultimately make better anglers than those who do not, because, in this action, like most things, there is really but one step between the sublime and the ridiculous: and the poor fellow, who makes no attempt with energy, will most probably in this, as in other pursuits, remain all his life in the back-ground. Walton, in speaking of throwing a fly, says we should fish "*fine and far off*:" but we must except *very* windy weather, or the result of a very long line may, with a very good angler, be *crack and whip off*. If therefore you have got into a particular current of wind, where this is the case, wind up your line a few turns, or you may soon lose another fly. Sometimes the wind blows very strong, directly across you, from the *right*, insomuch that it becomes an exertion to raise the rod enough to prevent the line from being blown back. Throwing with the *left* hand is then a convenience; but for those who are not able to do this, I can suggest no better *makeshift* than to raise the rod over the *left* shoulder, and throw the line by a motion similar to that used with a whip when lightly hitting a leader on the near side. (Any one who has driven in double reins will know what I mean.) I made a point of killing some fish this way, in order to try the experiment; which is, of course, a mere substitute for the best method of throwing. So much for *throwing*. Now for what few finishing touches I can think of:—Avoid, if you can, going too close to the edge of the water. Throw, if you are *au fait* enough to do it well, rather for the fly to become for a moment suspended *across* the wind, than directly down the wind; as it then falls still lighter, and, from this circumstance, is, of course, more likely to deceive a large fish. Prefer dropping the fly just under a bush or hedge, or in an eddy, to the open river, because your line is then more obscured from the light, and the largest fish generally monopolise the possession of such places, in order to find, and devour, the more flies and insects: and, also, to be near their places of security. If the spot is quite calm, watch the first good fish that rises, avail yourself immediately of the ripple that has been made by the fish himself; and drop in your fly a little *above* where he last rose. Never let your line lie too long, as by so doing you either expose your tackle to the fish by leaving it stationary, or draw the line in so close, that you lose both the power of striking your fish, if he rises, and that of getting a good sweep for your next throw. The *first fall* of the *fly*, in *fishing*, is like the *first sight* of a *bird* in *presenting a gun—always the best.*

KILLING YOUR FISH.—A small fish is, of course, not even worth the wear and tear of a reel. But, if you happen to hook a good one, *wind up immediately*; and the moment you have got him under command of a short line, hold your rod well on the bend, with just purchase enough to keep him from going under a weed, or rubbing out your hook by boring his nose into the gravel. (Observe a fish, and you will always perceive, that, after he finds he is your prisoner, he does all he can to get *down*, as the best means of escape.) After getting your fish under the command of a short line and well-bent rod, let him run, and walk by the side of him, keeping a delicate hold of him, with just purchase enough, as I before observed, to prevent his going down. When he strikes, *ease him at the same instant*; and when he becomes faint, pull him gently *down* stream: and, as soon as you have overpowered him, get his nose up to the top of the water; and, when he is nearly drowned, begin to tow him gently towards the shore. Never attempt to lift him out of the water by the line, but hawl him on to some sloping place; then stick the spike of your rod in the ground; with the rod a little on the bend; crawl slily up as quick as possible, and put your hands under him, and not too forward, as a trout thus situated is apt to slip back; so that handling him this way must be rather a different touch from that of *weed-groping*. If you use a landing net (which for saving time, and particularly where the banks are steep, is *sometimes* a necessary appendage), let it be as light as possible; very long in the handle; and *three times as large* as what people generally carry. Take care that neither that, nor the man who may assist you with it, goes even in sight of the water till the fish is brought well to the surface, and fairly within reach; and then you have only to put the net under him, or keep his eyes above water, and tow him into it. *Mind this;* or the landing net and your man will prove enemies, instead of assistants, to your sport. Nothing will so soon, or suddenly, rouse a sick fish as the sight of a man or a landing net. With regard to the time and weather for fishing, it is now well known to almost every schoolboy. But it may be proper just to observe, that however favourable the time may be to all appearance, yet trout will seldom rise well *just before rain,* or when they have *been filled by a glut of flies.* Moreover, trout will frequently cease to rise well, even at the best of times, from being *every day whipped at, by anglers, from the same bank.* My plan, in this case, is to go to the opposite side, and throw against (or rather under) the wind. A friend and I once caught two and twenty brace by this means, while a whole tribe of professed anglers, who were fishing from the windward side, caught (as we afterwards heard) but three fish between them.

TROLLING, or spinning a minnow, is the other most general mode of trout fishing; or, I may almost say, trout *poaching.* It is however very rarely done in a proper manner, though every man, as a matter of course, upholds his own system. I, like all the rest, did the same, till after fancying for years, that I could challenge any one, was beat and laughed at by a *trout-killing divine.* Now, however, I have not only got master of his plan, against which all others that I had ever seen, read of, or heard of, had no chance whatever; but have remedied a few trifling defects that it had, and put Chevalier in possession of the improvement. The great advantage of it is, that it takes the trout when they run and *bite short* by means of fly-hooks, that play round the other, on a *separate branch of line ;* so that I have often killed three or four brace of trout, without the minnow being in the least injured, or even touched by the fish. To describe the tackle *properly*, without giving a plate of it, would be difficult, if not impossible. After all, however, knowing how to bait the hook is the chief art; and even after being shown, requires practice on the part of the fisherman who adopts it. Supposing, however, that some angler might have confidence enough in what I have said to get a set of this tackle from Chevalier, I will endeavour (having *now a minnow in my hand)* to direct him as to baiting it. After choosing a *white-bellied* minnow, of *rather small size*, and hardening it in bran for an hour or two, first draw back the plummet, and put the *large* hook into the minnow's mouth, and out through the right gill, taking care not to tear the mouth or any part of the bait: then draw the line three or four inches to you, so as to be able to get the hook back again into its mouth. Then take the minnow between the finger and thumb in the left hand, and the large hook in the right hand, and run the hook *all down its back, close to the bone*, to the very end of the fish, and let it come out about the *centre* of the *tail fin*. Then with your right hand pull the minnow out as straight as it will lie, and press it into natural form with the finger and thumb. Afterwards *nip off* the *upper* half of the *tail fin*, in order to prevent a counteraction to the spinning of the minnow.

Having done this, draw down your plummet again, and see that your branch-line falls smoothly by the side of your bait-line; and if not, rub it with Indian rubber till it does. Your hook is then ready for action, and action indeed it may be called if properly done. I should observe, that a new gut seldom spins the minnow so well as one that is half worn out (by reason of the stiffness which encircles the minnow's gill). Therefore ten minutes soaking in water, and sometimes a little hard friction of the gut, just above the large hook, may at first be required; besides the working it with Indian rubber. So much for this plan; there *may* be many better; but all I can say is, that I have not yet *seen* one fit to be named with it.

The *rod* for *trolling* should be from eighteen to twenty feet long, and made as light as possible, though *neither too pliable nor top-heavy:* except just the top and bottom, a *minnow rod* is best when made of cane. This rod of course requires two hands: no matter therefore where the reel is placed. If the top is *too stiff*, you *strain a fish's mouth* so much as to run the risk of breaking out his hold, which is nine times in ten on one of the three small fly-hooks. But, if the top is *too pliant*, the fish will frequently *make his escape* on first being pricked. Here therefore, as in all things, the medium is best. A *minnow* must of course be *thrown underhanded*, and the line got well on the swing before it is sent out. You should throw it till it comes to its end, and then, by drawing in the hand, give it a little check, so that it should be laid delicately in the water, and not thrown in with a splash. *The very instant your minnow is in the water begin drawing* it at *one unvaried pace, down* stream, and then towards you, till near enough to require a fresh throw; and in *this, as well as fly fishing, never keep trying too long in the same place.* If a fish comes after your minnow, *never stop it*, or in any way alter the pace, or he will most likely be off again directly; though, if you can tow your minnow into a rougher place, without giving it any sudden motion, the fish will most likely follow it there, and be still more easily deceived than in the smoother water. To get your bait, use a silk casting net, and remember, that the chief art in throwing it is to hurl the right hand *well round horizontally*, instead of inclining it upwards. Keep your bait, with bran, in any thing but tin or metal, which is liable to heat in warm weather. This, I believe, is all that need be said on the best mode of trolling.

I have sent for, and read, the whole of this article, on the subject, to his piscatorial reverence, who, after the most rigid criticism that he could make, approved of it in the extreme, as well as of the improvement in the tackle, with which, before he would pronounce his judgment, he fished for a whole morning. The previous one, on fly fishing, I have submitted to the very best fly fisher I ever saw; but as it would ill become me to repeat his remarks, I must leave the correctness of it to the judgment of the reader.

There are generally known three other modes of trolling. The first is the *diving minnow*, which is precisely on the same plan as the gorge-hook for pike. This answers well in very deep holes, where you may frequently kill trout when the sun is too bright for the more common mode of trolling. On *this* plan, you must, of course, loosen the line, and allow the trout some time to pouch his bait. The second is the *artificial minnow*, which is the worst of all; because it does not, in general, spin so well; and, particularly, because it is too frequently made of *hard* materials, on which a fish, unless very hungry, will seldom close his mouth enough to get hooked. The third is called the *kill-devil*, and although, in appearance, not near so like a real fish as the other, yet it spins so well, and is so much softer in the mouth, that it answers, I think, the best of all plans, when you cannot procure the natural bait. Any good fishing-tackle shop will furnish these articles, and therefore it would be a waste of time and of paper to give a minute description of them.

WORM FISHING.—Though fishing with a lob-worm cannot be called trolling, yet it may be right, *en passant*, merely to state, that this is the best way to kill fish in a *mill-hole, when* the *sun is too bright* for the *fly*, or the *minnow;* and also a very destructive plan for *night work*. But I name such a diversion only as a pastime for the juvenile performer, though not with the contempt as does Dr. Johnson, who says, "Fly fishing may be a very pleasant amusement; but angling, or float fishing, I can only compare to a stick and a string, with a *worm* at one end, and a *fool* at the other."

If, however, the poor angler should feel sore at the wit, he might, in his turn (if scavenger enough to descend to verbal criticism), have a little pleasantry with the philologer, by brandishing his rod and exclaiming,

————————"almost as bad, good" doctor,

as—a wag and a worm-fisher, with a *comparison* at one end and *nothing to compare with* at the other! And when he has put away the stick and the string (and washed his hands) he may substantiate the propriety of his retort by looking out the words "*compare to*" in the doctor's own dictionary; which we should be as unkind to the doctor, as he has been to the angler, if we did not estimate as the best authority in existence.

The foregoing subject has led to a wide digression, or, to have recourse to a musical comparison, has thrown us into an extraordinary modulation, which, as the great Albrechts Berger observes, "*may astonish*," but "*not please*." By this rule, therefore, I should not have presumed to speak on what is foreign to my subject, by introducing that of fishing, if I had not some example of exception as authority to do so. Isaac Walton appears to please every one; and this gives me a sort of licence to consider that I may now even go further on the subject. Before dismissing it, therefore, I may as well tell a gentleman's cook how to dress a trout in my shooting book, as he introduce a milkmaid's song in his fishing book, particularly as eating is a more general concern than singing; and, above all, as there is not more than one cook in a thousand that does not spoil every trout in the dressing.

If a trout is out of season, or in poor condition, it would be needless to attempt dressing it in the *ne plus ultra* way; and, perhaps, the best simple recipe might be to split it, and broil it, with an occasional touch of cold butter. But when fresh caught, and in high season, the way to dress it is thus:—

Directly you have caught the trout, crimp it, with about four cuts on each side, taking care to let the *blade of the knife* be in a *sloping direction*, so as to make every incision rather circular and parallel to the gills; instead of having the blade of the knife perpendicular, by which you would cut too much across the fleaks, and the fish would not be near so firm. Then, if you have a pump at hand, let the trout be pumped upon as hard as possible, for about ten minutes; and if not, the laying it in cold spring water will do nearly as well. Having done this, put the fish away, *not* in *water*, but on stones; or, in short, in the coldest place that can be found.

When dinner is nearly ready, clean the trout, leaving the scales on, and pump on it for a few minutes more. Then have a kettle of water, with a large handful of salt, and when the water properly boils *(but not before)*, put the fish in; and an average-sized trout (say one of a pound weight) will be done in about ten minutes, and should then be sent immediately to table.

A trout, if possible, should always be dressed the day it is caught; and never put to soak and soften over the fire, in cold water, as is the general custom.

Remember, also, that if trout are suffered to remain in the water after being sufficiently boiled, they will directly become soft, and lose all the firmness which is given by this mode of dressing them. The same fish, if a large one, may be brought to table a second time, even for days or weeks after it has been first served up, by being put away in pickle enough to cover it, consisting of three-fourths of the liquor it was boiled in, and one-fourth of vinegar. These should be boiled up together, and poured over the fish, which must have with it some spice, bay-leaves, and either oil or fresh butter. The fish may then be taken from the pickle, when wanted; put, *over the fire, into boiling water*, for a few minutes, and then served up. This is a convenient recipe where a man has dressed some extraordinary fish, and then been disappointed of his dinner-party.

It has been remarked by many other people, as well

as myself, that, of all fish in existence, there is not one that you can partake of so many days in succession, without ceasing to enjoy it, as a trout, provided it be fresh caught, and well in season. Almost every sportsman, and every fishmonger, has his own way of fancying that he can tell when a trout is in season. As to the red spots on the skin having any thing to do with it, the very idea is absurd and fallacious. But the more general criterions are a small head and high crest, a full tail, and the roof of the mouth, or, what is still better, the flesh *under* the *tongue* being rather of a pink colour. Another excellent criterion is the *smallness* and *tightness* of the *vent;* for the better the trout is in season, the smaller will be that venthole which is formed just before the under, or belly, fin. After all, I prefer this, and one other, way of deciding; which is by the *bright and silver-like appearance of the scales.* Take twenty trout, and, I think, if you dress them all, and previously mark that one on which the scales shone the brightest, it will prove to be the best fish. This may be frequently ascertained, even before you land a trout, as a bright one, on being first hooked, generally gives two or three leaps out of the water.

Before you send trout on a journey, have them gutted and washed, but *leave the scales on*, and let them be laid on their backs, and closely packed in *willow* (not flag) baskets, and with either flags or dry wheat straw. Packing in damp grass or rushes is apt to ferment, and therefore liable to spoil your fish.

Having had some experience in sending trout to, as well as receiving them in, London, I may venture to prescribe for those who are in the habit of doing the same. Trout should be sent, as soon as possible after their arrival, to be laid *on* (not in) *ice.* I have repeatedly tried the efficacy of this. The trout which I received, the day after being caught, were soft and watery, in consequence of the journey; though they had travelled only by night. But those from the ice on the *next* day, were almost as good as if taken fresh from the river; for, by this process, the curd becomes set, and the fish recover their firmness. Trout will retain their flavour pretty well for two or three days, by being laid on ice, and turned, about once in twelve hours; but, if merely put on stones, they will be scarcely eatable, and frequently quite spoiled on the third day after being caught. This plan, by the way, holds good for other fish; insomuch that the ice will preserve them for many weeks after the flavour is quite gone. Thus it is that people are so frequently taken in with a fine-looking piece of salmon; which, although apparently fresh, and perfectly sweet, has been so long in a state of petrifaction as to have no more flavour than a bit of old leather.

*** I have been solicited, by sportsmen on the continent as well as of my own country, to enlarge on angling in general. But, as my experience has been chiefly limited to *trout* fishing, I should be sorry to impose on that confidence with which they have honoured me, by attempting to write on other branches of the art where I have but a superficial knowledge.

A LIST OF BIRDS,

&c. &c.

WHICH ARE MOST COMMONLY FOLLOWED BY SHOOTING SPORTSMEN,

ALPHABETICALLY ARRANGED,

WITH

THEIR PROPER NAMES, AS SELECTED BY BEWICK; THE LATIN AND FRENCH FOR THEM, AS GIVEN BY LINNÆUS AND BUFFON; AND OCCASIONAL DIRECTIONS RELATIVE TO SHOOTING THEM.

IN selecting this list, it becomes a question where to draw the line between those which are, and those which are not considered *sporting* birds; but as many shooters would be eager to kill what others would scarcely deign to fire at, it is presumed that the better way will be, not only to insert those which are followed by the keen sportsman, but all that are commonly shot at for diversion or practice.

With regard to the proper names of *land* birds, there is little difficulty in selecting them; but for those of *water* birds, and particularly *wildfowl*, there are so many provincial terms, that it would be a dull and endless task to construe the appellations given them by the decoymen, poulterers, and *gunners*, into their proper names in natural history. For example: the *dunbirds* are called *redheads* on the South and West coasts, and *Parkers* or *half-birds* in the fens. This is also a general term *here* for all birds under the size of the common wild duck. The *morillons** are called *douckers* in Scotland, and *gingling curres* in the West. The *tufted ducks* are *blue-billed curres* on the Western, and *dovvers* on the Eastern Coast, in many parts round which the *wigeon* are only known by the name of *winder*. The *golden-eye* is commonly called *pied curre*; and the *scaup-duck* is known by the name of *gray-back curre* in the South and West, and that of *teal-drake* in the North. For these, and all the various tribes of smaller wildfowl, the decoymen and poulterers have a sort of *sweepstakes* appellation, by putting them down as *dunbirds and divers*. Again, there are many absurd names for other birds, such as *Tommy Loos* for the *divers*, *Isle of Wight parsons* for the *cormorants*, and so on.

On the French coast, the same. We here find the *dunbirds*, and others of their kind, provincially called *vignons*; the *wigeon*, *sarcelles*; and *coots*, *marcareux*, &c. &c. In short, it would be a waste of time to explain the nonsensical terms by which only birds are known in many places; and more particularly as the naturalist or sportsman should be provided with "Bewick," which has not only the advantage of being portable as a pocket-companion, but will answer his purpose far better than any other work, during his pursuit in sport, or search of natural history.

The birds marked thus (*) are those of the *Anas* kind fit to be eaten, and which are usually considered as *wildfowl*. For the general pursuit of these, specific directions shall be given in another part of the work,

* Or young golden-eyes, according to Leadbeater.

as my young readers will be able to understand them better, after they have received a few lessons in shooting from a punt. The following alphabet, therefore, is chiefly intended as a directory for the more common mode of shooting.

In getting at all wild birds, approach them circuitously, instead of going directly up to them; and avoid looking full at them until you have got within shot, or till they shall, if flying, have come sufficiently close for you to fire. If you see a wild bird, when unprepared for him, either continue your course without looking at him, or instantly retreat, and he may then probably sit quiet till you can advance with caution on him a second time.

If a valuable bird lies wounded, always go up to him prepared to shoot, lest he should rise again, and make his escape.

BITTERNS.

To know if there are any in the fens, send out in the evening, when they may be seen on the wing, and heard making a hollow booming noise. The following day you may beat for them, with dogs, that will either point them, or hunt near enough to spring them in shot; as they will lie so close among the rushes, as to be sometimes nearly trod on before they will rise. If you wing a bittern, be careful that he does not strike you with his beak.

There are two sorts of bittern; the Common one, otherwise called Bogbumper, Bitterbum, or Miredrum *(ardea stellaris—le butor)*; and the Little Bittern *(ardea minuta—le blongios)*.

BUSTARDS.

From the open plains, which they frequent, you have fewer opportunities of approaching bustards than most other wild birds. They will, however, sometimes suffer carts and carriages to pass very near them, from which they have been frequently shot; and they are also killed in places where they have been used to see shepherds, by means of the shooter carrying a hurdle to conceal his gun.

There are two kinds of Bustard; the GREAT, or Common *(otis tarde—l'outarde)*; and the LITTLE BUSTARD *(otis tetrax—la petite outarde)*.

COOTS,

When found in rivers, are scarcely thought worth firing at; yet they are in great *requisition* when they arrive for the winter *on the coast*, from the immense numbers that may be killed at a shot, as they roost on the mud-banks. They are generally sold for eighteen-pence a couple, previously to which they are what is called *cleaned**. The recipe for this is, after picking them, to take off all the black down, by means of powdered white rosin and boiling water, and then to let them soak all night in cold spring water; by which they are made to look as delicate as a chicken, and to eat tolerably well; but, without this process, the skin, in roasting, produces a sort of oil, with a fishy taste and smell; and, if taken off, the bird becomes dry, and good

* A coot shot in the morning, just after roosting, is worth three killed in the day when full of grass, because he will then be whiter and milder in flavour. A Poole man is very particular about this, as the sale of his coots much depends on it.

for nothing. After all, however, these birds are in no way delicate, except when skinned, and, after being soaked twenty-four hours in cold spring water, repeatedly changed, made into a pudding, by which, as with all such birds, when in puddings, pies, or soup, you can get rid of their strong skins without losing the juice of their flesh; and their fishy taste is, in a great measure, drawn off by steam. (*Moorhens* may be cleaned in like manner; and, if in good condition, *they* will then be nearly equal to any wildfowl.) Coots, when on a large pond, generally swim or flutter out of reach, on being approached by a shooter; and as they are not worth bestowing much trouble on, the best way to kill them is to place yourself somewhat concealed under the leeward bank, while another person goes round, and fires a gun to windward, *before they can swim into any rushes.* They will *then fly* up in great confusion, and most likely, for some minutes afford employment for a dozen guns. *Shoot well forward,* as one shot before and under the wings of a coot will stop him sooner than ten in the hinder parts. *This,* by the way, *should be observed with most other birds.*

Coots, when on the coast, usually travel to *windward,* so that a west wind brings them to the west, and an easterly wind to the east, instead of vice versâ, as with other fowl. These birds take such a hard blow, and are so tenacious of life, that you may often stop ten or twenty at a shot, and by the time you have got on your mud-boards, or made your dog go after them, not above three or four may be left on the spot, and the others, if they have a spark of life, will swim, or what the gunners call "skitter" away. The plan which I have found best for slaughtering the coots by wholesale, is either to listen for them before daylight, and rake them down, at the gray of a white frosty morning; or watch them at some distance in the afternoon, and set into them as late in the evening as you can see to level your gun, taking care, if possible, to keep them under the western light.

If you think your wounded coots worth collecting, you will find nothing like a double gun to give them the *coup-de-grace*, as they are sometimes most tormenting birds to catch with a dog, or kill with a pole. *Coots*, instead of drawing together before they fly (like geese and many other fowl), always *disperse on being alarmed;* and as they generally fly to windward, the *gentlemen*'s system of wildfowl shooting answers well, which is to embark with a party; sail down on them; and, as they cross, luff up and fire all your barrels. When an infant at wild sport, I used to be mightily pleased with this diversion. When on the coast, you may easily distinguish coots from wildfowl, by the *scattered* extent of their line; their *high rumps;* their *rapid swimming;* and their *heads* being *poked more forward.* Beware of a winged coot, or he will scratch you like a cat.

N. B. If a gentleman wishes to have plenty of wildfowl on his pond, let him preserve the coots, and keep no tame swans. The reason that all wildfowl seek the company of coots, is because these birds are such good sentries, to give the alarm by day, when the fowl generally sleep. But the *mute*-swans will attack every fresh bird that dares to appear within reach of them. But not so with the *hoopers—they* are "the peaceful monarchs of the lake."

Naturalists have so far agreed, that there are two sorts of coots (the GREATER, and this, the COMMON BALD COOT), that for the one, Linnæus gives us the name of *fulica atra,* and Buffon that of *la foulque,* or *morrelle ;* and for the other we find, in the Latin, *fulica atterima,* and in French, *la grande foulque,* or *la macroule.* But, after all, some consider the one bird a mere variety of the other.

CORMORANTS

Have generally some regular evening course to the cliffs, where they roost ; and as they *fly low* towards *sunset,* they repeatedly balk the young shooter, who fancies them *Brent geese.* But as they seldom appear so very late as not to be distinguished, he may perceive the difference by the *extra length* and *sharpness* of the *head* and *tail;* and their occasionally ceasing to flap their wings as they fly. These birds may be easily killed in the breeding-season, if a shooter chooses to run the hazard of concealing himself about the middle of the cliffs. This many people do by being let down, for which some use a kind of saddle, and others a strong basket, or finding places where they can climb up for some distance. But as such dangerous schemes are by no means to be recommended, I should prefer the use of a *rifle,* or content myself with the few chance shots, that could be fired from a place of safety.

There are three sorts of Cormorants. The Common Great Black one, alias Corvorant, or Colegoose *(pelicanus corbo—le cormoran) :* the Green, Shag, Scarfe, or Skart *(pelicanus graculus—le petit cormoran,* or *le nigaud):* the third is the Crested Corvorant, but for this we have neither the names of Linnæus nor Buffon, as it was not ascertained to be a distinct species till a *dissection* of one took place, subsequent to the works of these great authors.

CURLEW. *Scolopax arquata—Le courlis.*

To get at a flock of curlews on the sea-shore, go in a small punt or canoe, when it happens to be high water *just after dusk*, or *before daybreak* in a *white frost.* They will then be assembled by hundreds on the small *headlands* of the *beach*, where they are at first so cautious in alighting, that the various plans of burying casks, &c., to wait in, do not always answer. In approaching these birds, be careful to keep *close alongside*, and *under the shade of*, the *land.*

In autumn, the curlews from all parts round the neighbouring coast will congregate in one enormous cloud, when they have generally two or three favourite roosting-places. To drive them to any one in particular, send a person towards the others with a *lantern;* on seeing which, they will immediately take wing, and may be heard repairing to their next evening haunt, with cries, which echo through the air for miles.

For curlews always contrive to have a second gun in reserve, because, if you happen to wing a curlew, he will generally cry out, and thus entice the flock to hover round, and sometimes to pitch down again. You will then most probably get much nearer than you might have been able to do previously to your first shot.

THE LITTLE CURLEW, or WHIMBREL. *Scolopax phæopus —Le petit courlis.*

Whimbrels appear on the shores, in small flocks, about April, and are much easier of access than the other curlews. These birds are called "Titterels" in, and about, Langston Harbour; and "Chikerels" in the district of Poole. They are very common in Romney Marsh, where they are called "Curlew Jacks," and may be killed in great numbers, without much trouble or difficulty. They are then in condition, and excellent eating.

THE STONE CURLEW. *Charadrius œdicnemus—Le grand pluvier.*

This, being altogether a *land bird*, is *classed among* the *plovers*, and called the *great or Norfolk plover*, and *thick-kneed bustard.*

This bird, although not amiss in flavour, is in general so dry and tough as to be scarcely eatable, except when young. There are few sportsmen who have not sprung these birds while crossing fallow fields in September, when the young ones are often found by the dogs, in beating for game.

DEER.

The art of killing deer with a rifle is so well known to every park-keeper, that it would be needless to mention more than the most approved methods of shooting them. For a deer standing *sideways*, take the *fore-legs*, the *neck*, or the *head;* but, in firing at the latter, be careful not to shoot *too forward* or *too low*, as you would then *only break his jaw.* A deer *facing you* affords the *worst chance* of all; but, if he is standing *from you*, it is the *best*, as you may then take him in the *poll*, or the *back of the head;* and, if struck anywhere in *these* parts, he will come down. For a bad marksman, or a long shot, the surest way to *hit* him (so as to have any effect) is to fire *just behind the fore-leg*, and *pretty low down:* this is the best and easiest target that he can present, and here you will have a chance of taking the *heart.* He will, however, unless shot through the *neck*, *brains*, *spine*, or *forelegs*, generally bound away, and apparently unhurt, till he has gone a considerable distance: he will then begin to stagger, and fall.

If you have an *outlying* deer, and are without bloodhounds to hunt him back to the park, or wish to save your corn by shooting him, go out in a summer morning just after sunrise, while the dew is on the grass, or unripe corn, and look with caution into every enclosure, and particularly among young *peas*. You must be very *silent*, because, if a buck *hears you*, he will probably *lie down* so close as to escape your notice; but, if you go carefully and silently, you will *see him feeding*, and most likely at no great distance from a hedgerow.

If he happens to be near some hidden place, that you can approach without being smelt* (by going to windward), seen, or heard among the boughs, you will probably get a good shot; but, if not, your best chance is to send some one *round* to the field beyond, and there to walk, or ride along the other side of the hedgerow, nearest which the deer is feeding. On hearing this person, he will, in all probability, either lie down so close as to *let you walk up to him*, or *come directly away from* the *hedgerow*, opposite to which *you should be concealed.* If he is pretty wild, and sees the man behind him, he will come bounding with such rapidity, that the most expert rifleman may miss him. In this case, a pretty stout gun, loaded with a mixture of mould and A or B shot, would be your best chance. If with this, however, you *even mortally* wound him, the chances are twenty to one, that he continues his course with unabated speed; so that, instead of beginning to despair, you must follow him up as fast as possible, by doing which, you will most likely find him dying in some

* There is a remedy to obviate this, which frequently answers; and that is, to carry before you an armful of very sweet *hay*.

hedgerow, a few fields distant. For this purpose a Newfoundland dog is very useful, as the moment the dog has run up to him in the covert, he will begin bellowing so loud as to be easily discovered.

To approach a buck in an open field, crawl as low as possible on the ground, and hold before you a *green bough*, which, *if there is a hedge or wood* behind, will *appear so confused with it*, that he will often suffer you to come within rifle shot.

The outlying deer usually *browse* all day among the thickets, where, amidst the verdure of the summer leaf and herbage, they are very difficult to be seen. They are particularly fond of apples, and the poachers in the cider counties, well aware of this, make frequent use of the apple pummice.

The three sorts of deer *common* in Great Britain are the FALLOW, already mentioned *(cervus dama—le dain)*; the RED, or Stag *(cervus elephas—le cerf)*; and the ROEBUCK *(cervus capreolus—le chevreuil)*.

The two last are now chiefly confined to the highlands of Scotland. The latter of them, being very small, is generally killed with common large *shot*. The sportsmen place themselves at the leeward end of a long wood, or *planting*, which the keepers go round for a great distance, in order to draw regularly down the whole range of coverts. By this means the hares and roes are at last driven out before the guns.

With regard to red deer, I regret to say, that I have never had any opportunity of shooting them, and therefore I should be a *quack* to pretend giving instructions on the subject. I do not, however, abuse this pursuit because I am ignorant of it; on the contrary, I should conceive it to be most noble sport.

DIVERS.

To shoot a diver, when he is fishing up a creek at low water, contrive to get your boat below him; as although he will perhaps rather dive close by you than suffer himself to be hunted up to a shallow place, yet he will, at last, be so much in need of breath, that, by *firing the instant he comes up*, you may be able to kill him. The large divers are most savage birds, and will, if wounded and driven to extremity, attack either man, dog, or boat. To kill divers along shore, peep over the banks in windy weather, when they are not so apt to *duck the flash*. Suffice it to say, that of those birds, which are literally and properly called *divers*, there are *seven kinds* to be found in Great Britain, exclusive of *six others*, which are separately classed as the *Genus Mergus*.

DUCKS.

Including all the various kinds of *wild* fowl, which are common in, and occasionally migrate to this country, there are *sixteen**, which come under the denomination of *ducks*.

* BIMACULATED, or CLUCKING DUCK. *Anas glocitans*—French not given.

BLACK DUCK, SCOTER, or BLACKDIVER. *Anas nigra—La macreuse*. I fell in with several of these birds during the last hard winter; and, in my life, I never saw such creatures to

* But if there is truth in the new discovery, that the *golden-eye and morillon are the same bird*, the number would then, of course, be *fifteen*.

Since the sixth edition, I have pretty well proved that Leadbeater is right, and Buffon, &c. all wrong. I have now scarcely a doubt that the "morillon" *is* a golden-eye under two years old.

swim, dive, and carry off shot. They take as hard a blow as a swan; and will even swim, for a short time, after being shot in the head.

BURROUGH DUCK, or SHELDRAKE. *Anas tadorna—La tadorne.*

The young sheldrakes, directly after being *hatched in the rabbit burrows*, are taken by the parent birds to the sea, where they may be seen in what the boatmen call *troops* of from thirty to forty; but, as the female seldom hatches more than fourteen eggs, it is clear, that each flock is formed by two or three broods. On their being approached, the old ones fly away, and leave the young to shift for themselves by diving. They may be easily shot when they come up; but you can seldom kill more than one or two at a time, as they always *disperse* before you can get very near them.

These birds show but tame sport with a gun, and are good for nothing when killed. But, in winter nights, they often give you a fine shot on the mud, though they are so *white* that you can seldom perceive them, even afloat, without a good moon. Be prepared to fire directly you rise; as they, being *very quick-sighted* birds, will give you but little time to present your gun. We had a great many Burrough ducks on our coast during the last hard winter. They were the *wildest* of birds till half starved by the freezing of the shellfish; and *then* they became the *tamest* of all wild-fowl.

You may keep young Burrough ducks for five or six weeks, provided you give them crums of bread, and *only a little* water three times a day. But if you let them *get into the water*, or even *drink too much*, *before they are full-grown*, and fit to be turned out on your pond, you are almost sure to *kill them.* This appears quite a paradox with birds that, in their *wild state,* are always in the water! But, such is the case.

* COMMON WILD DUCK. *Anas boschas—Le canard sauvage.*

The *male* bird of which is called *mallard,* and the young ones *flappers.* To find a brood of these, go, about July, and hunt the rushes in the *deepest* and most retired parts of some brook or trout stream; where, *if you spring the old duck,* you may be pretty sure that *the brood is not far off.* When once found, flappers are easily killed, as they attain their *full growth* before *their wings are fledged;* and for this reason the sport is often more like *hunting water rats* than *shooting birds.*

If you leave the brood, after having disturbed them, the old bird will remove them to another place long before the following day.

When the *flappers* take wing, they assume the name of *wild ducks.* About the month of August they repair to the corn fields, till disturbed by the harvest people. They then frequent the rivers pretty early in the evening, and show excellent sport to any one who has patience to wait for them. Our sporting writers in general have given no further directions for duck-shooting than to walk quietly up a brook, and shoot them as they rise. In doing this, if you have only a single gun, and should spring a bird at an uncertain distance, *halloo out* before you shoot, as there may be others under a bank, and much closer to you, that would spring on the discharge of your gun.

You need not be at a loss to know a *wild* duck. The *claws* in the *wild* species are *black.*

Some sportsmen recommend common land spaniels for duck-shooting, and nothing is more common than to see, in a picture, a smart-looking Tyro attacking a flock of wild fowl with two open-mouthed dogs of this description. This is an art we have yet to learn; and, I conceive, the best recipe to acquire it would be, first to tie the ducks by their legs, taking care not to do as the Italian once did with a hare, that he bought and tied up, in order to win his wager of shooting one—blow off the string, and set the game at liberty. I must, therefore, to be on the safer side, recommend *my* young pupils to use either a Newfoundland dog, a *mute water* spaniel, or an old pointer that will keep close, and fetch dead birds.

EIDER, St. Cuthbert's, or Great Black and White Duck. *Anas mollissima—L'eider.*

* FERRUGINOUS DUCK. *Anas rutila*—No French to be found for this.

* GOLDEN-EYE DUCK. *Anas clangula—Le garrot.*

* GRAY DUCK, or Gadwall. *Anas strepera—Le chipeau.*

LONGTAILED DUCK, or Swallowtailed Sheldrake. *Anas glacialis—Canard de miclon.*

* MORILLON. *Anas glaucion—Le morillon.*

Leadbeater, whose authority I consider as emanating from the fountain-head, says, that we have been all in the dark about the morillon. He positively affirms, that the bird so called by Buffon and other great men is merely the *female* or *young* male of the *Golden-eye*, and that, as most of the males never come to their full size or plumage till just before the breeding season, it is no wonder our ornithologists should be thus deceived about a bird that only migrates to us for the winter.

* PINTAILED DUCK, Winter Duck, Sea Pheasant, or Cracker. *Anas acuta—Le canard à longue queue.*

* SCAUP DUCK. *Anas marila*—For this we have not the name by Buffon, though I am pretty sure I have seen scaup ducks on the coast of Normandy, where, with the dunbirds, they are collectively called *les vignons*.

* SHOVELLER, Kertlutock, or Broadbilled Duck. *Anas clypeata—Le souchet.*

Birds of this kind are more common in the fens of Norfolk than in those other marshy parts of England which lie farther from Holland. The Shovellers breed in Norfolk, where they are called "*Becks*," and, in some places, "*Scopper-bills*." The flappers of this species are easier found, and show more sport, than those of the common wild-duck. Their flesh, too, I think, is of a superior flavour.

There is a variety of this kind, called the *red-breasted Shoveller*, for which, as well as all other varieties of wildfowl, I have found the coast of Norfolk to be the best. This, no doubt, is in consequence of its being the nearest to Holland; from whence there are driven across the channel, by a strong easterly wind, many birds that will seldom travel farther to the westward.

* TUFTED DUCK. *Anas fuligula—Le petit morillon.*

Why this is called by *Brisson* "the *little* morillon" I am at a loss to discover, as the *other* morillon is in every respect the *smaller bird* of the two. This is well known to all wildfowl shooters; and Mr. Bewick corroborates it in his quoted statement of weight and dimensions.

VELVET DUCK, Great Black Duck, or Double Scoter.
Anas fusca—La grande macreuse.

*DUNBIRD, Pochard, or Greatheaded Wigeon.
Anas ferina—Penelope, le millouin.

FIELDFARE. *Tardis pilaris—La tourdelle.*

As long as the berries remain on the hedges, fieldfares continue in the uplands, and are very fat; but afterwards they betake themselves to the water meadows, and feed on worms. These birds are then the "head game" for schoolboys, and people who go hedge-popping during the Christmas holidays. They are, however, scarcely tame enough for this diversion till they have somewhat lost their condition by hard weather. As fieldfares are so dispersed when feeding, the only way to get five or six at a shot is to hide under some place near the trees, which they fly to on being disturbed, and on which they will collect, if some one goes round to drive them from the water meadows.

GANNET, Gan, or Solan Goose. *Pelicanus Bassanus—Le fou de Bassan.*

Gannets are occasionally seen on almost every coast, at times when the shoals of herrings are most abundant; and, in stormy weather, they come pretty near to land, where, like large seagulls, they may be seen hovering over the foaming surge. These birds may be easily distinguished from the gulls by the additional length of their necks, and the sharp black ends of their wings, the motion of which is, at times, more like that of the *heron*.

The sailors sometimes catch these birds, by fastening a fresh herring on a floating plank, against which the gannet's neck is broken, when furiously pouncing on his prey.

With regard to the swarms of *solan geese*, which breed on the islands near North Britain, and the manner by which the fowler may distinguish their alarm, I find, that precisely what I should have observed is already so much more ably described, that I consider it better to quote the accounts from Dr. Harvey (as translated in Pennant), Bewick, and Martin, than attempt any one of my own, which would be a mere corroboration of what these authors have asserted.

"There is a small island, called by the Scotch, Bass Island," in the Frith of Forth, "not more than a mile in circumference: the surface is almost wholly covered, during the months of May and June, with nests, eggs, and young birds, so that it is scarcely possible to walk without treading on them; and the flocks of birds in flight are so prodigious, as to darken the air like clouds; and their noise is such, that you cannot, without difficulty, hear your next neighbour's voice. If you look down upon the sea from the top of the precipice, you will see it on every side covered with infinite numbers of birds of different kinds, swimming and hunting for their prey; if, in sailing round the island, you survey the hanging cliffs, you may see, in every crag or fissure of the broken rocks, innumerable birds, of various sorts and sizes, more than the stars of heaven when viewed in a serene night. If from afar you see the distant flocks, either flying to or from the island, you would imagine them to be a vast swarm of bees."

This island is "farmed out at a considerable rent for the eggs of the various kinds of water fowl, with which it swarms; and the produce of the *solan geese* forms a large portion of the rent; for great numbers of their young ones are taken every season, and sold in Edinburgh for twenty-pence each, where they are esteemed a favourite dish, being generally roasted and eat before dinner."

"The solan geese have always some of their number that keep watch in the night-time; and if the sentinel be surprised, as it often happens, all that flock are taken one after another; but if the sentinel be awake at the approach of the creeping fowlers, and hear a noise, he cries, softly, *grog*, *grog*, at which the flock do not move; but if this sentinel see or hear the fowler approaching, he cries softly, *bir*, *bir*, which would seem to import danger, since, immediately after, all the tribe take wing, leaving the disappointed fowlers without any prospect of success for that night."

Notwithstanding that the young gannets may be considered a delicacy, the old ones are so fishy as to be, in general, scarcely eatable.

* GARGANEY. *Anas querquedula—La sarcelle.*

Birds of this description are frequently killed in the fens of Norfolk, where they sometimes breed, and are called summer teal.

GEESE.

There are *six wild* sorts which visit Great Britain.

* BEAN GOOSE.

A variety of the common one.

* BERNACLE, TREEGOOSE, or CLAKIS. *Anas erythropus—La bernacle.*

Most common in Scotland and Ireland.

* BRENT GOOSE. *Anas bernicla—Le cravant.*

To kill Brent geese by day, get out of sight in a small punt at low water, and keep as near as possible to the edge of the sea. You will then hear them coming, like a pack of hounds in full cry, and they will repeatedly pass within fair shot, provided you are well concealed, and the weather is *windy* to *make them fly low*. Before you fire at them, *spring suddenly up*, and these awkward birds will be in such a fright as to hover together, and present a mark like a barn door.

COMMON WILD GOOSE, GREYLAG. *Anas anser—L'oie sauvage.*

This, for the market or table, is a far inferior bird to the ***Bernacle***, or even the ***Brent goose***, and has but little to recommend it further than the pleasure of killing it. The *common* GRAY *wild geese* may be always distinguished by their flying in a *figure*. These birds, instead of repairing to the coast, like other geese, prefer keeping inland, where they feed on the green wheat by day, and in the flooded water meadows at night. Wild geese, when feeding by day, take care to choose an open plain. You have therefore no means of getting near them, unless they are very tired, from having just arrived after a long flight. I have once or twice, however, got shots at them by taking one of the horses from a plough-team, and walking under cover of him, with a large gun. Some use a stalking-horse, the skin of a cow, and various other contrivances; which, after all, seldom answer for geese, although they may for golden plover, and other less artful birds. The surest way, therefore, to kill them, is to let any one, who works in the water meadows, ascertain what parts they have used (which he will see by their dung and feathers), and then wait for them at dusk, in some ambush, that commands the fresh places adjoining. Contrive, if possible, to get the line of a dyke or drain, so as to take their company on the flank.

Let the man who goes after geese, or any wild birds in the *snow*, dress as *white* as he can, and take a white cotton nightcap ready to put on before he begins crawling after them; or to a certainty they will catch sight of his head, and be off.

[EGYPTIAN GOOSE, GANSER, or GAMBO *goose. Anas Ægyptiaca—L'oie d'Egypte.*

Two of these birds appeared some years ago in Norfolk, one of which was killed by John Ponton, Esq., and the other by his keeper. Three Egyptian geese were, for some days, in the winter of 1823, in the fields of Longparish, and after being fired at about ten times, the old gander was killed by one of the labourers. I was informed that they were at first so easy of access, that I then concluded they must have taken flight from some gentleman's pond. The next year again, during the tremendous gales from the *west*, a flock of about *eighty!* appeared near the same place, and two more were killed, and sent me, by the same man. I have, therefore, no doubt of their importation, instead of migration, to this country.—I suppose these birds were, till of late years, very scarce, as Mr. Bewick could procure no specimen for his admirable work.]

* REDBREASTED, SIBERIAN GOOSE. *Anser ruficollis.*

A rare and very delicate species.

* WHITEFRONTED, or LAUGHING GOOSE. *Anas albifrons—L'oie rieuse.*

These geese were quite unknown to the gunners on the Hampshire coast, till the last severe winter, when they arrived here; and were, more or less, dispersed over other parts of Great Britain. One *Sunday* morning, when birds really appear to know their day of safety, about eighty of them pitched in a field, close to the village of Milford; which is literally a garrison of pop-gunners. Three at a shot were killed with a mere pop-gun—and by a tailor too! Our friend Snip, feeling himself a privileged man where a *goose* was concerned, and having, no doubt, seen on the livery buttons (and had construed to him) the motto of "*carpe diem*," had a fair "set-off" against his transgression, and breach of game-laws: and all ended well, as he shopped his game without getting shopped himself.—The poor geese, finding there was not even one day of safety inland, betook themselves, for security, to the salt water. Here their reception, the next day, was a volley from my two large barrels, which "stopped" about twenty, though I only got twelve, as we had not sufficient water to get very near them: otherwise, something great might have been done, as these geese appear to be much easier of access than any others. Captain Ward tells me that he got almost close to them; and, had not his gun flashed, would have nearly cleared off the company.

The laughing geese fly in more regular order than

the Brent geese; but not so much in a figure as the gray geese; and, I observed, have a cry which I can only describe by manufacturing, and twice repeating, the word "*kirrit*."—These geese are between the size of the two others, and are very little better eating than the gray ones. Their breasts are barred, like a pattern for a waistcoat; and seldom two alike (another good excuse for the tailor!)—They take a tremendously hard blow; and, if not well shot, will recover, after being knocked fairly down, and then fly away for miles.

Hudson's Bay is the grand depôt for geese of this description.

GODWITS.

There are *seven* sorts of godwits, including the small *redshank*. In my previous editions, I said *eight*.

The "*red* godwit" was spoken of as a delicious and scarce bird, and I observed that I had killed several of them on the coast of Kent; but always considered the *gray* godwit as the best worth shooting. But here we have all been in the dark again! The *red* godwit is no more nor less than the *gray* godwit in his *summer* jacket. These birds, like hussars, have a summer dress and a winter dress, and have thus out-manœuvred the logic of our generals in zoology. There are many birds which change their plumage in like manner, though perhaps not so much as these. My remark, as to the gray godwit being best, was an excusable error, because all birds eat better in winter than in summer. There is no great art required to kill godwits. In hard weather they are scattered on the shores, and in spring they may be easily shot when flying about in the marshes.

GREBES.

There are *seven* sorts, including the little river *dob-chick.*

These birds, in evading the flash of a gun, are even quicker than the *divers.*

The large grebes are worth shooting for the sake of their skins, which make excellent tippets and travelling caps.

GROUSE.

There are *three* kinds of grouse, exclusive of the *wood grouse,* or *capercaile,* a Swedish bird, that is given in Bewick as having formerly been known to visit this country; the same species of which so many are brought to London from Norway, and sold at the poulterers, some times for a sovereign each, by the name of *kappercally.* The natives, just before the breeding season, entice these birds, by an imitation of their call, towards an ambush, from which they shoot them *.

BLACK GROUSE, or BLACK COCK. *Tebrao tetrix—Le coq de bruyere, à queue fourchue.*

To shoot a black cock (in the winter), when he becomes wild, you should wait near, or in the direction

* For all particulars about the capercaile, and, in short, every thing relating to Norway and Sweden, I refer my readers to an excellent and interesting work called "Field Sports of the *North,*" by L. Lloyd, Esq.—This is something like a book, and quite original. Not a compound of errors, trash, and piracy, compiled by a paper-filler, who never shot but over a pitcher or a bottle, and crammed down the throats of inexperienced sportsmen, by the sheer puffing of an experienced flat-catcher.—And, by the way, another, beautifully written work, which may be considered as field sports of the *East,* has been lately published, under the title of "Sketches in India" by Captain Mundy, and dedicated to our former gallant

of, the larch firs, for which he flies to perch: and send some one round to drive him from the stubble, where,

Brigadier General in the Peninsula—Lord Combermere, who concluded his distinguished services as commander in chief in India, and with whom Captain Mundy served there as aide-de-camp. These are books which every sportsman should not only purchase, but have bound and placed in his library, as standard and original works.—Both the authors are utter strangers to me.

We have also now "Wild Sports of the *West*," written by a jolly rattling sort of gentleman, who gives us no name; so we must suppose him to be the "Wild" man "of the West." He "goes large" about his cornetcy in the Blues; his 12,000*l*. a year; the ladies dying in love with him; drinking till cock-crow; duelling; housebreaking; a blind seal; missing both barrels at a stag; and quizzing Sir Humphry Davy for not making a wine-butt of his inside; Colonel Thornton for not writing to please him; and your humble servant for high-treason against the dandies, and recommending Painter's gloves; and all this under a *sporting* title, after *one* summer's fishing with a cousin George in Ireland, who laughed at him and his tackle on his arrival, and part of a winter's shooting, of which he soon grew sick, and flew back to his London club (the refuge of the destitute perhaps) which, it appears, he never would have left, but to avoid being worried to death by the ladies who were in love with him, or his 12,000*l*. a year. We must all have his two volumes, if it 's only for the pleasure of seeing that

"On their own merits modest men are dumb."

But I hope this book is not a hoax! Now, if this, after all, should prove to be a fictitious affair, and merely got up by some romance-writer for the house of Bentley, we are properly taken in. But "to give the devil his due" (a coarse expression, though this author seems fond of "the devil," and therefore puts one in mind of him) the book, as a *fancy* thing, is by no means badly written; and (barring a little kicking over the trace now and then, for which he must take his chance about getting "pulled up") all in a gentlemanly style. But as for instruction in sporting——you might as well read Hudibras.

Oh dear! I had *all but* forgotten to notice another sporting author—the immaculate Mr. T. B. Johnson; and had I not done so, about sunrise, the black game may be seen feeding like rooks.—In the North, &c., the female of this species is called *gray-hen,* but in the New Forest both male and female are collectively named *heathpoults.*

The black-game rise somewhat like a young pheasant, and are, I conceive, to one divested of anxiety, and in good nerve, easy birds to shoot :—more so than a grouse or a partridge.

BLACK-GAME SHOOTING ON THE BORDERS OF HANTS AND DORSET.

At the commencement of the season, the black-game here lie tolerably well, and particularly if the weather is so hot as to drive them down to the bogs. The *gray-hen* generally remains with the pack, which seldom consists of more than five or six birds. Nine or ten is considered a very large pack, except in winter, when the cock birds all congregate together in one flock; and,

the poor old fellow would have never forgiven me; as he is now working hard "at all tacks" to attract notoriety, or rather the gold and silver fish of the gudgeon tribe. What an omission would this have been! Why he is the very Paganini of the book-makers! He can spin out any theme with his cranium as you would work up a lather with Naples' soap—ay, and *shave* as well, too! But really he is too severe on me. Now, this is bad policy on his part; because, no longer ago than within these six months, I burnt a bushel-basket full of discarded articles and memorandums, too stale for my work, that I could have sent him down by the Liverpool wagon, as valuable matter for one of his new publications, whereby his gleanings would have been only twenty, instead of fifty, years out of date.

So much for the two latter sporting authors who have thought proper to review my humble productions; and therefore it would be bad manners on my part not to return the compliment.

A sad digression from the capercaile! mais n'importe, it is not much the fashion to read notes, or (as some rod-of-iron critics call them) "blunder-marks," in the present age of intellect.

in general, defy every kind of fair shooting, as well as the few bungling artifices that gamekeepers are master of, with regard to wild birds. The keepers' only chance, therefore, is to wait concealed for their flight; as a black-cock, although one of the wildest birds in existence, will, *when once on the wing*, seldom break his course or raise his flight, let what will intercept him. The *old cock* birds, even at the *beginning* of the season, are very difficult of access; as, on being approached, *they* keep running forward instead of remaining with the pack.

The best, or, at all events, one of the best day's black-game shooting that was ever known, I believe, in *these* parts, I had with the late Mr. John Ponton at Uddens, on the 25th of August, 1825*. We *found*, on this gentleman's manor, *eleven brace in one day*, which was considered, by the keepers, extraordinary success; and we killed eight brace without missing a shot. But notwithstanding all our birds were as strong, and as large, as the old ones, we never even *saw* an *old* cock the whole day.

The black-game here are briefly called "*poults.*" The fagging for them is the hardest labour of any sport I know, because you have to work, in the hottest weather, through stiff heath, which is so much intercepted by fir plantations and bogs, as, for the most part,

* Black-game shooting, as will be seen by the game laws hereafter inserted, does not begin in the *New Forest*, nor in *Devonshire* nor *Somersetshire*, till the 1st of September. But *every where else* the first day is the 20th of August. Not being in the bounds of the *New Forest*, therefore, we began even five days *after* the time; consequently were not transgressing the law, as it might appear, without this explanation.

to prevent your riding; and, from the very few shots that you are likely to get in the day, you have not the same encouragement, as in the abundant sport of grouse shooting. But notwithstanding all, I was never so much pleased with any day's sport as with my first day's black-game shooting in England.

RED GROUSE, GORCOCK, or MOORCOCK (the common muir game). *Tetrao Scoticus—L'attagas.*

WHITE GROUSE, or PTARMIGAN. *Tetrao lagopus—Le lagopéde.*

These birds, instead of becoming wild in the winter, like the two others, may, at any time, be easily shot, if we can but reach the almost inaccessible parts of the northern mountains which they frequent.

They may here be seen on the ground, standing with the greatest composure, and looking like white pigeons; and are not unfrequently killed with sticks or stones.

GUINEAFOWL, PINTADO, or PEARLED-HEN. *Numidia meleagris—La pintade.*

Although guineafowls, as well as turkeys, and even peacocks, are sometimes turned out in gentlemen's preserves, yet they can only be considered as *poultry;* and my sole reason, therefore, for making mention of them is to observe what excellent birds they are to give the alarm, in the event of poachers entering a covert, or thieves lurking about your premises by night.

GULLS.

There are *thirteen* sorts of gulls; and as these are birds which no one would ever think of dressing, it is not generally known, that, although scarcely eatable in any other way, they make an excellent substitute of *giblet soup:* for this purpose their skins must be taken off.

If you shoot a gull, let him lie, and the others will keep flying about the place. You will always observe that gulls, *terns*, or sea swallows*, &c. contrive to *face you* in hovering round; knowing that they are almost *impenetrable when in this direction;* prefer therefore shooting at them in any other, as you will then have more chance of bringing them down, although at three times the distance.

HARES.

Always endeavour to shoot a hare crossing, and consider the *head* as your object. Withhold shooting at her when *coming to you*, until she is very close, or her skull will act as a shield against your charge.

If a hare canters past, and you are behind a hedge at feeding time, she will often stop, and sit up if you whistle. This I name to facilitate a shot for a schoolboy.

Of these there are *two* sorts; the COMMON *(Lepus timidus—Le lievre);* and the ALPINE or WHITE HARE, which frequents the Highland mountains, and goes to earth (or rather into the clefts of rock) like a fox.

HERON, or HERONSHAW. *Ardea major—Le heron hupé.*

Although one of the most difficult birds to approach

* These birds breed by thousands on the large tract of shingle, by Dungeness and Lydd, where they are called *kipps*. Their eggs are sold in great numbers among those of the greenplover or peewit.

by land, yet the heron is not quite so shy of a *boat* as might be expected. The best time to kill herons is to wait for them, at dusk or by moonlight, either near the brooks, rivers, or water meadows, or under the trees adjoining, on which they often assemble before they begin their havoc among the fisheries. The shooter may either remain in a *dark dress* against a *bush or hedge*, or in a *light-coloured punt* and *light dress on* the *water;* where he should keep by the side, or under the shade of the bank. The herons will, in either of these situations, come close to him before they can see him; and from the latter one he may float down stream (keeping *close* to the *leeward bank*) and kill them from his boat. He may bring them down farther than most other birds, as they are a large mark, and yet *require but very little shot.*

The best way to shoot herons *by day* is either with a *rifle*, or by the following contrivance.—These birds, when they have done fishing, generally seek the safety of an open plain, where, with their long necks, they can see an approaching enemy so well, that you can seldom get nearer (particularly if on foot) than about two hundred yards. Go, therefore, *when it blows a strong gale of wind*, on a *fast galloping horse*, and get as near as possible to them *on the leeward side.* The moment the herons begin to rise, charge for them at full speed; aud, before they can possibly make head against the wind, you will either *get under them*, or *they will fly over you*, and very seldom out of gun shot. The only obstacle is the chance of missing them, from the difficulty of keeping the horse sufficiently steady to shoot from his back, immediately after being pulled up from a gallop.

KNOT, Knute, or Knout. *Tringa canutis—Le canut.*

A bird which, like the *ruffs and reeves,* is more easily *caught* by nets than *shot;* as the knot, like the others, keeps running under the high reeds, where it cannot well be followed up, and then is apt to spring out of gun-shot. The knots, if they remain in England, when the fens are frozen, will sometimes repair to the coast. There they are much easier of access than either the curlews or gray plovers.

LANDRAIL, Corncrake, or Dakerhen. *Rallus crex—Le rale de genet.*

To find a landrail, always make choice of a *clover field;* and if that does not offer, try *beans, potatoes,* or beds of *young withey.* Landrails are now most plentiful in Ireland.

To call them in the evening, go behind a hedge near the swaths of corn, with two bones; one of which must be notched like a saw, the other plain; and by drawing the one down the serrated part of the other, you will produce a noise, which so far imitates their call, as often to draw them close to your place of concealment.

There are two sorts of *rails,* which may be named after speaking of the landrail; but, from their being *water* birds, or rather *waders,* which inhabit only the sedge and places near rivers, they are very widely distinguished in natural history. The one is the

COMMON WATER-RAIL, and the other the

SPOTTED WATER-RAIL, Spotted Gallinule, or Water Crake.

Notwithstanding these two are seldom regarded by sportsmen, yet there is scarcely a greater delicacy than either the one or the other.

In shooting *all kinds of rails* press them very hard, or you will have *difficulty* to *get them on wing*. If they are in a hedge, go a-head of your dogs, and shake it *before* them. Having once driven them up, you should fire, if there is any chance, as the difficulty of springing them a second time is tenfold.

LARK. *Alauda arvensis—L'alouette.*

To shoot larks (or any other small birds) in hard weather, sweep away the snow, and sprinkle a long train of *scearl**, corn, or chaff, within shot of some hedge or place that you can walk to unseen, and occasionally give them a sweeping.

OXBIRD, Purre, or Stint. *Tringa cinclus—L'alouette de mer.*

To get a shot among the clouds of oxbirds, which frequent the shores, go in your canoe, and either take them *on the mud from* a *creek* at *low water*, or *on a gravelly point* at *high water*. A white frost is the best time for this, and they are then most commonly interspersed with gray plover.

Oxbirds are sometimes so *tame* in *windy weather*, about the month of *August*, that, at high water, you may walk along the beach, and shoot them openly with a little double gun. Perhaps, after killing a dozen with your first barrel, the remainder of the flock will pitch

* A provincial term for those *light seeds*, that fall through the rudder, when cleaning the wheat, and of which the small birds are particularly fond.

among them, and present a shot equally good for your second. But these are no doubt mostly young birds, that have just flown, as the oxbirds are, in general, difficult of access; and *(like most other birds)* the *larger their flock*, the *more difficult it is to be approached.*

This is capital sport for a schoolboy. But the moment the tide leaves the mud—then is the time to get a punt and catch the oxbirds on the edge. A second barrel is the grand recipe for the slaughter of oxbirds; because if you happen to "stop" two or three, the rest are almost sure to pitch down with, or near them: and in this case as thick as they can possibly "stow" together. But if you have only a single gun, the moment you raise the barrel, to put the powder in,—away they all go!

The oxbird belongs to the tribe of *sand pipers.* Of these, including the *ruff* (the *female* of which is called *reeve)*, there are *fifteen* sorts: but, as they scarcely afford any particular sport, it will be wasting time to enter into any detail on them, or even to give a translation of their different names.

PARTRIDGES. *Tetrao perdix—La perdrix grise.*

RED LEGGED. *Tetrao rufus—La perdrix rouge.*

The latter has been of late years brought from the continent, and is now (as I before observed) plentiful on the estates of lords Hertford and Rendlesham in Suffolk.

The red legged partridges are fond of warm dry soil; and, from this circumstance, they are, in flavour, rather inferior to the common ones. Although called "*French* partridges," these birds are scarcely known in many parts of Normandy and Picardy, where the *common partridge (like ours)* is the only one commonly to be met with. In France they prefer the vine countries, for the sake of a warm sandy soil; but in Spain, Portugal, and the southern parts of Europe, they are universally diffused.

I remember, at the early part of the Peninsular war, getting some excellent shooting at these birds on the march between Castello Branco and Placentia; where, had there been time to follow a day's sport, the quantity killed might have been immense.

Red legged partridges will congregate *in packs, perch* on hedges, and, if wounded, often go *to earth.*

To kill them, you must press them hard to take wing, or they will run out of shot before they rise; and for this reason, they are apt to spoil your dogs. Red legged partridges being constantly on the run, are difficult to disperse; but by means of heading them, with men on horseback, their coveys, or packs, may be divided, and this being once done, they will lie like stones.

PHEASANTS. *Phasianus colchicus—Le faisan.*

Besides the common pheasant, there are now in *preserved coverts, as well as* aviaries, other beautiful kinds, which have been mostly brought from China; *viz.* the *golden pheasant; silver* or *pied pheasant,* &c.; and also two varieties of the common one, the one of which is precisely like it, except having a white ring round the neck, from which it is distinguished by the name of *ring pheasant;* and the other of pure *white,* which I had (it appears erroneously) supposed to be a mule bird between the common pheasant and the barn door fowl, partaking of the shape and habits of the former, with the colour and taste of the latter. What led me to think so was, that these birds appeared without any one having originally imported the breed, or even any variety, but where the common pheasants were often seen among the white barn door fowls. In a small covert of my own I had *one nide* of twelve, in which were hatched *nine common and three white* pheasants. But, since the foregoing surmise appeared in a former edition, I was favoured with observations from a superior ornithologist, which I am sure will be far more worthy the attention of naturalists than any thing I can insert of my own. I shall, therefore, take the liberty of subjoining his communication:

"In the second edition of the 'Instructions to Young Sportsmen' by Major Hawker, the author, in speaking of the different kinds of pheasants, says—"

Here he quotes from my second edition at considerable length. He then continues—

"The 'Instructions to Young Sportsmen' are evidently the work of a sportsman, who is a master of the subject on which he writes, and under a very moderate title contain a great deal of original and interesting information; information new, not only to the young sportsman, but capable of instructing the old. It is with great deference, therefore, that the writer of the following observations ventures to give a different opinion on the cause of white pheasants, or at least to submit that there should be assigned another cause for their production than that of their being mule birds, between the fowl and hen pheasant. He will speak of these two subjects in their order: and,

"First, on the probable cause of white pheasants.

"On reading the 'Instructions to Young Sportsmen,' the writer of the following remarks was struck with the observation, that 'the common pheasants were often seen *among the white barn door fowls;*' and recollecting the story of Jacob's contract with Laban, in the 30th chapter of Genesis, he began to think white pheasants were produced by the *impression* made on the hen pheasant, from having white fowls before her during the period of gestation. In the above account in Genesis it appears, that Jacob's stratagem fully succeeded, for we are told in the last verse, that 'the man increased exceedingly, and had much cattle.' These ring-streaked and speckled cattle of Jacob, and the brown sheep, were evidently caused by impression, or the operation of an outward appearance upon, and influencing, the senses, as will appear by reading, attentively, the story from the 25th to the 43d verse: and besides the peeled rods obtruded before the eyes of the cattle during the time of conception, he set 'the faces of the flocks toward the ring-streaked and all the brown in the flock of Laban.'

"If then beasts may be affected by impression, or the operation of an outward appearance on the senses, is it unreasonable to suppose, that birds may be affected in the same manner? and if by having peeled rods placed before them, and their 'faces set toward the ring-streaked,' an impression was made on these cattle, causing them to produce their young of that colour, may not the same cause have the same effect on pheasants? and the hen pheasant, by being among white fowls, and håving them before her eyes, be the mother of young, of a pied or white colour?

"But it will be said, 'Here are fowls of several colours besides white, with which pheasants are likely to mix in the fields, and this will destroy the probability of pheasants becoming white by impression made on the hen pheasant, since, as there are black and brown fowls, why should not pheasants become black or brown from the same cause?'

"It is submitted, in answer to this objection, that a white fowl is of a more glaring and obtrusive colour than any other, and consequently more likely to catch the eye, and make a stronger impression on the hen pheasant, from its striking peculiarity, and, as it respects the pheasant, *deformity.*

"But further, though we often hear of a variety of any particular species of bird, yet that variety is almost always either white, or a mixture of white with the natural colour. If among birds there be a lusus naturæ, she, in her freak, seldom deviates from this colour. And notwithstanding these white varieties may be fairly termed raræ aves, and although there are several species naturally black, yet a black *variety* always has been considered a *peculiar prodigy*, as we may remember in that well known line in the mouth of every school-boy. And among fowls there are none of a stronger colour than white fowls and black, and white is stronger than black. Other fowls approach more to the colour of the pheasant (the brown fowl particularly to that of the hen pheasant), at least than these two colours of white and black. Fowls of another colour than white will be introduced again soon after, as a concurrent proof, that white pheasants are not a mule breed between the barn door cock and the hen pheasant.

"In proof of the effect of the influence of impression on the senses from outward appearances, we might here allude to the human species, and the impression which is often unfortunately made on mothers, from objects of deformity.

"In the above remarks, the writer has ventured an opinion on the probable cause of white pheasants. He leaves it to others to judge how far he is right or wrong But however this may be, he will now endeavour to show, that whatever may be the cause of this lusus naturæ in the pheasant, yet that there are the strongest grounds for presuming, that the white pheasant is not a mule bird, between the barn door cock and the hen pheasant. And,

"First, it is conceived, that the white pheasant is not a mule bird, between the barn door cock and the hen pheasant, from the circumstance, that it is one of the laws of nature, that the young of all animals should be formed more after the male than the female parent, have more of the shape, nature, and properties, of the former than of the latter. This is well known to the breeders of cattle. If a horned ram be put to an ewe without horns, the offspring will have horns. On the contrary, let the ewe be horned, and the ram without horns, and the lamb will be without horns; in both cases taking after the ram. A mule was once pointed out to the writer of these remarks as something extraordinary, from its being the foal of an ass covered by a Portuguese horse, which happened to be brought over to this country by an officer. It was thought an extraordinary production, since the stallion refuses the she ass, and consequently all our mules are produced from the ass and the mare, and not from the horse and the she ass. But this mule, having *a horse for its sire*, was much more *like a horse* than our common mules, which spring from a more humble sire, and partake *more of the nature of the ass* than the mule here alluded to, and from this greater resemblance to the horse, it was pointed out rather as a curiosity. From hence the writer infers, that the white pheasants, if they were mule birds, between the barn door cock and the hen pheasant, would, according to this law of nature, take more of the shape, nature, and properties of the male than of the female parent. But the reverse is the case: white pheasants are *perfect pheasants,* in every respect but *colour,* and whether male or female birds, have neither the comb, the gills, nor the tail of the fowl; have no appearance of the fowl except in their white colour. Now the tail of the pheasant is so remarkable in its shape, as not to be found in any other class of British birds; and notwithstanding the rule of nature, that all animals should preserve more of the shape and properties of the male than of the female parent, yet the white pheasant, descended from the male fowl and female pheasant, retains the tail of the latter perfect and unaltered, and without any resemblance to that of the former.

" From this identity of shape in the white pheasant and common pheasant it is submitted, that the former cannot be a mule bird between the barn door cock and the hen pheasant.

" And with respect to the colour of the white pheasant, it will be presently urged, from the instances of white varieties in other birds, that this cannot be a satisfactory reason for its being a mule bird, or half a fowl.

" But it should not be forgotten, that in the ' Instructions to Young Sportsmen,' the *taste* of the white pheasant is mentioned as like that of the fowl. To this the writer of these observations can say nothing, but that it may depend on the imagination. Because it is known to be a white pheasant, and supposed to be half a fowl, the flavour of the bird may be judged rather from what is fancied, than from what is tasted. The *skin* of the white pheasant, when picked, is probably different (the writer says, *probably,* since he cannot speak to the fact, for he has never seen a white pheasant after it was picked) from that of other pheasants, and white, like that of the fowl, which may also change the appearance of the flesh. The whiteness of the skin will be owing to the colour of the feathers, which will probably have that effect on the skin. We see this in a pig; when scalded, and the hair taken off, the skin is either white, or stained with black, according to the colour of the hair.

" Secondly. It is well known, that other birds, besides pheasants, are white, notwithstanding the colour of their kind is quite different, and yet that these can be no mule birds is obvious. Every one has heard of white varieties of one species or other of British birds; and in Mr. Bullock's museum, in Piccadilly, there is a white jay, a white cuckoo, a white blackbird, thrush, and lark. But neither the male nor female parent of these birds could have been white, since among British small birds there is not one class or kind of that colour. And mule birds partake of the colour of both parents, as in the instance of the young of the goldfinch and canary. It is, therefore, clear, that the white varieties, just mentioned, cannot be mule birds; and, on the other side, if they may be produced white without being mule birds, why may not pheasants?

"Thirdly. If white pheasants were mule birds between the fowl and the pheasant, how does it happen that the mule breed between these birds is always *white* in all parts of the country? The writer of these remarks has seen two in a nide, and has heard of many other white pheasants. But he never saw or heard of any other variety of the common* pheasant than the pied, or white pheasant. And yet there are fowls of several colours besides white, with which pheasants are likely to mix in the fields; and the mule production between these fowls and the hen pheasant ought not to be white, but, according to the established law of nature, they should have a share of the colour of each parent. And thus the mule production, from a barn door cock of any one of several colours besides white, would be easily distinguished, but particularly if the cock were black.

"Fourthly. Again, if white pheasants be a mule breed between the barn door cock and the hen pheasant, how is it, that though we often hear of these white pheasants, yet we never hear of a mule bred between the cock pheasant and the hen fowl? The writer has already spoken of having seen white pheasants, and of having heard of many more, but he never saw or heard of a mule bred between the cock pheasant and the hen fowl. And yet he has seen pheasants

---

* Under the description of common pheasant, the writer here includes, for the sake of perspicuity, the ring-necked pheasant, though properly a variety of the common class, but he excludes, of course, all foreign pheasants. Neither is he here speaking of the mule pheasant, so called, which has the plumage of both cock and hen pheasant, and the cause of which phenomenon sportsmen cannot very well determine.

come into a lonely barn-yard, where there was no house, and where no labourers were at work, but where there were fowls. And he has known a cock pheasant to come early every morning in the breeding season to this barn-yard, and crow, often sitting on one of the hovels. And it is said a cock pheasant would beat a game cock, if unarmed with those barbarous weapons, steel spurs. If this be true, he would, of course, be more than a match for a dunghill cock. And as this superior prowess would enable him to defend his own seraglio from the violations of chanticleer, if attempted in his presence, so it would enable him more easily to invade that of his neighbour.

" Note.—White pheasants are seldom perfectly white, but are usually mottled, or variegated, or, as they are generally called, pied. When they are entirely white, the impression on the hen pheasant must be of the strongest and most perfect kind. But when they are pied, it is suggested, rather that the impression was not so strong and perfect, than that the impression was made by mottled or variegated fowls.

" With respect to the brown sheep mentioned in the contract between Jacob and Laban, it may be remarked, that as white is the natural colour of that animal, so the brown sheep may be to the white one what the white fowl is to the brown pheasant, the hen pheasant, at least, being of that colour.

" Here it may be added, that the fowl being about the size of the pheasant, and in its general form bearing some resemblance to it, so this general resemblance, in any other respect, will render its peculiarity, in point of colour, so much the greater deformity. Fowls, too, when they stray from the farm-yard into the fields to feed, and pheasants, when they leave the coppices and hedgerows for the same purpose, prowl and feed, both of them in the same manner. And while other birds are continually on the wing from place to place, and seldom remain long on a spot, the pheasant rarely rises unless disturbed, and is much more still and stationary. The pheasant, if undisturbed, continues in the same neighbourhood, particularly in the breeding season. Fowls, when they stray, since they cannot go far, must frequent the same fields; and as the pheasant from its habits is likely to meet them, and to remain with them, it is liable not only to a more durable impression, but subject to a greater exposure to that impression. And it is, perhaps, from these causes that there are a greater number of white pheasants than white varieties of any other single species of birds, for we much oftener hear of the former than of the latter. But what may be the cause of the lusus naturæ in other birds, the author of these remarks leaves to be explained, or attempted, by some more close observer of her feathered family."

PIGEONS.

The shooting of *tame* pigeons I have always had *want of taste* enough to consider as an amusement to be classed with *badger-baiting*. But as it becomes a glorious opportunity for assembling parties to gamble and get drunk, I must not be so unfashionable as to *moralise* about cruelty; particularly as the professors of this *accomplishment* might ask me, "Why is it worse than hunting a *bag* fox?" or "May not *every* sport be more or less condemned for cruelty?"

As pigeons are commonly turned out at twenty-one yards, it may be easily observed, that the knack of killing them consists in firing *the instant they are up*, and being careful *not to shoot under them*, as they take so hard a blow, particularly on the *rump*, that, if suffered to fly to any distance, they are apt to get out of bounds before they fall. The larger the gun and the charge, the wider the circle of shot; and therefore the better to assist that shaking hand, which, among the most expert marksmen, may be occasioned by anxiety. Plenty of powder, and a light charge (in proportion) of No. 6 shot will do better for a man while nervous than *very close* shooting; or, at all events, till he has become cool and confident, which he generally will find himself after he has killed a few birds in succession.

So little is the art of pigeon shooting the criterion of a good shot, that many of the very best performers at this are scarcely third rate shots at other birds, and some of them perfect cockneys in every other kind of shooting. It must, however, be admitted, that there is more difficulty in shooting pigeons *at a regular match* than many bystanders are aware of. The man who has to exhibit before hundreds of people, and is, perhaps, betting hundreds of pounds, feels in general a very different sensation from the one who stands merely as a spectator, perfectly composed; and while in this state, is confident of being able to beat those who are engaged in the match, although they may be shooting infinitely better than he perhaps could do if placed in their situation. In this, as in every thing else, therefore, it is far, very far, easier to be a fault-finder than a performer; because most things fall so decidedly short of perfection, that any simpleton may set up for the one, while, on the contrary, a man must have acquired some little knowledge, however superficial, before he can attempt the other.

Of *wild* pigeons, or (more properly speaking) *doves*, there are *three* kinds: the

STOCK, or WILD PIGEON. *Columba œnas—Le biset.*

RING, CUSHAT, or QUEEST. *Columba palumbus—Le pigeon ramier.*

TURTLE. *Columba turtur—Le tourterelle.*

The *second* of these, the most common, is almost universally known by the name of *woodpigeon;* and, if not too much fed on *turnips*, and kept till tender, is deservedly esteemed an excellent bird. The *turtle-dove*, however, is the *best* of the three; but being only a summer visiter, it generally escapes the notice of the shooter; except in the early part of September, when birds of this description are often sprung from the *pea fields.*

For shooting woodpigeons there are various contrivances, which, like those for *all other wild* birds, consist chiefly in *waiting for them,* as this always answers so *much better than attempting to follow them.* Some hide themselves among the trees, where they come to roost about sunset: others take them at perch, after the fall of the leaf, by moonlight* (the way poachers shoot pheasants); and many are killed by boys in the summer, who conceal themselves, in a harbour, near the ponds where these birds and the doves go to drink. But, after all, the most effectual way is to shoot them when they come to the *turnips* in *snowy weather.* If the frost is so hard that you cannot approach them, under cover of a fence, without making a noise on the white ice, you must, after moving them, wait, to leeward, for their return. If you can make a place in a hedge, it is preferable to the common plan of putting up hurdles covered with straw, as the woodpigeons are apt to notice, and feed out of reach of them. These birds are fond of frequenting beech trees, and feeding on the nuts that fall from them.

To get shots at woodpigeons round a fir clump, or plantation, send your man on the opposite side to drive them out before you; or they will, ten to one, go off *under cover* of the *tree* from which they fly. By waiting concealed in the covert, you may often stand in one

* This the woodpigeons will not allow you to do, unless the trees are clear of underwood; as the least rustling of bushes would put them to flight. For this reason (as Mr. Daniel very justly remarks) they are an excellent night signal, to keepers, when poachers have availed themselves of boisterous weather to attack a preserved covert.

place, where fresh birds will continue dropping into the boughs, till you have half filled your bag with them. Observe one thing, however, or you may not kill a bird in a week!—Recollect that a woodpigeon, directly he perches, begins to reconnoitre his safety in every direction; and if you move but a finger, *when* he *first alights*, he will instantly take wing. But if you will only wait perfectly still for half a minute, you may then present and fire at him as easily as at an owl.

Although the ringdove or woodpigeon seldom builds anywhere but in dark evergreen trees, such as yew trees, firs, &c., yet, in 1824, one of these birds entered a dove-house of mine; made her nest in company with the tame pigeons; and hatched her eggs there, notwithstanding a man was repeatedly going in to clean out the place, and take young pigeons. Here she brought up her two young ones, and then took them off with her. This is almost as singular as the circumstance of a partridge, in 1788, having reared sixteen young ones up in a pollard tree, through which went the bars of the stile in a public foot-path. This happened in Essex, on a manor of my late father, of whom Mr. Daniel had the deputation, and was an eyewitness to the circumstance. The particulars of this he very correctly states in his "Rural Sports."

PLOVER.

Of the plover tribe there are *six* sorts:—*viz.*

GREAT PLOVER (already named among the Curlews).

BASTARD PLOVER, LAPWING, or PEEWIT. *Fringilla vanellus —Le vanneau.*

The one famous for its eggs.

Old peewits, as we all know, fly round a dog, in order to mislead him from the nest; and I have observed, that the young ones, about July or August, frequently do the same: perhaps in imitation of the parent bird. With a dog, therefore, one, who agrees with the French proverb*, as to their being such a delicacy, may be able to kill several of these birds in the marshes where they frequent. The *afternoon* is the best time, as peewits prefer the uplands during the morning.

GOLDEN PLOVER. *Charadrius pluvialis—Le pluvier doré.*

GRAY PLOVER. *Tringa squatazola—Le vanneau pluvier.*

DOTTEREL. *Charadrius morinellus—Le guignard.*

RING DOTTEREL. RING PLOVER, or SEA LARK. *Charadrius hiaticula—Le petit pluvier à collier.*

The *gray plover*, and *ring dotterel*, are *coast* birds: the *others* chiefly frequent the marshes and fallows *inland*, where they feed on worms.

The golden plovers and large dotterels are worth more than all the others, either to shoot, or for the table. The former, when in large flocks, are wild, and must, therefore, be followed with caution; the latter are easier of access, though not so plentiful. Golden plover were formerly killed in great plenty by means of a *stalking horse*. If you fire at these birds as they fly over you, they will dart down for the moment, and spread in every direction; so that, by taking a random shot with your first barrel, you may often bring down the birds to a fair one for your second.

If admissible to bring together land and water birds, we may add to this list, the

* "Qui n'a pas mangé de vanneau, ne sait pas ce que gibier vaut."

LONG-LEGGED PLOVER, or LONGSHANKS. *Charadrius himantopus—L'echasse.*

This plover, and the *sanderling*, Bewick places by themselves, as a separate *Genus*, at the commencement of his second volume.

PREY, BIRDS OF.

To shoot the various birds of prey, which belong to the falcon tribe, such as buzzards, kites, hawks, falcons, &c. &c., the easiest and most destructive method is to watch the coppices in the *breeding season*, or induce the boys, by a trifling reward, to find out their nests. You should wait till the female sits hard on her eggs; and then go, late in the evening, with some large shot in a duck gun; by which means you may either take her as she flies out of the tree, or *blow up the whole concern* by firing through the nest.

This is a more certain, and a *much less cruel* way to destroy mischievous birds than by indiscriminately shooting, or catching, them at a distance from their nests; where, perhaps, their young ones, having been hatched, are *left* to be *starved* with hunger.

Ravens, carrion-crows, magpies, &c., may be killed in the same manner, or poisoned previously to the breeding season, by your putting in some of their favourite trees a few joints of horseflesh, well seasoned with *arsenic* and *nux vomica*. Another good way to kill these, particularly *magpies*, is to drive along the road with a horse that will stand fire, and shoot them from *a cart, gig*, or other *carriage*. I have known eight or nine magpies killed in a day by this means *(about the pairing season)*, when the keepers were constantly following them without being able to get a shot.

QUAIL. *Tetrao coturnix—Le caille.*

There is no part of this country where we can go regularly out for a day's *quail* shooting, as in France (where these birds abound in the month of August), or the more southern parts up the Mediterranean, where they sometimes cover the country for miles. The quails are so far plentiful on the left bank of the Tagus, that many of the officers, indifferent shots, while in winter quarters at Vallada, thought nothing of going over, and returning to their dinner with ten or twelve couple, although with every disadvantage in point of guns and ammunition.

These birds are so scarce in Great Britain, that to find a good *bevy* of them, and kill three or four brace, is considered as something extraordinary: and, although there is scarcely a sportsman, who has not occasionally met with a few, while shooting partridges in September, yet I have never known any one, who has had much sport with quails *in this country.*

RABBIT. *Lepus cuniculus—Le lapin.*

To shoot rabbits in the evening, sit in a tree; and, by your being above them, they are not likely to smell you, and will therefore play about close under the tree. Let your dead ones lie till you have done shooting, instead of putting an end to your sport by descending to pick them up. For *this* work you must take no dog*.

* As a specimen of criticism by the Wild man of the West—what think you of his here pronouncing "*in*conceivable the use of *a dog* among the *branches?!*" *con*ceiving, I suppose, that I should have dosed the public with a whole chapter to inform them that when a boy climbed a tree, his dog would have to wait below; and that a rabbit would not exactly like to come and feed under the mouth of

To kill rabbits, feeding in an *open* warren, keep a few hurdles pitched, and approach or wait for the rabbits under cover of them; taking care not to go directly to windward. For a regular attack, however, the better diversion is to ferret the holes, and stand about twenty yards off, very quiet, with your gun. This is more amusement for a man who is fond of shooting, than *netting* the rabbits; and the shots are not so difficult in this way, because a rabbit, when bolted by a ferret, does not, in general, go off so fast as when started by a dog. All other rabbit shooting is so well known, that my fancying I could give instructions on the subject would be like the Lisbon barber *informing* Baretti that grapes grew in Portugal. Though one word more (by the by):—In shooting a rabbit, always consider the *foremost half* of him as your *target*, or he will probably be shot in a slovenly manner; and if there is an earth near, most likely scramble to it, and make his escape.

REDWING, SWINEPIPE, or WIND THRUSH*.
Turdus iliacus—Le mauvis.

The redwing is a smaller bird than the fieldfare, and

a dog. By the powers, now, it seems strange that our elegant Emerald should have lost his lustre in such an *ould*-maid-*ish* critique; because he does really appear to be a volatile flash-parson, slap-dash, steeple-chase sort of writer. But

"Nemo mortalium omnibus horis sapit!"

(The never-failing college excuse after committing to living sewers the contents of a twelve-dozen hamper.)

Here, you see, we have a proof of the many instances where, (to give him beef, or in other words a bit of a *bull*,) rigid logic has been pumped in at one end till common sense is driven out at the other.

* The last of these three is in many places the provincial name given to the *missel bird*, or *storm thrush*.

not so wild; but its habits are much the same as those of that bird.

When redwings appear on the eastern coast, they as commonly announce the approach of the *woodcock*, as does the arrival of the *wryneck* that of the *cuckoo* in the south.

ROCKBIRDS.

Those, which are *commonly called rockbirds*, are the various tribes of the *Guillemot* and *Auk* or *Penguin* Genus, which, previously to the month of May, assemble by myriads, to breed among the cliffs that surround the British Isles. For brevity's sake, they are here placed collectively under the above name; and suffice it to say, that those most commonly shot, and the eggs of which are most in requisition, are the *razor-bill* and *puffin* of the *Auk* kind, and the common *willock* of the *Guillemot* kind. The puffins are most plentiful at the back of the Isle of Wight, and St. Alban's; the others on the cliffs near Eastbourne and Dover: but, for a farther variety, we must go more towards the *North* of Great Britain.

Although birds of this description can only be used for the sake of the *feathers*, or *to barrel* for *dog's meat*, yet many of the best sportsmen are tempted to amuse themselves with the diversion of "Rockbird shooting," from the number of shots that may be got in a day, and the uninterrupted opportunity of practice, and trials of skill. For this purpose, large parties of pleasure are made about the months of June and July, when, instead of taking only a full powderhorn and shotbelt, it frequently becomes necessary to be prepared with a cleaning rod, and an extra supply of ammunition.

The time selected for killing these birds *should* be

either before they hatch, or after they have brought down their young to the water, where they are able to shift for themselves: otherwise those, who destroy the old birds, have to reproach themselves with the cruelty of leaving the young ones to starve upon the rocks.

On approaching the stupendous cliff, in which these birds each deposit their one large egg, you see them, for miles and miles, blackening the air like swarms of bees: and what with the screaming of the gulls, the hollow croaking of the cormorants, and the various noises of the penguin tribe, you hear the caverned rocks in constant echo with discordant sounds.

On getting nearer, you will see the main body of the willocks and puffins standing, like ranks of soldiers, along the chalky chasms, but at such a height, as not only to be out of shot, but indifferent to the sound of a gun. Your plan, therefore, should be to let some one start, so as to be on the heights by the time you have arrived below. Having anchored your boat at a distance, where the birds sufficiently lower their flight, make a signal to the person above; who, by letting down about a hundred yards of line, with a piece of wood, a stone, or a bell at the end of it, will immediately put their armies to the rout, and keep them constantly pouring down upon the sea. To kill these birds, you must rather pick your shots, and fire well before them, as they fly with great rapidity, take a very hard blow, and your eye is apt to be deceived in distance, after gazing on a back-ground of chalk, which is, perhaps, two hundred yards in height. After all, however, the rockbirds will not always come near enough for you to make any extraordinary number of shots without missing, unless you descend in a basket, &c. (as I mentioned, when speaking of cormorants), *in the manner* by *which* the men *collect their eggs*, and *gather samphire.*

I remember, when a party went to shoot willocks near Dover, that those who were *under* the cliffs could scarcely get a bird to fly low enough ; while one person, who *stood above, and fired down*, very soon exhausted all his ammunition, without missing a single shot.

To take all chances at *rock-birds* and *sea-fowl*, with a small gun, use shot No. 3, instead of No. 7.

If your object is to bring home a large quantity of willocks, &c. merely for the fun of "taking the shine out of" some rival rock-bird shooter, choose a day when there is a good stiff breeze from *off the land;* so that, by having a smooth sea, and therefore being able to carry plenty of canvass, you can run in upon them under sail, before they begin to disperse, and either fly or dive. Thus you are enabled to cut them up, from three or four to perhaps a dozen, at a shot, with a good shoulder-duck-gun, and then have a right and left at them with your popgun as they come up after diving, and fly away, singly, within pistol shot of your boat. My skipper, Read, and I, adopted this plan in 1831, and had some good pastime at it last summer. By *this* mode of shooting, you may sail in any sized craft you please—indeed the larger the better, if manageable—and take out all kinds of refreshments, your party of ladies, and, in short, whatever you like, to make the thing agreeable. (For a net on my plan to catch up the dead birds without the risk of having to "put about" for them, I shall give you a little chapter under the head of wildfowl.) Read has since had many customers in this way for his large half-decked boat, which he now keeps, in my absence, to "commodate the quality," who, if not shooters, generally land at Alum Bay, where, after making their collections of the beautiful variety of chalks, for which a rock there is well-known, they generally proceed to a place called the "eating house"—Groves's Hotel, one of the best and most delightfully retired inns in the Isle of Wight. The *very* place, by the way, for one who has to draw, or to write a book; or for a couple who have to pass a honeymoon.

ROOK. *Corvus frugilegus—Le freux.*

Let those who find amusement in shooting *perchers* (or young rooks) be careful how they fire among rick-yards and buildings, and always *avoid loading* their guns with either *paper* or *tow*. For *this* kind of shooting, therefore, the *safest* and best kind of *wadding* is *leather*. But as this pastime is most frequently followed by those who never use a punch, or perhaps do not even know what the word "wadding" means, let me only advise, that they be requested to put green moss, or leaves, on their powder and shot, instead of using paper, which is so very liable to set fire to the buildings. Young rooks, by being first skinned, and then soaked all night in cold spring water, make pies, which are worthy the notice of the most scientific gourmand.

RUFF. *Tringa pugnax—Le combattant.*

Ruffs are birds of which the males are seldom found two alike in plumage, and of which the females are called REEVES.

As I before observed, when classing them with the knots, they are easier caught than shot in any great quantity. It is ludicrous to see these birds dancing round the hillocks in the spring, and particularly when they dance into the springes that are set for them.

SNIPES.

Of these there are the *three* following sorts:—

THE GREAT, or SOLITARY SNIPE. *Scolopax media—La grande bécassine.* (As Buffon does not notice the bird, we are to *presume* that this must be the French translation.)

THE COMMON SNIPE, SNITE, or HEATHER-BLEATER. *Scolopax gallinago—La bécassine.*

THE JACK SNIPE, JUDCOCK, JETCOCK, or GID. *Scolopax gallinula—La petite bécassine.*

To kill *jack*-snipes, a pointer that will stand them is the greatest possible acquisition, as *they* always lie so very close that you are liable to walk past them. *These* little snipes are easiest killed in a light breeze, or even *calm* weather, as in a gale of wind they fly more like butterflies than birds. Nothing teases a poking shot worse than jack-snipes; but to one who has the knack of pitching and firing his gun in one motion, they are, generally speaking, not much worse to shoot than other small birds, except in boisterous weather.

The jack-snipes are the best eating of all the tribe.

The "old hand" therefore keeps the jack for his own eating, and sends the fine-looking full snipe to his friend. As with pheasants, the *hen* is the *best* on the table; the cock the prettiest bird for a present.

STARLING, or STARE. *Sturnus vulgaris—L'etourneau.*

The time to shoot starlings by wholesale is just before the dusk of the evening, when they come down to roost among the reeds. Here they assemble in swarms, that darken the air; and, for some time, keep up a chatter, which even surpasses that of Frenchmen in their warmest political debates.

Having swept down some dozens with your duck-gun, let their *heads* be immediately *pulled off;* as this will, in a great degree, *prevent* their having a *bitter taste.*

Starlings are very good when stewed with rice, or made into a curry.

Before I conclude under the head of Starlings, I must ask leave to become my own trumpeter, in order to name a shot that I made at these birds, which will give some idea as to the manner in which they swarm together :—Happening, in November, 1825, to have my punt afloat on Lord Rodney's pond, at Alresford, I loaded my new double swivel-gun with a pound of small shot in each barrel *; and, a little before daylight, paddled across to a retired part of the pond, where the reeds were literally swarming with these birds. Having placed the punt "stem on," so as to command the eastern light, and shoot well clear of the reeds, I gave a little signal, as previously agreed on, to Mr. Macilwain (who, with Captain Hill, was in another punt behind) to discharge both barrels of my little double gun. On hearing this report, up sprang the whole army, consisting, I should say, of every starling in Hampshire, and making the valley echo like a peal of thunder. No sooner had they cleared the reeds than I opened my battery, and cut

* A pound *and a quarter* of shot, with two ounces and a half of powder for each barrel, is the proper coast-shooting charge for this gun.

such a lane through them as was thought scarcely possible; and the quantity of feathers which came flying back to leeward, I could compare to nothing but a fall of black snow. What number were killed and wounded we never could ascertain, from the extreme difficulty of getting the birds that fell among the reeds and quagmires, but we fairly bagged *two hundred and forty-three*, as fast as they could be picked up; and the workmen, when the reeds were cut down, declared that they *found between two and three hundred more:* for this, however, I have only their word; though there is no reason to doubt it, as we all felt confident that, *at least*, five hundred fell to this one volley!

It may be unnecessary to add, that the army of starlings took care not to quarter at Alresford the next night.

*** Many people "can't swallow the Starling story."—No! nor could they an orange, unless dissected;—so now let us dissect the "Starling story."—Those who doubt that starlings will sometimes assemble "ten thousand strong"—let them ask any *fen*-man:—that a huge swivel-gun will shoot with three times the *force* of a little game-gun—refer to the schedules of trial:—that there are 19,200 grains in 2lbs. of No. 8 shot—count an ounce of it and see:—that less than five grains would kill one starling with a *common* gun—ask any sportsman:— that the gun which killed these birds weighs but little under 200lbs.—ask Tom Fullard, who made the barrels.—Then where is the miracle? Why the miracle is this—that people, for want of one minute's calculation, should consider what is a matter of course as an impossibility! and that gentlemen who witnessed the performance should be laughed at when relating the circumstance!—In justice to *them*, I feel it right to explain it. But for my own part, I should not have wasted ink on the subject; because any good judge would know what large guns are capable of doing; and therefore a writer who gave false information would not only have his book soon found out, and crushed, as it ought to be, but himself exposed and hooted at for a quack. The thing speaks for itself. But

I find it more difficult to comply with my friends' request to be serious on the subject, than I should do to go and kill another such a basket of starlings.—While on the strain of scepticism, I should observe, that the account of Buckle killing thirty-five geese at a shot was ridiculed, though he tells me he did it *by night* and *on the mud.* This *may,* or may not, be true; but I *saw* Captain Ward, with *one* pound of shot, pick up twenty geese, and lose nearly as many more, *by day* and *in the water;* which for *difficulty* is treble the performance, in *comparison* with the other; as any old gunner will tell you. But as to these matters, it would be as unreasonable to expect the editor of a newspaper (who perhaps never saw a stanchion-gun fired), to pronounce a fair judgment on the performance of a coast-gunner, as to expect that a coast-gunner (who perhaps can scarcely write his own name) would compose a leading article for a newspaper. If some of our journalists were informed of *sixty* and *seventy* wildfowl having been killed at a shot, they would scarcely find ink enough for their notes of admiration!—And yet I can assure them from the *best* authority that *such things have been done,* though I admit but *very* rarely; and they are every day less likely to occur, from the increased number of shooters.

SWAN, WILD, or HOOPER. *Anas cygnus—Le cygne sauvage.*

If there are not two kinds of hoopers (besides the newly discovered species of wild swan), there is, at all events, a singular variety in the one, as will appear by the following observations: In 1822 I killed three at a shot—one an adult male, and two *young* birds; the latter, not having attained their white plumage; and in *all* of these the space above the bill was *bright yellow.* In 1829 I killed, at a shot, three more (besides wounding a fourth that escaped wing-broken), and these, above the bills, were *all* of a *pale flesh colour,* though one of the three, brought home, was an *old white* bird. Shortly after, I killed two more, an adult female with bright yellow, and a young one with the pale colour. Thus it appears that, whether male or female, young or old, some have the yellow, and some the pale colour. Putting all together, in 1828, 1829, and the following year, I killed about twenty more, and have occasionally observed this variety. Again Mr. Leadbeater tells me that the Linnæan Society have discovered *another distinct* species, it being considerably smaller, and *internally different* from the common hooper; and that there are not above four stuffed specimens of it in Europe; one of which he congratulates me on having. On the strength of this event, they have enlisted a W into the Latin language, and christened the bird Cygnus Bewickii, Mr. Leadbeater being sponsor for the correctness of the statement.

Since writing the foregoing observations, I have been favoured with the perusal of an admirable treatise, published by the very gentleman who made the discovery—William Yarrell, Esq. F.L.S. Here all the internal dissections are developed in the most scientific manner, and elucidated by lithographic drawings. But, as natural history is not our subject, I will conclude with a superficial extract from the work alluded to.—"Several examples of this new species are now ascertained to be in British collections. The museum of the Cambridge Philosophical Society contains one. There is one in the possession of Edward Lombe, Esq., of Great Melton, who has an excellent collection of British birds. A third was shot in the winter of 1827-28, by Colonel Hawker. These three were preserved by Mr. Leadbeater. A specimen was also killed in February, 1829, near Haydon-bridge, upon which bird some remarks have been lately made before the Natural History Society of Newcastle, by Mr. Richard Wingate of that town." [These, I suppose, are the four specimens to which Mr. Leadbeater alluded.] Mr. Yarrel then adds, "I have also had the pleasure of presenting three specimens, which furnished part of the materials for this paper, to the collections of the British Museum and the Linnæan and Zoological Societies."

"It is my intention, and on this occasion I anticipate the accordance of every British naturalist, to devote this species, which, I trust, I have proved to be distinct and unnamed before, to the memory of our late unrivalled engraver on wood, the justly celebrated Bewick."

Our naturalists are no less indebted to Mr. Yarrel, for his anatomical discoveries, and the good taste he has evinced by rendering so just a tribute to our immortal Bewick, than to Bewick himself, for his unrivalled engravings in ornithology.

The hoopers are, at certain times, easier of access than some other wild birds; and if, when flying, they are fired at *directly under the hollow of the wing*, or, when swimming, *through the head*, they may be stopped, at a reasonable distance, with a common double gun and small shot; perhaps even farther than other wild-fowl, as, when struck in the body, they become helpless from their *weight*, and *their heads* are less likely to *escape between the shot* than those of smaller fowl. But if, through eagerness, you happen to fire carelessly at their *upper coverts*, you may as well try to penetrate a woolpack, unless you have very heavy shot, or a ball. But more about hooper-shooting when we get afloat. Since the last edition, I tasted a hooper that had been kept three weeks, then hung up, with some onions in him, and buried for several hours. It was one that I gave my skipper, Read; and he, not being able to find a customer for it, reserved this bird for what he called his "Sunday's blow-out." He sent me a piece to try, and really it was very good. I conclude, therefore, that a *chef* with half the genius of Mr. Ude would make a hooper go down as well as a haunch of venison.

As for the tame swans—they, when young, are becoming quite a fashionable dish; and there is now a man in Norwich who serves the gentry round by fatting them at a guinea apiece.

* TEAL. *Anas crecca—La petite sarcelle.*

As a brood of teal, including the old ones, usually amounts to no more than six or seven, they are most commonly seen in very small numbers; unless they have collected on decoy ponds, and are driven from them by hard frosts, when they will appear on the adjoining rivers, in flocks of twenty or thirty together.

Of all the prizes that a wildfowl shooter could wish to meet with, a *flock of teal* is the *very first.* Independently of their being *by far the best birds of the whole anas tribe*, they are so much *easier of access*, and require such a *slight blow*, that no matter whether you are prepared for wildfowl, partridges, or snipes, you may, at most times, with very little trouble, contrive to get near them; and this being once done, you have only to shoot straight to be pretty sure of killing.

I have seen teal "duck the flash," though never but once, and then I had rather a slow shooting gun.

If you spring a teal, he will not soar up, and leave the country, like a wild duck, but most probably keep along the brook, like a sharp flying woodcock, and then drop suddenly down: but you must *keep your eye on the place*, as he is very *apt to get up again*, and fly to another before he will quietly settle. He will frequently, too, swim down stream the moment after he drops, so that if you do not cast your eye quickly that way, instead of continuing to look for him in one spot, he will probably catch sight of you and fly up, while your attention is directed to the wrong place. If the brook in which you find him is obscured by many trees, you had better direct your follower to make a large circle, and get a-head of, and watch him, in case he should slily skim away down the brook, and, by this means, escape from you altogether. You should avoid firing at random, as *this* may drive him quite away from your beat.

*WIGEON, WHEWER, WHIM, or PANDLED WHEW.
Anas Penelope—Le canard siffleur.

Wigeon * either choose their mates, or detach themselves into small trips preparative to so doing, by about

* Strickly speaking, we should say "wigeon*s*" in the plural number, as well as "pigeon*s*." But so generally is it the custom, among those who have any thing to do with wildfowl, to leave out the *s* here, that the introduction of it feels to me like hearing a "*flock* of partridges," or a "fox's *tail*." Let me, therefore, see if I can scrape up any authority for having thus deviated from the rules of our language. Yes! by the way; the plural of substantives ending in *out* should have an s; and yet, by habit, all modern sportsmen say, for the plural, "trout," and not "trouts." Well then, let the shooter, as well as the fisherman, appeal for a licence to kill languages.

Now therefore to the comparison:—It may be argued, that although in old works we read of "fish*es*," yet in modern language, or rather by habit, which gives a sort of licence, the word *fish*, speaking collectively, is generally used without a plural. Most people, for instance, would say, "a basket of *fish*," or "the river is full of *fish*," notwithstanding the plural of other nouns ending in *sh* should have the addition of *es* to distinguish it from the singular number. For instance, "dishes," "wishes," and so on. Again,

Valentine's day; and therefore killing many at a shot, after this time, is generally only to be done when they are fighting together, or in the event of cold weather.

speaking of them separately, some fish have, and some have not, an *s* for their plural; as, for instance, " herring*s*, " pilchard*s*," " sprat*s*;" on the other hand, " carp," " tench," " mackerel."

In comparison, too, I observe, that the word " *wildfowl*" is used without a plural (and yet translated in Latin, *volucr*ES *palustr*ES), notwithstanding we put a plural when the first syllable, or rather the adjective, is not used. For example, in speaking of poultry, we should say " a couple of fowls." We have, it is presumed, therefore an equal right to say " *wigeon*," " *teal*," " *plover*," though, on the other hand, we should say " wild-duck*s*," " dun-bird*s*," " curlew*s*."

Our lexicographers it appears still spell *Wi*D*geon* with a *d*; I suppose, because birds of this kind are not so much in the fashionable world as *pigeons*, and therefore the word has escaped the modern polish, or been neglected, which is the case with most things that belong to absentees. Mr. Bewick spells " *wigeon*" without the *d*. I shall, therefore, take the liberty of following his example, under the idea that lexicographers are not gods, but men; and therefore as liable to leave room for future improvement as are all other students and authors.

As the word *pigeon* was taken from the French, the *d* here should, I presume, never have been introduced, though we see it in the English translation of Anton Ernst Klausing's German dictionary, taken, as he states, from Nathan Bailey's English dictionary: (but, perhaps, from some *very* old edition). I have, however, seen it spelt with a *d* in subsequent works. The other bird was formerly spelt *Widgen*, as somewhat nearer to the Saxon, from which it was probably derived [See Scott's Bailey's Dictionary, in 1755, which says, " prob. of pɪȝȝenꝺ" (wiggend) " Sax. Fighting"]; and then, I believe, changed to *widgeon*. We may, therefore, it is presumed, follow up the improvement, and erase that consonant which is superfluous to the pronunciation; since it has, of late, become the custom to do so with *other* words.

A thousand apologies for (if I may use a vulgarism) such a *long-winded* note on one word, as this is quite unnecessary when a work

The wigeon, for coast night shooting, is like the fox for hunting—it shows the finest sport of any thing in Great Britain. We shall, therefore, hereafter make the pursuit of this fowl one of our leading subjects.

WOODCOCK. *Scolopax rusticola—La becasse.*

Although many sportsmen consider, that there are *two distinct kinds* of woodcocks, and Latham describes *three*, yet they are more to be considered as mere varieties of this bird, than any species that can be separately distinguished from it.

The feather of the woodcock, which is so acceptable to miniature painters, is that *very small one*, under the *outside quill* of each wing: to be sure of finding which, draw out the extreme feather of the wing, and this little one will then appear conspicuous from its *sharp white point.*

To *prove*, that woodcocks, on having migrated into this country, will repair to the *same haunts* for a succession of winters, I shall mention a circumstance, not as having pilfered it from Mr. Bewick or Mr. Daniel, but because it was *related to me by Mr. Pleydell himself*, when I was at Whatcombe House, where the bird is now preserved. In Clenston Wood (a covert belonging to the above place, in Dorsetshire), a woodcock was taken alive, in one of the rabbit nets, in the month of February, 1798. Mr. Pleydell, after having a piece of brass marked, and put round its left leg, allowed the bird to be set at liberty; and, in the month of December following, he shot *this woodcock*, in the very same coppice where it had been first caught by his gamekeeper.

---

is in the hands of a reviewer, or any other liberal reader. But I have inserted it merely for the amusement of the *word-catcher*; or, in other words, the little gentleman who looks more at the leaves on the tree than the design of the landscape.

Although it is here wished to abstain from all anecdotes, that may not be considered of some little *use* in the way of *information*, yet, while on the subject of woodcocks, I shall take the liberty of mentioning one circumstance, that occurred to myself on the 25th of January, 1810. It was, soon after, very correctly stated in a newspaper; but, no wonder, considered by many as an absurd and improbable assertion; and for this reason I shall, in quoting the paragraph here, add, that the circumstance took place in the presence of the Rev. W. Nourse and two other gentlemen. "A few days ago, a woodcock flew up the lawn, and dropped close before Longparish House, in Hampshire; and was *shot from the window*, by Captain Hawker, who, having been wounded in Spain, was there confined to his room. What makes the circumstance more remarkable is, that it happened in a country where it is very rare to see three of these birds in a season; and that a friend of his had laid a bet, he would be well enough to shoot a cock before the winter was over."

TO PRESERVE AND CHOOSE BIRDS,
&c. &c.

To distinguish specifically the foregoing birds, I refer my readers to Bewick; presuming, as I have repeatedly hinted, that no one, who has the least interest in shooting, either as a sportsman or a naturalist, could willingly be without such a portable, cheap, and yet such a very superior work.

If you shoot a curious bird, and have not the means of getting it stuffed while fresh, you may preserve the skin of it for many months by putting therein dry tow and powdered ginger. *May and June are the worst months for the moth*; and just then camphor is a good addition. But for MOTH, IN EVERY STATE, the *never-failing*, though *poisonous* REMEDY, is CORROSIVE SUBLIMATE, dissolved in SPIRITS of wine. To skin a bird, open him either on one side, or down the back.

I have, as proposed at the beginning, marked only those of the broad-billed birds which *are fit for the table;* and this has been done as a caution against the imposition of marketmen and poulterers, who, for instance, would have little hesitation in serving you with a couple of *gray* geese or *burrough* ducks, by way of a "delicate bottom dish for your second course."

Although it is not meant to dwell here on a subject, which more properly belongs to a *cookery* book, yet it would be very hard not to have *some* consideration for many, who would rather see one bird roasted and well frothed up on a table, than ten thousand springing from a stubble, or feeding under the moon. Let it therefore be observed, that, in *choosing* birds, you cannot be guided better than by selecting those, which, of their kind, are the *heaviest* in weight and the least beautiful in plumage.

Young birds may be distinguished by the *softness* of their *quills*, which, in *older* ones, will be *hard* and *white.* The females are, in general, preferable to the males; they are more juicy, and seldom so tough. For example, a hen pheasant* or a duck is to be preferred to a cock pheasant or a mallard. The *old pheasants* may be distinguished by the *length* and *sharpness* of their *spurs*, which, in the younger ones, are *short* and *blunt.* Old partridges are always to be known, during the *early part of the season,* by their legs being of a *pale blue,* instead of a yellowish brown; so that, when

* Provided it is not a very *dark*-coloured one, which would denote its being an *old barren hen.* Such birds, by the way, should always be destroyed as *vermin,* because they take to *sucking the eggs* of the others.

a Londoner receives his brace of blue-legged birds in September, he should immediately *snap their legs, and draw out the sinews,* by means of *pulling off the feet,* instead of leaving them to torment him, like so many strings, when he would be wishing to enjoy his repast. This remedy of *making the leg tender* removes the objection to old birds, provided the weather will admit of their being sufficiently kept; and indeed they are then often preferable, from having a higher flavour.

If birds are *overkept,* their *legs* will be *dry,* their *eyes much sunk,* and the *vent* will become *soft* and somewhat *discoloured.* The *first place* to ascertain if they are beginning to be *high* is the *inside of their bills,* where it is not amiss to put some heather straw, or spice, if you want them to keep for any length of time. Birds that have *fallen in the water,* or have not had time to get *cold,* should never be packed like others, but sent *openly,* and dressed as soon as possible. Partridges are often spoiled in September by being put to ferment in a large bag or pannier, which is carried by men on horseback.

It may perhaps be asked, by some one, on seeing the frontispiece (for which, by the way, it has long proved difficult to select any thing original in common field-shooting), why are the partridges carried on a *pole?* The reason is this:—if you put many birds together in a bag, when the weather is hot, and fag about with them, *particularly on horseback,* the *under* ones, at all events, are only fit for *entrées,* or cats' meat. If you hang them up in any thing—still they are liable to be shook, as well as to have *their heads pulled off.* But a pole, from requiring two people, cannot be otherwise than steadily carried; and thus your birds are kept cleaner than by other means. Here we have a hint for both the *chasseur* and the *gourmand.*

Sportsmen are often heartily abused by their acquaintance (I cannot yet bring myself to hackney the word *friends* quite so fluently as I ought to do) for sending them "tough and good-for-nothing game," while all the blame should, in many instances, rest with themselves, or their pudding-headed cook, who, may be, dresses an old pheasant, or hare, the very day after it was killed, or perhaps, while engrossed in a story or argument, leaves it to roast away, till there remains neither juice nor flavour.

All game, &c. should be kept till properly tender; or, *if wanted in a hurry*, it may be picked, wrapped up in a cloth, and *thus buried* in the earth for a few hours, before it is dressed. This is the custom abroad, where I have supped on wildfowl, *perfectly tender*, that were killed since an early dinner on the same day.

Birds, that are dressed so soon after being killed, as scarcely to have become cold, are more tender than if put by, for a night, and afterwards not kept long enough. On the other hand, if you want them kept a very long time, for any particular purpose, powdered charcoal (for game, venison, or any thing) is the best recipe that I have yet been able to procure.

P. S. When I wrote this, I had quite forgotten to mention also chloride of lime. But if you have an *ice-house*, put your game there, and you want no further prescriptions.

Keep your game in a *safe*, or a well secured larder, to avoid *flies:* and to get rid of *rats*, you have only to leave out, for their supper, a *red herring*, which you must first split open, and then occasionally heat before the fire, while you put over and into it about as much *corrosive sublimate of mercury* as would lie on a half-crown. The rats, when they have eaten of this, will shortly afterwards adjourn to the water; and, instead of returning, there drink themselves to death. This is a far more certain recipe to destroy rats than the mercurial ointment, which was before named in this work. It may be worth while to observe also, *en passant*, that the corrosive sublimate of mercury is a *never failing remedy to destroy bugs*, if mixed with spirits of wine, and well worked, with a paint brush, into the joints and crevices of furniture. But you can never depend on completely annihilating the *breed* of them, till you *do away with papering the walls of town bed-rooms.*

N. B. *Be very careful how you handle, or where you leave, this preparation, it being* POISON.

Q. What has this last recipe to do with *sporting?*

A. The citizens have been enlightening us country shooters with a new system of instructions for killing *our* game, and therefore the least that I can do in return is to give them a short recipe for killing *theirs.*

With regard to *dressing* birds, there are so many various methods, for which every cook or epicure has his favourite receipt, that it would be absurd to enter on the subject; but, as so many fail in adapting their sauces to *wildfowl*, I shall take the liberty of giving one that has been preferred to about fifty others; and was, at one time, not to be got without the fee of a guinea.

RECIPE FOR SAUCE TO WILDFOWL.

Port wine, or claret	1 glass.
Sauce à la Russe* (the older it is the better)	1 table spoonful.
Catsup	1 ditto.
Lemon juice	1 ditto.
Lemon peel	1 slice.
Shalot (large)	1, cut in slices.
Cayenne pepper (the darkest, not that like brickdust)	4 grains.
Mace	1 or 2 blades.

To be scalded, strained, and added to the mere gravy, which comes from the bird in roasting.

To *complete* this, the fowl should be cut up in a silver dish, that has a lamp under, while the sauce is simmering with it.

Let a goose, or any strong or fat wildfowl, be roasted with the addition of a small onion, and a *pared* lemon, in the inside; as this will draw out the strong fat, and give the bird a milder taste.

Hares and rabbits, *when old*, have blunt claws; are broad across the back; their ears are very tough; and, when cut, their *flesh curls up*, and remains dry. The first joint of their foreleg is larger and stiffer than in young ones, and their jawbones are very hard. In *young* hares and rabbits all is the *reverse* to this: *their* ears are easily torn, and *their* jawbones may be cracked with the forefinger and thumb.

* Introduced by the late Mr. Aveling, in Albemarle-street, and now sold there by his successors.

DOGS

HAVE been such a universal subject for every sporting writer, that scarcely a word can be said about them, but that of which we may find the counterpart in some publication or other. Every one has his own caprice, or fancy, about pointers, setters, and spaniels; and we meet, almost every day, with some fresh man, who has *got the best dog in England.*

Let it be observed, however, that, with all the perfection to which we have brought both the breeding and breaking of these animals, we are not always sufficiently particular. In the one, we are apt to let them degenerate for want of a proper *cross;* and, in the other, we are too well contented (provided they have "plenty of hunt in them") with their merely being broken well to back and stand, without regarding the importance of their *lying down to charge,* and being *stanch from chasing* hares or rabbits. Putting the credit of our dogs entirely out of the question, we forget the number of shots they spring by committing such faults.

If you *want game,* take *old dogs.* Young ones, however fleet and well broken, know little more than the A B C of their business, while old ones are up to every kind of trick.

I shall now give engravings, of a check collar, and an iron puzzle, that will, at once, do more towards dog-breaking than a whole treatise, which would be redundant to those of my readers who are sportsmen, and set all the others asleep.

CHECK COLLAR FOR BREAKING POINTERS, &c.

EXPLANATION.

A. Pin which screws out, to let the dog's head in. The rope, on being suddenly pulled, draws the rings into a corner of the triangle; and almost chokes the dog, by the pressure of B. B.

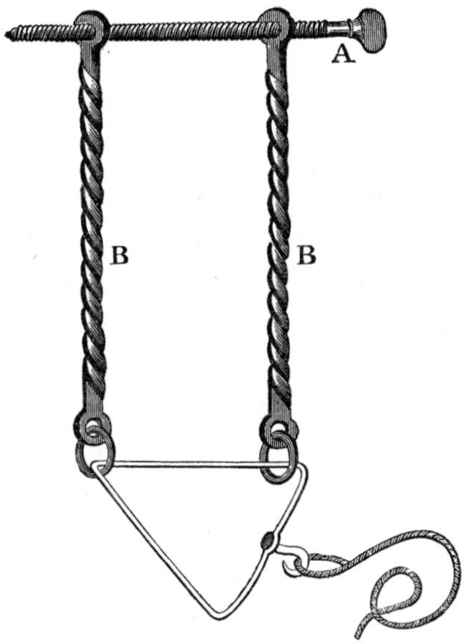

IRON PUZZLE

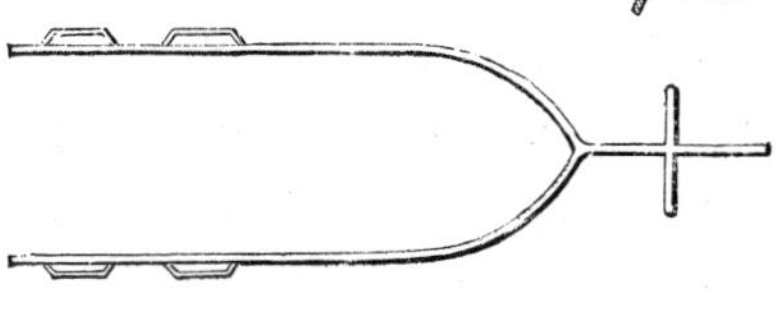

for ditto; to be put on with two leather straps: the hind one to be buckled over the dog's head; and the fore one round his lower jaw; so as for the cross to project under the front of it.

I shall, however, make one observation, which is, that a dog is far more likely to become a first-rate one, by being made a companion of, and corrected by *rating* and *shaming* him, than by being kept entirely away from the breaker, except to be taken to the field, and there *flogged for every fault* he commits. I had a friend in Dorsetshire, who was not only one of the best shots that ever lived, but who had, perhaps, the very best dogs in Europe, and I know this was *his* plan.

[In the fourth edition, I observed that any one who had been much in the west of England would know who I meant; but I now sincerely regret to add that this gentleman died in 1825. While he lived, the public mention of his name might have been thought a liberty; but now that he is no more, I feel it a duty —a tribute due to his memory. The sportsman alluded to was Bayles Wardell, Esq., who, take him for every thing, was one of the very best shooting sportsmen that ever went into a field! To say of any man that he was the *best* shot in England, would be as bold an assertion as to say that there was any man in England who could shoot better than Mr. Wardell!]

With regard to spaniels, they are, nine times in ten, so badly broken in, as, in general, to be only fit to drive a large wood; but, if taught to keep always *within half a gunshot*, they are the best dogs in existence for working among hassocks and briars. They should be trained very young, or they require an unmerciful deal of flogging; and it is sometimes advisable, at first, to hunt them with a forefoot tied up in the collar.

If you have occasion to punish a dog, which I should recommend having recourse to as little as possible, never kick him, for by such means you may do him an injury. I know a sportsman in Hampshire who had the misfortune to lose his dog by giving him one unlucky kick! Always, therefore, flog your dog with a whip or switch. To do this, and, at the same time, avoid the risk of his getting loose, or biting you, hold his head between your knees, by which means you properly secure him, and have a full command of his back, without being liable to strike him in a tender part.

If an obstinate dog will not come out of cover when repeatedly called—*be silent*—then he will begin to listen for you—and, through fear of being left behind, will most likely come sneaking out, so as to be caught for a timely flagellation.

NEWFOUNDLAND DOGS.

Here we are a little in the dark. Every canine brute, that is nearly as big as a jackass, and as hairy as a bear, is denominated a *fine Newfoundland dog*. Very different, however, is both the proper Labrador and St. John's breed of these animals; at least, many characteristic points are required, in order to distinguish them.

The one is very large; strong in the limbs; rough haired; small in the head; and carries his tail very high. He is kept in that country for drawing sledges full of wood, from inland to the sea shore, where he is also very useful, by his immense strength and sagacity, among wrecks, and other disasters in boisterous weather.

The other, *by far the best for every kind of shooting*, is oftener *black* than of another colour, and scarcely bigger than a pointer. He is made rather long in the head and nose; pretty deep in the chest; very fine in the legs; has short or smooth hair; does not carry his tail so much curled as the other; and is extremely quick and active in running, swimming, or fighting.

Newfoundland dogs are so expert and savage, when fighting, that they generally contrive to seize some vital part, and often do a serious injury to their antagonist. I should, therefore, mention, that the *only way* to get them immediately off is to put a rope, or handkerchief, round their necks, and keep tightening it, by which, means their breath will be gone, and they will be instantly choked from their hold.

The St. John's breed of these dogs is chiefly used on their native coast by fishermen. Their sense of smelling is scarcely to be credited. Their discrimination of scent, in following a wounded pheasant through a whole covert full of game, or a pinioned wildfowl through a furze brake, or warren of rabbits, appears almost impossible. (It may, perhaps, be unnecessary to observe, that rabbits are generally very plentiful, and thrive exceedingly, near the sea shore. It, therefore, often happens, that wigeon, as they fly, and are shot by night, fall among furze brakes, which are full of rabbits.)

The real Newfoundland dog may be broken in to any kind of shooting; and, without additional instruction, is generally under such command, that he may be safely kept in, if required to be taken out with pointers. For finding wounded game, of every description, there is not his equal in the canine race; and he is a *sine quâ non* in the general pursuit of wildfowl.

Poole was, till of late years, the best place to buy Newfoundland dogs; either just imported, or broken in; but now they are become much more scarce, owing (the sailors observe) to the strictness of "those ——— the tax-gatherers." I should always recommend buying these dogs ready broken; as, by the cruel process of half starving them, the fowlers teach them almost every thing; and, by the time they are well trained, the chances are, that they have got over the distemper, with which this species, in particular, is sometimes carried beyond recovery.

If you want to make a Newfoundland dog do what you wish, you must encourage him, and use gentle means, or he will turn sulky; but to *deter* him *from* any *fault*, you may rate or beat him.

I have tried poodles, but always found them inferior in strength, scent, and courage. They are also very apt to be sea-sick. The *Portland dogs* are superior to *them*.

A water-dog should not be allowed to jump out of a boat, unless ordered so to do, as it is not always required; and, therefore, needless that he should wet himself, and every thing about him, without necessity.

For a punt, or canoe, always make choice of the *smallest* Newfoundland dog that you can procure; as the smaller he is, the less water he brings into your boat after being sent out; the less cumbersome he is when afloat; and the quicker he can pursue crippled birds upon the mud. A bitch is always to be preferred to a dog in frosty weather, from being, by nature, less obstructed in landing on the ice.

If, on the other hand, you want a Newfoundland dog only as a retriever for covert shooting, then the case becomes different; as here you require a strong animal, that will easily trot through the young wood and high grass with a large hare or pheasant in his mouth.

DISEASES IN DOGS

Are so universally prescribed for, and in so many different ways, that it will be needless to treat on any thing farther than the most common evils that happen to them; the Distemper, the Mange, Sore Feet, getting lamed by Thorns, &c. &c., with the prescription, which I have *found to answer best* for each.

DISTEMPER.

To enumerate the various recipes for this *sometimes incurable* disease would require a volume; but, of all that I have yet tried, none has answered better than the one I shall here give; and, as the remedy is so innocent, it may be safely administered, where there exists even a doubt as to a dog having the distemper.

The following prescriptions are each about a dose for a full grown pointer. They must, of course, be increased or diminished in proportion to the size and strength of the dog.

RECIPE.

Opium	3 grains.
Emetic tartar (an invaluable medicine) .	5 grains.

To be given at night.

Repeat the dose, every third night, till the dog is recovered; taking care to keep him in a warm place, and always fed with a warm liquid diet, such as broth, gruel, &c.

If the nostrils should discharge, have them washed, or syringed, twice a day, with a lotion of alum, or sugar of lead; putting about half an ounce of either to a pint of water.

The following is a recipe, which no bribe could tempt the vender to part with; but, by means of some very clever chymists, I have ascertained it to be simply as follows:—(after some trouble in discovering the proportions, and discarding the ingredients by means of which it was disguised in a pill.)

RECIPE.

For a Half Grown Pointer:—

Jalap powder	25 grains.
Calomel	5 grains.

Made into a pill with a little gum water.

For a Full Grown Pointer:—

Jalap powder	30 grains.
Calomel	8 grains.

Mixed as above.

One of these doses, mixed with butter, or in a small piece of meat, should be given to the dog every other morning, on an empty stomach. The food should be light, and easy to digest; and the lotion, if required for the nostrils, should be observed here, as before mentioned.

Notwithstanding the trouble we had to discover this simple recipe, I should prefer the *one first given*, because there is less chance of a dog *taking cold* with that, than with any kind of *mercurial* preparation.

Since my earlier publications, I have been favoured with the following recipe from Dr. Taylor, of East Yarmouth; and from its great repute, as well as that of the gentleman to whom I am indebted for it, I am induced (though I have not yet tried it) to give this recipe insertion.

RECIPE.

Gum gambouge	20 grains.
White hellebore powder . . .	30 grains.

To be made in six balls.

One to be given to a full grown dog, six following mornings (or half the quantity to a puppy).

The dog to be kept warm, and fed on milk and gruel.

The following extract is from the letter of an old sportsman to a friend of mine—

"3rd February, 1832.

"The recipe, No. 3, for distemper, I can assure the Colonel, on the authority of the Duke of Bedford's old keeper (Brooks), is invaluable. Dr. Taylor, it appears, first communicated it to your friend.

"For the YELLOWS—a disease little less destructive, the same experienced sportsman gives, with invariable success,

3 grains of calomel,
6 ditto of rhubarb,
12 ditto of jalap,

made up in three balls, one to be taken each morning on an empty stomach.

"I may remark that, in alluding to the first mentioned recipe for the distemper, the quantity

30 grains of white hellebore,
20 ditto of gambouge,

shou'd be made up in nine balls instead of six, as the 'Instructions' say (Page 253).

"With every deference to so perfect a sportsman as Colonel H. is, I venture to offer these hints for the next edition of a work that has become the standard in Field Sports."

By an anonymous letter (for which I beg leave to thank the author of it, whoever he may be), I was induced, with the able assistance of a medical sportsman, to try, as a *preventive* to the distemper, the *vaccine inoculation*. We made the experiment on several dogs, and we could not afterwards hear that any one of them had taken the disease. But whether this was the effect of chance, or whether the remedy can always be depended on, I must leave to the decision of those persons, who are better versed in dogs than myself. At all events, the remedy is so innocent, that there can be no harm in trying it; and I shall conclude under this head, with the insertion of the letter, which, after what I have said, it would be negligent to omit.

"SIR;

"As a stranger I know not what business I have to trouble you, but, from the subject of my letter, you will, as a sportsman, probably pardon the intrusion. I should tell you I have lately purchased your 'Instructions to Young Sportsmen,' and I do not intend to flatter, when I say, it is by far the best book on shooting I ever read. And since, from its originality and excellence, I have no doubt it will go through another edition, I am induced to hope you will, in a future edition, say something on a preventive of distemper in dogs, which has been lately tried, *if after a trial you should find it to answer*. About two years ago, when in Sussex, I had frequently heard at table, that inoculating a dog with the cow-pox virus would prevent it from having the distemper. About half a year afterwards, having a pointer puppy, a few months old, I inoculated it. The dog has never had the distemper *yet;* but since dogs sometimes escape this cruel disease till old age, and sometimes entirely, this can be no proof. However, you may possibly deem the supposed preventive worth a trial; and, as no one is a greater friend of the dog than I am, it would afford me the sincerest pleasure if you should find it succeed, and make it known. After reading your publication, Sir, no one can doubt of your being a sportsman, and as such you must feel an affection for your faithful companions in the field; and since this will plead for me, and I shall ask your bookseller whether he cannot make this reach you without putting you to the unnecessary expense of postage, I shall make no further apology. But I am, Sir,

"Most respectfully,

"Your obedient humble servant,

"London, October, 1816. "CANIS AMICUS.

"P.S.—I should observe, the part where I inoculated my dog was on the inside of the foreleg, under the shoulder. It was done by cutting a very small place with a pair of scissors, and rubbing the bone, or quill, charged with the virus, into the wound. From the appearance of the wound, a few days after, I was afraid the virus had not taken effect, but I have been told that this slight appearance is usual.

"P. Hawker, Esq."

1832. I have ever since adopted the plan of vaccination; and so little, if any, has been the effect of distemper after it, that I have not lost a dog since the year 1816. Many thanks to my anonymous friend for the hint.

MANGE, COMMON OR RED.

RECIPE.

Sulphur vivum . . .	4 ounces.
Hellebore powder . . .	2 ditto.
Bay-berry powder . . .	2 ditto.
Spirits of turpentine . . .	1 ditto.
Hogslard (to form it into an ointment) .	½ pound.

The dog to be first washed with lime water; and, when dry, to be well rubbed with some of the ointment on the parts affected. The washing and dressing to be repeated every two days.

Give the dog half a drachm of nitre and a drachm of sulphur daily, for ten days.

It will be best to keep the dog free from getting very cold or wet during this process, which, by the by, very rarely fails to cure in two or three applications.

The following is another remedy, during the progress of which dogs may be worked, or even go in the water. The simple article required for this can only be procured on the sea coast.

> Rub the parts affected every other day with the strongest bitters, which are extracted from the salt, and are to be had at the salt-urns, by the name of *glauber*. This kind of embrocation may be kept, for some time, in bottles, if wanted to send inland.

I now decidedly prefer this to all other remedies.

SORE FEET.

To keep a dog's feet hard and sound, the best way is to wash them with brine, or pot-liquor, *every day after coming in;* because, if once suffered to get raw, they are so apt to smart (and particularly if any thing is applied), that the dog makes them worse, by gnawing and biting at them to allay the itching.

If any farther remedy was required, I should prefer the following

RECIPE.

Oil of vitriol	5 drops.
Tincture of myrrh	1 ounce.

A little of which should be applied, with a feather, after first washing the feet.

THORNS.

"For thorns," says Mr. Daniel, "a plaster of black pitch is the best cure for man, horse, or dog; and has succeeded after all other things have failed." I must, however (to speak as I have found it), observe, that a *poultice of linseed meal* surpasses every remedy I have yet tried, provided the thorn cannot be extracted, or cut out. But if the thorn can be got rid of, I should let the dog complete the cure with the *most healing* of all applications—*his own tongue;* by which there is no risk of softening or irritating his feet.

PHYSIC

Should be given to dogs before they begin their hard work. Nothing is better than a mixture of *one ounce of jalap* and a *pint of syrup of buckthorn.* With a large table spoonful of this mixture every dog should be drenched twice in each of the two weeks preceding the sporting season. The dogs should also, in hot weather, have some pieces of brimstone in their water-troughs. If people would only take this trouble, we should not so often hear of dogs going mad, or dropping down dead in the field.

STRAINS OR BRUISES.

I have always found, that an immediate and long continued application of water, *as hot as it can possibly be borne*, is, in these cases, the best fomentation that can be applied to man or beast.

After this, you may use, with wet rags, the following saturnine lotion:—

RECIPE.

Acetated lead	2 ounces.
Vinegar, and water, of each . .	½ pint.

Mixed together*.

When the inflammation is completely removed, rub the parts with the following embrocation:

RECIPE.

Soft soap	1 ounce.
Spirit of wine	1 ditto.
Oil of turpentine	1 ditto.
Green elder ointment . . .	1 ditto.

POISON.

Give, *as soon as possible*,

Emetic tartar, dissolved in warm water, 15 grains:

and, after this has taken effect,

Castor oil . . . . 2 ounces;

keeping the dog warm during its operation.

BITES OF VIPERS, &c.

Apply the following mixture:—

Green elder ointment, and savin ointment, equal quantities.

Let the dog be kept on a low and cool diet.

* I think it proper to express my thanks for an amendment to this recipe in the "Sporting Magazine," which, I am proud to see, speaks so handsomely of this work; though, by the way, I regret that I should have led the editor to suppose I was attached to the old game-laws. On the contrary, though I wished them at all events to have been made clear, yet I always disapproved of them.

"The medical advice in the diseases of dogs is rational, but we would not advise any one to depend on the Turpeth mineral, as a cure for madness." [This is Mr. Beckford's remedy, and merely *quoted* by me.] "In the embrocation for strains, the water should be omitted, and the quantity of vinegar doubled. Distilled vinegar, decomposing the lead entirely, makes the neatest, if not the most efficacious medicine."

I have been told, by a friend in Norfolk, that the *fat of vipers*, taken out, boiled down, and kept (like goosegrease) is a never-failing remedy for this, and almost every other, poison; but that it gives pain on the first application. From the confidence I have in every thing which this gentleman states, I am induced to insert the recipe; but, not having tried it, I cannot answer for its efficacy.

BITE OF A MAD DOG.

If a dog is bitten, or suspected to have been bitten by a mad dog, let him immediately be conveyed, with the greatest caution, to some very detached place; and, in the latter case, if no remedy is used, a short time will determine whether he has been bitten or not.

The following is the recipe preferred by Mr. Beckford, than which, it is generally considered, nothing can be more effectual. (That is to say, if any medicine in existence *can* be depended on for *this* horrid disorder.) It is simply

Turpeth's mineral*, 1st morning	8 grains.
————————, 2d morning	16 grains.
————————, 3d morning	32 grains.

The dog should be bled the day previously to taking the first dose; which, as well as the other, should be given on an empty stomach. He may have warm broth or pot liquor in the afternoon; but nothing else during the three successive days of his taking the medicine. Let the Turpeth's mineral be given in a piece of butter, and care taken that the dog does not throw it up again.

Mr. Beckford, in his "Thoughts on Hunting," says, "The whole pack, belonging to a gentleman in my neighbourhood, was bitten; and he assures me, he never

* Strong doses of this medicine—from fifteen to thirty grains, for two or three days successively—have been recommended in violent cases of the *distemper*, and performed great cures.

knew an instance of a dog, who went mad, that had taken *this medicine.*"

I am now induced to add something further on this subject; though, as yet, unable to vouch for its efficacy.

Hearing of a recipe to cure hydrophobia, in the possession of Mr. Potter, I made a point of having an interview with him, who has since favoured me with, and also given me leave to publish, the following letter:—

"11, Old Compton Street, Soho,
June 4th, 1830.

"Sir,

"In compliance with your request, I beg leave to submit the following.—The remedy of Mr. Coster, an eminent French surgeon, against hydrophobia is—Take two table spoonsful of *fresh* chloruret of lime, and half a pint of water; mix them well together; and, with this wash, bathe constantly the wound, taking care that the wash is frequently renewed. Continue this treatment for one or two hours, or more, in proportion to the extent of the injury. In this process, the chlorine gas seems to be the active agent, decomposing, by an energy peculiar to itself, the almost omnific virus, the cause of hydrophobia.

"I have the honour to be,
"Sir,
"Your very humble servant,
(Signed) "WILLIAM HORATIO POTTER,
"*Operative Chemist* *.

"To Col. Hawker, &c. &c."

OBSERVATIONS ON MAD DOGS.

With regard to mad dogs in the metropolis, it is the general opinion, and particularly of foreigners, who

* Cutting out, or burning, the part, has I believe been the ordinary mode of treatment in cases of this frightful disorder; and therefore I dare not presume to *recommend* any *substitute;* though I have thought it right to give *publicity* to the foregoing letter, from the *reported* excellence of the prescription.

visit our country, that this evil chiefly arises from a want of the dogs being properly supplied with water. For instance—in Paris, what with the fountains, and the dirty water forming kennels in the middle of the streets, there is always a plentiful supply for dogs. In many parts of Italy, where there is not that advantage, the inhabitants make a point of having little holes to receive water for the dogs, as a preventive of hydrophobia. Again, in Lisbon, where there are droves of large dogs, without owners, that literally run wild about the streets, and are tolerated, because they act as scavengers, to rid them of the filth, there is always a plentiful supply of water; and, if I remember and understood the language right, some of the inhabitants told me that they were obliged, under penalty, to put out a supply of water for the dogs. Now in all these *hot* countries hydrophobia is very rare; and *yet in London*, no sooner does *even* the *warm* weather commence, than we are in alarm with mad dogs. It could therefore, at all events, do no harm to try the experiment, now that we have a regular police, who could attend to it. But if this should prove ineffectual, and our climate be still destined to this annoyance, we should have recourse to more severe measures; and declare war against all the useless mongrels that infest the metropolis. Among the many lamentable cases of persons and animals getting bitten by mad dogs, we may safely say that nineteen in twenty of them originate from people keeping useless curs, which they turn loose to forage on the town, and for which there is paid no tax. (I always invoke the tax-gatherers, when I want to get rid of a nuisance; but, Lord knows, for no other purpose!) Let me suggest, therefore, that every one should have on his dog a collar, with the name and address, by which the owners of dogs may be found, and made to answer for any depredations committed by, or default in payment of duty for, them. A muzzle may be added; or a penalty for not having one. Let all dogs that are found loose without collars be taken by the *police*, and advertised in their district; and if, within a certain time, no one comes forward to take charge of a dog and pay the tax (which, if an animal of any apparent value, plenty of people would be glad to do, on speculation, or for the chance of reward from the owner), let the magistrate have the full power of passing sentence of death. This may appear cruel; but the riddance of useless curs is a minor evil when compared to the distressing events that have so lately occurred in the metropolis. It may be asked, how are the dogs to be *caught?* But it would be bad policy to publish the *many ways which there are of doing this*, at the risk of giving finishing lessons to dog-*stealers*.

June 24th, 1830.—In consequence of *more* distressing cases that have *just* occurred, I have been induced to hastily pen down the foregoing suggestions, with which there is barely time to save insertion, under the head of "dogs," for the sheet on which the printer is now waiting; and on which, therefore, I have no time for reflection. But if these observations should lead to any better measures, I shall then have fully gained the desired object; and therefore shall not care how ridiculous they may be thought, or in what a slovenly manner they may be sent to the press. While writing this "article" (as an editor would say), a little before midnight, "our" ears have been, the whole time, assailed, by a grand philharmonic of Marylebone dogs, producing such a serenade of complicated canine counterpoint, as "we" defy even a modern composer, or the monosyllable-gentleman himself, to have dovetailed into a symphony.

Annexed is the rough sketch of a mad dog, presented me, for this work, by Sir Anthony Carlisle.

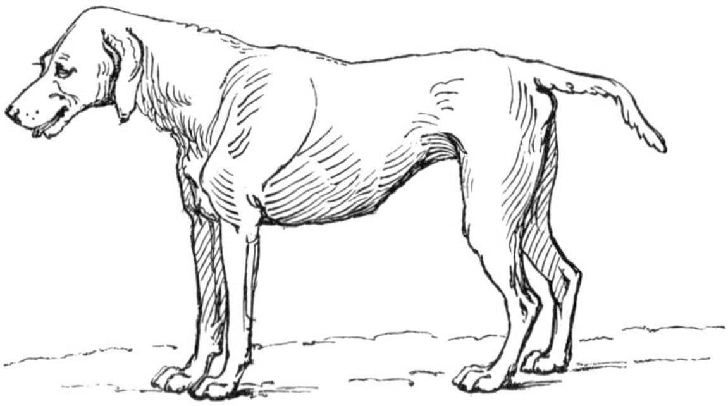

TO PHYSIC MODERATELY, AND GIVE A FINE COAT TO, DOGS.

Take a small handful of the leaves of the wood-laurel; boil it in a quart of water, till reduced to a pint, and mix it with sufficient liquid food to serve five or six dogs. This given, about once a month, in hot weather, I have found to answer better than any thing; but, as the wood-laurel in any great *quantity* is *poison*, it must be used with the utmost caution.

If a sportsman had his pointers *rubbed down and brushed* every day, immediately after they came home, and particularly if wet or cold, they would not only have fine coats, but be serviceable to him at least half as long again. This I have proved beyond all doubt.

I here conclude all that I shall say relating to " dogs," as the subject has already been done ample justice to by Mr. Daniel, Mr. Scott, Mr. Johnson, and many other authors, in their voluminous compilations on field sports of every description: and, though the last named, yet not the least, by William Augustus Osbaldiston, Esq., in his admirable work, which is called the "British Sportsman." On the merits of this gentleman's work (putting aside some of the plates) I cannot forbear making a few remarks, although he is (perhaps I should say *was)* an utter stranger to me. I bought his book when I was a lad, many years ago, and I cannot say that I have since met with any thing more purely original. Mr. Osbaldiston's "British Sportsman," it is evident, is faithfully drawn from nature, by a thorough-bred sportsman in the field, instead of being imperfectly copied from other works, by a hackney quill-driver in the metropolis. This work, in short, as well as Bewick's, may be considered as one of the fine old standards, from which many a book-pirate has torn the colours that he sails under; or, as the peacock, in whose feathers have strutted half the jackdaws in the book-making world.

PRESERVATION OF GAME.

HAVING said enough on the *destruction*, let me now proceed to the *preservation* of game.

A man, who, as a friend, had been hospitably entertained, or, as a stranger, accommodated with a day's shooting, would scarcely deserve the name of a gentleman, if he afterwards, clandestinely, set his foot on the ground of one, to whom he was thus far indebted; and it is, therefore, extremely illiberal to infer, that a good shot cannot sport like a gentleman; or that, when invited to shoot, he would destroy an unfair quantity of game; so far from it, a first-rate sportsman takes a pride in showing mercy to what is in his power, and piques himself upon strictly conforming to what he thinks would please his host, and being called a "nice gentleman" by an honest gamekeeper. Not only this, but, from being cool and steady, he has better nerves to withstand all temptation, than a raw shot, who has scarcely any command of himself on springing a forbidden bird. There are many 'squires, however, so hoggishly tenacious of their game, that, in spite of all reason, they continue their prejudice against a cracked shot so far, as studiously to avoid his acquaintance; because there are some greedy destroyers, who take an unfair advantage of their own skill and their host's indulgence; and, on the other hand, correct men, who have been known to kill an immense bag of game, at his particular request, for the supply of an election dinner, or some other reasonable purpose.

Thus many lords of manors, who would rather lose an ounce of their own blood than a brace of their pheasants, have been striving to preserve *every head* of game *by day*, while the poachers, unmolested, were *clearing it* by *wholesale* during the night. Sometimes, too, notwithstanding all their caution, their manors are invaded *even by day*, with *old stagers from a garrison*, who select market days, when the tenants are absent, and windy weather, when they can *manœuvre to leeward* and *outflank the keepers*.

Others again manage to create a diversion in favour of their trespass, by having the keepers drawn to opposite points, with the discharge of double guns and pistols; or, getting some bad shots, on promising them a share of the booty, to throw themselves in the way of the lookers out, and occupy their whole attention; first by running away to give them a chase that will prolong their distance from the real point of attack; and then, by warmly arguing in a wrong cause, so as to engross their attention with a triumphant explanation of their own knowledge, and their prisoner's ignorance in the game laws.

Many *gentlemen poachers* have, by running away, through pretended fear, drawn a gamekeeper off his boundary, who, being possibly there followed by his dogs, and having only a *gamekeeper's licence*, becomes so far in doubt as to his own safety against information, that he is too happy to compound for the day's sport being finished in peace, by those before whom he may have committed himself.

Some, with a polite bow and shrug of the shoulders, have pretended to be foreigners, who do not understand a syllable of English, and by this means deterred keepers from asking those questions, which, *if once put*, the usual *penalty* of twenty pounds would *bind them to answer*.

Others, regardless of either word or credit, most faithfully assure the keepers, that they have got leave from their master, inquire after his health, pretend to be on the most intimate terms with him and his aquaintance, and (probably, knowing him to be from home) have even had the effrontery to call at his house, in order to give still more plausibility to *their word*. A keeper should, therefore, *always serve the notices* on every one, who is not perfectly well known to him. This may be done with a degree of respect and civility, that could offend no gentleman, and would often be the means of outwitting many, who are regardless of all pretensions to that name.

Some attempt to carry their point by sheer bullying; threatening to box with, or shoot the keepers, and (under a hope that their masters would not offer themselves as a target to every puppy who came to poach on them) talk of "satisfaction—" "pistols—" "fighting in a sawpit—" and hold forth vaunting proposals, in which, if they were once *taken at their word*, they would, in all probability, like most *bullies*, or *soi disant* heroes, who *prattle too much* about "fighting," be the very first to *sport the white feather!* They are not all men of war who strut about with colossal brass spurs, and ten shillings' worth of hair, like a magpie's nest, pasted round their jowls.

Though last not least, among the successful plans of

the day poacher, is that of taking a double gun, and an old steady pointer, when travelling, and *cutting out* the game from the farther end of the preserved fields, which flank the turnpikes (as a cruiser would a flotilla from under a battery): or, if the fields are so large that he might be *coursed and caught*, simply to draw them within a *short run* of his carriage. A keeper, in this case, would do well to gallop quietly round to some likely field *in advance*, for which our friend would be pretty sure to turn out again; and here the keeper, by *hiding himself*, might pop on him, with all the necessary articles to put an end to his progress. For stopping one, who carries a gun to shoot *birds feeding* as he *travels along the road*, the better way would be to tie down the innkeepers, by a threat of withdrawing your custom, not to allow their postboys or coachmen to stop for *such purposes*; and, through a fear of getting in a scrape, these men would most likely contrive to pass by, or frighten up the game. *Now however the power of seizure and the 2£ penalty,* WITHOUT NOTICE! *alters the case: though, unfortunately, this summary penalty is calculated to annoy only the open, and perhaps fair, sportsman, instead of the run-away shooter, or secret poacher.*

If you owe a greedy shooter a grudge, give his dog, in *hot weather*, a *carte blanche* at a large tub of buttermilk, just before he takes the field. He will then have many points;—but few birds.

It would far exceed the limits of this work to insert every *ruse de guerre* that is successfully practised, for a tolerable shot to come home with a full bag. All keepers and lookers out, therefore, should be constantly on the alert, and made strictly acquainted with the game laws, at least as far as they relate to themselves; but although this may be learnt by a little conversation with almost any attorney's clerk, or a few written instructions, yet not one in ten knows how to serve a notice correctly, or even the most common points of what so materially concerns the duties of his situation.

Keepers should be as widely distributed as possible, by which means a marauder would have some difficulty to steer clear of them all; but these men *(like markers)* are too apt to get idling and chattering together, instead of minding their business. Each gamekeeper would do well to have with him a *witness*, for which, any common labourer would be sufficient; and, above all, a *spy glass*, by which he would most likely be able to distinguish any man, who might beat him by being longer in the legs than himself, or having a horse which was a better *fencer* than his own; and who he may, by this means, be able to recognise hereafter, so as to find him out, and proceed against him. A few words more, with regard to gamekeepers:

Be careful how you trust any of them with guns, under the pretence of their killing vermin; for it is an undoubted fact, that many of those, who are considered very honest men by their employers, are yet so much the contrary, that they will take every opportunity to destroy game, when not under the immediate observation of their master. For instance—a gamekeeper is in a covert: he fires his gun, and *pockets* a pheasant or a partridge, or kills a hare and *conceals it:* his master, who is perhaps not out of *hearing* of the *gun,* comes up and says—"John, what did you shoot at?" "A d——d hawk, sir," replies the *trusty* guardian of the *preserves.* "Did you kill it, John?" "Oh, no, sir, he was too far off; but I 'm sure I properly peppered him." "Where is he now?" "Lord bless you, sir, he's been out of sight these five minutes!"

Be very cautious whom you trust with fowling-pieces; they are not so often required, as keepers would *wish to persuade you they are;* and do not be led away with the *mistaken notion*, that it will be a protection to your game to have a dozen fellows running about with *guns* in their hands. It may be asked, How then are the various kinds of vermin to be destroyed? To which I would answer, that, if a keeper cannot effect this by means of traps, gins, poison, and the various other artifices, he is by no means qualified for his place. And, with regard to hawks and other mischievous birds, these underlings have only to keep a sharp look out, in the breeding season, to find their nests, and then take the head keeper, or some one proper to be trusted with a gun, to shoot them.

In case it should be considered unsafe for keepers to go their nightly rounds without fire-arms, I should rather recommend the use of *pistols* than guns, though I have little doubt but a *fierce dog*, and a *sabre* or a *bludgeon*, would effectually answer the purpose of defence against poachers. If you have reason to expect a gang of poachers, that may be too strong for your keepers, let some one go through your covers, and thrash away at all the trees till he has driven the pheasants from their roost. Having then spoiled the night's sport, you may go home and sleep in peace. This was the plan of my friend, the late Mr. Ponton, who, with only one regular keeper, had plenty of pheasants, in the midst of poachers.

The poachers, when not in bed or at their work,

generally frequent what were formerly called "*bough-houses*"—*un*licensed places where beer was sold, but *now* regularly *licensed*, as "*beer-houses*;" much increased in number; and therefore a ten times greater nuisance than ever!—The very ruin of the lower classes and their families. [If beer must be sold, it should be taken home by the poor man to his wife and children, and not guzzled by himself, in half a day's idleness, among, and perhaps under the tuition of, a den of thieves. We sadly want some amendment to regulate this abominable bill!] In haunts like these, it may be contrived to discover a whole gang of poachers, by having them closely watched, or buying over, for a spy or keeper, some well known "old hand." In short, if these fellows are *never lost sight of*, they *must* be taken, sooner or later; but, if only watched for in the fields and woods, they may escape their pursuers till they have stripped a manor.

The most scientific poacher, and the least likely to be detected, is the one who snares partridges, in the open country, or catches hares and pheasants, in covert, in the middle of the DAY. Take a covert, for instance,—the poacher with snares and silk nets goes through it, and quietly sets them. When this is done, throughout the whole extent of covert, where there are paths or runs, the coppice is then disturbed by a mute and unsuspected cur, and the destruction immense, if well supplied with game. The grand time for this is on a Sunday; or on a wet day, when no sportsmen are likely to be out. The fellow, if caught, has of course some prepared excuse, such as that of nutting; of cutting a stick—having lost his way, &c. You find no game upon him, and therefore can do nothing with him!

While possibly his fifty brace are hid away in sacks to be brought off at midnight to the *receiver*—perhaps the ci-devant man-cook of a country inn, or some such "deep old file," who generally contrives to keep out of all scrapes, and pass himself off as a respectable man.

The real way to keep up a good stock of game, we may rest assured, is, *first*, to be well guarded against such incursions as those previously alluded to. *Secondly*, to get the poachers watched at *their own houses*, by concealing people during the night, near *both* their *front and back doors;* also to have, *up the road, an eye on the stage-coaches;* and, above all, some *spies over the wagoners*, who are often their *very employers*, and who are enabled to *smuggle to London both* your *game* and *poultry*, not only *better concealed*, than if sent by the coach, but in much *greater quantities*. *Thirdly*, to keep *on good terms with the farmers*, who, it should be remembered, have a right to *tread on their own ground*, though the nest of a *partridge* or *pheasant* be *under their feet!*

In a few words, a gentleman, who, living on his estate, is liberal and popular with his neighbours, his tenants, and the poor, will seldom have much difficulty in preserving his rights of every kind. Few will be disposed to infringe on them, while every one is ready to offer assistance for their protection. But, on the other hand, the tyrant, hated and despised by all, when shot over by day, poached on by night, or even robbed of his property, becomes only the laughing-stock of his villagers, who would perhaps rather succour than inform against the offenders!

Nothing will *keep pheasants at home* better than

stacks of *buck wheat, oats, white peas*, or *barley;* provided you dispose of them IN coverts, where there is *access to water*. It is equally as well known, that high turnips will be a shelter for your partridges, as that *Swedes* will attract hares, and strong furze be the means of preserving game of every description.

I may add, that *woodcocks* have been often collected together by *decayed apples*. This discovery was first made in consequence of their having frequented the orchards in some parts of Dorsetshire, where they have appeared in numbers, and are called " ditch-owls."

In the three last editions, I observed, that there remained much to be done for the effectual preservation of game, to which the legislature would no doubt attend, when matters of more serious consideration were happily adjusted; and the game laws would, in all probability, undergo the improvement, for which there was ample scope.

Since our last edition, we have the NEW GAME ACT, which I have the very best authority for believing will, sooner or later, undergo further, and necessary improvements. I shall therefore, in *this* edition, reserve it as the last article, in order that it may remain open for future alterations.

DUCK GUNS.

[GENERAL DIRECTIONS FOR.]

I OBSERVED, in the two last editions, that with regard to a duck-gun—If a sportsman could afford to have one of the very best that could possibly be turned out of hand, he would, I was confident, get better served by Mr. Joseph Manton, than by any one in the trade; because *his* fine boring and other finishing were done entirely by picked workmen in his own house, under the immediate eye of himself, or his agents. Here he had rooms, with a good light to work in, and the very best of tools, and other conveniences, instead of having the different parts of the gun hawked about the streets from one poor journeyman to another; at the risk of ultimately requiring patchwork, in order to disguise from the customer their not fitting together in a sound and workmanlike manner.

[Notwithstanding this establishment of Mr. Manton has been broken up, I have reprinted the foregoing observations, as a hint for other tradesmen to follow his example.]

If, on the other hand, the shooter is content with a good serviceable duck-gun that will kill well, and answer every purpose, and is not *au fait* enough to send his own specific directions to Birmingham, he has only to go to the fountain head at once, and order Mr. Fullerd to send him a barrel *ready-bored for shooting*, and then get it fitted up to his own fancy by any tolerable mechanic *.

My reason for preferring this plan is, because I know by experience that if Fullerd is left alone, he can bore a barrel to shoot well; but when interfered with, he becomes a mere journeyman who dares not open his mouth, insomuch that if he was ordered to bore a barrel like a blunderbuss; a bugle; or a gas-pipe; no matter which—he must do it.

It has been a grand object with some gunmakers to suppress the reputation of Fullerd, and also of Lancaster, when he served the trade, by punching their names out of the barrels, and putting on their own. This may be all fair when barrelmakers are only employed for the rough work; but this is frequently done even when they have finished the boring, and completed almost every part of the barrels, and breechings, except the mere polish with sand-paper. It therefore often happens that, for this second baptism, and a few dandy ornaments, which are quite out of character for duck guns, the customer is made to pay an enormous per centage above the fair trade profit. Several of these gunmakers declare to me that they get nothing by what

* I know but one man capable of fitting up a *very large* duck gun without specific directions from the shooter—Mr. Burnett of Southampton, who has, for these last five years, been working for gentlemen-gunners under the directions of Buckle, Singer, and other professors of those secrets afloat which it would take a dandy-gunmaker more time than he can spare to learn. Mr. Burnett is not only a clear-headed ingenious workman, and most reasonable in his charges, but also a good practical shot.

they call "*making!*" duck guns. Very well, then: if so, by placarding the following name, where it cannot be punched out again, I shall be doing them essential service.

THOMAS (late William) FULLERD, No. 57, Compton-street, Clerkenwell—as good a large barrel forger as ever faced a fire, or swallowed porter.

(But with regard to common sporting guns, the case alters; because the fitting up of *them* is now pretty well understood by every one; and they require so many little appendages that the least trouble, as I before observed, when speaking of them, is to go at once to a gunmaker or a pawnbroker.)

Many will tell you, that *a large gun will do no more execution than a small one;* and, by the same rule, they may say, that *a gun will kill no farther than a pistol.*

The advantage of a duck gun is, that it *will carry large shot more compactly*, and may be fired with double or treble the charge for a piece of an ordinary size. You are therefore enabled to use the largest shot, with the same advantage, that No. 7 may be fired from a double gun; by which means, *at a large object*, you may kill considerably farther; and, in a flock, *many more birds at a shot.*

In comparing *small shot from a double gun*, as having the same advantage over large, *that a pin, with a moderate pressure*, would have over a *nail*, in *piercing the feathers of game*, by the same argument it may be said, that *large shot, from a duck gun*, would have the effect of the *nail driven by a hammer* through the *strong bones* and *feathers* of *wildfowl.* A large gun, to carry *twice* as much as a small one (say three or four ounces), should not weigh less than 12, nor exceed 16*lbs.* and be used with No. 1 or 2 shot; *and the same proportion of powder as before recommended.* One to carry five or six ounces should not weigh less than 18, nor exceed 20*lbs.*, and be used with A or B shot; and so on in proportion; but this is the most that can well be fired without a rest.

The recoil of a duck gun can only be checked *by weight of metal,* and there are *two ways to dispose of it:* the one, *immense thickness,* whereby the gun may be *short, portable,* and easily managed; and the other, *considerable length,* by which you may kill farther, and take a *much more accurate aim.* The former was the plan of Mr. Joseph Manton, the latter that of the late Mr. D. Egg: and, in order to partake a little of *both* advantages, I should *steer between the two,* and have my barrels *never less than three feet eight,* nor *more* than *four feet four inches, unless I used a rest;* by which means a gun being top-heavy is rendered quite the reverse of objectionable. In this case, I should adopt the plan of Mr. D. Egg, *as the best* in every respect. (Since the first edition of this book was published, Mr. Joseph Manton had generally adopted the proportions therein *recommended,* and made some of the best duck guns that could possibly be turned out of hand. He declared to me, that he gained a more perfect knowledge of his business by *making duck guns,* than by any other branch of practice.)

A *broad heel-plate* contributes greatly to *lessen the recoil;* and, in some of the largest sized *shoulder* guns, a sponge has sometimes been found necessary, to prevent the guard from cutting the second finger.

As to the best length for duck guns that are used without a rest, and must therefore be made to mount tolerably well; I will lay down a simple rule for those of every size: *viz.* measure the barrels of your best double gun, and see how many times they are in length the *diameter of the punched wadding;* and order your duck guns to be never less than from four to six *more* diameters in proportion. That is, if your double gun, of fourteen gauge, should be of the common length, (2 feet 8 inches), which is forty-four diameters, let your duck gun of seven gauge, and of 13*lbs.* weight, be never less than from 3 feet $6\frac{1}{4}$ to 3 feet 8 inches; (or, *if you can manage 4 feet, so much the better;)* and so forth on a still larger scale. The latter gun at forty-four diameters would be 3 feet $2\frac{1}{2}$ inches, but with *this* length it would scatter more at long shots; and, if properly loaded (say with $3\frac{1}{2}$ ounces of shot), would, by flying up forward, be felt too severely to the shoulder.

Recollect, that although the same ratio might hold good for *guns,* yet neither the *weight of the atmosphere* nor the *muscular power of a man* can be made to serve in proportion. If a duck gun is *too large* in the *caliber,* in proportion to its weight of metal, it will *recoil* considerably; and if *too small,* it will not have the desired effect of allowing the shot to *lie compactly* together.

A gun fired from a *rest* is *felt more than* if *held out,* because the left hand, when grasping it, checks the recoil. The stock of a heavy duck gun should be *more bent* than that of a common gun, as, when we are holding out a great weight, it is not so easy to *lower the head:* and it should also be observed, that the *curve in the stock* tends to lessen the recoil.

I have of late years had the duck gun stocks, which I use on the coast, made with a pistol grip, and whipped with waxed end, round the handle, similar to a cricket bat, which rather lessens the jar; and the upper part of the but very much cut away, in order to prevent it from hurting the shoulder bone. I also paint and varnish the stock, by which means it does not get cracked, after being wetted with salt water. The gun-makers' stocks I found were always a great plague on this account, as well as from the trouble of keeping them in order, after being exposed to the spray of the sea. Add to which, they recoil most unmercifully, and are therefore only fit for light charges. I should always have these stocks rather short; as one that would mount well in a shooting jacket, would be unmanageably long in a gunning dress.

The following is the average of several shots, tried at twelve sheets of thick brown paper, to ascertain the difference between two *common* duck guns, and a *very superior* double gun, made by Mr. Joseph Manton.

	Weight.	Length.		Gauge.
	Pounds.	Feet.	Inches.	
Large duck gun	14	4	6	7
Smallest ditto	$12\frac{1}{2}$	4	5	
Double gun	9	2	8	14

With No. 2. Shot.

	Yards.	In the 1st sheet.	Through the 12th sheet.
Duck guns	60	32	25
Double gun		20	18
Duck guns	45	34	34
Double gun		26	26

The large guns were loaded with precisely *double* the charge of the small gun, which is one-fifth *less* than that with which they always killed best.

The paper was nailed up close to a sheet of water, and two men placed to *observe* the effect; which was, that the outside shot (that which flew wide of the paper) appeared to be driven with much *more force* from the heavy guns, and, of course, spread a much *larger surface.*

This *proves*, that although, *if both accurately levelled,* the difference between a wildfowl gun and a small gun is not so *very* considerable, at a *single* bird; yet, from the *immense circle,* which the large gun spreads, you have more chances of killing with *an indifferent aim;* and, of course, in a flock (as before said), would kill *many more birds at a shot.*

At the same time an opportunity was taken to prove the *advantage* of shot *lying compact; viz.* after loading the double gun with a *full charge of powder,* and placing within the muzzle a round of pasteboard, I put thereon forty-five grains of No. 7 shot, shook them *all into one tier* on the wadding, and, after having laid on them another round of pasteboard, carefully rammed down all together:—the result was, that, at thirty yards, *twenty grains* were *well distributed* in a newspaper.

Subjoined is another trial, made in 1820, between the smallest sized duck guns, and fourteen gauge double guns (at thirty-eight yards), with twelve sheets of thickest brown paper put up afresh for each shot.

		Number of Grains in 1st Sheet.			Ditto through 12th Sheet.			Remarks.
		1 Shot.	2 Shot.	3 Shot.	1 Shot.	2 Shot.	3 Shot.	
With oz. and half No. 5. Shot.	*Old Joe* (a gun never yet beat, for its regularity of pattern on the paper), right barrel	156	143	116	73	74	80	Most regular.
	Ditto, left barrel	111	140	196	71	70	72	
	A newer gun of precisely the same size, right barrel .	189	150	124	62	86	41	Closest in 1st Sheet.
	Ditto, left barrel	145	122	145	54	69	80	
	Detonating gun, right barrel	166	127	124	102	89	91	Strongest*.
	Ditto, left barrel	164	137	128	82	90	72	
2 oz. and half only of No. 3 Shot, in heavy single guns.	A 13lb. gun (7 gauge, 4 feet barrel), by D. Egg . .	175	164	172	128	122	138	
	A 10lb. detonating gun (7 gauge, 3 feet barrel) . .	162	170	145	120	104	142	†
	One shot, for trial, against heavy single guns, with No. 3, in *Old Joe*, to show that even the best double guns will not throw large shot like duck guns . . .	88			71			

General Remarks.—A damp, windy day; and therefore much against the force of powder. The eighth part of a sheet of letter paper was pasted on every front sheet, as a bull's eye; and, on an average, received about five grains of shot. All the barrels were made by Charles Lancaster, except the one of Mr. D. Egg, and were well worked and dirtied previously to being tried. The same *measure* of powder as of shot.

* On Mr. Joseph Manton's first principle, which was discarded from being so troublesome to clean; and which owed much of its strength to having more weight of metal; and so small a vent-hole, that it was repeatedly missing fire.

† Recoiled severely, if loaded higher, from being too short in proportion to the

In comparison with the table of shots originally given, I am now enabled to add, the performance of a duck gun, made expressly to my order by Mr. Joseph Manton, the barrel of which was prepared by Lancaster.

WEIGHT.	LENGTH.		GAUGE.
Pounds.	Feet.	Inches.	Not quite an inch.
$17\frac{1}{4}$	4	2	

With four ounces and a half of No. 2 shot, *well shaken down,* after being put in the barrel, and an equal *measure* of *powder strongly wadded:*

Yards.	In the 1st sheet.	Through the 12th sheet.
60	50	48
45	92	92

The following table of a gun trial, which I have just found among my papers, and which I perfectly remember making (though I see it is without date, and without the size of the target or the shot being specified), may yet prove as well worth insertion as any, because it plainly shows the decided advantage in the increased size of guns.

bore, and therefore would not answer my purpose for wildfowl. This gun was made to my order by Mr. Joseph Manton, and is the same with which Mr. Osbaldiston, in 1824, won a five hundred guinea match, and since that, several others. This gentleman refused one hundred and fifty guineas for the gun.

DISTANCE SIXTY YARDS.

	In 1st half sheet.	Through a double quire of brown paper.
Best double gun, 9lbs.	4	4
Fisherman's old gun of 12lbs. (common breeching)	8	3
Joe Manton's duck gun, $17\frac{1}{4}$lbs.	14	14
An old Birmingham swivel gun (common breech) about 70lbs.	40	38

Query. Does this corroborate the assertion, then, that a small gun will kill as well as a large one?

For shooting in *windy* weather, and killing birds that would *dive at a flash*, there can be no question as to the superiority of *detonating* duck guns.

In loading a duck gun, the *farther* you wish to reach a flock of birds, the *more powder* and the *less shot* you must put; because you may often make good a few random shots into flocks of wildfowl, by putting a considerably larger measure of powder than of shot; when by the usual mode of loading, you might only hear the shot rattle on the wings of many, without bringing down a single bird.

To conclude this subject, it need only be observed, that the same directions as those before given will hold good for the *choice, care,* and *cleaning* of *duck guns.* They cannot, however, be made to balance quite so well as guns on a small construction, without an unmanageable quantity of lead; and, in these, the scrollguard, or, what is far better, as I before observed, a pistol grip to the stock, may be adopted, in order to prevent the right hand from being driven against the face, in the event of a recoil. But, if they should have been *loaded some time*, it is best to *loosen the charge of shot*, which, *otherwise*, would be *felt severely*.

If one of these guns should be laid aside for a season or two, your filling it with *mutton suet* will entirely prevent rust.

TO MAKE AN OLD GUN SHOOT WELL.

THIS may be done, if the barrel be of sufficient substance; of tolerably good iron; and perfectly sound; first by *boring it** (as before mentioned) so as to have *friction downwards*, and this *gradually relieved forward;* secondly, by putting in a *chamber* plug (vide plate); and, thirdly, by *giving immense strength* to the *mainspring* of the lock.

This recipe may not only be worth the observation of those who cannot afford a new gun, but useful to officers on service; who, from not wishing to increase their baggage, when constantly engaged, take no gun with them; and are, perhaps, after a summer's campaign stationed in winter quarters, where they have plenty of leisure, and the finest shooting, though with no other fowling-piece than a regimental musket. This was the case on the expedition to New Orleans, in the country near which place the wildfowl were innumerable.

A regimental armourer (even if he had the means) might not be perfectly master of the *boring;* and if he was, where, *on service*, would he get a lathe? but the *perforated plug* and the *strengthening* of the *main-*

* In a stout barrel, even the *deep flaws* may be easily got rid of, by means of making it red hot, and beating them in, before you fresh bore it.

spring would very much accelerate the firing of a musket; and some of these barrels, if properly loaded, often make a very effectual substitute for a duck gun; and particularly if eased a little at the muzzle by the hard working of sand-paper. (This, by the way, would be very near the right bore for a *detonater.)*

The proper charge for them would be about two tobacco pipes full of powder, and the same measure of large shot: but, as this had better be regulated by the degree with which they are felt in firing, I shall lay down a rule, which, by the way (with a very trifling alteration, according to circumstances), may be applied to all duck guns, and most other guns, that are fired with a *flint*-lock.

Load with POWDER *and* SHOT *by* EQUAL MEASURE *in as large a quantity as can be fired with ease to the shoulder; putting your* WADDING STRONG *on the* FORMER, *and* LIGHT *on the* LATTER.

As this alteration is all *inwardly*, it cannot affect the *appearance* of the musket; and (omitting the boring) it would, *if kept clean,* be all the better for his majesty's service. The perforation of the plug, however, should not be too small; and particularly in cases where it may become necessary to use it with cartridge powder.

Before concluding the observations on improving common guns, it may not be amiss to mention the following circumstances: An old fisherman, in the country where I was residing, had killed more wildfowl than any other man on the river, with a gun which he had picked up for thirty shillings. A few seasons previously to his death, he gave up shooting, and I bought this gun, from the reported excellence of the barrel, which fully answered my expectations. Finding, however, that the plug and touchhole were rather too much worn to be safe, I had them both replaced by the same country maker who put a new stock and lock. The barrel afterwards shot so slow and weak, that it was perfectly useless; on which I sent it to be altered by Mr. John Manton, who very civilly undertook the job; and, by *putting in* a common *chamber plug*, and *fresh perforating a common touchhole*, made this gun shoot so admirably well, that it was not till I had received five best finished duck guns from London that I could get one to equal it.

We are often laughed at for our expenditure in guns, when an old gamekeeper will sometimes beat them all with a " piece" that has scarcely a choice, whether to prefer *firing*, or being *fired at* with it. I admit, that if his barrel *happens* to be *well bored*, his *mainspring strong*, and his touchhole and chamber plug well put in, there will perhaps be very little difference in the *killing*, between his " piece" and the best gun that ever came out of London. But if we consider, that the excellence of a lock and soundness of a barrel, although not absolutely requisite in *killing*, are indispensably necessary for the *safety* of our persons; and that, although practice may bring a man to point accurately with a broomstick, yet we must allow the advantage, not to say the comfort and neatness, of having our guns turned out in a handsome and workmanlike manner.

DUCK SHOT.

No. 1 and 2 for a *seven gauge*, and A. or B. for a *five ditto*, or *inch bore*, are preferable to the very largest shot, by the same reason that No. 7 is best for game.

Mould shot *alone*, therefore, in any caliber less than that of a *stanchion gun*, is like No. 1 in a *double gun:* it *may* do wonders, for which you relinquish the certainty of what other shots *will* do.

To prove, that *even one of these* pellets *may be carried off* by a *wildfowl*, I should mention the circumstance of having seen a brentgoose, which, after having been brought down, flying, with No. 2, was discovered to have, *under the wing*, an old wound, considerably more than *an inch deep:* and out of this was taken one of the *largest mould shot*, which had *rolled up in feathers*, and formed a sort of *tent*.

The following is a table of what I find the best shot for wildfowl:—

	No.	
Common sporting guns; or what the gunners call "*Pop*"-guns .	3 for fair 1 long	shots
Shoulder duck-guns	1 for fair A long	shots.

	No.
Punt-guns	3 for starlight. 1 for fair shots (or in the dark, when birds are wilder than in starlight).
Packed by *regular layers* in cartridges	S. S. G. Above 100 yards. L. G. Wild random shooting.

A. or AA. are the best for *geese*, particularly by day, provided they are so tame as not to require S.S.G. In my second edition, I talked of mixing shot; but have since had reason to doubt whether it answers so well.

General Shrapnell tells me, that some man in Ireland had contrived to imitate his shells, or spherical case shot, with which he did wonders at the wildfowl. I have been favoured, by a gentleman in Kent, with the recipe for making and adapting them to small guns. But lest it might prove improper to publish it (which I could not well and clearly do without an engraving) I shall say no more on the subject, but leave this admirable invention as the valuable property of the British ordnance.

DUCK GUN WADDING.

To avoid book-making, I shall now cancel six pages, the experiments for which had cost me much time and expense, and say no more about paper, pasteboard, cork, leather, &c. &c., but, in a few words, name what I have proved to be the best wadding for duck-guns. For all shoulder duck-guns use Wilkinson's felt wadding, about a third in thickness the size of your caliber. But for long punt-guns, and all other *water*-guns that are *opened behind*, you will find that, after all, nothing beats a *tight-wound ball* of the *best picked oakum;* because it springs to every gradation of the caliber. I could publish fifty original pages on the subject, but who would take the trouble to read them? and what would be the use of this, after the sporting world has done me the honour to confide in what I recommend?

WATER BOOTS

ARE absolutely necessary for those who shoot in wet places, or wait, in cold nights, for wildfowl; and, *if good*, will effectually repel the water for a long time.

Water boots, that I have always found to answer, are made (for thirty shillings a pair), by a Mr. Cox, in Poole, whose principal business is their exportation to Newfoundland. Mr. Short, of East Yarmouth, is also a particularly good maker of these boots, and is so clever in other parts of his business, that he is in the habit of sending boots and shoes to gentlemen above a hundred miles on the other side of London. Some of the fen sportsmen call him the "Emperor of the boot-makers."

All boots, for going in the wet, answer much better if kept at least half a year before they are worn; and they should afterwards never be suffered to get too hard. *Water boots should be invariably worn over an extra pair of coarse yarn stockings, without which you do not give them a fair trial.*

So far from being hard to the feet, they are the softest possible wear, and may be made very light. They should always be made to draw, when required, very far above the knees, in order to protect them from cold or wet. Nothing, by the way, would answer so well in rain or snow for stage coachmen, if these gentlemen would just then condescend to wear them.

Various dressings are recommended, though, perhaps, almost any grease may answer; but the first and most effectual application might be tar, tallow, and bees' wax melted *(not too warm)*, and then poured *into* the boots; which, after having this shaken into every part of them, should be hung up to let it run out. By this dressing, and the sacrifice of the first pair of stockings that follows it, we may walk in the river with more comfort than a "Swell-kiddy" would cross the street after a shower.

This recipe, however, though a double defence, I do not mean to say is absolutely necessary; for I have latterly found that *neat's foot oil* answers every purpose.

As another good recipe, I should prefer the following one:—

RECIPE.

Drying oil	1 pint.
Yellow wax	2 ounces.
Turpentine	2 ounces.
Burgundy pitch	1 ounce.

Melt these over a slow fire, and then add a few drachms of essential oil of lavender (or thyme). With this your boots are to be rubbed with a brush, either in the sun, or at some distance from the fire. The application must be repeated, as often as the boots become dry again, until they are fully saturated.

If your heel should become galled by walking in a water-, or any other, boot, you will immediately remedy the inconvenience by applying a piece of gold-beaters' skin, and over that a little court plaster, in order doubly to defend the part. But even in this trifle there is a right and a wrong way of going to work. Instead of cutting with scissors, and merely wetting the plaster, let it be for a moment *heated by the fire, as well as wetted,* being previously stamped with a *wadding-punch,* by which means, from having no angles, or corners, it will stick as fast as your own skin; provided that, when on and *dry,* you put over it a little cold cream, or any kind of grease, in order to repel the damp.

The application that has been usually recommended to me by surgeons is diachylon-plaster, which, in cold weather, curls up, and torments you so much in walking, that you soon become lame again, and then wish the doctor at Jericho. Go to Godfrey's, or some other first-rate chemist, in order to get the sticking plaster in perfection, as many a one has poisoned his skin by not having the genuine article.

Let this edition supersede the recipe for *cure,* by giving what is better,—a *preventive.*

Get a square silk pad, similar to a kettle-holder. Then have sewn, on two opposite corners of it, pieces of list long enough to go twice round, and tie on, the ancle. No wrinkle of a water-boot can then cut or bruise your "tendon Achilles," or back sinew, provided you secure the pad firmly, by putting it *over* your common *stocking,* and under your yarn stocking. I was stupid enough not to think of this plan till 1828. Thus, if we were to shoot for a century, we should always be finding out something useful; however frivolous it may appear, when mentioned to a reader who is not in immediate want of it.

WATER-PROOF DRESSING FOR SHOES,

ETC.

TAKE a piece of Indian rubber, about the size of a walnut: cut it in small pieces, and put it into a phial with four ounces of highly rectified spirits of turpentine. Cork it up for about a fortnight (more or less, according to cold or hot weather), and shake it every day. When this mixture has come to a consistence about the thickness of treacle, it is fit for use. You may then work it, with a paint brush, into leather, rope, or what you please. But, when used for the soles of shoes, leather trunks, or any thing that does not require flexibility, you should add, to this composition, three times the quantity of copal varnish. The most effectual mode of application is to anoint, not only the outside seams, but also the whole inside of the soles.

If you want this dressing in a hurry, and an extra expense is no object, you will find that *æther*, or *naphtha*, will dissolve Indian rubber, *and dry*, much quicker than spirits of turpentine. The powder colours, for painting, either with or without oil, will mix perfectly well with this composition.

The foregoing recipe was given me by Mr. Cornelius Varley, who tells me that he sent it, many years ago, to the Philosophical Magazine. Not wishing, however, to enter it without some kind of investigation, I applied to Mr. Fisher, the celebrated chemist in Conduit-street, who was good enough to make for me as many experiments as the limited time would admit of. The preparation which *he* found to mix the best, was *three oz. of Indian rubber, boiled for about three hours, in a pint of linseed oil**, which thus became immediately of a good consistence; but it required such a time to dry, that he afterwards found it necessary to *add spirits of turpentine.* In short, it has long been known that the solution of Indian rubber is a valuable recipe for making things waterproof. But there are so many ways of doing it; and, perhaps, among them all, the *best* not yet discovered, that we must, for the present, dismiss the subject by merely giving the hint, with the hope of putting our speculators on the scent, to bring to perfection what would be to their own advantage, and worthy the notice of the public.

* *This* comes very near to the recipe given in our former editions, and *now very much in use,* for dressing Russia duck.

CORNS.

To walk with corns, and without torture, get a piece of chamois leather, spread with diachylon plaster. Cut, with your wadding-punch, as many rounds as will form a sufficient *thickness to prevent the boot or shoe from pressing* your stocking on the *corn;* for the reception of which you must punch a *small hole through the centre.* By this simple contrivance, I have known many a dot-and-go-one gentleman start off as bold as a dog just uncoupled.

CORN-PLASTER.

The following recipe was given me by the Earl of ——— on purpose for this book; and I set my man to try it on several unfortunates, who have given him their blessing for the cures he has made.

Mercurial plaster . . .	2 drams of each.
Diachylon ditto, with resin . .	
Diachylon ditto . . .	
Sugar of lead	20 grains.

All mixed together
And spread on leather.

Apply a piece of this plaster for 3 or 4 days. Then soak the foot; and rub the corn with a piece of pumice-stone. Again repeat the plaster; and the corn will soon disappear. N. B. The corn never to be cut.

DRESSES FOR WILDFOWL SHOOTING.

If you attempt to go out for wildfowl, without being properly clothed, you will not only frighten them away, and kill nothing, but you will experience those very miseries which are merely imaginary with persons who do not understand this pursuit. How many do we see, who fancy that they would catch their death by cold if they went out at night for a few hours in a punt: and yet these very people are in the habit of doing what is ten times more dangerous:—walking in a wet day from the west end to the city, with thin boots, without galoches, and in cotton stockings; and there, perhaps, with damp feet, sitting on business for a whole morning!

Having mentioned that water boots should, even for walking, be worn with an extra pair of coarse yarn stockings, I should advise those, who go out in cold nights, to have their boots made easy enough to admit, instead of these, a pair of the thickest *wads*. They should reach nearly up to the middle. This will be found quite enough, provided the under stockings are of the warmest quality. Such, for instance, as the "Sanquhar hose," that are sold (and, I believe, were first introduced from Scotland to London) by Mr. Otley, in Sidney's Alley. Having put on the boots, there must then be drawn over all a pair of short loose sailcloth * (or, if cold frosty weather, Flushing-coating) trowsers. This, and only this, will defy the cold, and have its solid comforts, by not only keeping off the sleet, or snow, but any little spray that may fly from the splash of the windward oar.

It is needless to say, that (except the feet, which we have already defended) every part of the body should be clothed in *flannel.*

With regard to farther covering for the body, could we ensure not getting wet, *leather* would, perhaps, be the *warmest;* but, at all events, the waistcoat, both before and behind, should be made of either *shag*, or Bath-coating, which certainly, taking all weather, answers best, and is the most comfortable. Under the waistcoat should be worn a Flushing-frock, and over it, a short jacket, of either drab cloth or swanskin. But the *sheepswool wove into cloth* (an article which the guards of coaches bring me from Exeter) I now find beats every thing; this material, however, is too thick for the *sleeves.* The cap may be made of cloth, or any thing you please; because a *Welsh wig* may be "shipped" when going into birds; and, by the way, kept on, with the cap, if the weather is so cold as to require it. Mr. Lloyd, 13, Old Bond-street, has invented an excellent, though simple, defender for the chest (which he calls an "*Anglesey*"); and a large shawl handkerchief may be worn over the collar. A

* *Sailcloth* is so strong, so durable, and such a good defence against rain, that it answers better than any thing for making game bags; or defending the mahogany gun cases of those who would wish to avoid the expense of leather; and, if dressed with tar, it makes the best possible gun-cover.

pair of worsted wristbands (sold by the name of " muffatees") should be worn with cloth gloves, and, over gloves and all, a large and long pair of double *swanskin* cuffs, which are as warm as any muff, and may be drawn, or shook, off in an instant, when you want your right hand for the trigger.

Which of the two colours for the jacket and cap is to be used will depend on whether you have sun or moon; on which occasions you and your boat should appear in a light drab, or you will occasionally shine so much, as to be quite conspicuous. But at *all other* times a *bluish white* is *indisputably* the *best colour;* except in *starlight* or *snow*. Then you cannot possibly be too white; insomuch, that a clean *linen* frock and cap might take you forty yards nearer to your birds than even flannel or swanskin. All further covering, such as a cloak, white hat, &c., may be at your own option, as you would, of course, " douse" it when you began to " work to birds;" and, indeed, the greater part of that beforementioned would be too warm, except for one who had nothing to do but attend his gun.

I shall now add one recipe for a surtout, by way of a dread-nought, which, as wet weather has of late years been " so much in fashion," will, I trust, be doing service, not only to gunners, but to every class of the community, except the tailors, who might lose business by it, and their satellites the dandies, who would faint at the sight of it. It is but fair that the man who gave me the recipe should be immortalized by its introduction, and not I, who am the mere copyist. I got it at Winterton, in Norfolk, from the factotum of all the wet work, one Larry Rogers, who calls it his " *Sou'wester*," and gets it all for nine shillings. In this dress, with water boots and overalls, every thing (but a man's eyes, which he may defend with goggles, and his mouth and nose, which he may fortify at Messrs. Fribourgs') is as independent of rain as *was once!* a Corinthian " Charley" in his watch-box. Add to this, it is so light and convenient for the arms, that you may walk, ride, row, or take any exercise without being heated, as with other surtouts. Oil-skin might do likewise; but this very soon wears out, and comes to six times the price. [In case the logician should condemn the arrangement of *this* latter sentence, I must humbly beg leave to argue that he would be wrong; because it is the fashion to *wear out* the coat *first*, and *pay* for it *afterwards*—I mean if paid for at all.]

Now to the point:—

Make, with an article called ***Russia duck*** (which, *as well as swanskin*, should be previously wetted and dried, to prevent shrinking), a loose over-all frock coat, and a hood; or a cap, with a flap behind, similar to a coal-heaver's hat, and dress them as follows:—

Take three quarts of linseed oil, and boil them till reduced to two quarts and a half, the doing which will require about three hours; and when the oil is sufficiently boiled, it will *burn a feather*. The addition of some Indian rubber was suggested to me; but of this I did not make a trial; because the dressing (for ***Russia duck***), answered so well without it. When the oil is quite cold, take a clean paint-brush, and well work it into the *outside* of the whole apparel, and it will soon find its way to the inside. Let the apparel then be put out in the air every dry day, for a fortnight or three weeks; and, at the expiration of that time, provided the oil on it be thoroughly dry, take the remainder of your prepared oil, and give it the second coat, which will dry much quicker than the first.

I was told that one coat of oil would do, as the dressing could be renewed at pleasure. The difference, however, was this:—The first coat would barely stand a hard day's rain; but after the *second* coat was on, this garment, if held up, would hold gallons of water as tight as the pail from which I poured them.

In short, this recipe has, *after eight years' trial, proved* to *answer* so *well*, that I have no doubt if it had been disguised, and "set a going" by some gentleman who was a "dab" at preaching, puffing, and wall-chalking, he might soon have made a little fortune by it, and set up for an E-S-Q.; with his "cad," and his "cab," and his —, &c.

N. B. Tell the person who boils the oil to beware of getting burnt; and let him do it out of doors, or he might run a risk of setting your house on fire. Add to this, the smell of it, when boiling, is a great nuisance; although the dress, *after* being thoroughly *dry*, will retain scarcely so much of it as common oil-skin.

This garment, if made double-breasted, with buttons *only* on the *right* side, and *none* on the *sleeves, which* should be *sewn close*, is, without exception, the best I ever used for throwing a casting-net. In addition to the coverings herein named, I find that a very large old umbrella, fitted up with brown Holland, *and thus oiled*, is the greatest possible comfort and shelter to those who go in a punt. Moreover, it makes a capital mizen-sail when going before the wind; and is a complete shield to you and your man, from the shaking of a wet dog, should you have no following-boat to rid you of this annoyance.

Here, I conceive, is all the covering that can be required for *real* wildfowl shooting; and as for the little pastime of tramping the water-meadows, or waiting for the flight, I need only observe, that wearing a *hat*, and particularly a *black* one, should be avoided, and *drab* is, on the whole, about the best colour. For the latter pursuit, the shooter should have a gunning-coat, lined with shag, that has pockets convenient for loading; a flap to fall over his lock, and a quaker's collar, which will not interfere with his gun. [The pattern for this coat, and the recipe for the *Sou'wester*, I have given to Mr. Davies, late Christie (deceased) and Davies, 49, Poland-street*.] This coat, with a shawl handkerchief, should be worn over his shooting jacket; and, of course, not put on till he ceases to be in motion; or he might, otherwise, get heated, and take cold.

If he wishes to sit down, never let him be so imprudent as to sit on the damp ground, but have either a hand-basket or a bag full of straw, or something of this kind; and the *lower his seat*, the *better* he will be *able to shoot at fowl when they are going over his head.*

The foregoing directions, I trust, explain all that is requisite on the subject; and, in this article, as well as in many others, I have to beg pardon for the style in which I have written. But in a work where the poor author is left without a single muse to inspire him, the subject will often become, both to the writer and the reader, like a dreary journey, where any trifling observation may be admissible to lighten the way. For

* I likewise gave him one for a common shooting jacket and waistcoat; having observed that but few of these articles are comfortably made by the dandy tailors.

instance, when we give a dissertation on water boots, hot oil, and Russia duck, the hero of his own tale might, it is presumed, crave a little indulgence for what the sceptic might consider playing the fool with his pen; or, in another point of view, taking the advice of Æsop to the Athenian philosopher, and unbending that bow, which, the sceptic himself admits, has been already strained too hard by the generality of authors and travellers.

TO PRESERVE GUNNING CLOTHES FROM THE MOTH.

To keep your gunning-dresses, and indeed all other cloths, furs, &c. free from the moth, let them be perfectly *well aired*, and then *sewed up* in a *bag* of brown Holland, or other *linen*, which if sewn tight, and *kept dry*, will rarely ever fail to preserve them. But, if you wish to be doubly sure, you may put, in the bag with them, either half a pint of pepper-corns; or, what is still better, equal quantities of camphor and carbonate of ammonia. A bladder filled with turpentine is another good remedy.

TO PRESERVE GUNS FROM SALT WATER.

For this recipe I shall copy Mr. Daniel, from whom I took it.

"Three ounces of black lead, half a pound of hogs' lard, one quarter of an ounce of camphor, boiled upon a slow fire; the gun barrels to be rubbed with this; and, after three days, wiped with a linen cloth. Twice in a winter will keep off the rust, which the salt water is otherwise sure to be continually bringing out from the iron."

This recipe I had adopted, ever since taking it from Mr. Daniel's "Rural Sports;" and, up to 1822, found it to answer *infinitely better* than any thing I had before tried.

In that year, however, I was recommended to use *mercurial ointment*, which, I find, gives less trouble, and answers quite as well, if not better.

When on the *sea*, always use *neat's foot* oil for every part of your gun, *except the works of the locks;* because *sweet* oil has not body enough to repel the effect of the salt water.

I have lately found this to answer so well as to become a very good substitute for the other dressings.

If the salt water should have stained your barrels, you will, I think, find yellow soap and warm water the best recipe to restore their colour.

My reason for now using *neat's foot* oil is, because I have found that *linseed oil* is apt to *stain the barrels.* Nothing can surpass the neat's foot for *every* part of a gun, except among the works of locks, for which it has too much body.

WILKINSON'S OIL.

Mr. Henry Wilkinson, of Pallmall, has discovered a method of purifying oil for chronometers, gun-*locks*, and other fine pieces of mechanism, for which the Society of Arts rewarded him with their gold medal, and published an account of the process in the forty-seventh volume of their Transactions, with certificates from some eminent watch-makers who had used his oil for seven years; and, as I have myself *proved* its *decided superiority* for *all gun-locks*, I give the recipe to make it for the benefit of those who will undertake the trouble which it requires, and in the very words that Mr. H. W. has been good enough to write on purpose for mé to publish.

"The finest olive oil is first exposed to a temperature of about 32° F. by which a large portion becomes solidified, as seen in the oil shops in the winter. While in this state, it is poured on a filter of bibulous paper, and the fluid portion allowed to pass through; the solid which is left on the filter being rejected. It is now raised to a temperature above 212°, but not exceeding 230°, for about one hour. This process drives off all the water and acetic acid it may contain, by evaporation; and the purification is completed by repeated filtrations through recently prepared *animal*-charcoal *."

This oil is sold by Mr. W. under the denomination of "*Pure Vegetable Oil;*" and, with the addition of

* Prepared by burning *bones,* in a crucible, without access of air.

half a pound of camphor to one gallon of this oil, by the name of "*Persian Oil*," which he has used for many years to preserve the *out*side, or iron and steel work of guns from rust on a long sea voyage; as it acts like a fine transparent varnish, and does not injure the appearance on opening the gun-case.

While speaking of Mr. Wilkinson, it may not be amiss (though I confess rather out of place *here*—but my other sheets are printed off) to mention that he has recently obtained a patent for a new and improved mode of loading rifles and pistols at the breech, which greatly facilitates the operation of loading; but, as an engraving would be required to give a correct idea of this invention, which, after all, is more for *service* than for *sporting*, I must refer to him for a full explanation of its advantages.

He is also engaged in some other ingenious schemes which certainly possess *novelty*, and evince great mechanical talent; but whether they will or will not succeed, time alone can determine.

WILDFOWL SHOOTING.

THIS amusement is generally condemned, as being only an employment for fishermen, because it sometimes interferes with ease and comfort; and bucks (who shoot as they hunt, merely for the sake of aping the Adonis at breakfast, or recounting their sport over the bottle) shiver at the idea of being posted, for hours, by the side of a river, or anchored, half a night, among the chilling winds in a creek.

This, however, is only the actual service of the sport, as it may, like all others, be enjoyed with moderation.

The usual way of sallying forth, for this purpose, is to drive to an inn on the coast, call the waiter, who recommends an *honest* boatman, for whom the boots is immediately despatched. On his arrival, he sees how eager you are to set sail, fixes his price accordingly, shows you thousands of birds, where he knows a boat can never get at them, obliges you with a few of his own killing, at double their value, and your day ends with a ten pound bill, and, perhaps, bagging a couple of sea gulls.

If even there *was* a chance on the shore, or in a fen, to see a flock of fowl well pitched; send a gentleman-sportsman after them, and he generally comes back without a bird; while a common fellow would get a shot, and kill three or four. Why is this? The gentleman thinks his cracked shooting is to do every thing, and will not go low enough, for fear of dirtying his knees; while the rustic, not minding dirt, or any thing else, pulls off his hat, crawls to the fowl, and is generally as sure of getting, as the other is of *not* getting, a good shot.

The average of shooting, *on the coast*, is now far inferior to that in many private rivers and ponds, by reason, that, where the wildfowl contribute to the winter subsistence of the fishermen, they are for ever followed, and not *only by them*, but every vagrant, who can raise a *few shillings* to purchase an old musket; so that, on their appearing in numbers, there is generally assembled a *levy en masse*, who, by indiscriminately firing at all distances, make them so difficult of access, that, although thousands may be *seen*, few will fly or let you come *within reach*.

Indeed, the sport is sometimes so completely ruined, that I have heard the poor men, who earn their livelihood by it, express a most earnest wish, that some kind of licence was required, which they could pay for tenfold by the number of shots that are now spoiled by the idle, drunken, mischievous rabble, that frequent the alehouses about Christmas, for the nominal purpose of wildfowl shooting. These fellows would, by this means, be deterred from infesting the shore, and the poor fowlers would be better paid for their hard labour: add to which, this would prevent the depredations that are not unfrequently committed by these armed vagabonds. As it is, however, the lords of manors may forbid their carrying guns, or otherwise trespassing, in parts where the *tide does not flow*, such as the waste land, &c.

In some, though *now very few*, retired places, where all this is not so much the case, the diversion of what is called flight shooting is excellent to those who are neither prepared nor disposed to follow wildfowl in a more scientific manner. I shall, therefore, endeavour to give a few hints on the subject.

It is well known, that the generality of wildfowl keep constantly passing in small "*trips*," about the dusk of the evening; and that, after having collected in the night, they return in a few large flocks at, or before, the dawn of morning. No plan for a *small* gun, therefore, answers so well as to wait then patiently for them, and fire as they pass to and fro. They will, *at these times*, seldom take notice of one who stands against a bush or bank, provided he remains *perfectly still*, is not *conspicuously* dressed, and wears a seal's-down, or other kind of *cap*, instead of a hat. If such places are not to be found, an ambush may be easily made. Thus situated, he will be able to distinguish the different sorts of fowl, long before they come within shot, and be struck with the wild retirement of the scene. He will observe the whistle, which announces the approach of wigeon—the similitude to a storm of the rapid flying dunbirds—the shrill sounding pinions of the wild ducks—and the mournful notes of the plover, with the roar of a bursting surge, and discordant screams of sea-fowl.

Flight shooting is always followed with most success in very *boisterous weather*, provided the course of the birds happens to be against the wind; as this not only obliges them to *fly low*, but doubles them well together. You may then keep two guns employed faster than yourself and a servant can load them. Never look up while loading; you can do no good by it; and you will only put yourself in a flurry; and, perhaps, break your ramrod. If your man (*knowing you have no gun loaded*) says, "Look out, sir!" Why—I had almost said—knock him down.

Should the weather be clear, and the birds *come in high*, your best means for getting a good chance is to conceal yourself *in a canoe*, between the banks of some *small creek;* as they will *lower their flight* on *reaching the mud*, and, in all probability, give you as many fair shots as you can fire during their arrival; which may continue about half an hour. Be careful to shoot well *forward*, and, *if they are fifty or sixty yards above you*, at least *two* or *three feet* before their heads, with a *flint*, and about *half the distance* with a *detonater*.

In choosing your station, select either a bank or wall, that divides the sea from detached pieces of water, or marshes, or any other point, which can intercept the flight of the birds from their nightly feed. Should their *course* be generally *up some channel*, you may there *anchor a boat or two*, and either conceal yourself in one of them; or keep your station for the chance of their *turning the birds* towards you.

In *rough weather*, you may sometimes have sport for the whole day, by digging a masked intrenchment at the extreme end of some promontory, that divides one well-stocked bay from another.

If the coast becomes *too much frequented by shooters*, and you can hear of a neighbouring *pond* or *lake*, take a walk to it in the course of the day, and see if the birds *use it at night*. This you will ascertain by going to the *leeward* side, where you will most likely find some of their *feathers*, which will have drifted to the edge of the water, and which, in case other shooters may be coming to explore also, you will do well *to gather up* or *conceal.*

When evening comes, take your station at the part *nearest the spring which supplies the pond;* or *otherwise,* anywhere to *leeward,* with a *good light,* and there remain in ambush, with your largest gun.

Here the birds will probably come in faster than you can count them, and you have then only to wait till they are *well packed together;* in which case, you would probably get from *ten* to *twenty at a shot.*

If the pond is large, place some one concealed on the opposite side, who (should the birds be feeding out of your reach) will, by a *gentle* noise, be sure to make them swim across; but, if he *overdoes his part;* goes directly to windward; or *shows himself;* they will *fly up. Never fire at random on such occasions.* If you wish to make the birds *forsake one pond,* with the view of their using another more convenient for shooting them, you should put, in the former, either some *train oil* and *quick lime;* a bushel of soot; or two winged birds, well rubbed over with asafœtida.

The *dunbirds* and *divers** may be easily known, by

* *So called by the decoymen:*—These birds have different provincial names on almost every coast: in some places, they are called *curres,* in others *duckers;* and, by many, are indiscriminately classed with the *dunbirds.* Their proper names, however, are scaup duck, tufted duck, gadwall, and golden-eye. They are remarkable for their *rapidity of flight,* expertness in *diving,* and *carrying off a* great deal of shot. *These,* as well as the *dunbirds,* will very often, what is called, *duck the flash;* that is, pop under water like a dobchick, and completely escape the shot. If, when shooting at night, you whistle, or make any *little noise,* before you draw the trigger, they will put up their heads to listen (though they will not *fly* unless the noise is *repeated),* and you are then sure to cut a good lane

the disturbance they make in the water, and they will generally swim over the *whole* of the pond in a few hours; so that, in *moonlight*, you would be almost sure of them.

Should the pond be frozen over, you might sometimes have a very fine shot, *by breaking open a large place in the ice*, where they would collect together for the *fresh water*, and most likely be accompanied by *duck* and *mallard*. The chief of the shooting on the ponds by night is at the *dunbirds*, which are vulgarly called *redheads*; for, with the exception of the *tufted* and *scaup duck*, the other diving birds prefer feeding by day. The *golden-eyes* go out every evening to sea, where, until the winter is nearly over, they will remain all night; though perhaps tossed on billows in the most tempestuous weather.

through their ranks. If you see a single curre by day, when he *dives* you must *run*; and the moment he *comes up*, *squat down*. So you may go on till within ten yards of him, and then stand ready to shoot him as he flies up, which he will do on coming up again, and seeing you suddenly appear so close. There are various contrivances for shooting birds that dive, such as cormorants, grebes, &c.: some fire the moment they come up; others shoot under them, or under their heads; and many hide the flash, by putting a shield of pasteboard before, or a cover over, the gunlock; but, after all, the best recipe is to have a good *detonating* gun.

LAUNCHING, AND CANOE SHOOTING.

HAMPSHIRE LAUNCHING-PUNT.

A HAMPSHIRE punt is made so light and narrow, as just to hold one person, with a gun of about seventy pounds weight, and six feet in the barrel, fixed on a swivel. This gun is so arranged, that it rests on the bow, and may be raised, or turned a few inches, by a mere *stump*, which some of the gunners here now have, instead of a *but*, in order to take up less room in the punt; and to admit of their firing higher, in case the birds should rise.

They row with their backs to the gun till they see the fowl, and then turn round on their faces; lie down, and either work along, with the *leaded stick*, A., or, if the water be too deep for this, with two paddles, like B.

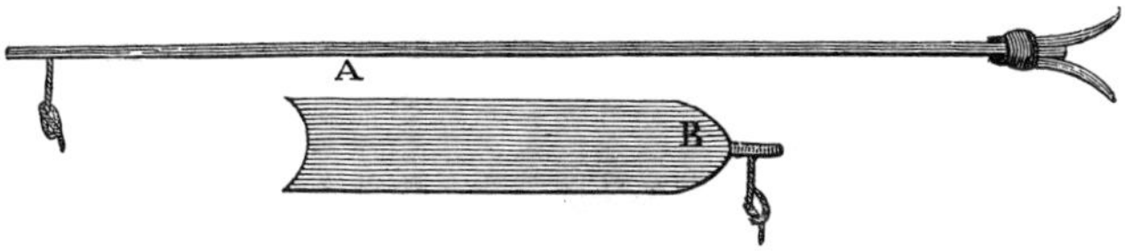

On having arrived within shot, they relinquish the one on their *right* side, which, in order to prevent its floating away, is made fast to the gunwale with a piece of string. They then keep straight the punt with the one on the left, while with the right hand they regulate their aim and pull the trigger.

The Hampshire punts are now built rounder at the stern, and the recoil of the gun is received entirely by a knee *fixed only* to the *bottom plank* (instead of a cross piece), which is far safer, and decidedly less likely to tear away the sides of the punt. The bottom is now made of *one* elm plank, an inch and a quarter thick, to which this knee is fixed by bolts and screws; and, consequently, as there is *no recoil on the sides* of the punt, every part, but this plank, is made as light as possible.

DIRECTIONS.

Punt 14 feet long; bottom 15 inches broad; sides 10 inches high, after increasing to about 2 feet 6 inches at the gunwales. This punt must not exceed 80 lbs. weight. [A solid block of elm is best for the knee. A 50 lb. gun, to carry 12 oz., answers best "for all tacks" in launching. The old 70 lb. guns of these men are too heavy when you get foul of grass and "winkles."]

NEWLY RIGGED MUDBOARD.

12 inches square.

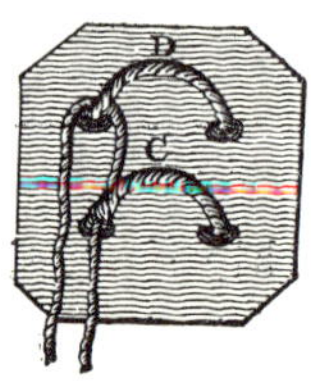

N. B. Put your heel to that part of the long rope (or "*pot-line,*") which goes under D, and is *spliced both to C and D.* Then cross the rope over your instep; put one end of it under D, and the other under C, and then tie them, on the instep, in a hard sailor's knot.

As a proof of my former argument against the safety of the Hampshire punts, I need only observe, that, since my second edition, three men (Vincent, Jones, and Tanner) were drowned, and another (Harnet) was killed, by his gun. These regular western channel gunners are now, therefore, become very shy of shooting afloat, for which, by having punts that are so *crank*, and draw so much water, and guns proportionally so short in the barrel, they have always been the worst equipped of any "*big* gunners" (as they call themselves) on the British coast.

They have, of late years, therefore, adopted an entirely new mode of getting at the birds, for which that vast track of ooze near Lymington is better calculated than perhaps any other mud in the world.

They start off, generally in the afternoon (provided the tide serves, so as to be low enough at the proper time), keeping as close as possible to the shore, and going before the wind, till they arrive at the leeward end of their beat; the whole track of which, for one night's work, may be about five or six miles. They then go ashore, and either get into a pot-house, if they have a sixpence to spend (which is not always the case), or lounge about the shore till day-light disappears, and the birds begin to fly; having first put all "*in order*;" that is, to draw out their mould shot, which they generally have in, for the chance of geese "going down along;" put in smaller shot; and regulate their gun so that it will bear about eighty yards, when the punt is on the dry mud. No sooner are the wigeon pitched than off they set, in tarpaulin dresses; and looking more like chimney-sweepers than gunners, crawling on their knees, and shoving this punt before them on the mud. No matter whether light or dark, few birds or many, *bang!*

goes the gun ;—and no sooner have they picked up what few birds are readily to be found, or missed the fowl, which they very frequently do, as the punt, by even a few periwinkles, might be thrown off the line of aim, they proceed again; thus travelling all night (by "launching" over the mud, and rowing across the creeks) in a direct line, similar to the march of an *army of coots*. I should not omit to mention, that, as the birds will seldom allow them to get into the punt to fire, some of them draw the trigger with a string at the end of the ramrod, and others creep up on one side, and pull it off with the finger.

A launching punt, in severe weather, may *sometimes* be used to great advantage *by day*, when it blows such a gale as to drive the wigeon in from sea, to the channel's edge, where they shelter themselves under the lee of the mud; and keep sufficiently in the "wash" to prevent their legs from being frozen. Then it is that a Hampshireman hauls his punt across the oozes, if they are too hard frozen for him to launch her, and gets into one of those little creeks, which, in *very* rough weather, and at low water, can be approached by no other means. He then paddles down the creek to where he suddenly pops on his game. If he can then catch the birds clear of the rounding mud, he perhaps makes a capital shot; and, if not, he is obliged to hoot them up, and do the best he can on the wing. As all this is more or less among the breakers, he frequently half fills his boat in the scramble; but, as the channel's edge is generally hard and shallow, he is in no serious danger, provided he does not attempt to follow his outward-bound cripples. After having made the shot, he catches up what birds he can get; and then hauls his punt upon the mud, in order to empty out the water, and proceed for a fresh attack. Thus, by undergoing misery of this kind, the Hampshire launcher may be filling his bag, while a man who could only shoot afloat would be obliged to stay at home. Thus the mud, and the *mud only*, affords the chance for *his* sport.

But when the water flows over the ground, and "knocks up" a sea that would make his little craft totter like a walnut shell, then his reign is at an end; and the proper gunner, with a long decked punt, would be killing half a sack full, where the launcher "dare not show his nose," by being able to work against a head sea, that would swallow him up; or, if going to leeward, to ship twelve yards of canvas, and go by him, as a frigate would pass a sand-barge.

Launching is perhaps the most laborious, and the most filthy work in all the department of wildfowl shooting; and not only that, but it so ruins the country, that in a very short time it entirely "breaks the haunt of the birds," without having yielded any material advantage to those who adopt the system. As some corroboration of this, I need only observe, that a family, who were the leaders in this way, and who (except Read) are by far the best launchers in Hampshire, have of late been reduced to absolute distress for a livelihood!

Till about ten years ago, off Lymington was one of the best gunning coasts in England, for this reason— IN THESE PARTS the VERY NORTH-EASTER WHICH BRINGS THE FOWL "CUTS THE TIDES," so much that *even* at the "*full and change*" they most frequently do *not* "*make over the ground;*" and the birds thereby formerly got such a "strong haunt" that, when the tides "lifted" again, from the change of wind, nothing would make them forsake the place. But now the new system has put an end to this; and sent most of the birds to Poole Harbour, and other places where the mud will not admit of launching. On this point there is a difference of opinion by the two cleverest men in the "profession." Buckle says that "launching is the ruination of a coast." My man (Read) says that it may be had recourse to, without injury to the ground, provided you allow the birds to feed till they are full, before you shoot at them. I am of Buckle's opinion, which is now pretty well *proved* to be correct, by the *ruination* of the *Lymington country*, for all *night* shooting, *except launching*.

I have, therefore, made a great sacrifice in wild sport, by continuing to rendezvous—at Keyhaven; because, *on that part of the coast, when the water begins to flow over the mud, at night, the birds, in general, leave the harbour, and fly out to sea; and even before a single shooter appears afloat!* But I became attached to the quarter, from the inhabitants being such—as we may hold up for an example to those of other country places. The neighbours are gentlemanly—kind—hospitable—people who know the world, and mind their own business;—the tradesmen civil and obliging;—and such is the honesty of the half-starved coasters, that I never lost so much as a thowl or a mud-board, in the twelve years that I have frequented the place. (Such people deserve a higher encomium than could be penned by a poor scribbler on guns and shooting!)

With regard to the *day* shooting in these parts, the state of the Hampshire coast, last winter, was so truly and ably described by "the Admiral" (Buckle) that, after him, any thing I could attempt would fall very short of doing justice to the subject. I must therefore endeavour to recollect what he said to me, one day, on landing at Keyhaven. (After heaving a sigh from the very waistband of his tarpaulin unmentionables; relieving his gorge by the ebullition of some originals, that any boy would have remembered better than his lesson; and then composing himself, by a smooth-down of the hair;) he commenced, with action suitable to every word, the following oration.

"Mr. Hawker,—Sir,—It 's all up with gunning now! The poor gunners 'll be starved! The birds 'll be all banished off the coast! I come all the way from So*w*thampton here, and never shot a gun!! What with them Itchen Ferry lubbers, in their washing-tubs—and the poppers along shore—and them young monkeys of boys rowing about to look for cripples—and the gentlemen jokers knocking about, at all tacks, in every kind of craft, from Royal yachts down to launching-punts—they won't allow the poor birds one minute to pitch! —There they were! some firing a pound of mould-shot, at every little trip that passed by, half a mile off!—Some of 'em had got cannons o' board, to heave boluses after the geese!—and another lot had got half a ship-load of muskets and rifles!—But I can't larn as e'er a one among 'em got a bird, except two of my cripples, as got away last night. I should have had a noble shot at them large curres just abreast of Calshot:—I suppose there was three hundred of 'em, as thick as ever they could stow; and, just as I let go my starboard paddle, to give it 'em home, some dandy chap pops off at one of them little gulls! so I rows up, and axes him, if 'twas to be as he was a poor man, how would he like to have the bread took out of his mouth in that there manner?—Well, thinks I, this 'll never do! so I gets my punt o'board my craft, and sails down to Leap. This was worse and worse—here they were on all day, and all night too! and fellows, from all parts, had come here, to quarter, on purpose for gunning. Well! the next day, I drops down here, as you see, sir; and I *never* could have believed *any* thing *could* be so bad as *this!* I brought up, off Lymington, about low water; and I 'm burnt if there wasn't some chap or other stowed away in every spreader, besides them bird-frighteners from Itchen Ferry, that had got down here; and buried theirselves the same as the launchers do—and there they kept peeping out of their holes," (here he became quite dramatic), "and popping up their stupid heads, and looking, for all the world, like so many dead people rising out of our St. Mary's church-yard! This is a precious pretty pass for gunning to come to! To have all the birds drove away by them as kills none theirselves, nor won't let others, as *do* know how, kill 'em—and by stupes too—wot knows as much about gunning, as gunning knows about them!! Ah, Sir! prowising 'tis to be so another winter, with the blessing of God, I 'll get off to Wexford in Ireland, or to foreign parts, or somewhere or other, where we can get a few heavy shots in peace!!"

Thus concluding, as he began, with a symphony of hearty oaths, he tapped his tobacco-box, for a fresh "quid," and held forth on the more cheerful subject of what he had done in better times.

LAUNCHING-SLEDGE.—For a man who goes long distances on the mud, it would of course be dangerous not to have a boat that would *carry both himself and his gun, in case* he should be *overtaken by a quick flood-tide before he could escape.* But to one who was content with merely having that, in which, with high land behind him, he could just shove off, and catch the birds under the moon, in such a place as the edge of some river, where the mud is pretty level and clear of holes, I shall prescribe one much lighter, and in which he can never be tempted to endanger his life afloat. The drawing will at once explain it sufficiently, and the only caution that can be required against accident is, that, as his gun must be cocked before he advances, he had better have a bit of cork to intercept the flint or detonater, which can be drawn away with a string (as the noise of cocking a gun might spring the birds), and which must not be removed till he has crawled sufficiently on one side of his punt to be quite clear, in case the gun should go off.

This punt is so much lighter than any thing which you can float in, that you may move it with one hand, and by leaning your weight on a hand patten, which, being a little "*kammelled,*" *slips along* without noise, and with the greatest ease, you may, with good water boots, go two or three hundred yards without getting the least wet.

The best time for launching is rather before half ebb, after the water has been over the ground, and made it slippery. "Dead low water" is, of course, a bad time; because you have then great trouble to get your punt upon the mud; and treble the distance to go after having done this.

The gunner should not be black like the Hampshire men; but recollect, that, as all extraneous bodies appear darker, he should *be* at least a few degrees *lighter than the mud,* in order to *appear* precisely of the *same colour.* Indeed, the lighter the better, *if no moon.*

SUSSEX MUD-BOAT.—There is another contrivance for traversing the oozes, which is simply a very slight board, with sides, somewhat in shape like the fore end of the Hampshire punt, sawed off, and a tail board, or bench put across it. This is used on the Sussex coast, in places where there are but very few creeks to interrupt its progress. The way to manage it is this:—The gunner first lays his piece (a large hand gun) into the "mud-boat;" and then kneeling on the bench with one knee, he kicks along with the other leg, and advances with a rapidity that you would hardly credit;

and when that leg is tired, he changes it again, and works away as before. Having got pretty near to his birds, he lies down in the " mud boat," in which, if the mud is soft, he can work along with his feet; but if hard, he must "hold on," and shove this kind of sledge before him. He lies close on his chest to fire, and has a stock cut away at the but, which is filled with horse hair. This so much eases the recoil from his collar bone, that (unless in a sharp frost, when guns are apt to strike harder) he can manage to fire half a pound of shot at a time. Birds may be approached much nearer by this means than by any other kind of " *launching*," as the whole concern is so much lighter, and smaller.

So much for the new system, by which the ancient mode of shooting on the Hampshire coast, so well described by Mr. Gilpin, and quoted by Mr. Daniel, has *long ago been totally superseded!*

Although I cannot, for a moment, suppose, that the generality of sportsmen would ever think of adopting *this* method, yet I have given directions for it, because I am fond of any thing original; and for this reason I have made it the subject of a little drawing. Here the light launching sledge is in the fore ground; the Hampshire gunner contending with it in the centre, and the Sussex mud-boat looking after other birds in the back ground; the latter is shown with a man in the position in which he traverses the oozes *before* he begins to crouch and advance to the birds. In order to tell the story, I have found it necessary to put this, and other subjects, a little " out of drawing." Here I hope the R. A. gentlemen will pardon me, with that liberality which is inseparable from men of talent.

Since the last edition, Buckle has beat us all, by con-

Inv.d & Sketched by P. Hawker. Eng.d on Steel by H. Adlard

MUD-LAUNCHERS, on the oozes, off LYMINGTON, shoving their PUNTS up to WIGEON.

London. Published by Longman & C.o 1844.

triving a punt in which he can *work himself over the mud without getting out!* But, as this would be of no use to gentlemen, and as, by giving an engraving of it, I might only be serving other gunners, to *his injury*, I shall say no more about it; particularly as I, of course, make it a rule never to publish the particulars of any thing that I consider as having been explained to me in confidence.

POOLE CANOE.

(For shooting from the creeks, with a large shoulder gun.)

The Poole canoe is built sharp at both ends, *on the plan of the Greenland whale-boat*, except being so flat at the bottom as to draw but about two inches of water, and so light as to weigh only from sixty to a hundred pounds. For this canoe, &c. see the plates and instructions, with the assistance of which a carpenter ought not to mistake in building one.

DIRECTIONS.

Dimensions.—From stem to stern, 12 feet; length of bottom, 10 feet; bottom, at centre, 3 feet 2 inches; width at ditto, from gunwale to gunwale, 3 feet 7 inches; height, 11 inches at centre, rising to 13 ditto fore and aft; weight, about 100 lbs.

N. B. Timbers yew or oak. Bottom to be three pieces of elm or pine, an inch thick. Each side one plank of elm, one-third of an inch thick. Caulk the seams with oakum: then pour in hot rosin, softened with a little oil to prevent it from cracking: and paint the bottom (outside) with red lead.

CANOE FORESHORTENED.

For a guide to builders, if ordered inland or abroad.

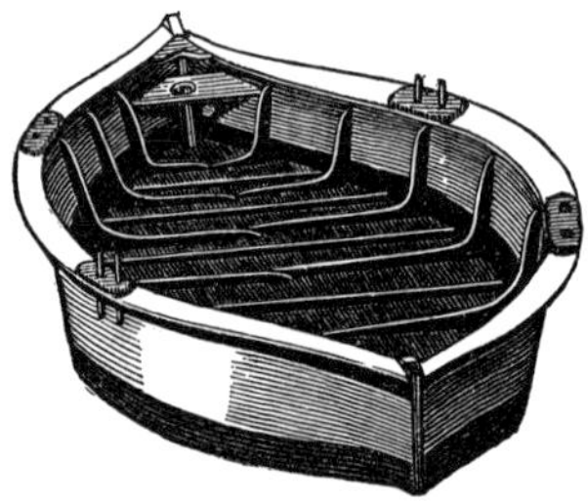

SETTING POLE.

The bit of lead round fork makes it sink better.

POOLE MUD-BOARDS.

Sixteen inches square.

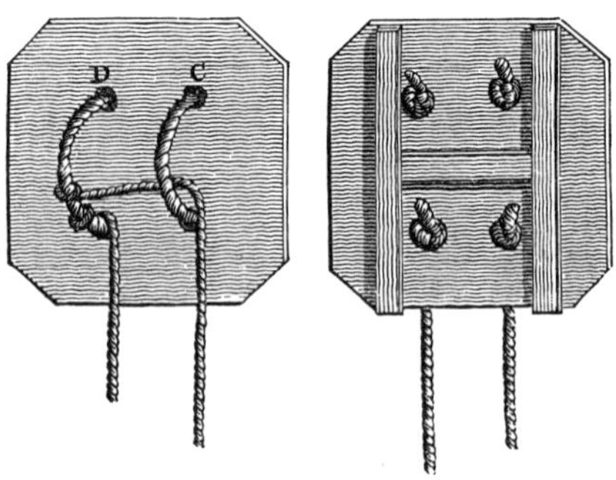

Upper side. Under side.

Put your foot into C, with your heel hard against D; place one of the small ropes on each side the foot, and under C; then over it, and under D. Having done this, draw the ropes together, as tight as the foot can bear them, and tie them over your instep. These boards are, of necessity, larger, and fitted up with stronger rope, than the others, because the Poole ground is so very soft.

But the Hampshire boards, with our improvements of double splicing, and having strong pot-line, to "lash" over, are now by far the best, and the quickest to "ship and unship."

In making all canoes for gunning, the builder should be careful to have the *bottoms* of them a *little rounded* (say about half an inch of convex, "amidships," for a bottom three feet broad); and, what is of still more consequence, a little "kammelled," or sprung; that is, gradually rising "fore and aft," in order to "give them life." They will otherwise row miserably heavy, and, when they get aground, suck the mud or sand so much, that, in order to get them off again, you might be forced to stand up; and this would frighten away the fowl. If, however, the bottom of a canoe is *too* much kammelled, she will never keep steady in going to birds. Some people, for this reason, leave hollow grooves between the bottom planks. I should say, that to every five feet of plank I would give about one inch of "kammel;" so that the bottom of the canoe here engraved, being ten feet, would, by holding a string along the centre of the bottom *(outside)* prove convex about two inches. If a little more, she would be none the worse; perhaps better; provided that she drew water enough to give a bearing to every part; otherwise the ends that were sprung would, by being *out* of the *water*, "*cluck*" so much as to *make birds swim away in the night.* In short, *let your draught of water be the chief guide, to regulate the kammelling, or springing, of your punts and canoes.* If not required for rough work, or a fixed swivel-gun, I should recommend that the planks be not more than three quarters of the thickness specified in the foregoing directions; as nothing, *provided* it be *perfectly safe*, can be too light for getting to wild birds. It is the *large size* of a boat, *not* the *substance* of the wood, that makes her safe in a sea. If the builder puts some tarred oakum round the heads of the principal nails, before he drives them in, so much the better. Notwithstanding all that the boat-builders have said, I now find that *copper nails are* the best. For dressing and painting, vide directions hereafter given.

This kind of canoe, although built for other purposes, is, on the western coast, generally preferred, for shooting, to one of *any other kind.* It answers best, when used (no matter whether by day or night), from low water to half, and sometimes to full, flood. You manage it thus:—

Sit down, on some straw or rushes, with your gun by your side, and take with you a *small* Newfoundland dog. Row about, till you can see or hear a flock of wildfowl on the mud. To find them sitting, if by night, look at first very low, so as to bring the surface of the mud in contrast with the horizon, by which means you will overlook the black edges of the creeks and holes, instead of seeing, and perhaps mistaking them for, birds.

When you have rowed within three or four gunshots of the fowl, take in your oars, and reconnoitre the creeks. Having ascertained which is likely to be the best, lie down, and *push along* with the "*setting-pole,*" (or "*gunning-spread*"), and, while the mudbanks stand above the little channels, you are so completely hid, that you will seldom fail to get a shot, *provided there is a creek within reach of the birds,* and you do not *go directly to windward of them* *.

* The *decoymen can* go to windward of the birds by means of the smoke from a piece of *dutch turf,* or common *peat,* which, after having it well dried, they are able to *carry lighted in the hand* for the short time that is required to *drive the wildfowl into the pipes.* Another recipe, of which some pretend to make *a great secret,* is a

On arriving sufficiently near, should the water be so low that you cannot present your gun at the birds without kneeling or standing up, you must get aground at the side of the creek, or steady your canoe by means of forcing each oar from between the *thowls* into the mud, otherwise the recoil of the gun will *set her rocking*, and thus you might possibly be tipped out. Having *made all fast*, rise up and fire. Take care, however, to rise high enough to be WELL CLEAR OF THE MUD, or NOT A FEATHER WILL YOU TOUCH; and present as follows:—By *day*, or moonlight, if the birds are close, *directly at* them: or if beyond forty yards, shoot at their heads; unless they are feeding in a concave place, where the tide has left a kind of plash, in which case you must level rather *under* them, or you will only graze their back feathers. In *starlight* take your aim just on the top of the NARROW BLACK LINE, IN WHICH BIRDS ALWAYS APPEAR, TO ONE WHO IS LOW DOWN; and when so dark that you cannot see your gun, present, as you think, about a foot over, or you will most likely shoot about a foot under them.

Should you have been successful, you will, if at night, generally *hear* your cripples beating on the mud, *before*

paste of *cowdung and chopped straw;* but, before this will ignite properly, it must be *baked in an oven* for about *thrice as long* as the time required for *making bread.*

All these things may answer very well *behind the screen of a decoy;* but in a canoe, or punt, the fire could not be so easily concealed, and there would be some danger in lighting it where one, *without a retreat,* was *sitting on straw,* and with *gunpowder* on board. The burnt turf, &c. may be used with success by a person walking behind the high banks of a pond, or river, who may light it, when required, by carrying on a match a little *hyperoxymuriate of potash,* and dipping it into a small phial of *vitriolic acid:* another more simple remedy is the "*German tinder*" that is used for lighting cigars.

you can sufficiently recover your eyes, from being dazzled by the fire, to *see* them. Your man then puts on his mud-boards, taking the setting pole to support him, and assists the dog in collecting the killed and wounded; taking care to secure *first* the *outside* birds, lest they should escape to a creek. During this time you are left in charge of the punt; and should, if possible, keep a look out, in order to see if any more birds fall dead, or wounded, from the company, before they have flown out of sight.

The *gunner* generally calculates on bringing home the half only of what he shoots, from the difficulty of catching the whole of his winged birds, which he calls *cripples*, and those that (to use the pigeon phrase) *fall out of bounds*, which he calls *droppers*. If birds fly up he generally declines firing, knowing that the moment they are on wing they become so much *more spread*, that he could seldom get more than three or four, for which it would be hardly worth while to disturb the mud; particularly as wigeon, by night, if not fired at, will, in cold weather, probably settle again at no great distance.

The Poole men sometimes go partners, by which means they can, with a very light punt, use two poles at a time, and shove up a creek that is nearly dry, and then fire two guns to a whispered word of command. This they call a "double gun," and, by such means, they, some years ago, could frequently secure forty or fifty wigeon at a time.

But, within these very few years, Poole harbour, as well as almost every other part of the English coast, has been ruined for all the poor hand-gunners, by the introduction of punt-guns, that carry from one to nearly two pounds of shot; which, as the sovereign remedy in the present time, I shall hereafter explain to the very latest improvements.

The gunners' principal enemy is the *curlew*, which often springs up from the edges of the creeks, alarms the whole place, and sometimes spoils them an excellent shot.

GENERAL INSTRUCTIONS

FOR

SEA COAST WILDFOWL SHOOTING, WHEN AFLOAT.

I SHALL now more briefly explain my reasons for entering into the minutiæ of wildfowl shooting. It is very rare to meet a gentleman, that *can*, or a good professional gunner that *will*, give any information on the subject. The art is, therefore, the least understood of any sport in existence. No man, who had a large gun, and could earn five pounds in a day, or night, would be bored with a gentleman for the sake of his five shillings; and therefore the only man likely to be hired, *at a good time for this sport*, is some boatman, who has little to recommend him beyond a local knowledge of the harbour; and who therefore requires some one to direct him how to manœuvre the birds.

In following wildfowl, it is easier to get within twenty yards of them by going to *leeward*, than a hundred and fifty if *directly to windward*, so very acute is their sense of *smelling*.

The best time, therefore, to have sport with a canoe and a shoulder gun (provided it be *low water*, or *half ebb*, while you are *hid in the creeks)* is in clear, frosty, moonlight nights, when the *wind* happens to *blow towards you as you face the moon*. It is then impossible for the wildfowl to smell you ; and you may, by getting them directly under the light, have the most accurate outline of every bird, and even distinctly see them walking about, at a much greater distance than a gun could do execution. From thus being on the shining mud-banks, they appear quite black, except some of the old cock wigeon, on the wings of which the white is often plainly to be seen.

It does not follow, however, that nothing can be done without a *bright moon.* So far from it, that the old Poole men, among whom there were, formerly, some of the best shoulder gunners in the kingdom, prefer but little moon, even for the *mud.* Here, by constant habit, they can easily distinguish the black phalanxes of wigeon from the shades on the places they frequent, and particularly if they are feeding among the puddles which have been left by the tide.—(Speaking of what the Poole harbour gunners *were,* I should not omit to mention, that there still remains one particularly good "hand," who has attended me for some years, during the winter—James Read, who came from Greenland, in the Isle of Purbeck, and who, take him for *every thing,* is one of the most extraordinary performers that ever put an oar in salt water.)—In this pursuit, and when not favoured by the best of light, there are a few cautions to be given to an inexperienced shooter. First, to ascertain that the black patch to be seen *is* a flock of birds, which he will do, by observing the occasional change of feature in the outside of it. Secondly, on approaching them, to be careful that their enormous masses and tremendous noise do not deceive him in the distance, and tempt him to fire out of shot. And, thirdly, not to be too eager in getting his dead birds; as it sometimes happens, in hard weather, that the remainder of the flock will again pitch down among them; particularly if he has winged some of the *younger* birds, which have not the cunning to make off for a creek, like the old ones. In this case, a reserved gun would, probably, more than double the produce of his first shot. It should be understood, that this night shooting is chiefly at the *wigeon*, as the *geese*, of late years (since there have been so many shooters), have seldom ventured much in harbour by night; except sometimes at high spring tides, with a full moon; and the greater part of the *ducks, teal, dunbirds*, and such like, repair inland to the ponds and fresh springs, unless driven to the salt "feeding ground" by severe frost.

A *company* of wigeon, when first collecting, may be heard at an immense distance, by the whistling of the cocks and purring noise of the hens; but when they are quietly settled, and busy at feed, you sometimes can only hear the motion of their bills, which is similar to that of tame ducks.

Wigeon are never so readily disturbed by *hearing* a noise as by *smelling* or *seeing:* in both of which they are very quick; though, in the latter, less so than many other birds. *Sea pheasants* and *teal* are sometimes with them.

On the Dorsetshire coast, the shooters' terms for a large flock of wigeon are a *company;* for about thirty or forty, a *bunch* or *trip* of birds; and, for about ten or twelve, a *little knob:* a *string* or *skein* of *geese*, and other such provincial appellations. They also call a creek a *lake;* and the smaller creeks, or drains, *latches.*

Drawn & Sketched by P. Hawker. Eng.d on Steel by H. Adlard.

Approaching WILDFOWL, preparative to the flowing tide.

The former is a *general term* among people on the *coast;* but the latter, in the neighbourhood of Lymington, is called a "*spreader.*"

If we can neither find a creek nor a "latch," with sufficient water to *set up to birds,* it is sometimes thought necessary to put the canoe in one of the latter, and there await the return of the tide, with which we may gradually approach them, as the water flows. But if this advance cannot be made under an hour or two, we may as well go away; and, if no better chance should offer, return to the place when the tide has risen to within one or two hundred yards of the birds, instead of waiting idle for so long a time.

Here, unless disturbed, they will remain, as long as the tide allows them a place to stand on; and, as the mud begins to disappear, will concentrate themselves on the last uncovered spot; where, to use the words of a gunner, as soon as the water begins to "*whiten the mud,*" thousands may be *seen,* literally wedged among one another, and from whence they are so unwilling to fly, that they will seldom stir till the water actually *sets them afloat**. With proper management, therefore, you have, *at this time,* every chance of approaching them. To do this, let your punt or canoe be kept well fore and aft, and lie down in her, as close as having to push, or paddle, her will admit of. But do not advance on your birds till you have just sufficient water to carry up your punt. Then "work up" to them; and be careful, all the time, to guard against any sudden motion. By attending to this, and having *every thing*

* This is *now* all over in the *Lymington* country, where the birds are so "ill-used" at night, that they generally go off to sea before the tide flows within two hundred yards of them!

white (except in *moonlight*, when a *drab*, or *canvas colour*, will be less glaring), you may safely approach the unsuspecting mass of fowl, which will, at first, *appear like* the indistinct view of an *island;* and, on getting near, it will look more and *more black*, till, at last, you will plainly distinguish the shape of the outside birds. Now, then, is the critical moment to decide whether your exertions are to be crowned with success, or a severe night's hard labour is to end without your getting a shot. Perhaps, unless you have a " good loom " (that is, high black land) to advance from, the moon may suddenly come forth too bright for *this* sport. Perhaps some straggling bird may be so near you as to give the alarm ; or perhaps some fellow may ruin all by firing a shot ; and you may have the mortification to hear the sonorous host rising, like a roar of thunder, to take their departure for the open sea.

On the other hand, you and your boatman may have the good fortune to open your masked battery among their black columns ; and, by cutting a lane through them with a pound of the smallest duck shot, you may possibly secure 50 *or* 60 *wildfowl* as fast as yourselves and a dog can collect them. I formerly recommended the addition of discharging also two large hand-guns ; but it so rarely occurs that we can sufficiently see through the smoke to fire them in time, that I have latterly considered them not worth taking out, except for shooting at *low water*. (As a proof of what *may* be killed at one shot when birds are wedged together, I need only say that, on the 9th of January, 1825, my man, James Read, when sent to reconnoitre the creeks about two o'clock in the morning, killed and fairly bagged 12 wigeon, 5 ducks and mallards, 2 pintails, and a gray plover, with a common shoulder gun, that carried only 5 *ounces of shot.* This, however, is such a shot, with a *small* gun, as I never heard of before, and perhaps may never hear of again. There were, he thinks, about 30 birds in the company. They were all in a lump; and, to use his own expression, he "got almost o' board 'em before he let drive.")

Having thus succeeded, beware not to let your eagerness be the means of endangering your personal safety. Many have lost their lives by *both* having quitted the boat, which might soon drift away, and leave you "an inevitable prey to the returning tide." Let one go out for the birds, taking with him the *setting pole,* which will not only be useful in supporting him on his mud pattens, and finding out the deep places, but very handy, with the fork at the end, in pinning down the wounded birds. The other person should be all this time close to him in the boat, rowing or pushing with an oar, with which he may occasionally assist in killing the crippled birds that are afloat.

This opportunity of shooting wigeon may be also taken by *going out,* when the evening is not too light, *at high water,* and keeping at a distance till the *tide begins to leave the mud;* on and round the *first appearing* part of which the birds will probably collect.

There is no time of tide at which birds are so easily approached as at, what is called, the "*ground-ebb;*" because the receding tide makes the shallows, on which they stand, or swim, appear so white, that the birds are easily distinguished, and causes a sufficient ripple, on the deeper water, to give it, at all times, rather a darker colour. Thus the gunner has the advantage of catching his birds in the white water, while the birds have the disadvantage of his advance from the dark water; by which means we calculate that it is easier to get within fifty yards at the ebb, than within seventy yards upon the flood. I now allude to *night* shooting, as such close quarters are very rare by day, and particularly with a large company of birds. I cannot repeat too often that, except in a glaring moon and sun, it is impossible for the gunner to have his punt and his dress too white for calm water. To prove it—except in a moon, who ever saw a burrough-duck at night?—Look at the hoopers again—you *may* discern those which are under two years old, because they are dusky; but the old swans, notwithstanding their size, are almost, I may say quite, invisible. While, on the other hand, a wigeon, which is only brown, appears as black as a crow; and a coot looks as large and as black as a chimney-sweeper.—(Read this to any old gunner, and he will know, though he may not say, that I have told you right. In short, appeal to the *most finished* performers, as to what I have asserted on all that relates to wildfowl.)

On *this* occasion, the shooters *must* be provided *each* with mud-boards, or they may be left all night on the mud, for want of being prepared to haul their boat to a creek.

[A canoe or punt may be successfully used on a lake, pond, or river, by keeping it in parts where the water is shaded with the reflection of land objects, with which a small boat appears so confused, that the birds would, most likely, not perceive it, before you got a fair shot. Be careful, however, not to appear in a colour conspicuously different from the background; approach with caution; and, above all, beware of getting directly to windward of the birds.]

As the punt and canoe, previously treated on, are used most frequently for *night* shooting, which, as I before observed, is chiefly at the wigeon (or birds of *similar habits*, that join them in hard weather), I cannot, I trust, class the subject better than by concluding, under this head, with what further remarks may be useful as to wigeon, and reserve those for hoopers, geese, and curres till after we have taken up our heavy artillery, without which but little can be done with these, or any other birds that are commonly killed by *day*.

WEATHER.—*Fog*, *snow*, or any other hazy weather, is very bad, as it makes every thing on the water appear large and black, and then it is that these birds (and indeed *all* others) soon take alarm. The novice fancies just the reverse! Fog in the *fens* and *marshes*, however, is sometimes the best weather, although quite the *reverse* on the *sea*.

Bright starlight is the *very best of all times* for getting at birds, *as the tide flows over the mud;* particularly if there is a little breeze, without wind enough to blacken the shallow water. If a cold black frost, so much the better.

Even in moonlight, wigeon are easier approached than in hazy weather. In white frosts wigeon are often restless. In rain they are constantly flying and pitching. In very dark weather they are suspicious, and more on the watch than in starlight; but, if the wind blows fresh enough to drown the noise of a launching-punt, some "heavy shots" may now and then be made, by sweeping the surface of the mud to the sound of where the flock is walking and feeding. But as in *dark* THICK weather the chances are fifty to one against doing much, I should recommend every gunner in the kingdom to—go to bed at such a time. Rest assured, that if all the gunners would allow their birds to get a "strong haunt" in dark nights, it would be pounds and pounds in their pocket, before the end of the season, if not the very first week that it became clear and starlight.

It is not sufficient, however, to be starlight *over head only;* we must have it *clear* also *round* the *horizon*, or the birds, as in thick weather, will all disperse, and keep *walking away* from you *in different directions.*

In *mild weather*, wigeon are generally *scattered* about, like rooks, till after midnight, unless they become concentrated by the flow of the surrounding tide. But in cold weather they sit thick together.

The first night or two, of thaw, after a sharp frost, is the best opportunity for this sport.

Such is the effect that the change of *wind* has on the *movements* of *wildfowl*, that I am induced, as a specimen, to name the following circumstance.

A few years ago, I was detained in London during three weeks' easterly wind, till, at last, I received a pressing summons from my man, to inform me that the coast was swarming with birds. I directed him, by return of post, to have the punt ready to get afloat at nine (it being high water at ten) the night after I received his epistle. I mounted the coach-box at eight the next morning, hoping to breakfast in London and make a heavy shot at wigeon, at above one hundred miles from town, before eleven o'clock the same night; which, had I gone *even one* day *sooner*, I should have been almost sure of doing. But, before we had got half way through our journey, the wind suddenly flew from east to west! and no sooner had we reached the coast than there came on a tremendous westerly gale and rain, which it was impossible to weather that night. The next morning I had the mortification to see the whole atmosphere darkened with birds that were mounted high in the air, and making the best of their way out of the country. The day before my arrival, my man had killed twenty couple, with a light 45 lb. stanchion gun;—*the second day after, not a fowl was to be seen or heard of!!* Again, vice versâ, I had once been three weeks on the coast without seeing a bird, and after about ten days' easterly wind, there suddenly appeared at least three thousand wigeon and geese, though we had not seen a single wildfowl the day before! I had first to weather sixteen blank days; and then killed one hundred and twelve fowl in eighteen hours! They talk of the "glorious uncertainty of the law," and I am sure we may "sing out," by way of parody, on the diabolical uncertainty of the fowl.

TIME.—Was it possible to preserve a public harbour, wigeon should never be fired at till they had fed for some hours, and got well together; because a shot fired in the evening, when birds are scattered, seldom produces much, and is apt to make them forsake the place altogether. If, indeed, they were left till just before day-break, so much the better. A man who gets upon the mud, or in the creeks, and amuses himself by popping away at evening flight, has, of course, the curse of every regular gunner; as, by such a practice, he ruins a small harbour in a few nights. Though the best of all shots is when the birds are "*on their last legs*," before the tide flows high, yet shooting at them when *actually afloat* is not near so well. They are then more scattered: their feathers are not so open: and shooting them at *this* time is apt to make them *forsake* their "feeding ground."

SOUND.—The thicker the weather, the more silent the wigeon, when pitched. A shrill clear pipe denotes a single cock wigeon, as does a long loud "purre" a hen: but when the call of the cock is one short, soft note, and not so often repeated, you may expect to find a company. If so, you will probably soon hear the birds " all in a charm" (that is, in full concert), if you have patience to wait and listen, which a good gunner always repeatedly does, every now and then, before he ventures on the final approach. The birds might otherwise steal away, and totally mislead him. When wigeon are " in a *charm*" they are *not minding you ;* but when they are *quite silent,* they are, as likely as not, *suspecting an enemy.* At this moment, you must keep still, till they open again ; and so on, till you see them ; and then, in *starlight,* you are generally near enough, at all events for a large gun, to give them your royal salute.

Be sure and choose, if possible, the best background to advance from, in order to disguise your profile from the horizon. Even a black cloud is better than nothing. But if (before the mud is covered) you hear birds walking away, and neither feeding nor " speaking," it is a bad omen. It shows that they have some suspicion of an approaching enemy, and are half inclined to fly. When birds are about one hundred yards off (or much further, in very calm weather), you may hear them feeding ; the noise of which, at this distance, is like the falling of a little water, and is often mistaken for it at *ebb* tide.

Here are (in the fewest words I can give them) all the necessary requisites for night-shooting ; and, if well understood and well managed, you are just about as sure of getting a fair shot (in a *favourable time),* as you would be with a young partridge to a dead point in standing clover. As to all the old plans of burying punts, casks, &c. &c., they are *now* of so little avail in almost every part of *England,* as to be no longer worthy of insertion.

STANCHION, OR PUNT-GUN.

I HAVE, by practical experiment, since the earlier editions, found, that the gunmakers have another lesson to learn!—Although a gun of this description must of course be *supported* by some mechanical means, yet the universal system of *entirely confining* the gun under the barrel, so that it cannot be relieved even one inch in the recoil, is the worst that can possibly be adopted. It not only (when properly loaded) jars every thing so much as to require extra strength, and therefore extra weight to a punt, which we want as light as possible, in order to go in shallow water; but the sudden check throws the muzzle so much out of the proper direction, that we are frequently obliged to take level very far under, or over, the mark; according as the gun may spring, from being either heaviest or lightest forward: and, what is worse than all, this sudden check, at the moment of ignition, materially injures the shooting of the gun in every respect. This experiment was tried, in my presence, by Elijah Buckle, one of the best stanchion-gunners in England, and *by far* the *best I* ever saw, who left the coast of Essex for Southampton; who has been frequently in my employ; and to whom I am, most probably, indebted for not having remained much longer in ignorance on the subject. Indeed nothing but ocular demonstration would have convinced me of this argument. What pride and folly it is, then, for any one to hold himself above being shown, even by the most humble individual!

The gun was loaded with a pound of shot, and two

ounces of Messrs. Curtis and Harvey's best coarse powder. I fired from the confined swivel, that is generally used by the *London gunmakers !* in doing which I levelled at least a *foot over* the object; and, by this means (as the water and the paper proved), shot perfectly accurate. Buckle then fired; having taken level *at* the *centre* of the object, from the swivel: and the whole charge went into the water, before it had gone ninety yards, where the target was placed. I then began to abuse the late Mr. D. Egg, and said, I hoped that Buckle, as an experienced gunner, and an engineer (he having been a long time in his Majesty's service), was convinced of the fault of the gun; on which he said, and with justice I own, that both "the London gentlemen," and I, had " a little to learn yet." He then, to use his own words, "hove away that humbugging swivel;" and, by means of a large bolster of sheeps'-wool, *fired the gun from his shoulder*, with the same charge as before; *which I put in myself.* He presented as usual, *directly at* the object, and *made such a shot as this barrel had never before been known to make, both for strength and closeness.* I then, to be convinced of his veracity, as to *taking aim*, fired the gun in *his* way with about ten ounces of shot, not quite fancying the pound to my shoulder. I levelled *at*, instead of over, the mark, and the shot were delivered with the greatest accuracy. The gun, with this charge, went under my arm precisely five inches, as I afterwards measured. If a gun, when fired this way, was to swerve in going back, it would be dangerous; and therefore the under part of the stock, in order to lie firm on the bench, ought either to be *made flat*, or *fixed in a piece of wood*, that was *flat at bottom*. It then occurred to me, that if this gun (of eighty-five pounds weight) was fired with *ten ounces* from the *swivel,* it might go so easy as not to interrupt the shooting. I accordingly tried it, and so little appeared to be the recoil, that it could not be felt; notwithstanding which, by aiming *at* the mark, the charge was, as usual, from the *swivel, entirely under it.* On the other extreme, I saw a gun fired by the owner of it, Samuel Singer, at Poole (which weighed 141lbs.). This was on a swivel, and mounted very *light forward,* and he told me, that he was always obliged to present very far *under* the object, or his whole charge went over every thing; and that he should "douse" the swivel for a rope breeching. The latter, however, is *apt to break,* and has *often proved dangerous.* But, I have since used my 85lb. gun with a rope breeching that reaches all the way from, and goes through a hole in, the stem of the punt. The breeching has then so much play as, with the help of a padded but, at the shoulder, to ease the recoil tolerably well. It is, however, not to be compared to the spring swivel; though the best plan, that I know of, to fire any gun, that is not *forged on purpose, for* the spring swivel; because the fore part of the punt then takes the pull, upon the same principle that an arch bears a heavy weight. It was Singer who showed me this plan; and, for my mode of simply fixing it to the gun, vide plate of the "*Invisible Approach.*" The gun, with a breeching, goes nearly as far back as the rope will stretch (say an inch or two), and then *springs forward again for about a foot;* unless checked by a notch in the stock, which should butt against the gunning-bench.

The question—the grand object—therefore is, how

to *take off the recoil* in the *best* manner? I mentioned the experiment of the swivel to several of the leading gunmakers, and, although they had all plenty to *say* on the subject, I could not meet with one who was able to *do* any thing towards the proper attainment of the object.

It would take pages to state their different plans. But enough of them: a few lines are sufficient; and these to say that however plausible their inventions may appear in a counting-house conversation, not one of them would answer *all* purposes, when fairly brought to trial.

I was, therefore, notwithstanding all their consultations, turned adrift to seek my own means of accomplishing the object; and I shall therefore, under the next head, give a sketch of the plan to which I have had recourse.

(I must crave the indulgence of nine-tenths of my readers for having trespassed on them with this insipid detail, as I have some few brother sportsmen in this way, who would value it more than all the rest of the book put together. Moreover, it may be the means of preventing accidents, which frequently happen to those who use swivels, and particularly if they do not fix them with judgment.)

The barrel of a punt-gun, to be in good proportion, should, I conceive (including the patent plug, of about six pounds weight, and from two to three inches in length), be about seventy or eighty pounds weight, from seven to nine feet long, and from an inch and a quarter to an inch and a half bore, according to the one length and weight, or the other.

The smaller the bore is, in *reason*, the further you

can kill at a small number of birds; but the larger size of these two shoots the best, and most regular pattern. Any thing beyond that size seldom answers.

It may, of course, be made on the same proportion to any size; but, although a gun much beyond this size will kill more birds at a shot, I am inclined to think, from what I saw of the one at Poole, that it will not kill so far in proportion. As some proof that Singer was not very partial to this gun, I need only state that, some months after I saw it fired, I received a letter from him making an offer of it for sale; which, as he is a man of long experience in the business, I conclude he would not have done, if the gun had perfectly suited him. Not having been able to sell it, when I last saw him, he had then had it lengthened: but still it failed; and he has since got another.

The barrel, in forging and filing, should be left well filled up, and, in every part, substantial.

NEW PLAN FOR FIRING TWO POUNDS (OR TWO POUNDS *AND A HALF*) OF SHOT TO THE BEST ADVANTAGE; AND, AT THE SAME TIME, EASING THE RECOIL OF A SWIVEL-GUN.

As guns to carry a pound of shot at a time are now to be constantly seen on almost every part of the coast, as well as in most of the fen countries, the very few men who formerly had them are now surrounded by rivals; and therefore, in order still to keep the lead, some of them have had recourse to using guns that carry from one pound and a half to two pounds of shot. The recoil, however, from *these* guns is so tremendous, that most of the men who used them have met with some accident or other, and are therefore giving them up. The desideratum then is to accomplish this with no more recoil, or risk of accidents, than there is with other guns, and thus to have an advantage over the host of ordinary gunners.

The plan that I have adopted is as follows:—

A pair of barrels put together so as to fire *two circles, each one partly eclipsed with the other:* the *one* ignited by *percussion*, and the *other* by a *flint*, by which means the trifling difference of the *two separate modes of ignition* makes such an *immense difference in the recoil*, as to reduce it to a mere nothing in comparison. The eclipsed part of the circles, when the two barrels are fired together, puts into the paper at least a fourth more shot than any one barrel could be made to do; and the *enormous weight of metal* not only *gives additional strength* to the double discharge, but *also to either barrel* when you fire them *separately*, which, of course, you have the option of doing; and therefore you are never obliged to discharge an extra pound of shot in waste, as with the huge single guns before alluded to. Moreover, the gun, on my plan, cuts two united lanes through the birds, instead of wasting half the shot in the water, and in the air, which is the case when the charge is contained in *one* large *circle*. In short, this plan forms, as it were, a kind of oval to suit the shape of the object: and thus, at the moment that one part of the birds are being killed by the detonater, the others are just *conveniently* opening their wings for the flint barrel, though they have not time to rise; *because* I have here *eased the recoil*, and got the barrels together so as to do the business *point blank*.

The mode of easing the recoil is by means of a long loop, worked on, between, and under, the barrels; and the swivel-pin going through a *slider, on which rests the whole weight of the gun.* The space within this loop (about eight inches), with the exception of an inch and five-eighths that is taken up by the slider, is filled with a *spiral spring*, which has a play of rather more than two inches; (and if it had even four or five inches of play, I should think it would be all the better.) Consequently, before any *jar* can take place to *interrupt the point blank delivery of the charge*, the shot has left the gun, which is, afterwards, brought forward again by the reaction of the spring. The loop *should be* made of horse-nail stubs, and forged on to the barrels. Mine is not so; therefore if this part fails, the fault lies with Mr. Fullerd, and not with me. Suppose this *was* to give way?—which would be almost impossible, *if done as it ought to be*—then you have a ring in the *stock* (all of which, except a moveable but, is of *cannon metal*) with a reserve rope that takes up the recoil immediately.

It was the opinion of a distinguished officer in the navy, before whom I fired this gun several times, that my plan for easing the recoil would answer extremely well for the *carronades*, or at all events, for the *ships' swivels*, in His Majesty's service; and I therefore had made a rough model for the inspection of himself and friends. If, however, the Lords of the Admiralty should honour me so far as to think the suggestion worthy of notice, I have only to say that Mr. Westley Richards, of Birmingham, is the mechanic who so ably manufactured the one I have, after the model and instructions that I sent him. Indeed there is no one else yet capable of executing the order*.

Here is an outline of the plan in question, which has so amply repaid me for the trouble I have had, in overcoming all obstacles, that I shall, under the next head, give directions for it, assisted by explanatory engravings.

Before this gun, &c. was found to answer every purpose, it went through several hands:—Mr. D. Egg; Mr. Fullerd; Mr. Joseph Manton; Mr. Westley Richards; Mr. Parsons, of Salisbury, and Mr. Long, of Andover (now with Lancaster); besides journeymen in my own employ; and, consequently, as so many artificers have been *separately* occupied in completing it, I may have safely defied any one of them before I published it to turn out precisely the same kind of article.

Since the 5th and 6th editions, I have tried the gun and punt, in every possible way; and no plan that I had ever before seen was worthy of being compared to this. I shall, THEREFORE, NOW GIVE engravings of the WHOLE CONCERN; by which means I shall secure to myself the pleasure of being the first to publish what has cost me much trouble to complete; and which many are now imperfectly copying, and may perhaps be passing off for their own invention.

* The only objection at the Admiralty was "the trouble of keeping it clean!" Now I have had my swivel afloat, for weeks at a time, in all weathers, and never did any thing to it, except occasionally working into it, with a brush, plenty of neat's foot oil.

EXPLANATION OF MY PLAN FOR EASING THE RECOIL OF A SWIVEL-GUN, CARRONADE, OR SHIP'S SWIVEL.

The following are the dimensions of the apparatus for a swivel gun, which carries about a pound of shot. But if the apparatus is adapted to a carronade or ship's swivel, it must be more than proportionably stronger, because a carronade, from being so very short, has such a severe recoil.

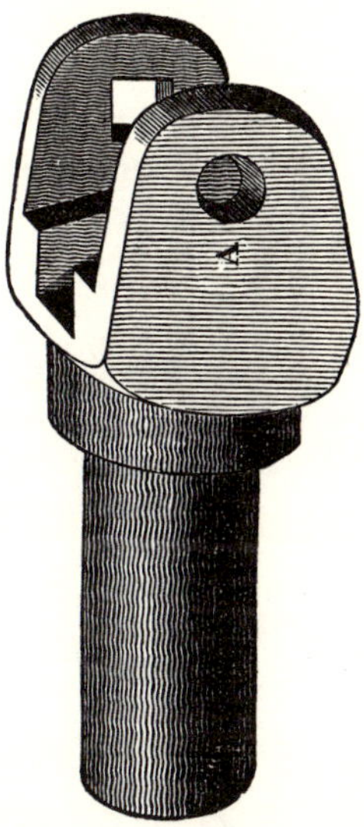

A. THE SWIVEL, on which the gun rests, and which, it may be observed, is made as short, and compact, as the working, up and down, of the gun will admit of, in order to avoid, as much as possible, all extra strain occasioned by lever; as, of course, the longer the ears of the swivel, the more severe the strain on the neck, and on every thing else below it.

Size. { Height, altogether $9\frac{1}{2}$ inches.
Thickness of the ears in the thinnest part (where the pin goes through), each one $\frac{1}{2}$ an inch.
Diameter of the upper circle, neck, or collar, $2\frac{1}{2}$ inches.
Diameter of the lower cylinder, or stem, $1\frac{1}{2}$ inch. }

Weight—$7\frac{1}{2}$ pounds.

The wooden block of the punt, or whatever the gun is fired from, *receives* both the neck and the stem, so that on this plan the lever, or strain, operates only as far as the lower part of the ears.

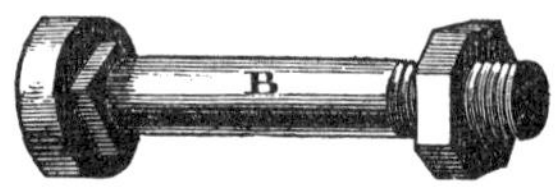

B. THE SWIVEL-PIN.

Diameter—of the cylindrical part, $\frac{3}{4}$ of an inch.
Length—(exclusive of the threads of the screw, and the head and square shoulder) 3 inches.

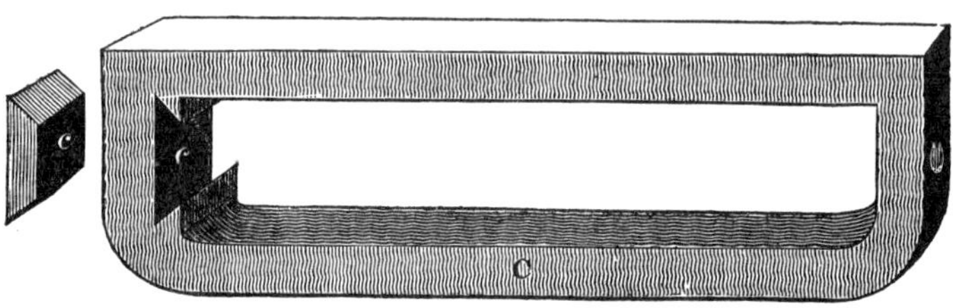

C. THE LOOP, which should be forged with, and made as a part of, the barrel; or, at all events, welded on, so that no recoil could tear off, or loosen it, because *if merely soldered on—I would never answer for its safety.*

Length—altogether, 10 inches. *(If longer, and therefore able to admit a longer spring, I should say all the better.)*

c. A little wedge of elm, or walnut-wood, which is pushed into the mortise, *c*, in order to ease the jar that is occasioned by the slider, G, coming in contact with the hinder part of the loop, on *re*-action taking place.

This piece of wood must, of course, be replaced with a fresh one, when nearly worn level with the iron.

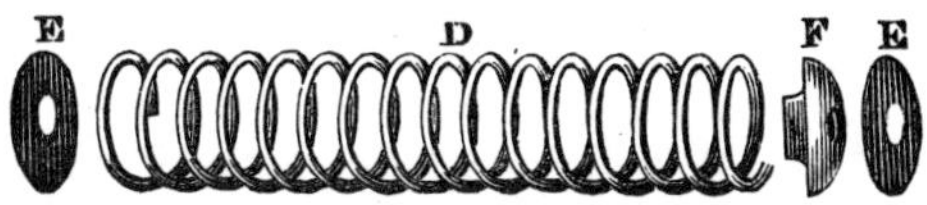

D. The spiral spring*, which is closed by the recoil of the gun, and which, *in the reaction*, sends the gun forward, and up to its place again.

Length—6 inches *(and if* 8 *or* 10 *inches, or more, in order to have so much the further play, I conceive it would be a great improvement on what is here sketched).*
Diameter—outside, an inch and half.
Substance of the wire, of which the spring is made—nearly $\frac{1}{4}$ of an inch in girth.

[In the last edition I mentioned (though would not, till tried, recommend) the late Mr. Fullerd's plan, and a *flat* spring. This has been since tried, and totally

* What are the odds that coachmakers do not some day apply this kind of spring to *carriages*?! The weight of one is only 10½ oz.; that of 8 stage-coach springs 254lbs.!!

failed. No springs have yet answered but those of Westley Richards.]

E.E. TWO ROUNDS OF LEAD, to save the spring, the boss F, and the shoulder of the pin H, from the harder contact of iron. COPPER is BETTER; and an *old* penny-piece the very model for it.

F. A BOSS, to fill up that end of the spring which has nothing to prevent it from swerving.

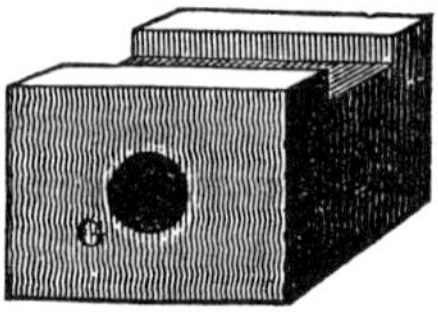

G. SLIDER, of solid iron, *on which rests the whole weight of the gun;* through which works the swivel-pin B; and into the female screw of which goes the male screw of H, which is the next, and last, comparti-ment here shown.

H. A LONG PIN, to support the spring, and prevent it from swerving. The thick end, or shoulder, on the left, *fits tight* into the inner circle of the spring. The cylinder (where the H is marked) is a bit of box-wood, put on to fill up the inside of the spring which, when forced together, by the recoil, brings the rounded end of this wood in contact with the boss, F; for which reason I put before it a piece of thick Indian-rubber, in order to ease the jar.

[When the recoil takes place, the pin is forced out

through the hole in front of the loop C, for as many inches as the spring has play; and this *pin*, by the way, *must have a square point*, in order to be unscrewed, with a key, when removed from the slider G.]

I shall now, to the relief of the reader, as well as myself, conclude these directions with a sketch of all the apparatus put together, for shooting:—

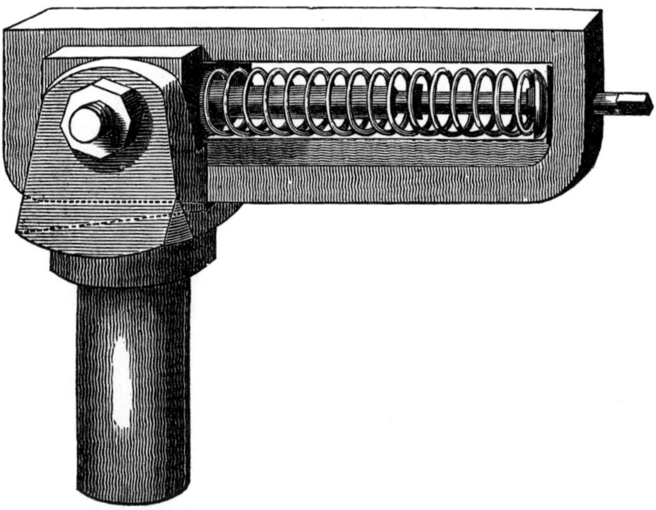

Intricate as this may appear, in explanation, I can assure my readers that I have used it on salt water for *four successive winters*, and had no trouble whatever in keeping it free from rust, except having to anoint it, occasionally, with mercurial ointment, and keep it always greasy, by means of working, with a brush, into every part of it, plenty of *neat's foot* oil. Moreover, I had no occasion to take the apparatus to pieces till the end of each shooting season.

TRIAL of the great double gun, after being fresh

bored by Tom Fullerd and John Hussey, in presence of Mr. Joseph Manton and myself (attended by Mr. Charles Manton, Penn, Hussey, Asell and son, and most of the best workmen), at Bayswater Firing-ground, May 2, 1827.

Target, 26 sheets of thick brown paper, 2 feet 4 by 2 feet 2. Distance, 90 yards.

Shot No. 1 (but the gun was not more than two-thirds loaded, for want of safe means of fixing it).

	No. of grains in 1st sheet.	Ditto through 26th sheet.
Flint barrel	75	31
Detonating barrel	64	30
Both barrels together	102	53

A round was then fired from the best barrel of a common double gun, at 26 sheets *nearly double the size of the above.*

8 0

Then a reputed good single gun.

9 0

We then stuck up a very large open sheet of brown paper, in order to try the difference at 40 yards, with No. 1 shot. Result—

One barrel of great gun	690
Ditto of little gun	50
Ditto of single gun	80

[N. B. Since this trial, we fired the barrels, at the same distance, from the punt, and on the water, where we could put the *full charge of* 20 *ounces in each barrel;* and the result was—

Flint . 106 Detonater . 102, and equally strong.]

By the foregoing trial we see how ridiculous it is to

draw any comparison (which many people are ignorant enough to do) between a common shoulder-gun, and a huge punt-gun; though the punt-gun had here every disadvantage, by being tilted out of its true aim, every time it was discharged; as the make-shift, by which I fired it, was merely a rough block of elm, with a hole for the swivel; and on such uneven ground, that I fired every shot in jeopardy, lest the gun should upset and break the locks, not to say a word of breaking my bones.

BEST MODE OF IGNITION FOR A PUNT-GUN.

With regard to flint or detonater, I have, till a few years ago, used only the former with a *swivel-gun;* but they have both been tried by the men who constantly use these guns, and the far greater proportion have decided in favour of the flint. They say that the recoil from a detonater is so sudden as to shake every thing too much; and also, that the birds, by night, set up their heads at the flash of a priming, just enough to be a much better target; and, therefore, the detonater does not kill so many. I merely give this report as I had it from some of the best performers. And, as to rain—a lock-cover, of either patent leather and sailcloth, lined with flannel, or the leg of an old water-boot (the East Yarmouth fashion), will keep the lock as dry as when in a house, if the shooter leaves it on, and either acquires the knack of taking aim under his gun, or has little elevated sights to project above the gun-cover.

Since the fourth edition I have well tried the detonater with the *double* swivel-gun, on the plan for which it became necessary. It killed better than I expected, though I was obliged to give up the *copper cap to it* as *not* being *safe.* I, therefore, got Joe Manton to put me a breeching for his copper PRIMERS, which *for these* LARGE DUCK-GUNS answer better than any thing I can describe; because THEY give the *only possible means of combining a* SHORT COMMUNICATION *with* PERFECT SAFETY. But, nevertheless, I agree with the gunners that, if I had a *single* swivel-gun, it should have a *flint* lock.

NIGHT CARTRIDGES;

AND

Improved Method of Loading a Large Gun.

The best method, among the old gunners, for loading their punt-guns, was to unship them; and, after wiping them out, to put the powder in a wooden measure that fitted into the caliber. [Why a *wooden* measure?—Because if a metal one dropped overboard—good b'ye to it!] Then to place the *gun perpendicular, leaving the measure in the muzzle;* in order that the powder may fall to the bottom of the breeching. Some used a powder-cartridge, and pricked it through the touch-hole, like a cannon; but this could only be done with a *common* breeching. They wadded with loose oakum; brown paper; pasteboard; or old hat;—loaded with shot, in precisely the same manner as with powder;—and then added just enough oakum, or paper, to prevent the charge from getting loose. But this plan always put the shooter to the inconvenience of unshipping his gun;

and was, of course, rendered impracticable where the gun was too heavy to be raised from the stanchion. What was the consequence? The powder and shot were not half rammed home; and the killing, and even the safety of the gun, became a matter of doubt. I shall now, with great pleasure, though it is against my own sport to divulge it, give my new plan to all my brother-sportsmen; and I flatter myself that those who have sufficient confidence in my advice to try it, will say that they never loaded with so much expedition or comfort; and that their large guns never shot so strong, so close, or so regular by the ordinary modes of loading. To the point, then, as I hate preface and prosing. Supposing your gun was from 80 to 100lbs. in weight, and carried a pound of shot. Take the same measure of powder as of shot, which in weight would be about two ounces; and, *with the gun in a horizontal position*, put it all the way to the breeching with the loading-spoon A.

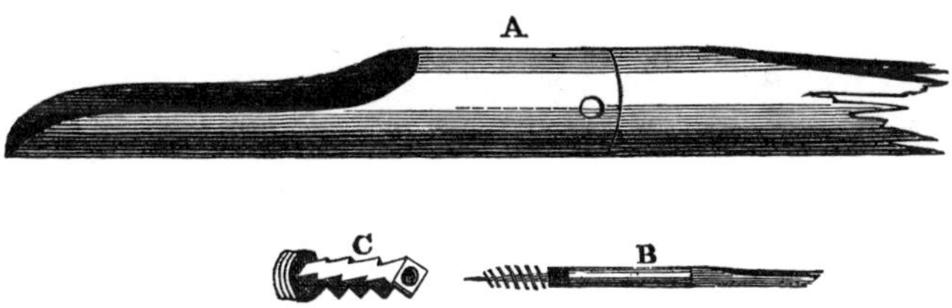

Taking care to keep *upwards* the *black*-painted, or flat, part of the loading-rod; by which you know that the *open part of the cylinder must be upwards.* The *upper part* of the *rod* is made *flat,* in order to *feel it* in the *dark,* when shooting by *night.* *When the powder is home, elevate* the muzzle as much as you can; turn round the loading rod; and, after giving it a shake, *draw it out* with the *black*, or *flat, part downwards.* Then reverse the rod, and *work the powder well into the centre-hole, with the small end of it,* C*; because *when loaded* in a *horizontal position* no wadding whatever will drive *cannon*-powder sufficiently home to fill the centre-hole of a solid breeching; the consequence of which is slow shooting with a flint; and repeated missing fire with a detonater. (This I never proved till last winter. The want of having discovered it before has cost me hundreds of birds; and had almost converted me to the opinion of many gunners, that "patent breechings never answer for large guns.") Having thus properly lodged your powder, you have then only to add the wadding; while doing which, elevate the gun as much as you can.

Now, then, to the plan for the *shot.* Why did cartridges always shoot in patches? Because the thickness of the paper interfered with the regular delivery of the shot. Why was not very thin paper adopted? Because the form of a shot-cartridge could not be preserved without some substance of paper; and moreover, without this we could not draw out the charge. But I have now remedied all these little inconveniences, by the most simple means; and, so far from claiming any credit for the plan, I think we were all in the dark not

* C should be small enough *to go well into the centre-hole,* in order to clean it out, if required. On *my* plan of loading, the little worm B, which will go well into the centre-hole, will be quite sufficient to draw out the wadding, or any thing else. The small end of this loading-rod cannot be too light; because, if heavy, it would overpower your hand, and make you spill the powder in filling it: particularly when loading afloat.

to have thought of it ages ago. Take, for a *punt-gun*, *thin cartridge*-paper (or, for a common gun, ladies' curling-paper), and place it thus to the mould, B.

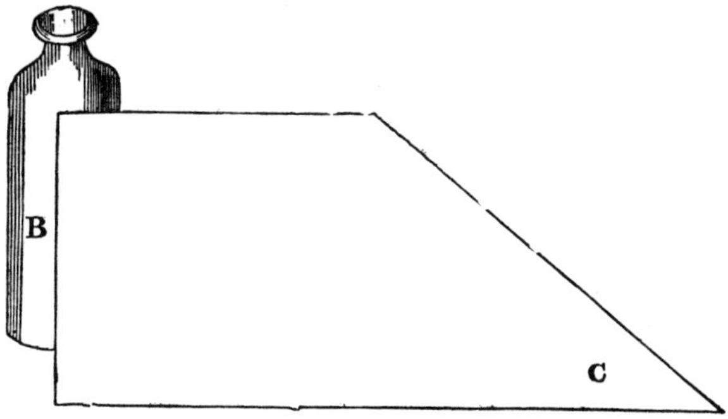

Roll the mould on a hard board, or table, till the paper has been wound as close as possible round it. Then tuck the corner, C, tight into the *concave bottom* of the mould; and afterwards press in all the lower edge, in order to form a bottom. Close it with sealing-wax, which is better than paste; as that soon gets damp. Having thus formed your cartridge, put the mould, with the cartridge round it, into the receiver, D, and press, or stamp, the mould hard on the table, to equalize the bottom of the cartridge. The receiver should be broad below, in order to stand firm on the table. The dotted lines show its cylinder, which should be just *within* the size of that of the gun.

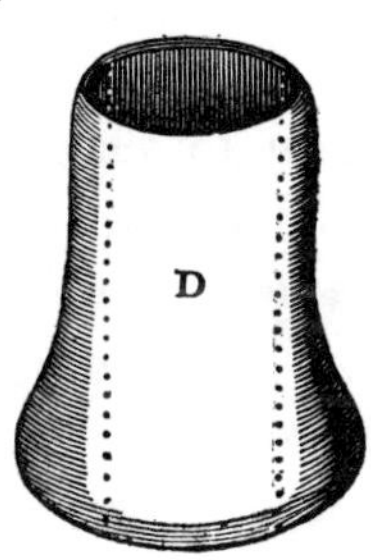

Then take the head of the mould; and, by giving it a little turn round, it will become disengaged, and draw out, leaving the paper in the cylinder. Put in your charge of shot; and, while so doing, shake it well down in the receiver; as this will make it shoot close and regular. Take off the receiver, and your cartridge remains, formed on the table. You have then only to close the top of it, by turning down the ends as compactly as possibly, and tie it together, *longitudinally*, with a piece of fine sailmaker's twine, in a hard *sailor's* (not a " grandmother's") knot. Put a piece of oakum, sponge, or any thing that may be held well by the worm of a ramrod. Tie round *that* another sailor's knot, and your cartridge is completed, thus—

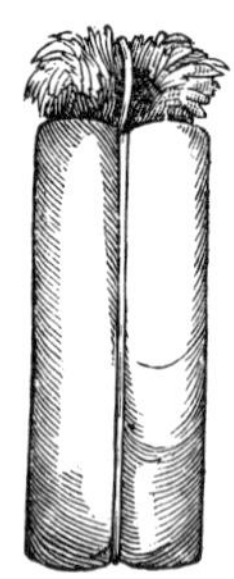

[I had, at first, used curling paper, even for a punt-gun; but I found that, when a little damp, it would burst *in loading;* and, although cartridge-paper is too thick for a sporting gun to shoot regular with, yet a *punt*-gun invariably does well with it; and particularly with my system of *mixing neat's foot oil with the shot.*]

Put the cartridge into the gun with the *oakum head upwards*, and you may *press* it down tight with the ramrod, as the smallest and worst of worms will draw it out with the greatest ease; and in any position, should you wish to unload your gun, change the size of your shot, &c. I made several of these cartridges for a musket, to stop crippled geese with; and, if I wanted to load in a hurry, I put the oakum end downwards, *without any other wadding*, and they shot very well. But, when I had time, I loaded as before directed; and found that even in a shoulder-gun, *these* cartridges shot better than the common mode of loading. If used in a *double* gun, the oakum heads must fit sufficiently tight to prevent the recoil of one barrel from jarring the charge of the other. But this very rarely occurs with any kind of *cartridge*, if it fits tolerably well. I have now tried at least five hundred rounds of these cartridges in my huge double gun, and they answer so well that I never use any thing else, unless I want Eley's for long wild day-work; and his cartridges, by the way, would never draw out, till I got him to put on them my oakum top-knots. But for *game* shooting all these little things are not required;—here we may "leave well enough alone," and be content with having every thing to the summit of our wishes, if we only know how to make use of it.

For a box to take cartridges afloat, and keep them perfectly dry, see the one that I have put in the plate with gunning-punt and gear.

Having now loaded our gun, nothing remains but the priming, for which I should recommend a small pistol-flask, with a *top* that *holds just enough for the pan;* by which means we are not so liable to overload the pan, or spill the powder in the dark. Clean your touch-hole after every shot with a clipped feather; poke a little of the *fine priming* powder into it, before you fill the pan; and always thoroughly wipe out your barrel with a ring-nosed ramrod (as shown in plate with gear) after every shot; not only for safety's sake, in case of a spark being left behind; but because you may have to put your gun by, loaded, for a night—or perhaps a week—before it may be fired again. Here is all that need be said on the unentertaining, though useful, subject of loading a large gun; and, when any one will favour me with a better plan, I will not only discard mine for it, but tear from my pages this tedious explanation.

I cannot resist stating, that when I invented this large gun, many people sarcastically observed, "How can he load it?" When the spoon and cartridges were contrived—then it was, "How is it possible to draw the charge?" Why, *without* the cartridges I can do *this*, by drawing the wadding and then shovelling out the shot with the loading-spoon. But the *other* we can do even *under sail*, by standing on deck, astride the gun, and using the rod over-handed. What other difficulties can they make out? Only let me know—and I am all ready for them!

CANDLE-CARTRIDGES.

We have now an improved method of making these cartridges:—Get a tin, or copper, cylinder, within the size of your caliber, and stop it up, at one end, with a piece of either wood or cork—no matter what—previously to filling it. Then melt some tallow, till quite warm, and pour it on your charge of shot, where the tallow will find its way into all the interstices. Let the cartridge remain till quite cold, and it will come out as well formed as any mould candle. You have then only to case it in thin paper, for which sufficient allowance must be made in the size of your moulding-cylinder; so that, *when all is complete*, the *cartridge* will *fit nicely* to the caliber of your gun. If you want many of these cartridges, you should have plenty of moulds; otherwise you lose much time in waiting for them to get properly cold and hard. The candle-cartridges (like Eley's) should be well rammed, in order to prevent their "ball-ing."

Though I condemn tallow confined in wire, I can see no objection to it when merely covered with light paper. I am indebted to my friend Captain Ward for this discovery, and a schedule of its excellent performance.

FIRING.

The firing of these guns, at long distances, requires some practice, by reason that, before the shot can travel a hundred yards, the birds, if quick-sighted, will be on the move, particularly if they see the flash. No one had ever the kindness to tell me this, when I first used a long gun; till, after some time, wondering what was the matter that I could not kill (not being able to see through the smoke), I fired at a mixture of curlews and gulls; the latter of which were killed, and the others never touched.

By this I discovered, that the one, being quick-sighted and active birds, sprung before the shot got to them; while the others, not being able to get out of the way, were killed. A little elevation for the *gun* (in which a few shots at a mark will direct you), and a pretty good *elevation* for the *springing of the birds*, *according to what birds they are,* is absolutely necessary, and practice alone will best teach this. Suffice it to say, however, that a man, to be a good shot, with a large gun, has even more to *learn* than to shoot well in the field; particularly when he comes to cross shots at flocks going past, where, sometimes, there may be required a yard of elevation, and ten yards' allowance for the distance they are at, and the rapidity of their flight.

As it becomes necessary, *when approaching wild birds,* to be well concealed *in your punt,* you are obliged to fire these guns, lying down as close as possible on your chest. For which some have a wedge to support the breast. If you put your *cheek to the stock,* your *shoulder-bone* in contact with the *but,* or your second finger *behind the trigger,* you run a risk of having them severely *jarred;* but, if you manage the gun properly, the sensation, with a *light* charge, is no more than that of firing powder from a small gun; and the report, *to the shooter,* seems a mere nothing. To fire a stanchion gun, put your *left hand over the but,* and regulate it to the line of aim, while your *cheek gently grazes the back of the hand.* Put *all* the fingers of your right hand *before the trigger, keeping the thumb out of the way;* and be careful *not to let your knees come in contact with the timbers of the boat.* By observing well these directions, a child might fire this gun with as much safety as the smallest fowling-piece.

In firing a punt-gun (without any stanchion) from the *shoulder,* you must *lean hard* against the upper part of the padded but; and have the gun as *top-heavy* as you can possibly overbear, by which means the *friction of the stock against the "gunning-bench,"* and the check of your shoulder, prevents the gun from running too far under your arm. Never attempt to shoot a barrel so short as six feet in *this* way, as it might fly up and hurt you. Always try these guns with a quarter of a charge first; and increase the loading with an ounce of shot each round. By this means you avoid the risk of a recoil, as you then gradually ascertain how much ammunition can be fired with perfect ease to the shoulder.

If you are so fortunate as to get a *line* of birds, shoot rather *beyond* the *first* of them, which *will then be taken by* the *lower shot.* You may thus (with *mould* shot) sweep the water *from one to two hundred yards,* and possibly kill some of them all the way, from one of these distances to the other.

The advantage of a *stanchion gun* over a *shoulder duck-gun* is far more than that of the *latter* over a *common sporting gun;* and so generally has this of late years been found out, that, now-a-days, but little can be done without one, on any part of the English coast.

PUNT
FOR THE USE OF A STANCHION GUN.

A gunning-punt, which is very narrow, although it may row fast, is extremely dangerous, and will not answer for going in shallow water, which is the grand object, in order to get up to the birds before the tide has flowed high enough to drive them off their legs, and disperse them.

All round-bottomed punts, such as are used at Southampton and Itchen Ferry, and most of those at East

Yarmouth, are on a bad construction, except merely to sail about with a shoulder-gun; because they have such unsteady bearings, and are so built, that the gun, and the man's head who fires it, must appear considerably above the gunwale. The consequence is, that he frightens away half the birds which he ought to kill; and can never regulate his gun for shooting in the dark. In short, clincher and carvel built boats are only used by those, who, whatever they may fancy, are not finished masters of their business.

All gunning-punts should be as flat as possible in the bottom (except having the necessary "kammelling," to "give them life"); by which they draw far less water, and are so stiff, that it becomes impossible to capsize them. If an accident did happen, it would be by their *filling* and sinking, but *not upsetting*, as the before-mentioned boats might do; and, as a still further guard against which, *these* boats may be decked all the way from "stern to mid-ships," and half way round the sides.

The most destructive gunning-punt, for *one* hand, that I had seen up to 1824 (when I adopted my new plan), was about nine inches high, and drew scarcely two inches of water, with a man and his gun. This punt should be full *three feet broad, from about a yard before the stern;* decked all the way from the gunning-bench to the bow; and so sharp forward, that, when required, the bow may be shoved for several feet up the edge of the ground, so as for the gun to be raised at the but, rested on the "stem," and fired over the mud, before the tide flows high enough for a large gun to bear in the ordinary way. But, as in this case the recoil must be checked by the shoulder, I have only superficially described the punt, knowing, of course, that very few who shot for pleasure would adopt the system. Moreover, by fully explaining it, I should, instead of serving *sportsmen*, be only taking the bread from Buckle, the man who showed me the minutiæ of it, to put into the mouths of his rivals, whom he says he will, and, I believe, he safely may, give seven years to find it out, and be perfect masters as to building this punt, and then knowing how to use that and the gun. Although as much as is here mentioned may, of course, be known by every one who has seen the punt in question. Many boat-builders have seen it, and ridiculed the idea of not being able to go home and make precisely the same thing. Several, however, have been built by them to order, and, as yet, not one has been done right, though, of course, much like it in *appearance*. There is not a boat-builder in a thousand who knows any thing about punts, as the best gunners generally make their own, and keep the secret to themselves; or, at all events, from the boat-builders, who would otherwise be making them for every shooter in the port. The best way, therefore, is to get an able gunner to find head, and a good inland *carpenter*, who *works much better* and *neater* at *this light board work than a boat-builder*, to find hands and tools. I never could get a punt that would answer till I did this.

Several boat-builders have overhauled mine when they could find a chance to do so; and every one of their productions, that I have yet seen, was quite laughable; though, to all outward appearance, a good imitation. If, therefore, they succeed now, it is but fair to infer that it will be through the help of the engraving.

Having treated further, perhaps, than was necessary

on shooting punts in general, I shall conclude with explaining the one alluded to, which I have found to answer best, taking in consideration comfort, safety, and every other point requisite for those sportsmen to whom is offered this part of the book.

IMPROVED NEW PLAN FOR A GUNNING-PUNT*.

In 1822 I contrived, and in 1824 built, a punt which I have been using, and improving on, ever since; and which is now, I believe, rendered as complete as any thing yet invented, for the purpose of carrying the heavy weight of a *double* swivel-gun, with two men, and gear; but which, by the way, like sportsmen, dogs, and every thing else, is beginning to be worn out, just as it approaches perfection. Here, however, we have our model to renew from, and perhaps to improve on;—not so with ourselves;—for, after we have been all our lives making the voyage of discovery, and are just arriving off the land-mark of perfection, we are cast away on the rock of declining years; and thus it is that we are for ever excluded from the port. But enough of the sentimental—and now for the punt:—She must be decked over in every part, except leaving just room enough for the

* My punts have always had more beam and more "flam" than those of other shooters. This was much admired by a first-rate seaman—my friend, Captain John Symonds, R. N. He was at the building of the "Vernon;" and I am told she has more beam, &c., than any other of our frigates; and as to her excellence—I believe there is not a question.

shooter to lie to his gun, and the man to work to the birds; in order to do which, without his hand being shown too high, a part of the deck, on each side, must be made to "ship and unship." The deck should be formed of the lightest possible board, and covered all over with strong canvas; which helps to strengthen it, and renders it doubly water-proof. The only parts of the deck requiring strong support are the front, where a man has to stand, if he loads the gun afloat; and the place where is fixed on the light metal thowls. The space left open must be surrounded with bulwarks, which continue rising, in proportion as the punt becomes lower forward, to about four inches in height, and ending in a little stem, or second bow, that "ships and unships." So that, when wanting to go through a sea, you have only to "douse" the moveable back-stock of the gun, and ship this stem-piece, which elevates it well clear of the spray, and keeps the sea from coming into your punt. You must also trig up your gun, in the same way, when rowing stern foremost with two "hands;" or, otherwise, the man who pulls what then becomes the stroke oar, would have the gun too much in his way to be able to row. *He* pulls merely by little copper thowls that ship into the bulwarks, and are carried in one small bag, next to the other which holds the spy-glass. See plate.

The mast ships, on either side the gun, in little cylinders that should be bored out of a solid piece of elm, and fixed so as to be water-proof. When under sail, both "hands" should get as much "aft" as possible, in order to prevent the punt from "griping;" and, as she will then be rather "by the stern," the gun will point too high, unless you lower the muzzle. For this purpose I have invented a moveable support, on which you may let down the gun; and then go forward enough to fire it, when running before the wind.

Where the birds are much used to gunning-punts, firing under sail, from this kind of craft, is a murdering recipe; because my punt, when under sail, at a fair shot from birds, appears like a large boat some hundred yards off. When others "set," I sail;—when others sail, I "set." (The only way to take a lead in any thing is not to copy other people, by which you are sure of doing nothing beyond mediocrity!)

While the stem-piece is on, so much of this punt is shut up as to be well defended from shipping a sea; and when the open part is closed with oiled Russia duck, which, by means of two large holes in it, is lashed round the waists of the shooters, she becomes a complete life-boat. But this "Esquimaux," as we call it, I never had occasion to use but once; and then more for trial than from necessity. It, however, makes a delightful covering in bad weather. This punt *may* be made air-tight, and a regular life-boat *without* the *cover*. But, on *this* plan, I found that we were much inconvenienced, for want of room to "stow" away the mast, oars, gunrods, &c., and therefore I opened her again all the way under the deck.

This punt should be rounded, athwartships, about an inch, and "sprung fore and aft" at least three inches. Mine is about four, by which she has more "life in a sea;" and I put on a little wooden shoe, just under her bow, which holds her on steady when you run her nose aground; and saves her from rubbing when landing on a gravelly shore. I have of course *also* a defence of thin sheet *copper*.

Except a few little cross-pieces of well seasoned *oak, each floor and timber should be formed all in one, with a piece of tough hoop ash,* which must be well boiled, in a large copper, and then rounded to the proper shape. In order to make these timbers fit without a vacuum, the sides must of course be filled up with angle-pieces, which should be cut to rather a square shape, where the sides and bottom meet, and of course be round inside, in order to meet the hoop timbers. These angle-pieces, being *merely to fill up the space,* require no strength, and therefore a long piece of deal, or, in short, the lightest wood, is best for them. Light bottom-boards are of course required, in order to protect the timbers, &c., and with them we can have sheepskins, rugs, or many other things more comfortable, and less likely to lose the "traps" in, than rushes or straw. (For this great improvement in timbers, I believe, we have to thank the Americans.)

The sides, "amidships," on this plan, being so very low, may be "flammed" out as much as you please; because they are not more than two or three inches above the water; and the rising deck looks just like the water itself. Thus all that the birds can see "end on" is the bulwarks, which appear much less than even the smallest launching-punt.

About eight inches above the surface of the water is the best height for the gun, in dark nights, or in a dead calm; but in rough water, the higher the gun is fixed, the more birds you will kill.

The stanchion should be "shipped" into a block of *elm,* which ought to be fixed *to nothing but the centre plank,* and this plank, *just where the bolts go through,* should be left an inch and a half thick. (The block and centre plank of the punt that I built are *carved in one solid piece;* but for this I was forced to cut down a fine elm tree on purpose.) The gun should be fixed *a little on one side.* To do this nicely, put your punt afloat, lie down to your gun, and *see* that all *is* "in trim" *every way,* before you bore the holes for the bolts. By this means of fixing the knee, or block, the jar of the gun is all thrown on *one strong point,* and every thing else is carried back with it; and therefore the sides, and every other part of the boat, may be quite as light as those of one which is only required for a shoulder gun.

Every thing should be slightly tacked together, and balanced afloat, with the gun "shipped," and the gunners on board, before the deck is put on, or the knee fixed; otherwise when the shooter lies down, to the left of his gun, the chances are ten to one that he finds his punt out of "trim." If means of easing the recoil are adopted, the punt may then be made of even lighter materials than the Poole canoe. I need scarcely observe, that a punt, of the *same size,* which is *light,* will *drown* a *heavy one;* as the latter, for want of "life," labours in a sea, and gets filled; while the other flies over every thing, without taking in a drop of water: add to which, a light punt may get out of danger, by being hauled across the mud, when the other is obliged to "weather it." But with a TWO *hundred* pound gun this cannot be done; and therefore we want a punt that we can "live in." I formerly observed that where *nothing but* the *shoulder* had to take the gun, I should prefer my boat principally built of *cork,* which it would be utterly impossible to sink. One with hoops and canvas would be still better; and, I have no doubt, might be made to answer both for launching and 'float-shooting.

In approaching birds, the shooter, *having nothing else to attend to,* may be constantly *ready* with his gun; so that, if they fly up, he can always ensure being able to fire before they have risen twenty yards; while *another person* has *only to manage the punt.* This *he* will do by a *setting pole,* or skulling in a little crotch with a single oar, according to the depth of water. As either the one or the other will be *under cover of the front bulwark,* they are less *visible* than *working-sticks* or *paddles* at the *sides.* Paddles on the principle of a bird's foot, and worked *inside,* would be desirable.

I have since built a long narrow punt for my single gun, with a rope breeching (as before described under the head of "punt-gun"), that goes through the stem. *This* punt will certainly row past the other as fast as if she was moored; and is much lighter. But I can always get at least twenty yards nearer to birds with the large one, because, from her breadth, she admits of so much lower a deck; and in her I can fire while quite out of sight; whereas, with the rope breeching, I must put my shoulder to the but, and thereby show my head to the birds. In rough weather, too, these narrow crafts are such "wet boats" as to make shooting more a misery than a pleasure. All punts of this kind should have no iron about them. All the nails, and every thing required in metal, should be of wrought *copper,* for which reason they cannot be completed in the *best* manner without considerable expense.

Let me now conclude this narcotic essay on punt-building by a reference to a new plate, executed, under my directions, by Mr. Varley and Mr. Adlard; with a scale of dimensions, which will, I trust, be found more agreeable than troubling my readers with marks of reference.

Explanation.

N.B. *Except* the *detached part* of the *gun*, all here shown is according to the scale; though the *lower* view of the punt is, by the perspective, a little thrown out of the proportion for *measuring*, as well as of her " rakish" (or prettily shaped) appearance. But this has been done in order to show some of the inside.

1. Broadside of the punt, shut up for the night; or for travelling on the carriage.
2. Moveable support for gun.
3. Enlarged view from part of the gun, as shipped in the block, showing the detonating lock, and the cannon-metal stock.
4. Travelling carriage on lancewood springs. The fore pieces take off (as shown by dotted lines), and then you have only to drag the hind wheels, (see chain;) roll your punt up, (see roller in front); and then refix the two fore pieces. Put some hay-bands under your gun, lash every thing on with a cart line, and you are then in marching order, for any part of the world.
5. " Truck," for shipping gun; and conveying ashore that and the gear, birds, &c.
6. Perspective view of the punt, which we will now overhaul from stern to stem.

N.B. Thin copper at each end, in order to cut through the ice. [*This proved invaluable during the last hard winter!*] One skulling-crotch shipped; the other stowed away, in the case, on deck. These should be made fast with a piece of string; or, being of copper, they would sink, if they fell overboard.—Starboard " trap-hatch," unshipped, for skulling or setting. This should be stowed away under the side-deck; but I have here thrown it overboard, in order to show it.—" Cleats;" to " make fast" sheet. Drawer for "cripple-stopping" ammunition. The moment the gunner has made a shot, he should " douse back stock," " up stem-piece," " on lock-cover," out with his little double gun, from the canvas curtain on the starboard side, and get " right aft" as quick

PUNT & GEAR FOR A 200 lb. GUN.

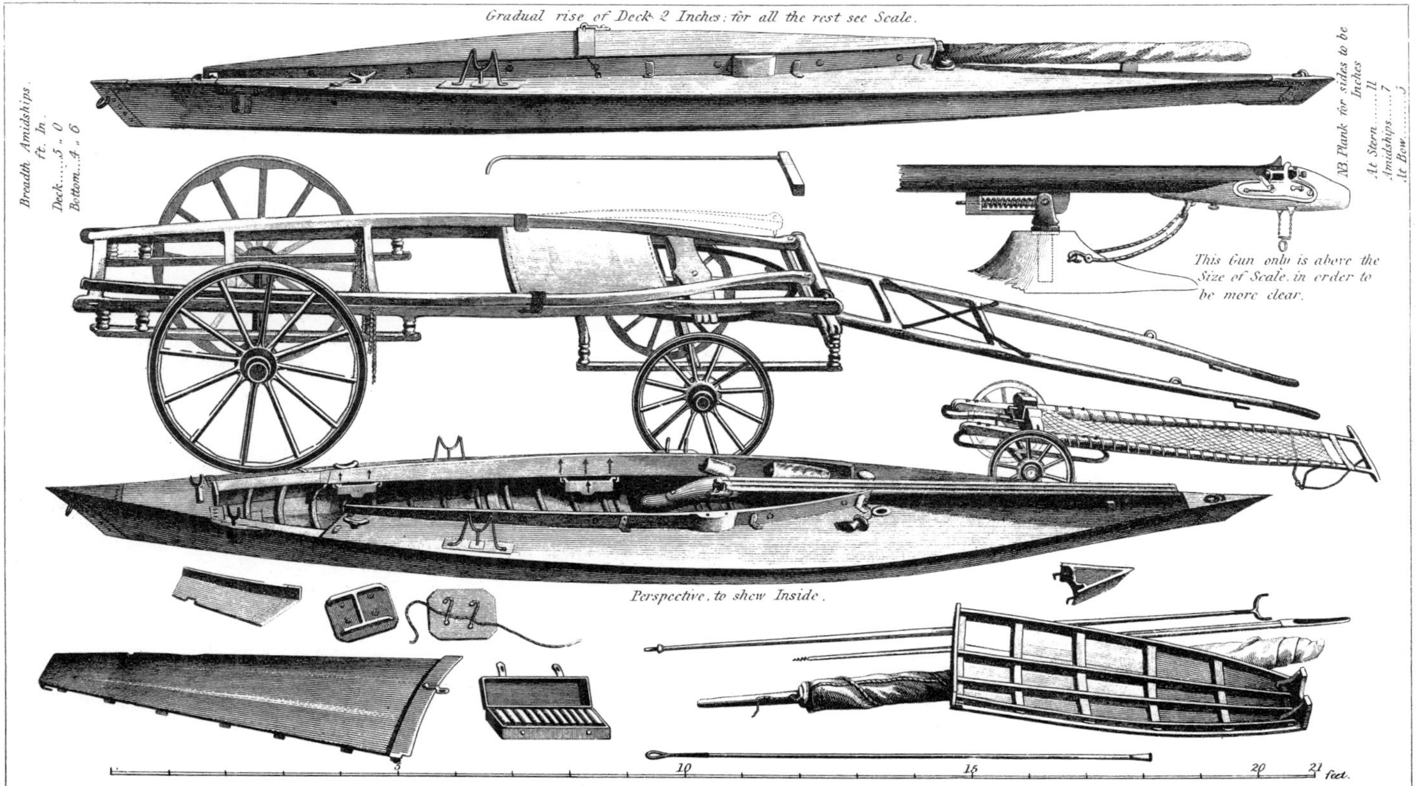

Invented by P. Hawker: Drawn by C. Varley, Engraved by H. Adlard & Published by Longman & Co. 1830.

as possible, and pop away at the cripples, while the skipper rows the punt in chase of them. [N.B. Sling this gun so that if it went off it could not injure you or your punt.]—The next drawer is for the small articles belonging to the large gun. These drawers should have just over them a small ledge, inside the bulwarks, or the wet will keep dribbling into them. They should be marked with black stripes, or you will have some plague in seeing where to ship them by night. The little marks round the outsides of the bulwarks are meant for the brass studs to which is buttoned on the "Esquimaux" cover.—The "*stem-piece,*" (or support for chest, when lying to gun), mudboards, covers, cartridge-box, setting-pole (or "sprit" for sail), loading-rod, sail, and ring-nosed ramrod (or cleaning-rod), conclude all the "traps" that it may be necessary to show; and then all you require is a few years' practice, in order to make a good use of them.

N.B. In the original plate I did not put those men which are in the gunning-punt in their *proper places for a "cripple chase,"* because *here* they have no sea to encounter, and have a dog, and other boats, to help them; and as *this* is *wholly* an *explanatory* plate, I have left out the men, in order to show better the interior of the punt.

*** In this edition I am now enabled to add that I have constantly used the punt herein prescribed for eight winters; and, had I followed my own advice, by making *every*thing of *copper,* I believe she would have been as good as ever for eight winters more. But, although she is yet serviceable, I have been induced to build another, which has not a particle of iron about her, except the two skulling crotches. She is nearly two feet longer than the one here shown;—has *two pairs* of *fixed* thowles—so that we shall always row *her stem* foremost—and the reserve-rope, or breeching for gun, is made fast to a ring in the extreme stem-piece, and comes from all the way *under* the deck on each side of the blocks with two thimbles, to which we lash, with a smaller rope, the ring in the gun-stock. Thus, from the great length, we have a spring of rope, in addition to the spring-swivel. Except having the centre-plank from the knee to the stem about an inch and $\frac{1}{4}$ thick (for the recoil), I have built this punt much slighter than any thing I had used before; and I have got the mast-steps further aft, by which improvement she never gripes, as the other would sometimes do, under a press of canvas. As far as I can yet judge, I am inclined to fancy her the best punt (for a *very* heavy gun) that ever went afloat. But as yet, I have only fired three shots since I launched her—one at a small trip of wigeon of which I stopped 8—the other at 3 geese, all of which I brought home; and, on my way into port, knocked down a single olive, flying, merely to discharge the gun. I was then unexpectedly called to town, in consequence of the 6th edition being out of print; so, in this one, can say nothing more about the new punt, except that the cost of her was just 35*l.* 14*s.* 10*d.*; and this by no means extravagant, considering the superiority of the workmanship. One to all *appearance* like her might be made for 6 pounds; and, after all, *for gunning*, not worth 6 shillings!

Having stated the foregoing improvements, the plate from Varley's drawing will be quite a sufficient guide for this punt, as well as for the original one.

Never use a punt which is too narrow or too upright in the sides—Captain Ward was near losing his life by being persuaded to do so. Beware also of *flat* decks,—they occasion miserably "wet boats," in every little breeze; and, in very hard weather, the water freezes on them before it will run off, and forms a mass of ice that makes your punt so heavy as to have no life in a sea, and therefore be liable to fill and sink.

The method of shooting wildfowl which I have last described is the best calculated for the amusement of a *gentleman*, as he may *go out between breakfast and dinner;* and, in *frosty* weather, perhaps kill his twenty or thirty couple in a day, followed by his companions, who may keep at a distance, to enjoy a sight of the sport; and afterwards join in the "cripple chase." [Vide plate.]

So far superior is this diversion to what people are aware of, that I have never yet met with a solitary instance of one sportsman, who had *seen it in perfection*, but what was quite elated; and preferred *even* a *sight* of it to the best day's game shooting in the kingdom. It is therefore condemned as an occupation for rustics only by those who know nothing whatever about it.

Invented & Sketched by P. Hawker — Eng^d on Steel by H. Adlard.

Commencement of a Cripple-Chase, after firing 2 lbs of Shot into a Skein of Brent Geese, & Two Wild Swans.

London: Published by Longman & Co.

Let those, who fancy punt-shooting such a dangerous amusement, compare the accidents that happen in it, with those in fox-hunting, battû shooting, or any other sport, and see in which they most frequently occur: though this pursuit is generally followed by poor men, who have the worst, the others, by gentlemen, who are provided with the best, of every thing. In Poole harbour, for instance, where the channels, at times, are far more dangerous than in most other places, I should, at a rough guess, say, there were, on an average, a hundred canoes; and yet, for these last twenty years, which is as long as I have known the place, I have never heard of but one man being drowned, and he was not only subject to fits, but had left the shore when in liquor.

I here allude to *open* punts, than which decked ones are of course infinitely less exposed to danger.

SHOOTING WITH A STANCHION GUN FROM A PUNT.

Now that we have *got* the *gun and punt together*, a few more words as to the shooting: those, who fancy that any one can shoot well into a large flock of fowl, will find themselves in a mistake. There is, I must repeat, much more knack in it than people are, at first, aware of; and, in my humble opinion, it is far more difficult than to kill double shots at game; because the man, who can quickly pitch his gun on, or just before, a partridge, has so little variation in distance, as the birds are generally from twenty to forty yards off, that without any further calculation, or practice, he might, in a slovenly manner, contrive to knock down the greater part of those at which he fires. But, in the other shooting, the different calculations of elevation, &c., are tenfold more difficult; and particularly if taking flying shots, at perhaps one hundred yards, from a boat that is rolling and pitching in a sea, and where one inch in aim might make the difference of twenty fowl at a shot, or not touching a feather. All this, however, is best gained by practice, though it may be right to caution the beginner against mismanagement, that might unjustly put him out of conceit with his gun.

In sitting shots, he must (as I before observed, and cannot too often repeat) remember, at *long distances*, to preserve a little elevation for his gun; and further, a good elevation for the birds springing at the flash, and perhaps being up *before the shot has time to reach them*.

On going to either hoopers or geese, he will, nine times in ten, have notice by the birds themselves when he is to fire, as *they*, previously to taking wing, *draw closer together and set their heads up*; so that he may keep on, even if it were to within forty yards, till they give the signal. And if at night (which is the only time he could get so near) they were still down, he should first take level; and then, previously to drawing the trigger, make some little noise, and by this means induce them to look up, before they receive their "allowance." By thus having their feathers open, and their stretched necks for a target, he will kill at least double the quantity that he would do when they were either sitting close down, or flying; as in the *one position* their *feathers* would be *closed*, and in the *other* the birds would be much *more scattered*, than when down.

The curres, dunbirds, &c. will generally give notice likewise. The ducks and wigeon not near so well; and the *teal* spring instantly, without giving the least notice; so that in shooting the *latter* birds, keep quiet, and fire as soon as you think you can make a tolerable shot. Always, however, get as near as you can. Rely on it, close quarters is the grand recipe for filling the bag, at this, and all other shooting. You must remember too that the sea, or any water, with a large flock of birds on it, deceives you extremely; insomuch that what many people *fancy fifty*, proves to be above a *hundred* yards. Take a novice afloat, and the first specimen he gives you of his ignorance in the art, is either to fire himself, or endeavour to persuade you to fire, at birds which are very far out of gunshot.

Curres.—We will now make a few short observations on the birds usually killed in this way. I will begin with the "*curres*" (a provincial term for all the various tribe of diving ducks), as they appear about October. These birds, when accustomed to the skirmishers of the coast, are generally worse to get at than any others; and you have then often no other alternative than paddling up a winding creek, so as to suddenly pop on them in turning a corner, and fire either sitting or just as they fly up. But when curres are, by frost, just driven to the coast from under the kind protection of some bird fancier's pond, they are a fine prey for a swivel gun; provided you hide the flash; get their heads up before you shoot; and are well armed with little double detonaters, to work away at the "cripples," after you have stocked the water with them, by the discharge of your artillery. For thus finishing the business, the percussion system is a *sine quâ non*, as these birds are sure to "duck the flash" *after*, if not before, being wing broken; and they will, when wounded, shrug themselves up so much, that you ought to get within fifteen yards, before you give them the *coup de grace*. Hundreds of sportsmen would be glad to take a punt, and follow you, on a fine sunshiny day, for this purpose; while you might either sit still and enjoy the fun, or be proceeding for some other attack. But the business must be done as quick as possible; or one half of the curres will be off, while you are killing the others. Cartridges and all other expeditious means are here desirable. *Curres* most frequently *keep afloat*, instead of going on the mud.

BRENT GEESE.—Towards November, or December, we have the brent geese, which are always wild, unless in *very* hard weather. In calm weather the geese have the cunning, in general, to leave the mud, as soon as the tide flows high enough to bear an enemy; and then they go off to sea, and feed on the drifting weeds. But when it blows so fresh, that they cannot weather it long enough to feed outside of the harbour, they *then continue inside the whole day;* though they most frequently take especial care to weather almost any thing, rather than trust themselves *there* at *night;* except when they are very short of food. If therefore you have water over the mud for your punt, you may often make a tolerable shot by setting, or sailing, even in mild weather, particularly when the tide has kept up high, and the geese, having become hungry, are just getting their legs, at the first ebb; and still more so if this happens towards sunset, when they feed greedily previous to leaving the harbour for the night.

In *mild* weather prefer following a small flock to a

large one. *Recollect, the more pairs of eyes, the wilder the birds.* A single goose is termed a "*pricked*" bird; that is—turned out of his company, which he is sure to be if he receives even the slightest wound.

Taking it for granted that my young reader now understands me, as to presenting the gun, I have only to give a few directions on the last, though not the least, thing, to be observed; his *getting the geese* which he may have *shot.* They take such a hard blow, that he will, generally, find the greater part of them, that are stopped by the shot, well enough to swim and dive with the greatest agility, and they will all invariably *make for the heaviest sea that is near.* The boat, which follows, therefore, should always *keep well on the outside of the birds;* and, if armed with some "*cripple stoppers*" (old muskets, or any small arms), so much the better; as, while you are rowing after one goose, the others may all get off to sea. If you are near enough to reach a wounded bird without a gun, take him *horizontally across the neck* with the *edge* of an oar, or you may thrash away at him to no effect, till you have splashed yourself from head to foot; so very hard are the upper coverts of his feathers. In shallow water, where he is not obliged to swim, a good light dog will do more in five minutes, than a party of men could do in an hour. But when once the dog is out of his depth, these birds are so quick in diving, that they will most probably escape from him.

When it blows fresh and the tides are very high, you will always do best by leaving the geese quiet: 1. Because they are then more dispersed, and there are then more *stragglers* to *catch a view of your broadside:* 2. because they are so buried in the waves that, if you shoot sitting, the water will intercept the shot; and, on their flying up, the wind is apt to disperse them, so much that you cannot kill many: and, 3. because they, finding no inducement to stay in one place, while there is no food to be got, have no other employment than to be constantly on the watch. Always, therefore, *wait till the "ground ebb;"* and then the birds, having been beat about, and starved, for perhaps all the flood, and all the after-flood*, will be so greedy for a good feed, that you will, at this time, get much nearer to them; and find them well congregated for a heavy shot; particularly if your punt draws so little water as to enable you to catch the birds on their legs. Moreover, you will have no difficulty in securing your cripples; many of which, in a high tide, escape to sea, while you are popping off the others.

HOOPERS, *or* WILD-SWANS.—When the winter further advances, and the birds are driven from Holland and the Baltic to the more genial climate of the south, and then followed by severe weather to the refuge they have chosen, their last alternative is to leave the fens, ponds, and decoys, and betake themselves to the sea-coast, in order to avoid starvation. Then, and then only, it is, that all this diversion may be enjoyed in perfection, and without much trouble or difficulty. We have then a variety of all kinds of wildfowl, and sport for every shooter. And it is at such a time as this only, we can expect to see the monarch of the tribe, the

* We have two tides on the Hampshire coast. The first as the water flows in from the Needles; the second as it comes down the Western Channel. The second is generally two hours after the first; so that, in high tides, the water sometimes keeps up for several hours.

hooper, or wild-swan. We had, during the hard winter in 1823, a fine specimen of all this on the Hampshire coast, the flats of which, off Keyhaven and Pennington, were, for some weeks, covered with ice and snow. Nothing could be more novel or beautiful than the appearance of the harbour, which was one solid region of ice, crowned with pyramids that had formed themselves of the drifted snow, and frozen like crystals; and, on the thaw, the harbour appeared like one huge floating island, as the ice which covered it was carried off by the fall of a high spring-tide. The effect of this huge body, with the wild-swans sitting upon it, while it receded, and looking as if formed by nature for the only inhabitants of such a dreary region, gave the spectator more the idea of a voyage to the arctic circle, than the shore of a habitable country. When the large bodies of ice were carried off, and nothing remained but those of a smaller size, the whole harbour was, of course, in arms with shooters, and had almost the appearance of a place that was besieged. The following morning, though it blew very hard, and poured with rain, every one was in arms for seven of the swans that again appeared, anxiously hoping that they might swim, or fly, near enough for a random shot; though the punters, from drawing too much water, required at least another half hour's flood before they could make the difficult attempt of getting at them in open day. By having a punt which drew less water than theirs, it was, therefore, my lot to have the first chance, if no one fired off a gun, in order to spoil the shot, which is a very common practice on this, and all other coasts. I, therefore, took the precaution of getting well round to windward; and when I had arrived as much to windward as one dare go to wildfowl, having previously covered myself and my man with clean white linen, and a white nightcap, to appear the colour of the snow, we floated down among the small pans of white ice that were constantly drifting to leeward; and, by this means, had a couple in the boat, and another that afterwards dropped dead, just as the other punts were coming up. This circumstance I think it right to mention, in case it should hereafter be found a useful recipe for getting at very wild birds, though it is with reluctance that I become so much the egotist as to introduce any thing that relates to my own performance. In giving further directions about swans, I must observe, that to take a sitting shot you need never be hurried, as these birds never can rise above the level of any swivel-gun till they have beat the water for several yards, in order to get their huge bodies on the wing. To shoot them while travelling past on their flight—make all possible haste to row (or if on land, to run) till you get under them, as they fly very low, and will seldom break their course. They may be frequently killed also, after they have pitched where you are unable to get at them sitting, by surrounding them with boats, and having a gunning-punt in advance, ready to fire as they pass. We afterwards got two more of them by this means. Be careful, however, always to let a swan *pass you*, so as to *shoot under his feathers*, or you may as well fire at a wool-pack. (This, I believe, I named before, as well as that his *head* must be your target, if you have only a common gun.) In 1829, and again this last hard winter, I had excellent sport with the hoopers; and if the tide, the ice, and the other gunners, would only allow me to proceed, I generally got one, or more, whenever they appeared on our coast.

But, before I launched the punt, that has been before described, I thought a great deal of killing two or three hoopers in a season. Before going up to hoopers, put a few large pieces of ice on the deck of your punt, in order to prevent these long-necked birds from seeing into it. If a swan rises out of shot, where he is likely to go entirely away, present your small gun very far *before him*, and *over him*, and by thus firing, you will sometimes make him "haul his wind," as a sailor calls it, and come across, a fair shot for your large gun.

Hundreds of common swans are mistaken for hoopers. In hard weather they are driven from gentlemen's seats, and still more so from the large swanneries; such, for instance, as that at Abbotsbury, in Dorsetshire. They then frequently repair to the shore; and by congregating in flocks, and there getting driven about and shot at, become quite as wild as the real hoopers, from which they are difficult to distinguish, unless you hear them *hoop*. But when near enough to *inspect the head* you can *be no longer in doubt*, as the naked skin above the bill in the *tame* swan is *black*, and in the *wild* swan *bright yellow*. *Under two years of age* the hoopers, like other cygnets, are not white, but more or less of a *dull fawn colour*, and then the yellow is much less brilliant; though still plain enough to distinguish them from swans of the tame species. Moreover, the tame swan has a protuberance just above the bill, where the forehead of the wild swan rises gradually in profile, though it is rather hollow when inspected from the centre. [I write this with a stuffed specimen of the tame swan, and each specimen of the hooper now before me.]

An octavo volume might be rapidly filled, without

reference to any other work, on the mere subject of shooting all the foregoing birds; but, through consideration for my reader's patience, I shall now conclude, sincerely hoping that I have given all the real information which is absolutely necessary for his pursuit of them.

BOAT SHOOTING, UNDER SAIL, OUTSIDE OF HARBOUR.

(As no one, I presume, would go afloat without either having sailors, or being pretty good amateur sailors themselves, it would be needless, as well as difficult, to write otherwise than in nautical terms.)

We now take our leave of the harbour, and will have one cruise *out of* harbour before we proceed for the shooting system to France.

To venture after fowl at sea you must have a large boat, with good bearings, that will carry plenty of canvas. *Rowing* after them scarcely ever answers; but when it blows fresh, a fast sailing boat may often run in upon geese, and sometimes other birds, before they can take wing; and after a coast has been for some time harassed by the gunning-punts, I have seen more birds killed *under sail* from a common boat, than by any other manner of *day* shooting. But to do the business *well,* a stanchion-gun must be fixed in the boat, and this, by all means, contrived so as to *go back with the recoil,* or you *run the risk of staving your boat,* and, therefore, of being really in danger. Recollect, when you get on the *outside* of the harbour, an accident is no joke; and you have, as Dr. Johnson observes, but one plank between you and eternity.

A boat for this work should have plenty of beam, and as little keel as she can well go to windward with, in order to get, at times, within shot of the mud and sands, and also to run through a harbour at spring-tides, without getting aground. You should, therefore, for *this* sport, always *make choice of* a day *when the wind is off the land*, and a time *when the tide is flowing;* as you have then no danger of filling your boat with the hollow sea of a lee shore, or running her so fast aground as not to be able to get her off immediately. In following wildfowl under sail, command, as much as you can, a windward birth, in order to bear down on them at pleasure; and if they rise out of shot against wind, as they usually do, luff up directly, and try to head them for a cross shot. As the gun, when on one tack, is in the way of the jib, you must have the man who attends the jib-sheets always in readiness to haul the weather one to windward; but this must be done only just before you want to fire, or you deaden the boat's way. Take care also to let the sheet be under the barrel of the gun, in order that your line of aim may be clear of every thing. In this pursuit, when the more wind sometimes the more sport, never go with less than three good hands; and *be careful, in squally weather, not to make too fast the mainsheet*, as nine-tenths of the misfortunes that we hear of have occurred from this very circumstance.

While on this subject, it may be useful information to many gentlemen, and it is but doing justice to an ingenious man to say, that, for building a boat, yacht, &c. I have never yet met with any one who could beat Mr. Thomas Inman, of Lymington. As a much better recommendation than my book, I need only say that he has been chosen by Joseph Weld, Esq. for building his yachts. Mr. Inman came from Hastings, and is now established in Lymington.

I will now conclude here with explaining the apparent inconsistencies of the plate by a dialogue, *à la Walton* :—

Critic. Why put all your wounded geese swimming one way?

Author. Because geese, directly they are wounded, always make for the heaviest sea.

Critic. Admit that: but why have you made birds falling where no gun is fired?

Author. Because, in wildfowl shooting, one third of the birds that are mortally wounded fly off apparently unhurt, and then drop suddenly from the flock.

Critic. Why is your wounded curlew on his legs, and the goose unable to dive, while the winged hooper is able to swim?

Author. Because the mud being convex, in some places, the water that flows over it is only about three inches deep there; while it may be nearly a foot deep a few yards further; and the *web-footed* bird always makes for the *deep*, while the *wader* seeks the *shallow*, water.

Before dismissing the plate, too, I should explain, that the man, who is taking the passing shot, is sketched for Buckle, with his punt: the yawl is with a party, and a swivel-gun, who are bearing down, in obedience to the punter's signal, while the other man is standing on his mud-boards, hallooing and swearing because he also cannot obey the signal (by walking across to intercept the cripples) through fear of leaving two city gentlemen aground; while their poodle dog can no longer contain himself, and on hearing another shot, jumps overboard. The Newfoundlander, in the foreground, is sketched from a bitch of mine, that was imported from St. John's.

In describing these subjects, however, I have unfortunately not the means of getting assisted as could be wished, because they are so totally foreign to artists. But for the original plate from which this was taken, I am indebted to the kind and able assistance of William Daniell, Esq. R.A.

BOATS USED IN THE SOUTHAMPTON RIVER, AND ELSEWHERE.

Having spoken of the Hampshire coast, I allude to that part of it all the way from Christchurch bay to Leap and Calshot; on sailing round which point we open the Southampton river, where the mode of shooting again differs. The order of the day here is to have *small carvel-built boats,* and many other miserable contrivances.

The gunners (or rather bird-frighteners) in these parts scarcely regard any appearance in dress or colour. These men, particularly the Itchen ferrymen, go sailing about all day, firing random shots, and so disturb the coast, that they spoil the sport of those few who really understand, and would assist their families by the pursuit of wildfowl. What few birds they kill are either geese, brought down on the wing, by constantly firing very large mould shot; or cripples which have escaped from other gunners, and got into a sea which their light high-sided boats are able to weather. Farther up this river, towards Millbrook, before it was so incessantly bombarded, they had formerly a more sensible plan; but this was chiefly for getting the *curres*. It was to set, at low water, lines, with horse-hair loops, in which these birds were caught and drowned, when diving to bite the weeds, and were thus left on the mud by the ebbing tide.

On other parts of the coast of England, I have observed the boats are more or less on the construction of those already mentioned. But when in Scotland, I could procure nothing *small enough* to answer the purpose in any way. This, however, was some years ago. Here (on the Clyde, below Dumbarton) the sport would have been excellent, and particularly at the bernacles; but since I was there, I hear that this, like all other places, is nothing like what it was in former times.

CRIPPLE-NET.

Of all the little "wrinkles" that ever occurred to me, for securing wounded birds in a sea, one of the best is a cripple-net, precisely similar to the landing net of an angler. The hoop of iron (or, what is far better, $\frac{1}{4}$ inch hard-drawn copper wire) should be nearly 2 feet in diameter, and made as light as possible, except just where it screws into the socket; as *there* comes all the lever or strain. The pole should be made with light Norway deal, and about 5 or 6 feet long. You then stow your net, on the bottom boards, under the skin that you sit on, and lay the pole alongside the other gear; so that you have no incumbrance whatever, even in the smallest punt. The meshes should be just sufficient to hold a teal, and you may have the net of silk. But I'll warrant that even twine will not hold wet enough to make any thing uncomfortable. I could write a sheet full to explain the many advantages of this simple contrivance, but my doing so would be a waste of time. Let any gunner therefore, and particularly if he has another "hand" in the punt, only try the thing, and I think he'll never, by choice, "put off" again without one. What have we all been thinking of to leave this till November 1832? How many hundreds of fowl would it have saved for hard-working gunners, instead of their falling a prey to gulls and Itchen ferry-men! The whole cost of my cripple-net (a rough one made for trial) was 2*s.* 6*d.* The first time of using it I caught up as many wigeon as would have sold for 12 shillings, where I had not time to load the "cripple-stopper," and where, by once "putting about," we should have let all the birds get into a rolling surf before we could have "fetched" them again. Every common boatman, much more a gunner, knows the difficulty of picking up even a dead bird, when scudding under canvas, perhaps eight knots an hour, in a "lop of a sea;" and the immense time lost if you miss the bird, and consequently have to "put about," and beat back to windward. Mark me, now, if most of the floating gunners, preventive boatmen, and rock-bird shooters do not provide themselves with this said cripple-net!

N. B. The net is not meant to supersede the use of a small gun; but merely intended to save many shots that you would be obliged to take with it if you had only the oar or your hands to depend on; and it will be found a great comfort, by saving you from getting wet about the wrist.

POPPING-PISTOL.

How frequently have I, when out on a windy day, got within a fair shot of wigeon, duck, and mallard, &c. where the water was so rough that it would have stopped the shot, and where the birds were so scattered as not to be worth firing at! In this case I had no alternative but to hoot them up, and shoot flying. What was the consequence? in spite of all the noise you could make, they would keep rising only a few at a time, and therefore present no shot worth firing at with a large gun. Again—when birds are on the mud, at low water, where no swivel-gun can bear on them, and you frighten them up,—they seldom rise within your "bearing" till they have flown far out of shot. But now I am up to them;—only get a short stout *pistol* with a good charge of *powder*, and, when well in shot, let your man pop it off:—Up they all go like a rocket;—and down many of them come, like the stick of it! Many may say,—why not let the man fire off your *small gun?* I answer—how is a man to manage a punt in rough weather, and use both his hands with a shoulder-gun at the same time? Moreover, the *gun* would of course have *shot* in it; and I should therefore beg to be excused from lying directly under it, lest his hand should drop.

This plan and the net I have only tried a few times; but they answered so well that I cannot resist inserting them, now that I am just in time to do so.

ARTIFICIAL ISLAND

FOR CURLEWS, PLOVER, OXBIRDS; AND, IN HARD WEATHER, ALL OTHER BIRDS.

I HAVE generally seen a great many curlews, gray plover, and oxbirds, at " the fall," as the gunners call it, which is towards the end of October; and sometimes even as early as the equinox. As these birds generally congregate sometime before the real wildfowl arrive, they frequently show good sport; and are, at all events, no bad substitutes for getting the gun and gear into play for the approaching season; particularly as the gray plover are delicious, and the oxbirds tolerably good eating. The first question therefore is,—How are we to kill them in any great quantity? The old gunners will tell you to catch them on a point at high water; or on the edge of the mud, just as the tide begins to fall. But I can tell the old gunners that " down our way," as the cant phrase is, no sooner does " the fall" arrive, than there is scarcely a point to be seen but what is garnished with the shock-head of some shore-popper or other; and, in many parts of the world, as likely as not, by some " hand" in the preventive service. Thus, while the vigilant examiner of pockets and portmanteaus, and rival of the hungry "saddle-back*," with his government-gear, is all eyes after a trip of birds, the "fair-trader," by wholesale, is, perhaps, with all hands, "working a crop of goods." But, to return to our innocent occupation,—at the ebb, there are generally shooters in proportion to the birds; and, at low water, the birds are several hundred yards in, upon the mud, which, on most parts of the Hampshire coast, is so flat, that even the curlews are washed off their legs, by the flowing tide, before a punter can find water to go into them. The plan that I adopted, a few seasons ago, when I happened to be staying on the coast, was to *make an island in the middle of the ooze*, where I was sure of the first shot; unless any one was there whose punt drew less water than mine, which happened not to be the case. The way to make an island, that will stand the overwhelming south-westers, is this:—Go, at low water, and drive strong poles, from nine to twelve feet long, into the mud, at about the interval usual for hedge-stakes, till they stand no more than two or three feet in height. Then make a hedge to enclose as much space as you may wish your gun to sweep. Fill in your fence with faggots, well lashed on; and then cover them with mud, sea-weed, and light gravel, taking care to leave a smooth up-hill surface, which your gun will play well upon; and without leaving any protuberance that would protect the birds from the shot. After your island has stood a few heavy gales, you will then see whether you have to replenish it or not; and, when all

* Coasters' term for the great black-backed gull, which hovers at a distance, till a shot has been fired; and then takes away the killed and wounded before your face.

appears to stand well, go and cut off your stakes, level with the island ; as they might, otherwise, wholly alarm the birds, or partly protect them from your shot. Let your island be completed a few weeks before the autumnal passage of the birds; and I'll warrant that the *first heavy gale and spring tide* will drive to it some home-bred oxbirds, if not curlews. These, provided they are not driven away by some premature tyro of a gunner, will bring down the birds of passage which migrate to the coast; so that, with the first *good tide,* and very *high wind,* you may expect to see—not one particle of your island—but only the rug, or carpet, as it were, which is formed by the innumerable birds that cover it.

WILDFOWL ARTILLERY.

CARRIAGE FOR USING A STANCHION GUN ON LAND.

Before we cross the channel, for France, we will now look at the artillery.

A stanchion gun may be fired from a carriage, that can be wheeled over land; which is much lighter than a common loaded barrow. But, with this contrivance, the person firing the gun must sit *on* the carriage and rest his feet on the strap, so as to *go back with it,* otherwise he would, by going directly behind it, stand a chance of being knocked down; or, at all events, of getting his shins broken.

Having contrived one, which answers well, I here give a representation of it, with directions for its management.

EXPLANATION.

A A Bands of copper.

B Plate of ditto to strengthen gun stock.

C C Handles to wheel carriage.

D Cord that goes over stock to elevate muzzle of gun, while wheeling carriage.

E Leather strap to support feet.

F Splinter-bar to carry a hurdle, bushes, or any thing to mask shooter, and apparatus, when approaching birds.

(To do which he must unhook the cord, and let the gun rest on the bar; then fix his ambush, and crawl along, pushing all before him till he is near enough to get into his seat and fire.)

DIRECTIONS.

A barrel made with trunnions, or a spring swivel, is best; as with this the copper is no longer required.

N.B. Block to be 22 inches wide; iron round the top of the hole; and the stanchion to go through the axle-tree below.

Keep the hole well oiled, to prevent rust; and for the facility of turning, or lifting out the gun.

The ramrod, &c. may go on the carriage.

Your shoulder and cheek should be kept just clear of the stock.

INVISIBLE APPROACH.

We have all been asleep about one invention—and that is the means of approaching wild birds in an open plain, or on a pond which affords no ambush. The old stalking horse was almost the only remedy for this, till I brought out the "wildfowl artillery;" and, with either of these, if birds only *fly round to reconnoitre*, you are exposed, and there is an end of your sport. But, at last, thanks to this wonderful "march of intellect," I have had the brains to contrive what I was a "flat" for not thinking of ten years ago—an invisible approach, over which birds may repeat their flight, like swallows or bats, and be as wise at last as they were at first. It is simply a little frame, on wheels, made of good and well seasoned ash, and thereon placed a moderate sized stanchion gun; the recoil of which is taken by a long rope-breeching, that closes a spiral spring, in order to ease the frame, and thereby enable you to have it light. You have only to lash down the but of the gun, so as to elevate the muzzle, and the machine may be wheeled about like a barrow, or "towed" behind any kind of vehicle.

To approach birds—lean with your chest and elbows on the sacking, and go on your knees, having, of course, knee-caps or water-boots, till you get within about a hundred and fifty yards of your fowl; then crawl into your shell, so far as to leave out *only* your *feet;* and work on with *them.* But, as this is rather harder labour, you may leave it till absolutely necessary. Be careful to approach as slowly as possible for the last fifty yards; and, if you see birds looking up wild, lie quiet, and wait till their heads are down again, before you move on.

This machine may be covered with boughs, &c., or masked, in front, with the skin of a sheep, deer, or what you please; and the birds will then let you approach them as well as if you were some harmless quadruped. (I would allow the critic to say—"*an ass*"—if the thing had not answered most admirably; as many people who have seen it can prove.) This invention being difficult to explain, and the subject a dull one to write on, I will now give three views of it, which were taken by Mr. Cornelius Varley, with his admirable invention, the *patent "graphic telescope."*

I have added a little "approach," or Birnam wheel-

INVISIBLE APPROACH FOR WILD BIRDS ON LAND.

Invented by P. Hawker, Drawn by C. Varley, Engraved by H. Adlard, & Published by Longman & Co. 1830.

barrow,—or march-of-intellect machine,—or whatever we are to call it—(the *clods* call it the "*nwisable proach*")—for the use of small guns. This was tried by a gamekeeper, at some leverets feeding, which, on seeing him, always ran into covert, three gunshots off. But when he advanced in this machine, he killed some with the greatest ease. I have withheld putting the boughs or covering on this, in order to show the wheelwright how to make it. The expense of my little one was about twelve shillings; so that I dare say even a rogue would make one for a guinea or thirty shillings. The large one is a heavier and more expensive concern. As an ambush to *wait in*, it answers comfortably for *all* places, whether wet or dry. But to *advance* with it on birds, we, of course, require tolerably good ground. Let me see the man who will invent any thing to work a *stanchion* gun over *bad* ground!

EXPLANATION OF THE PLATE.

The first sketch represents a bird's eye view, to show the machinery, viz.—the spiral spring, which closes by the recoil of the gun; the painted canvas that hides the fore-wheels; and the pockets convenient for stowing ramrods, &c.—Q. Why is the spring not in the centre? A. Because, if it was, that breadth which would correspond with the space occupied by the shooter, would give an unnecessary increase of size and weight to the machine. The second is a foreshortened view of the apparatus, dressed up with boughs, as it appears when approaching birds and under mask of a wooded background. The third is a broadside view, with the gun fixed, showing the rope-breeching, by the pull of which, on a sliding bar of wood, the spiral spring is closed: the sliding support, on which the gun rests firm, to whatever height you want to fire a sitting shot; and the canvas cover above, which, when put on, conceals the operations of the shooter. The small machine, near the centre of the plate, is for a common shoulder-gun, which may be rested on the front bar, and thus fired, like a rifle.

SHOOTING WILDFOWL IN FRANCE.

On the French coast, although they are all great shooters, and especially on a Sunday! I could never meet with a very small boat of any kind.

I remember going to a lake, called Gattemare, about a league from Barfleur, which contained more wildfowl (chiefly *dunbirds*) than ever I had before seen together. They floated with the greatest composure, while the *canaille* were firing at coots, &c. from the banks; and the lake being above a mile long, and nearly half a mile broad, these birds, aware of their safety (like the ranks of puffins on a cliff), remained indifferent to the noise of guns. Finding nothing could be done with them, I, and some friends, tempted the commissary of marine, by a promise of bringing birds enough to keep his family for a week, and giving him something from *Angleterre*, to exert himself most zealously in getting a boat overland. This having been accomplished, we started before daylight; but instead of finding a *petit canot*, as he and his *gens d'armes* had described it, we were ushered into a huge man of war's boat, that, in a few minutes, put the whole pond in motion with the rising of birds, and very soon after was nearly sending *us* to the bottom of it, by the rapidity with which it leaked. In spite of all, however, our sport, with common guns, was admirably good, and I have little doubt but that, with proper equipment and apparatus, we might have done wonders.

We afterwards agreed for the exclusive right of the shooting there, and protected it, according to the custom of this country, by an armed *garde-chasse*, which part was most ably performed by one of the commissary's *gens d'armes*, who, in addition to his military fusee, had provided himself with the terrific appendages of a *cutlass* and a *set of handcuffs*.

We found the French peasants very intelligent, and useful to assist in shooting; and, although quite ignorant of following birds *on* the *water* (in comparison with Englishmen), yet they were pretty well up to the making of bastions, huts, and every other trick for getting shots on, and from, the *shore*.

The French coast is plentifully supplied with wild-fowl; which *there* are far more easy of access than in our country. Taking from between Cherburg and Neville to Carentan, there is, I believe, no better place within the same distance, from the south of England, than this would be, for an enthusiast in the diversion. Here the birds are now far more numerous than on the coast of England; and the very few shots that are worth taking with the wretched *guns* and *powder*, which are used by the few people who here follow wild-fowl, render *their* sporting but a trifling impediment to your enjoying the whole range of country. (Although the powder is so execrably bad, yet the French *shot* is well manufactured, and of good quality.)

The only objection, however, after the ten or twelve hours' sail, which this would about be from Lymington or Poole, is, that the isolated situation of the country, and the misery of the inhabitants, preclude your having any farther amusement than the constant pursuit of sport.

FRENCH HUT-SHOOTING,

CALLED

LA CHASSE À LA HUTTE.

As the French hut-shooting is the only means by which a very bad shot, with a very bad gun, may kill ducks while as dry and as warm as if by his fireside, I made a point, on a subsequent excursion to France, of going up to Peronne *, which may be styled the university for *chasseurs* on this system, in order to make myself master of it, and insert it in the third edition, under an idea that its great facility, and little inconvenience, may better suit the generality of my readers, than the more scientific plans of wildfowl shooting. The lakes of Peronne are better calculated for a lover of comfort to shoot at his ease than any place I have seen. The water, being a part of the Somme, is not quite stagnant ; and is, in every part, about four or five feet deep, surrounded, and intersected, by innumerable islands and walls of rushes. The waters here are rented by different " huttiers" (hut-shooters), who get the chief of their livelihood by supplying the markets of Paris,

* The hut system is also tolerably understood near Calais. Monsieur Huret I found to be " *le plus fort huttier*" there ; and, if I remember correctly, it was him that I met one morning with forty-three wildfowl, that he was just bringing home, with his basket of call-birds, after one night's sport.

and other towns, with wildfowl, which they shoot, instead of taking them by decoys, as in our country. Though the French, in some places, are very expert at catching birds (particularly on that vast tract of wild sand between Crotoi and St. Valery, where I have seen the whole mouth of the Somme spread with nets and surrounded by lines of horse-hair nooses), yet shooting from the hut (la hutte) is the favourite, and most general, method of getting wild-fowl in France. The common way of making a hut is to dig a hole in the ground by the side of some pool or pond; and then roof it over with turf, so that not an opening remains, but one hole, into which you crawl; out of which you fire; and in front of which are fastened, to three separate pegs in the water, two tame ducks, and a drake. The *drake* must be in the *centre*, and the ducks *one on each side of him*, at about five yards interval; and the birds being thus separated, will, frequently, be calling to each other; and if so, there will seldom pass a wild one, but will come and drop with them. You cannot, in general, succeed with less than three call birds. Indeed I should recommend having never less than six; and, if you have twelve, or even more,—all the better.

The chief point, however, to be attended to in England, is to get, if possible, some young wild-ducks bred up, and pinioned. Or, by way of a makeshift, to select tame birds which are the *most clamorous*, even if their colour should not be like the wild ones. But in France you have seldom any trouble to do this, as the ducks used in that country are mostly of the wild breed; and three French ducks, like three Frenchmen, will make about as much noise as a dozen English.

The Italians, in order to make their call birds noisy,

for a "roccalo," burn out their eyes with a hot needle; a practice at which I am sure my English readers would shudder; though the translation of what they say in Italy is, that "these are the happiest birds in the world; always singing." (It may be necessary to explain, that a roccalo is a plantation, and a large silk net, into which various small birds are driven, as soon as they have collected, by a Signor, who is concealed above the trees, in a highly elevated box, similar to a small pigeon-house. Out of this he hurls down a large stick upon the birds; and they, flying down, as if to avoid a hawk, are all made prisoners in the net which is placed behind the trees.) But, to return to the huts of Peronne: they are very superior to the common ones. The way to make them is this:—Cut down a large square in the reeds, about eight feet by four; make a foundation of either stone, wood, or brick. Then drive in six piles on each side; and on them put six hoops, precisely like those to a tilted waggon. The foundation being then formed, nothing remains but to build up the sides with turf, or what else you please, and thatch the roof and the whole of the inside. In front there must be either two or four port holes to fire through (each one bearing clear of your call birds), and at the back a little door to crawl in at, which you enter by a labyrinth. This hut, being built among the high reeds, and afterwards strewed over with them, is completely invisible; although as commodious inside as a large covered cart. Here the *huttier* of Peronne goes regularly every night, wet or dry, and takes a great coat (if he has one), with a piece of brown bread, and a sour apple, for his supper. In front of his hut are fastened, to piles at each end, three separate ropes, about twenty yards long. On the *centre one*, he ties *four drakes*, and to the one on *each flank four ducks;* making, in all, twelve decoy birds; and these, being (to use a military term) dressed in line, whatever bird he sees out of the ranks, he knows must be a wild one: and as the lake, in moderate weather, is like a mirror, the night is seldom so dark but that he can see to shoot at the very short distance which his miserable gun, and miserable powder, will kill.

The great man of the *huttiers* here was, and perhaps still is, Monsieur Desabes*. To his services I was recommended by the proprietor of whom he rented his share of the water. He informed me, that the *huttiers* never allowed shooting from a boat, or at birds on wing, through fear of disturbing the pond; and said, that *his* plan was to take his night's rest, and leave the birds till a little before daylight; when they would be all doubled together; and when a shot would do far less mischief to the decoy than if fired before the birds had fed and slept. *Here he is perfectly right.* But that if a "*grande compagnie*" should drop, the noise would awaken him, and he could then take his choice whether to fire or not. After inspecting all his apparatus by day, he would make me go with him by night, and being unwell at the time, and unprepared, I was scarcely in the humour to do this, particularly as I knew that it was past the time of year for this kind of sport. I agreed, however, to go, and was conducted to one of his best intrenchments, where his twelve decoy birds,

* I may now say "*certainly* is" (unless he dies before this edition is out), as I have just heard from a French sportsman, who has been shooting with him; and who tells me how mightily pleased he was at seeing his name in the book of "Monsieur Aukare, le chasseur Anglais."

all in battle array, were placed under the light of a beautiful moon, within the quarter of an English gun-shot of his hut, which was *uncomfortably warm.* Here I remained, more likely to be suffocated than chilled, for I know not how many hours; but not a wild-duck ever came, though his three alignements of decoy-birds kept chattering away, like the other bipeds of the French nation; and although the whole valley, for a league, was resounding with the quacking of decoy-ducks, and defended by the masters of them, yet I could not have the honour to say, I had seen or heard the firing of a single shot. Had my experience ended here, therefore, I should have had but little inducement to recommend the French system. But I have since imported the French brood of decoy-ducks; tried it in England; and find, that, by this means, a gentleman with his little gun may sit at his ease, and kill more wildfowl than by any other plan I have ever seen; and without the risk of driving the fowl entirely away from his pond, which he would be liable to do by the use of punts, or any other mode of attacking them.

In this shooting, let it be remembered, that the *ducks* usually *quit* the *large ponds* at night, and therefore the huts for *them* must be made round the smaller waters, where they feed. But for the *dun-birds*, and all kinds of *curres*, the large pond will be the best place, as they seldom leave it; and, if not too hard pressed, *they* may be driven like sheep (by means of a person paddling to and fro, at a *distance;* and occasionally making a little noise), either by night or day, towards any of the batteries which the shooter may choose to open on them.

Coots may be driven in like manner, but will not double up for a shot, like the others. Ducks and mallards will not allow you to drive them; but on the first alarm will generally take wing.

As a proof of the superiority of the French decoy birds to the common English ducks, I need only mention, that a few winters ago, when I sent over some of them to Lord Rodney, for his beautiful pond at Alresford, Mr. Sparry, the late bailiff, in order to secure them, for the night on which they came, put them within a few hurdles, close before his house. When he got up in the morning, no sooner did he open his door than a number of wild-ducks flew up from within the little fence he had made, and into which these birds, of course, had enticed them. Several tame ducks had constantly been in, and all about, the place; but these had never decoyed the wild birds, in the manner that had been done by the *Frenchmen* *. These birds have since bred so well as to stock the whole pond; and, by their progeny being fed, when young, with oats on a *drum-head*, they would every day, while Mr. *Sparry's* family resided near the pond, fly in, from all parts, and *muster*, like soldiers, *to a roll of the drum!* [Should this, like the shot of starlings, be thought a touch of the Alresford marvellous, I only beg of the sceptic to appeal, for the truth of it, to any one in Alresford, from Lord Rodney himself, down to the very labourers of the place.]

* I sent a dozen French ducks to the Regent's Park; and, three winters ago, I observed that they had there decoyed at least thirty wildfowl: wigeon—tufted ducks—and dunbirds. This was, of course, a great novelty in the very smoke of London. But, on my return to town, after the following winter, I do not remember to have seen any. Perhaps the *skating* may have driven the wild birds off or perhaps the following winter was *too* severe for them to remain in fresh water.

If the hut system is adopted, two or three huts should be made, and then the *hutter* has a choice which to take, according to the light and the wind. [Vide plate.]

Critic. Why have you put all your call birds one way?

Author. Because ducks, when stationary, and *not feeding*, always sit facing the wind; or, if in running water, with their breasts against the stream.

⁂ The "Invisible Approach" will be the best of all apparatus for *this* sport, in places where the ground is not too boggy to admit of either wheeling or carrying it; because with this you have your hut ready made; and a sweeping charge to cut a lane through the fowl. The machine might be left all night, with the gun ready loaded, and the call birds planted. You have then only to steal down in the *morning* (*which is always the time that birds assemble and sit thickest together,* while "washing up" or sleeping, after their nightly feed); crawl into your den; take the oakum ball out of your pan; prick the touch-hole; prime, and cock: in doing the one, let your pan very quietly down; and, in doing the other, hold the trigger; or the catch of the scear may spring the birds. Then get back, and lie to your gun; and, when you find the company swimming to your fancy,—pull away.

Designed & Painted by P. Hawker

Engd. on Steel by H. Adlard.

HUT SHOOTING ON THE FRENCH SYSTEM.

London, Published by Longman & Co.

WILDFOWL SHOOTING IN THE FENS.

PUNT, GUNS, &c. USED FOR THAT PURPOSE.

HAVING returned from France, and learnt the system of that country, we will now finish our wildfowl excursions with a few observations on the fens, and other fresh waters, where it is the most likely to answer. The punts in the fens are now somewhat similar to that which I before named of Buckle's, only much narrower, in order that the gunners may be able to pull them through the reeds, in places where they cannot use their paddles.

The guns here, instead of having any thing to check the recoil, are, like his, merely *rested* on a broad *thwart*, or *gunning-bench*, about the centre, and in a groove at the bow, to support the muzzle; so that the shooters here fire in the manner before stated, *viz.* they lean with the hollow of their shoulders hard against their *fowling-pieces* (as they *here* call *punt* guns); and, after thus checking the recoil themselves, allow the gun to run under their arms. The fen guns are built *purposely to avoid a recoil*, and to *shoot very close, at a small bunch of birds;* and, consequently, they are *not* on the very *best proportion to make heavy shots in a flock.* For, notwithstanding they are from *forty to seventy pounds weight*, and from *seven to ten feet in the barrel*, yet they are only about an *inch in the bore.* Although, as an extraordinary circumstance, the fen-gunners sometimes kill from thirty to forty birds at a shot, yet they now-a-days consider it very good work to secure a dozen.

This is nothing great, in comparison with what has been formerly done on the coast; for instance, from thirty to forty wigeon, besides lost birds, killed from the *shoulder;* and from seventy to eighty different wild-fowl from a swivel gun. These, however, though shots extremely rare, are not to be set down as extravagant impossibilities, when we consider, that a shoulder gun of twenty pounds weight *may* be fired with *half a pound*, and a stanchion gun with *a pound and a half* of *such shot*, that any *one grain* of it *might stop a bird;* and this shot (say even the large letter A) has *fifty grains to an ounce.*

The winter shooting in the fens is not what it was; as they have been much drained for cultivation, by which the wild parts are less extensive; and the use of large guns having of late years been the order of the day *here, as well as everywhere else*, the birds are now much wilder, and not so plentiful. Putting this aside, however, the fens have not so many advantages as people are led to suppose; for, should there be a *hard frost*, the whole of the reed beds and meres become one continued *sheet of ice*, and without a vestige of food for the birds; unless, by the way, you take the precaution to *keep a place open* for them, which plan answers most admirably, to get the very best shots that can be made. But should the weather be open, the greater part of the wildfowl remain in the decoys during the *day-time*, and this marshy country is too much extended to select any particular spot for their *evening-flights:* consequently, save having a tolerable quantity of *bitterns*, occasionally most excellent *snipe shooting*, and in summer the flapper shooting, here is not much to be done till about the last fortnight in March, when the birds are distributed preparative to their breeding. Then it is that old ducks and teal may be put up and killed right and left with a double gun; and then it is that we have the greatest chance of *catching the ague!*

The fens from Holme to Ramsay were, at one time, the best I had seen: they lay to the right of the north road, when you are going down, within a stage of Huntingdon, and scarcely an hour's walk from Stilton. But afterwards, in 1816, I found those near Winterton, in Norfolk (the private property of I. B. Huntingdon *, and R. Rising, Esqrs.), far superior; and the variety of wild birds here was such, that, in the breeding season, you might kill from twenty to thirty different sorts in a day. Some, by-the-by, I had never seen before, and, if I mistake not, I was favoured with a sight of two or three, that were not even in Bewick, by an excellent sportsman, the late C. Girdlestone, Esq., which he had in his private collection, at Yarmouth. In many parts you could scarcely walk without treading on the eggs of terns, plovers, redshanks, and almost every other kind of marsh-bird. At certain times, in the winter, the fowl, on their passage from Holland to the south, dropped in here, and literally blackened the centre part of the lakes called Horsey-broad, and Heigham Sounds, where they fancied themselves protected by the surrounding ice. I was here shown by Rogers his plan of getting

* Now of Joseph Hume, Esq. M. P.

fowl on the ice. It was to cut four horses' leg bones, and after filing them smooth, like skates, to place them longitudinally under a very small punt; and then, lying on his breast, to shove over the frozen part, with two iron spikes. Any other means of passing a place that was partially frozen would be dangerous in the extreme.

I, however, went to this country again, in 1824, and found, that owing to the drains for cultivation, and increase of the decoys, the quantity of birds was, and has for some years been, so much reduced, that I was obliged to alter the MS. of this statement from the present to the past time. My account would otherwise have proved a gross exaggeration. This shows how few years will put a sporting book out of date!

The fens are famous for the ruffs and reeves; but these birds frequent such awkward places, and are so wild during the summer, when they come here to breed, that, as I before observed, they seldom afford much sport for the *gun*.

SHOOTING WILDFOWL ON VIRGINIA WATER.

I WAS here shown an ingenious mode of sweeping down the wildfowl, in large quantities, by Mr. Turner, His Majesty's keeper; who, in his younger days, was a great performer in the fens. His plan for killing the wildfowl here is to fix a great many large guns parallel to the edge of the lake and to cover them over with grass. He plants them about a hundred yards apart; and has a long wire, from the trigger of the foremost gun, to the but of the next one behind it; and so on. By this means he has only to plant, and then cock, all his guns; and, by pulling off the first with some hundred yards of line, he opens on the fowl an almost instantaneous running fire, which sweeps the whole edge of the lake, where, after their nightly feed, the birds generally come to take shelter; or to sun themselves on a fine, frosty day.

I think Mr. Turner told me that he had, by this means, once brought down seventy wild ducks, by one discharge of his battery.

DRESSING FOR PUNTS AND CANOES.

To keep gunning punts and canoes from leaking, or, as those who use them call it, *weeping*, melt a *pint of tar* with a *pound of pitch,* and either *half a pint of common oil,* or *a proportional quantity of suet.* You have then only to pour a little of this mixture into the seams of your punt; and, instead of bedaubing her all over the bottom, as we did in the old school, a dozen years ago, have the bottom painted, with one or two thin coats of *red lead,* which will last much longer, and with which the boat rows much lighter.

White rosin and mutton suet is even a better dressing, and by far the *lightest* of any. To avoid rubbing the bottom of your punt every time she is hauled ashore, have two small rollers, by which you will considerably save her.

Have your canoes and punts, previously to being put together, painted *under every timber with red lead,* and they will (to the no small annoyance of the builder) last you twice as long. But *where the other paint is to go, do not* put red lead, as white will neither look nor take so well upon it.

If you want good white lead for paint *(instead of whiting and water),* you can have it from Messrs. Walker, Parker, & Co., at the *shot* manufactory.

Have the outside of all your punts and canoes painted, with the *very best white lead;* and to make them drab, for sun or moon, use a little distemper colour, such as the scenes of the theatres are painted with; and this, either with, or without size, may be mopped off in a few minutes. Some of the gunners use a wet clod; but you must beware of *salt* mud, as that would *stain* your punt.

For shooting off at sea, when there is a breeze, a tint of lead colour has the best deception. But I seldom use it, unless very light, for two reasons—the one, that it is a bad colour for shallow water; and the other, that no prudent man would go off to sea in a punt, when there is so much "lop" as to darken the water.

To stop a chink, or crack, force in, with a caulking iron, some oakum, or stiff brown paper, *before* you pour in any kind of mixture. *Hot rosin, softened with a little oil, does very well by itself, if you do not wish to have the trouble of mixing the other ingredients.*

BEST MEANS OF CONVEYING PUNTS, &c. OVER LAND.

THE boat-cart, or canoe-carriage, here prescribed, will, I think, be found the best means of conveying any kind of punt to those places, where it would always be most likely to answer; such as ponds and other private waters, where no gunners are allowed to sport; and where the keepers scarcely know a punt from a pig-trough.

This carriage, if only required for the punt itself, might be made *much lighter*, with only *two* high *wheels*, similar to a long French cart. But when laden with baggage, the plan of four wheels becomes a necessary one, in order the better to support and save the punt. In either case springs would be a decided improvement, was it not for the duty on them. The best substitute is, first to put a good bed of straw under the punt; and then to fasten on punt, baggage, and all, with a line, similar to that used for binding a load of corn in harvest.

By unscrewing, and taking out, the thorough-pin, and the two pins which go through the block-supporters behind, this carriage may be taken to pieces; and, in two lots, rowed across the water in the canoe itself. This plan, therefore, gives a conveyance, over land and water, for baggage, &c.; and, by lifting the boat out, you have a light wagon, which may be serviceable on many occasions.

N. B. For carriage to travel with a *very long* punt, and swivel-gun shipped in it, refer back to the new plate of "punt and gear."

SHOOTING WILDFOWL ON A RIVER,

ETC.

For killing common wild-ducks, that frequent a river, you have only to go a little before sunset; place yourself against any dark bush or bank; and there wait, patiently, and out of sight, till they come down, and fly round you; which they will generally do several times, before they drop into the stream or marshes.

As wild-ducks most frequently betake themselves to the springs and rivers about dusk, you have no occasion to wait for them longer than just *the last hour*, or *half hour before dark;* but, if they have been much *disturbed* or *shot at,* they will not always fly sufficiently early to be *seen;* though you may plainly *hear* the shrill, and somewhat melancholy, *sound of their wings.* If, however, the twilight is *followed by a full moon,* these birds will often withhold coming to the river *till the moon has completely risen;* in which case you might have to wait till an hour or two after dusk. But then the sport is considerably better, and will last much longer, with the additional advantage of your having a continued good light for shooting.

Wild-ducks generally come to the same place, unless they have been shot at, or there should be a change of wind and weather.

It often happens, that wild-ducks, dunbirds, and other fowl, come down at night to large rivers, ponds, or lakes, which are so deeply surrounded by *floating reeds*, that no one can approach the water; and the birds, aware of this, *do not lower their flight till they come near them.* So far from this *defying* the shooter, it is one of the finest opportunities that can be afforded for death and destruction. Let him sit, in a small *punt* or *canoe*, fore and aft, among *the rushes*, where, towards dusk, he will be so completely hid, that he may either shoot at birds flying within pistol shot, or wait for a good chance on the water; from whence (his boat being hid on each side, and *foreshortened* to the *only point of view)* he will be pretty sure to escape the observation of the birds. This plan may be resorted to where there are no rushes, such as under the bank of an island, or in a small brook, near which there may be no hiding place. Here, however, nothing would surpass the French system, for those who had the means of adopting it.

All these *stratagems* may become unnecessary, in places which are strictly preserved, and where wildfowl shooting is interspersed with that of snipes and other birds; but as these places are now but rarely to be met with, I have thought it necessary to dilate at considerable length in the foregoing instructions relative to *shooting wildfowl*, which are now but seldom to be killed without *care, patience*, and *good management.*

Having now, I trust, sufficiently explained the best methods for killing all kinds of birds, on land; on fresh waters; by sea; in harbour; out of harbour; and in every situation, that I can think of; there remains, I believe, no more that need be said under this head. I shall therefore proceed to the other subjects of the volume; and, after giving a little advice, that may possibly be of service, for the health and comfort of a young sportsman, conclude with a short epitome of, and a few observations on, the Game Laws.

GENERAL ADVICE

FOR THE

HEALTH AND COMFORT OF A YOUNG SPORTSMAN.

THE last part of the work that it would afford me any pleasure to dilate on is that of cookery. For it is an old, though a just, observation, that we should eat to live; not live to eat. But when, by adding a short paragraph or two, I can, perhaps, put some of our young sportsmen, or young "foragers," up to what, in the language of the present day, is called a "wrinkle," I may possibly be the means of saving them from unnecessarily hard fare, when quartered in a small public-house, on some shooting or fishing excursion. As many of the little publicans live chiefly on fat pork and tea; or, if on the coast, red herrings; the experienced traveller well knows, that, when in a retired place of this sort, where, from the very circumstance of the misery attending it, there are the fewer sportsmen, and, consequently, there is to be had the best diversion, we have often to depend a little on our wits for procuring the necessaries of life. If even a nobleman (who is, of course, by common people, thought in the greatest extreme better than a gentleman without a title) were to enter an alehouse, the most that could be procured for him would be mutton or beef, both perhaps as tough, and with as little fat, as the boots or gaiters on his legs.

A chop or steak is provided. If he does not eat it, he may starve: if he does, his pleasure for the next day is possibly destroyed by his unpleasant sufferings from indigestion. He gets some sour beer, which gives him the heart-burn, and probably calls for brandy, or gin; the one execrably bad and unwholesome; the other of the worst quality; and, *of course*, mixed with water, by which adulteration is derived the greatest part of the publican's profit. The spirit merchants make it, what they call above proof, in order to allow for its being *diluted*, the doing which, so far from dishonesty, is now the common practice, not only with many respectable innkeepers, but by retail merchants themselves. Our young sportsman, at last, retires to a miserable chamber and a worse bed; where, for want of ordering it to be properly aired, he gets the rheumatism; and, from the draughts of air that penetrate the room, he is attacked with the tooth-ache. He rises to a breakfast of bad tea, without milk; and then starts for his day's sport, so (to use a fashionable term) "bedevilled" that he cannot "touch a feather:" and, in the evening, returns to his second edition of misery.

On the other hand, an old campaigner would, under such circumstances, do tolerably well, and have his complete revenge on the fish or fowl of the place.

His plan, knowing the improbability of getting any thing to eat, would be to provide himself with a hand-basket at the last country town which he had to pass through, before he reached his exile; and there stock it with whatever good things presented themselves. He then arrives at the pothouse, which the distance, or the badness of the roads, might oblige him to do the previous day. His first order is for his sheets and bedding to be put before a good fire. If he arrives too late at night for this, let him, rather than lie between sheets which are not properly aired, sleep with only the blankets. He then, supposing he would not be at the trouble of carrying meat, sends for his beef or mutton. Having secured this for the *next* day's dinner, he takes out of his basket something ready dressed, or some eggs, or a string of sausages, or a few kidneys; or a fowl to broil, a cake or two of portable soup, or a little mock turtle, ready to warm; or, in short, any other things that the town may have afforded; and with this, he makes up his dinner on the day of his arrival. If the beer is sour, and he does not choose to be troubled with carrying bottles of other beverage, he is provided with a

Little *carbonate of soda,* which will correct the acid; a little nutmeg or powdered ginger, to take off the unpleasant taste; and, with a spoonful of brown sugar and a toast, he will make tolerably palatable that, which, before, was scarcely good enough to quench the thirst.

He will know better than to call for brandy or gin, but will order *rum,* knowing that that is a spirit* which would soon be spoiled by any tricks or adulteration. He will have in his basket some lemons, or a bottle of lemon acid, and make a bowl of punch, recollecting the proportions of

One sour,
Two sweet;
Four strong,
And eight weak.

* If a sportsman likes to take a flask of spirit, as a guard against cold, a stomach-ache, &c., he will, I think, find nothing equal to the real Highland Scotch, or Irish, *whisky.* Or, if he cannot get this, a little *extrait d'absinthe Suisse;* from the celebrated Mr. Johnson, No. 2, Colonnade, Pall-mall; or Mr. Sargenson, at No. 5, who is one of the best and cheapest spirit merchants in London.

This is quite the focus for good punch, which any shallow-headed boy may remember, by learning it as a bad rhyme.

It may be necessary to observe, that, by first pounding the sugar fine, you can of course measure it to a nicety, by means of a wine-glass, as well as the lemon juice, and the other liquids. Also, that half the acid of Seville orange juice is better than all of lemon juice; and further, in making punch, the spirit should be used as the finishing ingredient; though put in another jug; and the SHERBET POURED UPON IT.

But as to the improvements of pink champain, hot jellies, arrack, limes, &c., it would be out of place to talk of such luxuries here, though of course, after professing to give the *focus* for good punch, it becomes a necessary caution against error, to except that which is composed with all the dainties of an alderman; who, by the way, is welcome to my share of them; as well as to that of the gout after them. Here we have spoken of *hot* punch. Now for *cold;* which, being merely intended as a cool beverage, requires to be much weaker.

For this, I cannot do better than copy a receipt that was given me, some years ago, when quartered at Glasgow, where cold punch was universally drank; and where its excellence was only to be equalled by the hospitality of the inhabitants. It is

"A wine glass *nearly* full of best refined lump sugar *pounded.*
Twelve ditto of cold spring water.
A lime, and half a lemon [or, if no lime, a whole lemon, which might yield about half a wine glass full of juice]
Two wine glasses *brim*full of *old Jamaica rum.*

Let the sugar be well melted, and the lemons thoroughly amalgamatedwith it, and the water, *before* you add the spirit."

Or, to be much more brief, I will say, for *cold* punch,

One sour,
  Two sweet;
Four strong,
  Twenty weak;

As here we have only to repeat the old rhyme, and change the eight into a twenty. If I could make it shorter, and more simple, I would.

For those worthies, who think it a good joke to metamorphose a man into what he would not like to be called, by making him drunk, this beverage, if introduced by way of a sequel to wine, is one of the most certain to answer their purpose: because it is so cooling, and grateful to the thirst, that the more he drinks the more he requires of it, instead of beginning to find it unpleasant, like wine, *hot* punch, or other more potent liquors. I name this, not as a *lesson* to the *wag*, but as a *caution* to the *unwary*.

With materials for making other cool portable beverage (merely to quench the thirst) almost every chemist can supply you. But, provided a packet, the size of a pint bottle, is not objected to, I should prefer that prepared by the late Mr. Farley, now Mr. Tabor, (Charles Street, St. James's Square), called "*effervescent lemonade*," which is quite free from the taste of physic. My name, when I first spoke of this beverage, was not even known at this laboratory; and therefore it can, of course, be merely to serve my readers that I mention it.

While on the subject of cool beverage, let us, *en passant*, just annihilate the Sedlitz powder conspiracy. There is no gentle *alterative* so pleasant a beverage as a Sedlitz powder. But if you ask for this medicine, otherwise than in decorated 4*s*. 6*d*. boxes, many of the chemists decline serving it, under plea of a 50*l*. penalty.

If they are liable to this, it will be an act of kindness to relieve them, from all pettifogging informers; and, if not, it will serve them right to put an end to the hoax. Let us therefore placard the recipe; so that a gentleman may either call for it as a *prescription*, or lay in his own cargo at Apothecaries' Hall.

Rochelle Salts, 2 drams.
Carbonate of Soda, 2 scruples.
Tartaric Acid, 2 scruples.

The two first may be kept together: the other must be detached, for effervescence, till you are quite ready to begin stirring and drinking.

If this is not thought sufficiently pleasant, you may add lemon and sugar: or if required *merely to quench the thirst*, you should omit the Rochelle salts; and then you have, at one good *swig* *, for about three-pence, three eighteen-penny " saline draughts!"

Our sportsman will then, having taken care to provide himself with a little good tobacco, or a few cigars, have recourse to smoking; which, next to the sovereign remedy of taking a little *purl*, before you inhale a vaporous atmosphere, is the best *preventive from catching the ague* when *fen*-shooting; and, perhaps, one of the greatest preservatives from cold and illness, of any thing in existence. Under particular circumstances, therefore, smoking becomes not only justifiable, but sometimes necessary. It is, however, the last thing that I mean to recommend making a constant practice of, when *not required;* as most people, it is presumed,

* " A *low expression*," but one that will surely be thought good enough for prescriptions, when swallowed, by wholesale, at a *low price*.

would consider it an idle habit to become every day absorbed in what might be thought an agreeable stupefaction only by a few jolly fellows, who, if I may speak in their own style, glory in being able to—drink like a fish—sit like a hen—and smoke like a chimney. The old sportsman then retires to his well-aired bed, where he is provided with the best of counterpanes, a good box- or gunning-coat, or a cloak; and, after passing a good night, he rises to breakfast. If he has brought no tea with him, he makes palatable that of the place, by beating up the yolk of an egg (first with a little cold water to prevent its curdling) as a good substitute for milk or cream, a little powdered ginger, and a teaspoonful of rum. He then, previously to taking the field, desires a man to prepare some greaves, which he might carry for his dogs, or get, for them, some meat; and deputes a person to the cooking of that intended for himself; which, if bad in quality, as will most likely be the case, there is but one good and easy way of dressing. This I shall now translate from my French recipe: *viz.*—Let your servant take

Three pounds of meat, a large carrot, two onions, and two turnips. [The Frenchman adds also a cabbage: here John Bull may please himself.] Put them into two quarts of water, to simmer away till reduced to three pints. Let him season the soup to the taste, with pepper, salt, herbs, &c. &c. He must then cut off square about a pound of the fattest part of the meat, and put it aside, letting the rest boil completely to pieces. After he has well skimmed off the fat, and strained the soup, let him put it by till wanted.

On your return, while seeing your dogs fed, which every sportsman ought to do,

Let the soup be put on the fire for twenty minutes, with some fresh vegetables (if you like to have them), and, for the last ten minutes, boil again the square piece of meat which was reserved. Another necessary part of the recipe also should be prescribed, lest the dish should fall into disrepute. To prevent the deputy cook from helping himself, and filling it up with water, let him have a partnership in the concern; and when he has occasion to quit the room, he should either lock the door, or leave one of your relay dogs for a sentry.

You will then have a good wholesome gravy soup to begin with; and, afterwards, some tender meat, which if

Eat with mustard, a little raw parsley chopped fine, and a few anchovies,

you will, it is presumed, find an excellent dish. A pot of anchovies might easily be carried in a portmanteau, being, of all the luxuries from an oil shop, one of the most portable and the most useful. But nothing is worse than a mock anchovy, which is merely a salted bleak, or other inferior small fish, flavoured with a little anchovy liquor. Within these few years, however, the supply has been so good, that you will generally be served with the real Gorgona fish at any respectable oil shop. But Mr. Burgess has now, I believe, the largest and choicest importation. Signor Bassano, who was also famous for anchovies, has now set up again at No. 27, Jermyn-street.

Be careful to keep anchovies in a small *stone* jar; as an earthen one might break with them, and spoil your clothes.

Let me now add the simple receipt for as wholesome a mess as any one who can "rough it" would wish for—the dinner, of all others, for an invalid—and an alternative against starvation, where there is not even a piece of meat to be got.

Have a fowl skinned and quartered;
Put it over the fire in a quart of cold water;
Boil it *full two hours:*
Then add two ounces (or a handful) of pearl barley;
Three blades of mace; about two dozen peppercorns; and
Salt to your taste;
Then let *all* boil *together* for *one more* hour:

And it may be eat immediately; or put by, to warm again whenever you want it.

The convenience of this camp cooking is, that it will serve for any kind of fowl. For instance, if you have an old barn door hen; old game that is shot all to pieces; two or three couple of gulls; coots; or even curlews,—by consigning them in this manner, to constant boiling and steam, you make those birds eatable and digestible, which, in roasting, or common cooking, would prove offensive in taste, and hard in substance.

N.B. The pearl barley (or *rice*, by the way, if you prefer it) does well with all poultry, and birds of white flesh. But with coarse birds (here we cease to have a dish for *invalids*), such as curlews, herons, gulls, or coots, it becomes necessary to omit the pearl barley; because you there require onion; fish sauce; lemon, and even a glass of madeira, if you can get it; similar to dressing a turtle, or making giblet soup. This you would, of course, make stronger, and boil, perhaps, an hour more than chicken soup. All such messes may be eat with anchovy, curry powder, or what you may fancy, to give them an additional *goût*.

An old sportsman, having thus far subsisted tolerably well, may, afterwards, with the help of his gun, or fishing-rod, be enabled to fare decently, and enjoy good sport; while some poor helpless exotic would have spurned the very soil of the place; left it in disgust, before he had killed a bird or a fish; and, as likely as not, be laid up and fleeced at the next inn, and there saddled with some country apothecary.

To be as brief as I can, on this uninteresting, though possibly useful, head, let me take a memorandum of the few portable articles that contribute to the health and comfort of a travelling sportsman.

A medicine chest is sometimes out of the question; otherwise, a chemist would direct him better than I could presume to do; but, as I speak solely by experience, I can, of course, speak with some confidence, on the very few things of no bulk, which may be here noted down, as likely to render him essential service. But, before I name a single article, I must take up in my own defence, one observation, lest that observation may be left as a powerful weapon against me in the hands of those who are versed in this subject, in which I do not presume to have the slightest pretensions, further than personal experience. In short, I must premise with saying, that, *what would be an effectual remedy in one constitution might not answer with another*. And though the philosopher tells you, that every man, before he attains the age of forty, must be either a fool or his own physician; yet the doctor, in answer, affirms, that he who knows a little of physic, knows a great deal too much! This point I leave for the philosopher and the doctor to settle between themselves; but I trust they will both agree with me, that there can be no more impropriety in suggesting a few common medicines, with which proper directions would be given by the person who sells them, than in entering any other kind of inventory of what might be useful to a young sportsman, or young traveller. All our sporting authors have boldly taken the field, so far as amply to prescribe for the dog; while I am left exposed, under Æsculapian batteries, by having to prescribe for the master.

A BOTTLE, OR PAPER OF MAGNESIA*.

As a generally recommended cure for the heartburn, by correcting acid on the stomach; a trifling preventive to the gout; a pretty good aperient medicine, particularly if taken with acid, which gives it somewhat the effect of Epsom salts; and a very good medicine when mixed with rhubarb, which counteracts its coldness on the stomach.

* *Carbonate of soda* is *now* so *generally preferred*, that I was on the point of erasing magnesia from the list; when I saw, in the "Age" paper, a letter from my friend, Sir Anthony Carlisle, which, by his permission, I here subjoin:—

"Langham Place, July 3, 1830.

"Sirs.—I have made several trials with your purified Magnesia, and common justice demands a statement of the results. During my long continued professional experience, I have had many occasions for seeking some harmless corrector of acidity incident to the stomach and bowels. I have generally found the magnesia in ordinary use to be hurtful to the digesting power of the stomach when repeatedly given; and, in some instances, both in children and grown persons, it concretes into balls in the intestines, which is a dangerous occurrence. If, as you assert, the purified magnesia, now offered to the public, is freed from lime, and the poisonous earth called barytes, it must be inoffensive to the stomach, and not liable to concretion. I have under these impressions, directed Lockyer's Magnesia to be taken, in several instances, with remarkable benefit. I think it is a more potent cathartic, and less hurtful to digestion, than any other magnesia; and when it meets with alimentary acid, it must become a purgative liquid solution, and therefore incapable of concretion. I have sometimes directed twenty grains of your purified magnesia to be mixed in an ounce of infusion of rhubarb, and half an ounce of decoction of the yellow Peruvian bark, to be taken as a corrector of heartburn, and at the same time as a gentle aperient.—I am, &c.

"ANTHONY CARLISLE.

"To Messrs. Aldwinckle and Bromfield, Lockyer's Magnesia Warehouse, 237, Tottenham-court-road, corner of Bedford-street."

(For *correcting acid,* however, *I* always *prefer* the use of *salt of tartar;* but this, I believe, is not the general custom. I merely speak of it as I find it.)

SOME ESSENCE OF PEPPERMINT.

See the paper round it, for its various good qualities.

N. B. Bottle a tea-spoonful of this in a pint of water (where you cannot immediately get a pint of peppermint water), and put with it *two drams of salt of tartar.* Keep this as a standing ornament to your bed-room chimney-piece; and *when you require it,* from having made too free with French wines, or hard stale port, take half a wine glass full going to bed *.

[Many who fancy themselves great judges of port wine keep it but a moderate time in the wood, and a long time in little quart bottles; instead of doing just the reverse; or of bottling it in two, or *four,* quart magnums. Port does not, like claret, turn to vinegar, unless drank within a short time after being drawn; and therefore the last glass of what was decanted, and occasionally drank, from magnums, would be worth a dozen glasses, even just uncorked, of that which had been *bottled* in *pints.* (The reverse would be the case with *spirits.*) The larger the body the wine is kept in, the more agreeable to the palate of a *good* judge, and the less injurious to the stomach. It is not sufficient for wine to be old and even genuine; but it should be made of grapes that have grown in a warm part of the vineyard, which give it a sweet and full body; and it should be free from green or blighted fruit, or it will get worse, instead of better, by keeping; so that you may produce a bottle of wine with a fine looking crust, "bee's wing," and all such nonsense, which, in reality, is neither better nor more wholesome than the stale beer of a country pot-house, where the poor landlord is a tenant at the mercy of a bad brewer.

Thus many of the trade are obliged to, what they call, "marry" the wine, in order, as with many other kinds of marriages, to turn the bad stock to good account; not to say a word of the innumerable tricks

* This mixture may be used also as a lotion to preserve the *teeth,* immediately *after* eating *acids.*

that are played by quacks and inferior venders. In places where you can do as you please, let no silly fashion dissuade you from drinking your wine out of a narrow-bottomed glass (somewhat longer, and more like a funnel than what is now made), as a glass of this form retains so well the *bouquet* of the fruit. Fashion is all very well; but reason has a prior claim to it. I make no apology for a digression to this subject (except my inability to do it justice), because what is here introduced relates to that which, more or less, concerns us all.]

A FEW CALOMEL PILLS,

and the ingredients for an aperient draught on the following morning;

in case a severe attack of bile, or any such illness, should require something beyond a mere alterative.

Calomel, although a *medicine to be used with caution,* I have always found to be the most effectual recipe to cure an *obstinate* stomach-ache, in case it cannot be removed by a cordial, hot water, essence of peppermint, or *tincture of rhubarb.* Calomel, however, being a strong mercurial preparation, would deprive you of *a day's* sport, by the *indispensably necessary confinement after taking it.*

I have lately been favoured with a recipe which is almost as effectual as calomel; and with which a sportsman need not be made prisoner. It is simply to take, at night, a pill composed of—

Blue pill, 2 grains;
Compound extract of colocynth, 4 grains;
Oil of carraways, 2 drops.

One pill is generally sufficient; but, if not, the quantity may be increased, or doubled, on the same proportions. If one large pill is objected to, the above articles can of course be made up in two.

(On showing this prescription to a medical friend, he said that it would be greatly improved by altering the proportions to *four* grains of blue pill; four grains of colocynth; with *one* drop of oil of carraways; and adding *one grain of ipecacuanha.* These to be taken, in two pills, at bed-time.)

The foregoing prescription was given me, for this work, by a medical gentleman, on his retiring from business; and it beats all the anti-bilious nostrums I have ever used. So, giving *him* thanks, and all the credit of it, I may now say—"*take my pill—read my book,*" and without the *3s. 6d.* a syllable for this advice.

(No one prepares colocynth, or makes these pills, better than Briggs, 48, Wigmore Street.)

On my naming the foregoing recipe to Sir ——, one of the first medical gentlemen of the age (but who might not like to have his name published, with a *prescription,* on a frivolous occasion like this), he kindly said that, as *he* had a great objection to *all mercurial* preparations, where they could possibly be avoided, he would present me, for this edition, with a "sportsman's pill;" or, in other words, as he observed,

"An opening pill, without mercury; and which may be taken as often as is needful, without offence to the stomach"—viz. "30 grains of Aloes; 30 grains of Scammony, and a sufficient quantity of Venice Turpentine to make *fifteen pills.*"

"*One* taken at bed-time generally acts on the morning following, without disturbing the sleep. If one pill is not enough, two may be taken, for a while; but the effect usually improves by use, contrary to other cathartics."

This remedy has been frequently tried, and much approved, since the last edition.

A LITTLE TARTAR EMETIC,

in case of severe indigestion, or a dog being taken ill. This medicine, given from a grain and a half to two grains, in warm water, will sometimes perform wonders among common people, who are subject to have the stomach disordered by eating voraciously of bad and unwholesome food.

A friend of mine, with nothing whatever but this recipe, has been, for a great many years, the successful quack of his village; and boasts of beating the doctors without having lost a patient. How far my friend may be justified in flying, on every occasion, to that which may tend to weaken the stomach, I leave it for those who are versed in medicine to determine; notwithstanding he may have gained the confidence of the village.

(After all, too, a couple of wine glasses full of water, taken as hot as it can be drank, without the astringent addition of either tea or spirit, I have found, would, in general, relieve indigestion.

Another remedy, which lately became in fashion, is to swallow, *whole*, two teaspoonsful of common mustard seed just before going to bed, and an hour before dinner. It may be taken in a little water. I have proved it to be an excellent remedy.)

Remember, that a DOG *requires, of tartar emetic, or any other medicine, at least twice as much as a* MAN.

I have been somewhat remiss in entering on this list what may be called physic, without first giving a receipt or two for a *mere alterative.* Far as my intention is from entering further into a subject on which I can have no pretensions, yet the three following prescriptions, being those of eminent men, may certainly prove worthy of insertion: for, when the stomach is the least out of order, the *nerves* are affected; and then how are we to *shoot?* But to the point—

Take, either an hour before dinner, or at bed time (*I* prefer the latter), a pill made with

$2\frac{1}{2}$ grains of rhubarb,
and $\frac{1}{2}$ a grain of cayenne pepper;

With a tea-spoonful of carbonate of soda in a glass of water. *Two*, or more, of these pills may be taken if one is not found sufficient.

Another recipe, perhaps more effectual, but less simple, and therefore less to be had recourse to, is—

Aloes—rhubarb—cayenne pepper—of each 1 scruple;
Carbonate of soda, 2 scruples;
Extract of poppies, 6 grains;
All made into 24 pills.

Two a dose.

I find in my MS. box also the following excellent recipe for a weak stomach, which was written down for me by my friend the late Sir Hutton Cooper.

$2\frac{1}{2}$ grains of rhubarb;
5 ditto carbonate of soda;
10 ditto Peruvian bark.

To be taken in a glass of hop tea, or cold ginger tea, an hour before dinner, and continued, every day, for a fortnight.

So much, and quite enough too for *me* to take the liberty of speaking about, on the subject of alteratives.

HUXHAM'S TINCTURE OF BARK,

as an effectual stimulus to brace the nerves of a bad shot. The sportsman has only to take a dessert spoonful in a glass of water before he goes out. [THE LESS, HOWEVER, ALL STIMULI, AND INDEED ALL MEDICINES, ARE HAD RECOURSE TO, THE MORE EFFECTUAL THEY WILL BE WHEN TAKEN.]

When for a short time in Holland, I always kept

well by taking a teaspoonful of this medicine in a glass of Madeira, before inhaling the air of the marshes *.

CONCENTRATED CAMPHOR JULEP

is another good remedy to compose a nervous man for the rising of a cock pheasant. Fisher and Co., in Conduit Street, make this in perfection.

WHITEHEAD'S ESSENCE OF MUSTARD;

which *I* have found to be *one of the finest recipes that ever bore a stamp,* for preventing or curing the rheumatism ; or for cuts, bruises, &c. &c. The real inventor of this embrocation is Mr. Johnston, (the famous soda water man), who, being an apothecary, thought it *infra dig.* to appear as a trumpeter of patent medicines ; and therefore used the *nom de guerre,* as the French call it, of " Whitehead."

A PIECE OF FLEECY HOSIERY,

in case of a pain in the chest, to which application the rubbing in a little of the above essence may be added ; and continued, for a day, after the fleecy hosiery is no longer required ; in order to prevent the pain from returning when you leave it off.

[No sportsman who is subject to pain in the chest, or severe rheumatism, should be without the " Poor Man's Plaster," which is sold by Mr. Sterry and Sons, oilmen, 156, High Street, Southwark.

---

* The new *French* remedy for the ague is now in general use, and nothing has yet been found more efficacious. After clearing the bowels with a good dose of medicine, give FIVE GRAINS OF SULPHATE of QUININE in treacle, jelly, &c. directly after the cold fit ; and continue it, three times a day, for nearly a week after the appearance of the disease has subsided. The dose is sometimes increased to ten grains thrice a day, and there is no danger resulting from an overdose. [I insert these directions precisely as they have been forwarded to me, under an idea that nothing could be more desirable for a work that professes to treat chiefly on wildfowl shooting, than a recipe for the ague.]

I went there in order to ascertain if they had any agent in the more fashionable part of the town. But, it appears that Messrs. Sterry have as much custom as they want in their own district, without taking further trouble. They told me, however, that if a shilling was inclosed in a letter, post paid, eight sheets of this plaster should come back, by return of the twopenny or general post: or, of course, four sheets for sixpence. I have well tried this admirable recipe; and let those who use it say whether or not I am right for recommending it.]

SOME COURT STICKING-PLASTER,

to enable you to walk in comfort after being galled by a water-boot.

(See directions under the head of "Water-boots.")

I have now, I believe, mentioned all the articles of my pharmacy, and next to them must come the

DENTIFRICE.

Brush your teeth every morning, with Spanish Sabilia snuff (which may be had in perfection, from Fribourg and Treyer, 34, Haymarket, or Hudson, 132, Oxford Street), and every night with a little arquebusade, or brandy; and keep, in the bottle containing it, a small piece of *camphor*. This will not only make it a tenfold greater preservative, but will prevent the vassals of the place from drinking it.

Never put cold water to your teeth, but always use it lukewarm.

If any thing will prevent or cure a tooth-ache, except aperient medicines, to reduce the inflammation, or the sovereign remedy of the new patent instrument, it will, I have reason to think, be that which has been here mentioned. At all events, some of the first dentists in London and Paris admit, that this remedy is a most excellent *preservative*. I, therefore, do not hesitate to say, that for a sportsman, and particularly for a wild-fowl-shooter, it may be worthy of insertion.

I was told by a friend who rarely errs in his prescriptions, that the best *cure* for a tooth-ache is

One tablespoonful of rum,
Another of vinegar,
And a teaspoonful of salt,

mixed together, and then held in the mouth. But, of this I have never had occasion to make a trial.

But if the foregoing directions, as a *preventive*, are attended to, we are not very likely to require prescriptions for a *cure*.

I shall now conclude with the following little hints:—

First, If you or your dog should, at any time, get a severe blow, let the wounded part be instantly fomented with water, as hot as can be borne, for at least half an hour; and you will thereby reduce your suffering, or impediment from sport, to at least half its duration.

Secondly, If you burn yourself in shooting, or otherwise, wrap the part affected immediately in *cotton*, the application of which, it has been proved, acts like magic with a burn.

This I was told as a recipe that had been adopted in Paris; and found it to answer extremely well. But, on proposing it for insertion here, to an old friend, one of our greatest surgeons that ever lived *, he assured me that a better recipe was the

constant application of *vinegar*.

Thirdly, If you should take cold, bathe your feet in hot water; if a little salt or bran is, or both are, added, so much the better. Get into a bed warmed, with a little brown sugar sprinkled on the coals; and take some whey, or whatever you can get, to promote perspiration.

* The late Sir Everard Home, who was kind enough to carefully inspect all the medical directions here given, before they went to press.

This remedy, simple as it is, will often prevent your having recourse to James's powder, &c. and may sometimes, perhaps, save you the expense of twenty pounds for medical attendance.

Fourthly, *Never fast too long;* and avoid, whenever you can, fagging *too* hard,

or, *when you come to a middle age,* you will most likely begin to feel it; and perhaps insomuch as to become nervous, and lose your good shooting. Remember this advice, and see who will last the longest; you who do, or those who do not, follow it.

Fifthly, Never go out with quite an empty stomach to wait for wildfowl; particularly in the morning. Should you wish to start before any one is up, you might always have left for you, over night, a crust of bread, or a biscuit, with a glass of milk, which, with a little sugar, nutmeg, ginger, and the yolk of an egg, may be made good in a moment. And this is better than what is called a "*doctor*" (rum and milk); because you then dispense with taking spirit in a morning, the very bad habit of which should always be avoided, except in a country where the chances of ague might justify your taking a little *purl;*

Which, by the way, was recommended to me by one of the first medical gentlemen in the profession. Do not have recourse to any such liquors, unless absolutely required to defend your health against a pestilential climate; or in case of being taken with a sudden chill; when a small quantity of spirit and beer, mixed together, if not thought too disgusting a beverage, might sometimes prove one of the most powerful stimuli to warm you, of all things that an alehouse, or perhaps any other house, could afford. If *going out,* take it *cold;* if *going to bed,* you may have it *warm;* for in the one case perspiration is as objectionable, as it would be desirable in the other.

Sixthly, Never sit down in wet feet *, or with wet clothes on any part of your body; but, if a change is not at hand, keep in motion, or go to bed, till one can be procured. Or, if you want to start again, when refreshed, first wet your feet with either spirits, or essence of mustard, and then be as quick as possible in taking your refreshment. Many people prefer *applying* the spirit to the *inside,* instead. This is not so well; because spirit alone always flies to the *head*; while strong *beer,* on the contrary, would warm the *body.*

I shall here conclude, under this head, with the *multum in parvo* advice of the great Dr. Boerhaave: Keep the BODY OPEN; the HEAD COOL; and the FEET WARM.

*** I am proud to say, that some gentlemen who are the very heads of the profession, with that liberality which distinguishes all men of talent, have approved of the humble advice here given *(of course, without the slightest pretensions, and merely as a refuge for the destitute)*: and there are only some of the little doctors who bark, and cry "quack," at what they think an infringement on their sacred rights. But, if they knew to whom all here had been submitted, before it went to the press, they would, perhaps, to use a vulgar phrase, in language most opposite to their overwhelming rhetoric—"knock under."

Having now mentioned the few things that happen to occur to me, as deserving the small space they would occupy in the baggage of a sportsman, who we all know is sometimes in an exile, where he might die before he could get medical assistance; I shall just note down a few articles as desirable for his comfort, as the foregoing ones might prove for the preservation of his life; *viz.*

Canastre tobacco, or cigars †.
Cayenne pepper.
A pot of anchovies.
A phial of lemon acid.
A bottle of the best olive oil.

---

* To keep the soles of shoes dry, you will find no ready-made article better, or cheaper, than Mr. Hunt's "water-proof composition."

† The mildest, and perhaps the pleasantest, tobacco, for those who are not much used to smoking, is that called Syrian; which (although

With these ingredients, and half as much knowledge as usually belongs to all our old campaigners, he may perfectly enjoy his dinner on fish, flesh, and fowl, in those wild places where they are most abundant, but where we are the least able to have them dressed in perfection. For example:—

There is no better sauce for a wildfowl, plover, or snipe, than *equal quantities of olive oil and lemon juice.* Cayenne pepper, when mixed with a little vinegar, gives a fine relish to a pheasant, or any other game. With good oil you can, in most places, during the fishing season, have a French salad made with the young leaves of the wild dandelion; or, in the shooting season, a German salad, called in some parts of Germany, I believe, "*kartofel salat,*" with *slices of cold boiled waxy potatoes.* Either of these, with a few onions, an anchovy, and two spoonsful of oil to every one of vinegar (or *equal quantities* of each to the *German* one), make a very good salad; or, at all events, a good substitute for one, where perhaps the lettuce, cress, or endive, are scarcely known to the inhabitants. *Tarragon* vinegar, for salads, is generally preferred to the other vinegar. (Let me observe, by the way, that the chief art of dressing a salad consists in *wiping perfectly dry* whatever it is made with, and cutting off the flabby parts from the leaves of the herbs.) If you have no good butter, for your fish, you will find, that with a little cayenne, a spoonful of the liquor from your anchovies, and some lemon, or vinegar, *olive oil,* and mustard, it will be perfectly good. Nothing is better than a dish of small birds *fried,* and eat with oil and lemon juice; and if you have no good butter to fry them with, here again some *oil* must be your substitute.

If you have no biscuits to eat with your wine, or, what you may drink for want of it, cut some slices of raw potatoe very thin; have them broiled, or fried, brown and crisp with your oil, and sprinkled

---

to be had at a reasonable price of Mr. Ward, 16, Piccadilly) is not so generally known as it deserves to be. For expensive and fancy tobaccos, of the very best quality, we should go to Mr. Hudson, in Oxford-street; but an insertion of all their names here would be as great a bore as a Greek lesson.

with a little Cayenne pepper; but, in dressing them, let the *slices lie independent of each other,* or they will become soft by fermentation. If you wish for a hash, or any thing dressed by way of variety from plain cooking, you can always give it a flavour, if you have cayenne, lemon, and anchovy.

In short, the ingredients here named, as general acquisitions to your eating in comfort, will be found, I trust, some of the most useful; and I therefore need add no more, as I neither profess, nor wish, to gratify the palate of an epicure; but have merely attempted to show, how one man could make himself comfortable, where another would starve, by the foregoing hints to young caterers and young sportsmen.

Having now said enough as to taking care of, and providing for, my young readers, we will suppose one of them to have arrived at the miserable hole alluded to, and that the first salutation, after the knock at his bedchamber door, in the morning, is, "*A wet day, sir!*" and, instead of being able to pursue his sport, either after breakfast, or at noon *(the most usual time for the weather to clear up,* if it clears up at all), he is consigned a close prisoner to the pothouse; looking alternately to the windward clouds, and the plastered walls of the room; hearing, through a thin partition, the discordant merriment of drunken fellows; and inhaling the breezes of a smoky wood fire, with the fumes of their shag tobacco! In such a predicament, then, how can I prescribe for him? and in this predicament, I believe, there are very few sportsmen that have not often been. Why here again, then, I will endeavour to give him a little advice, though I hope he will not think I am beginning to write a sermon. I shall now first observe, that, of all things on earth, to make a man low spirited, unhappy, or *nervous*, is to get into a habit of *idleness*: and, although there are many young people that would pay little attention, and perhaps laugh at me, if I told them that "idleness" was the "root of all evil," yet some, among those very persons, might listen most earnestly, when I remind them, that being *nervous* or *low spirited* is of all other things the most likely to put even a crack *sportsman* off *his shooting*; or to make a young angler *whip off his flies; or be too eager, and therefore unskilful, in killing his fish.* Always, therefore, let him be *employed*, and think no more of the weather, till his man comes, with a smiling face, and says, "*Sir, it will do again now!*" when, if he is a man of genius, and has proper resources, he could almost have wished for another hour's rain, in order to complete that in which his mind was become absorbed. Supposing the hole in which, for the sake of a few days' good sport, he is immured, contains neither books, nor newspapers; nor even stationery good enough to write a few letters in comfort (which, by the way, he should always be enabled to do, by carrying a quire of paper, and one of Clay's new steel pens), still there is no excuse for his being in *sheer idleness*. The mere pocket will always contain enough to employ successfully many a leisure hour. If he is studying any thing particular, he may be provided with some little volume, the most useful to his subject. If he draws, he may, at least, make a sketch of the hole he is in, for a laugh when he gets home; or, if in another style, practise, according to his fancy. If he is a "musician," and away from an instrument, let him learn to do some exercises in harmony, for no man should be called a musician till he does know harmony. If he is an author or a poet, he can never be at a loss:

or, if nothing greater, perhaps he may be a merry fellow, who sings a good song over his bottle, and therefore, on this occasion, by being provided with a "Pocket Nightingale," he may stock himself with songs enough to enliven all his associates on his return. If he is a dry fellow, an enemy to the Muses, and an admirer of only that which is tangible, he may in his retreat con over his pounds, shillings, and pence; and be amused with sketching his affairs, and thinking of what will be most to his advantage. But if he is an *idler*, destitute of all resources—why I will not say "Lord help him!" —but—let him help himself. Let me advise him to embrace, in this day, a moment for reflection, and consider it as an example, perhaps of many hours and days he may have to spend, at an age when he has no longer youth and vigour to distinguish himself among the field of sportsmen; and make a determination to embrace some pursuit, that will be to him a source of future amusement; and he will then, I think, have reason to consider this as one of the most successful days on his calendar.

LIST

OF THE

LONDON GUNMAKERS.

Alden and Smith, 55, Parliament Street, Westminster.
Anderson, Robert, 6, King Street, Westminster.
Ashton, T. and C., Swallow Walk, Goodman's Fields.
Atkins, Alexander, 44, Coldbath Square, Clerkenwell.
Baker, E. and Son, 24, Whitechapel Road.
Barnett, J. E., 134, Minories.
Beckwith, William Andrews, 58, Skinner Street, Snowhill.
Blake, J. A., 253, Wapping, High Street.
Blanch, John, 29, Gracechurch Street.
Blissett, Isaac, 69, Leadenhall Street.
Bond, William, 59, Lombard Street.
Bond, E. and W. 45, Cornhill.
Bowstead, Frederick, 6, Little Alie Street, Goodman's Fields.
Braggs, Robert, 37, High Holborn.
Child, W., 280, Strand.
Egg, John (late D., deceased), 1, Colonnade, Pall Mall.
Egg, Joseph, 1, Piccadilly.
Fisher, Charles, 8, Prince's Street, Leicester Square.
Forsyth, A. and Co., 8, Leicester Street, Leicester Square.
Gameson and Williams, 67, Threadneedle Street.
Garratt, Jos., Rufford's Buildings, Islington.
Golding, William, 199, Oxford Street.
Golding, William, 1, Duke Street, Grosvenor Square.

Grierson, Charles, 10, New Bond Street.
Gulley, Joseph, 254, Oxford Street.
Hall, Collinson, 52, Upper Mary-le-bone Street.
Harding, James, and Son, 82, Blackman Street, Borough.
Hill, John, 76, Tooley Street.
Jackson, Richard, 19, Prince's Street, Lisson Grove.
Jackson, Jane, 28, Wigmore Street, Cavendish Square.
Jackson, T., 17, Upper George Street, Bryanstone Square.
Lacy and Witton, 13, Camomile Street, Bishopsgate.
Lancaster, Charles, 151, New Bond Street.
Leigh, James, 49, Leman Street, Goodman's Fields.
Lindsay, Alexander, 28, Coventry Street, Hay Market.
Ling, William, 16, Church Street, Soho.
London, Edward, 51, London Wall.
Manton and Son, 6, Dover Street, Piccadilly.
Mills, William, 120, High Holborn.
Moore, Charles, 77, St. James's Street.
Moore, William, 78, Edgeware Road.
Mortimer, T. J., 34, St. James's Street.
Nock, Samuel, 43, Regent Circus.
Parker, William, 233, High Holborn.
Potts, Thomas, 70, Minories.
Pritchett, R. Ellis, 37, Chamber's Street, Goodman's Fields.
Probin, John, 46, Lisle Street, Leicester Square.
Purdey, James, 314½, Oxford Street.
Reynolds, T., 47, Great Prescott Street, Goodman's Fields.
Richards, Westley, his agent, Bishop, 170, New Bond Street.
Ridley, T., 22, Chamber's Street, Goodman's Fields.
Riviere, Isaac, 315, Oxford Street.
Sherwood, J. and W., 12, Wellclose Square.
Smith, S. and C., 64, Princes Street, Leicester Square.
Stevens, Thomas, 43, High Holborn.
Tatham, Henry, 37, Charing-cross.
Wilbraham, George, 123, Leadenhall Street.
Wilkinson, James, and Son, 27, Pall Mall.
Wilson, William, 154, Minories.
Wright, Robert, 44, Great Prescott St., Goodman's Fields.

PRESERVERS OF BIRDS, &c.

(I give the names in reply to numerous inquiries which I had hitherto been unable to answer.)

Leadbeater, Mr., 19, Brewer Street, Golden Square, who stuffs for the British Museum, and whose competitors, since he left Mr. Bullock's, had reported him dead. For this reason, it became my duty to let the public know that "poor Mr. Leadbeater" was, and I am happy to add he still is, alive and well; and stuffs better and cheaper than any one I have met with. I luckily found him out just in time to clip the wings of their ornithological fudge, by putting his name in the last sheet of the fifth edition.

Ware, Mr., of Southampton; and Wiltshire, Mr., of Winchester (a very good performer); are our principal bird-stuffers in the country.

GAME LAWS,

FOR

JANUARY, 1833.

So little was the prospect of our ever getting rid of the diabolical old Game Laws, *notwithstanding almost every Member, in both Houses, admitted their absurdity and inconsistency!* that we are highly indebted to Lord Althorp for carrying, as a ministerial measure, any thing like an amendment on them; and reducing them *(as I expressed a hope that they would be)* "*into one Act of the present reign.*" By a reference to my "Suggestions for New Game Laws," of which I made memorandums at least ten years ago, but which I did not publish till 1824 (*vide* the earlier editions of "Instructions to Young Sportsmen"), it will be seen that the present Bill, though similar to what was therein suggested, is, in many clauses, open to great improvement. But never mind!—any thing in lieu of the old and inconsistent statutes is an acceptable pledge for further alterations, till the legislature shall be less occupied with matters of more vital importance to the country.

The General Qualification is good; but the Sporting License should have been increased to 5*l.*; or, at all events, to this amount for those who use *double* guns.

Every thing between Landlord and Tenant had better have been settled by themselves. The legislature will do more harm than good by this interference. And with regard to the tenant being liable not only to the penalty of 2*l.* for allowing people to shoot, but also to that of 1*l.* for every head of game killed!—the clause, to say the least of it, is not one calculated to put the farmers in good humour—and if *they* are in a *bad humour*, the poor *game*, I fear, will be in a *bad way!*

The sale of game, I have no doubt, will prove as severe a blow to the business of poaching, as would free trade to that of smuggling; and the one experiment may be safely tried, because it does not, like the other, interfere with the revenue or commercial interest.

The PENALTY *for trespass is the best law that was ever enacted.* But at present it is inefficient. The grand object that I had in recommending a penalty for TRESPASS ONLY, was to have the power of taking up a man whom you *knew* to be a poacher, but who was too well versed in his art to suffer himself to be detected in the "PURSUIT OF GAME:" and also to have the means of trouncing a dandified marauder, to whom the paltry sum of 2*l.* would be no more an object than a bottle of champagne or a bundle of cigars. But, on the other hand, giving fair play to both of these worthies, by making them subject to a penalty *only* as WILFUL trespassers; or, in other words, for continuing or repeating the trespass after they had been warned off by the proprietor or occupier of the land. To be more fully understood, however, I shall now take the liberty of reprinting a part of what I before published, under the head of "Game Laws;" and by a reference to which it will be seen precisely how far the suggestions therein contained are analogous to the Bill which has now passed, and the Abridgment of which (with that also of the old laws still in force) shall conclude the following pages.

P.S. Dec. 1832.—I have now the best authority for saying that the ministers admitted several provisions (of which they entirely disapproved) to be introduced in the new bill, and, in short, were obliged to compromise with their opponents, on the best terms they could, for the sake of attaining *two* great *objects—legalising the sale of game,* and the *general qualification.* The one, to say the least of it, an act of common justice to all gentlemen who are not possessed of landed property, or sporting rights—the other the extinction of a law that subjected even the second sons of noblemen to the same penalty as the lowest tradesman, when shooting on the property of their own fathers—not to say a word of its gross absurdity and inconsistency!—What objections there are to *these* two clauses I am at a loss to know! But as to the *other* sections of the present Act—it becomes quite a mystery to learn from whence they emanated! Certain, however, it is that almost every one is exclaiming most violently against the new game-laws; and swearing that, unless they are altered, field sports will soon cease to be the occupation of gentlemen. But is there any such great difficulty in discovering the evil that now exists, and renders the new game laws (which might be made excellent) even worse than the old ones? See how the matter at present stands—we have, on the one hand, legalised the sale of game, and thereby opened the market an hundred fold; without, on the other hand, having taken any one additional step against the wholesale destroyer of it—the poacher. We may proceed against the fair sportsman, like a common felon, if, by chance or absolute mistake, he crosses one little strip of land, without a formal permission; while the *poacher*, unless you can *prove* him to be "*in search or pursuit of game,*" is wholly exonerated from the penalty of the present Act. No man should be subject to a penalty unless he has received a *notice*, and *then* let the penalty be made even more severe than that in the new game laws. And, above all, let the PENALTY be for WILFUL TRESPASS, WHETHER IN PURSUIT OF GAME OR NOT. How could the poacher then go to reconnoitre—or to set his wires—or to take the eggs of game?—But, as the law *now* stands, it destroys the sport of the gentleman, whose interest it is to preserve the game; and, by an enlarged market, affords additional facility to the wholesale destroyer. As the law was (except qualification), and STILL IS, any man with a license and permission may CATCH game, in the day time!! Only refer back to my "Hints for the Preservation of Game," and see what may be done in this way by the DAY-*poacher*. Again—walk through the streets of London, or any other large town, and see how many hundred head of game are hanging in the poulterers' shops, *without one feather being touched with* SHOT!—Is it possible that we can *do away with qualifications—keep an open market*—and *at the same time* have no effectual remedy against the trespass of the *secret poacher*, or the *murderous havoc of the net and snare?*—But, following up the same bad policy, we make war with the very men of all others who have the power to be our best assistants—who are constantly on the ground, and about at all hours—and who have the lower classes under their immediate control—I mean the *farmers*. They, who feed the game, are to be subject to *even* a *greater* penalty than the unknown trespasser; and to pay 1*l*. *for every head of game, in addition to* the 2*l*. penalty for trespass! Can any man of common sense imagine that, while such a law exists, a farmer will exert himself to prohibit his labourers from poaching, or feel the smallest interest in preserving the nest of a partridge?—Impossible! With a general qualification and an open market, a three and a half guinea license is not sufficient. Though the *legal* attainment of game, by fair purchase or otherwise, is the undoubted right of the subject, yet the *shooting* it is an *amusement*—a *luxury;* and, for this reason, there can be no hardship in raising the price of a certificate. Why not also make every one who shoots wildfowl, plover, wood-pigeons, &c., any where but on his own land, pay a small license for his diversion, similar to a French *port-d'armes?*

In short, after all, there has been an immoderate deal said, and but very little done, with, this everlasting subject, the game laws. Let us however hope that, before the sports of country gentlemen are completely annihilated, something will be settled to the satisfaction of all fair and rational men:—and as to those who are not of this number—whether they are pleased or not—is a matter of very little consequence.

SUGGESTIONS FOR NEW GAME LAWS.

[*Published in* 1824.]

By making observations on the inconsistence of the present Game Laws, I have involved myself in the unthankful office of having to point out where, in my humble opinion, the evil exists; and therefore, at the same time, of having to prescribe a few brief suggestions for its remedy. Of all subjects that ever came to a revision of the legislature, this, although comparatively insignificant, is perhaps one of the most difficult, by reason that to please all parties here, I firmly believe, would be an utter impossibility.

One simple question, however, may be asked by every one:—Let any Member, supposing that he is an advocate for the present Game Laws, advert no further than to the Act relating to *qualifications*, and to the *Mutiny Act*, and see whether they are not *inconsistent*, or, in other words, *contrary to justice and to common sense?*—Can that Member, therefore, say, that he would be strictly doing his duty, if, when called on for his vote, he tacitly admits, that those Acts which are *inconsistent*, or *contrary to common sense*, should remain among our code of laws? But, as to the *general principles* of the Game Laws, we should, instead of putting ourselves out of temper, make every allowance for the errors of those who may be inclined to vote in their favour. We should recollect, that many of the cleverest men in existence, when you come to the subject of their *game*, cannot divest themselves of feeling, in some degree, personally interested; and it need scarcely be observed, that although a man may have the highest sense of honour, and the most consummate talent, yet all men have, more or less, one favourite pursuit, their attachment for which evidently points out where their weak side exists; and here, therefore, it becomes difficult to give them satisfaction. Let what will be proposed, depend on it there will be a host of public speakers and public writers to disapprove of it; and as every suggestion on such a *tender* subject is not only open to criticism, but to public ridicule, I am justified in repeating, that whoever speaks or writes on this subject, undertakes a most unthankful office.

I shall, therefore, withhold going far into detail, and conclude with a few hints, that are entirely founded on experience; and pretty good information as to the secrets among poachers of every description. Not presuming, however, that I am capable of dictating even to the lowest member in the legislature; but merely with a view of pointing out a few of those evils, which may have escaped notice among persons of far greater abilities than my own.

We are all highly indebted to Lord Wharncliffe for his exertions towards improving the Game Laws. For, as Sir Robert Peel justly observed (if I may quote from newspapers), "the Bill went to provide remedies for two great evils, which sprung out of the present laws. *First, it empowered the sale of game;* and, *second, it made a great and necessary change in the qualification.*" But with regard to making game private property—much as the measure would be to my own private interest, yet I cannot conscientiously say that I think it would give public satisfaction. The most correct man would for ever be liable to get into difficulty, by which means there would be more, instead of fewer disputes between sportsmen and occupiers of land. To conclude then: I shall here repeat, with a few trifling additions, what I before suggested through the medium of the "Star" evening paper; and, at the same time, apologise for presuming to give a public opinion, which, in many respects, may differ from that of men with whom it would be the height of folly for me to suppose that I could cope in either talent or argument.

"April 12, 1824.

"SIR,

"I beg leave to suggest, through the medium of your paper (and I have also taken the liberty to send to Members of both Houses of Parliament), the mere outline of what, in my humble opinion, would be the best improvement that could be made on the Game Laws.

"Yours, &c. &c.

"To the Editor."

Do away with qualifications (or at all events arrange them so as to be strictly just and consistent).

Any further observations on this law, as yet existing, for *qualifications*, would be an insult to the understanding of my readers.

A five guinea license for every one who shoots *game* (except a keeper, who should pay two guineas).

An extra guinea and a half, once in a year, could be no great object to a man who can afford to buy a gun, and can also afford to give up a considerable portion of his time, and to keep dogs, and supply himself with ammunition. At all events, if this duty should reduce the number of shooters—so much the better for the *birds;* if not—so much the better for the *revenue.*

A two guinea license (similar to a French *port d'armes)* for every one who carries a gun, in any place whatever (off his own premises), but with *this* license only a *gamekeeper* can kill *game.*

(Let a man who shoots without a license be surcharged by the collectors of taxes, as they are the most vigilant informers).

There could then be no complaints about the "liberty of the subject," more than his paying for any other diversion. If he can afford to carry a gun for his amusement, let him assist the revenue by paying for it.

This duty would only operate on the mere idlers of the country, who, in winter, neglect their work to go about with a gun, to the ruin of themselves, and risk of their own as well as other people's lives. Lest it should be argued, however, that this might throw on the parish-books those fishermen on the coast, who could, otherwise, support their families by shooting, I must beg to inform you, that these are the very men who are most anxious that a duty should be laid on guns, in order to prevent their being constantly annoyed by the idle. I am credibly informed, that a few years ago, a petition to this effect would have been presented to the House of Commons by (I think) a Mr. B——, from the fishermen on the coast of Essex, had they not disobliged this gentleman by poaching, or some other improper conduct.

Let farmers' bird-keepers be confined to the use of a pistol, or fire-arms not exceeding a foot in length, and be liable to a surcharge if they shoot at game or water-fowl.

Many a "*bird-keeper!*" have I caught, both at dusk and at dawn, crawling behind a hedge after a covey of partridges that were feeding on a barley stubble. Such little exercises in rural sports frequently go on, either in the morning, before sportsmen are in the field, or in the afternoon, while the legislator is at the first course of his dinner, his head-keeper at his tea, and the under-keepers watching the coverts.

Many a "*bird-keeper!*" too, have I seen leaving the good farmer's corn to the generosity of rooks, while he had skulked off to the river, to try the quality of his master's gun and ammunition at a duck or a moor-hen.

A freeholder of five hundred acres (or a tenant, with the consent of his landlord) may depute a gamekeeper.

As the law now stands, many a gentleman is living on his estate, which consists of more than a thousand acres, and yet has no means of obtaining game from that very estate on which the game is bred, unless he is a sportsman himself, or invites others to come and shoot for him.

Thus the man of ONE *thousand* acres, if he is not the lord of a manor, is to be left dependent for ONE BRACE of birds; while the lord paramount, with his FIVE *thousand* acres, could perhaps command his FIVE THOUSAND head of game in a season! And, what is even harder again on the former, while the *occupier of not so much as one hundred* acres *has a right to appoint a keeper*, because he happens to be the lord of the manor! All this may be thought very clever and very proper! but, unfortunately for me, I am so blind as not to be able to *discover* the propriety of such a law, though it requires but little penetration to perceive its monopoly and injustice.

Have licensed dealers subject *only* to the magistrates.

Every person should have the power of legally obtaining game, by which means it would be thought the less of; and there could be no excuse for dealing with a poacher, or other unlawful vender. It is very hard, that not only a respectable tradesman, but even a gentleman, perhaps with high rank and immense funded property, cannot command a brace of birds for his table without being liable to a penalty. The unjust severity of such a prohibition, therefore, induces many opulent persons to encourage this illegal traffic. It does not follow, however, that the gentleman is to turn *game-poulterer*, or that game must be made private property, for the purpose in question. For if it was, the farmer might possibly spoil the gentleman's sport, by making a trade of it; or, if thwarted in his views, might then destroy the nests of half the birds on his land. But let those who, from having a certificate, and permission to shoot, are lawfully in possession of game, be allowed also the power of selling it to persons who are duly licensed to deal in that article. In short, let the matter be so arranged, that every one may have a lawful means of procuring game, as well as venison, or any other luxury.

One hundred pounds penalty for buying game of one who has neither a certificate to kill it, nor a license to sell it; and let the *vender* have the power of *turning informer.* The same penalty of course for one, who, with neither certificate nor dealer's license, shall *sell* game, or offer game for sale.

Perhaps many of those who prescribe laws are not aware, that most poachers are in a society, and have a stock purse to support each other; by which means they are enabled to snap their fingers at a *five* pound penalty. But a few *hundred* pound penalties would soon reduce their fund to a state of bankruptcy, and thereby overturn the whole concern.

The Mutiny Bill to be altered, so that it must be the *proprietor* or *occupier, not* the *lord of the manor,* who gives leave to officers*.

For, as the Articles of War now stand, it appears, that an officer is liable to a penalty of five pounds for shooting, without the *lord's* leave, on the ground of his own father, where this very lord has, perhaps, no right to sport himself!

[I might go more into detail, but to write any thing *too long* is the sure way *never to have it read.*]

The foregoing suggestions having met with great attention, I was induced to address to the Editor of the "Star" another communication on the subject; which will here follow, with some additions:—

"SIR,

"As you did me the honour to publish my last letter of the 12th ult., on the Game Laws, I beg leave

* 1831. The Mutiny Bill NOW IS altered, as herein formerly prescribed. This will be seen by an extract from it hereafter given.

to propose an amendment in the Act for the punishment of trespass; and, at the same time, to transmit you a few more observations on the subject of the Game Laws in general. I am," &c.

TRESPASS.

FIVE pounds PENALTY *(open to mitigation)* for one who goes, or wilfully continues, on the land of another, *after he has received notice.* One half of this penalty to go to the collector of taxes for government, and the other half to the poor of the parish wherein the offence is committed.

The defendant, if dissatisfied with the decision of the magistrates, may refer his case to trial at the assizes, &c.; but, if he lose his cause, he must pay the *5l. in addition* to the damages that may be awarded by the jury; and, in *this latter case,* the *5l.* should go to the *plaintiff,* in order to liquidate his costs, or any expense that might have been incurred by the trouble which the defendant would have given him.

No *compromise* to be taken for this, or any other, penalty, unless before, and with the consent of, magistrates. It should, of course, however, be arranged so that information for the penalty of TRESPASS could be only laid by (or by order of) the person, or persons, on whom that trespass was committed.

By this means we can at once take a warrant against the poacher, who, if a shrewd fellow, and master of his business, would clear off half the game in a small manor, before he might be detected in the pursuit of it, much less in the very act of poaching. All seizures, bloodshed, and danger, might thus be almost wholly avoided. Only see him, even with a *spyglass,* at any time on the forbidden ground (so as to be able to swear to his person), and have a warrant for him as a wilful trespasser *. By this means also, the poor farmer, who *has no money to go to law*, has some protection against infringement on his rights by the man who tramples on him, from this very circumstance. But having no share in, and therefore no profit on, the penalty, he has no temptation to take any advantage merely for the sake of getting the 2*l.* 10*s.* himself. Any person thinking himself aggrieved, should have the law open to him; and the risk of an extra 5*l.* in such a case could be no object.

For the second, and all future wilful trespasses, on that same person to whom the offender had before been made to pay the 5*l.*, *to be not less than* 5*l.* *nor more than* 50*l.*, *at the option of the magistrates.*

---

* I one day happened to be, for some time, in conversation with one of the shrewdest fellows, and most finished poachers, that ever lived; who, after defying all his pursuers, has left off the trade, and retired to a lawful business. He laughed at the game laws. I then named to him the new laws, as lately proposed. (Here I alluded to the late bill which was thrown out in the Lords.) He smiled, and said, "that won't do." I next named what I before, as well as what is here, suggested; as if another Act contemplated by parliament. He then put on a very serious face, and said, "Upon my soul, sir, that's the only plan: that would properly *do* them. No one would trust a man for 100*l.*; but 5*l.* is no object to either a buyer or even a poor man, if he has got plenty of *friends under his thumb!* A man, too, must be a *poor hand* to let people *see him at work*; but if a gentleman could *work him* for a mere trespass, he could not go to *his ground*, to '*plant his men* †' *before feeding time.*"

IT ABSOLUTELY REQUIRES A VERY OLD SPORTSMAN, WHO HAS DISCOVERED ALL THE SECRETS OF POACHERS, TO STRIKE AT THE ROOTS OF THIS EVIL, AND NOT LEGISLATORS, WHO ARE WORTHY OF A BETTER OFFICE.

† Poachers' term for *setting wires.*

Who should have a great extent of discretional power to mitigate the penalty; as this law, like all others, must of course be open to the abuse of tyrannical persons, and there might occur some extraordinary instances, where it would become desirable to mitigate the punishment as much as possible.

If the defendant appeals from the decision of the magistrates, to a court of law, for a *second* wilful trespass, whereby the penalty here proposed would be from 5*l.* to 50*l.*; let him, *if he loses his cause,* pay, in addition to the damages, whatever sum had before been awarded by magistrates.

Amend the 57th statute of Geo. III. for transporting a man who is found, at night, armed with intent to kill game; and let it be, that, *if he makes any* RESISTANCE *on being apprehended,* he shall be transported.

If not, his "footing it," for a month or two, in the tread-mill, would be quite sufficient punishment; and *particularly*, to a *poacher*, who, except when at his nightly business, is generally one of the *laziest* drones in existence. This little "training," too, may perhaps be the means of getting him "in wind" for a more industrious life; and, therefore, of tending to the support, instead of the starvation, or incumbrance on a parish, of his unfortunate family.

All game shooting (except black game, muir game, and ptarmigan) to begin on the 1st of October.

By such an arrangement thousands of very young partridges, that are not fair game, would escape being massacred by the gentleman-poacher, and falling a prey, when in hedges and hassocks, to the dogs of the pot-hunter. There would be avoided many disputes between farmers and eager young sportsmen (perhaps the sons of their landlords), who sometimes cannot resist following their game into the corn. There would be an end of destroying a whole nide of young pheasants in standing barley, which is so frequently and so easily done in September.

The hot weather of September was never meant for hard fagging. September is a month that the agriculturist should devote to his harvest, and the man of pleasure to sailing, sea-bathing, fishing, and other summer pursuits. But when *October* arrives, the farmer has leisure to enjoy a little sport after all his hard labour, without neglecting his business; and the gentleman, by a day's shooting at that time, becomes refreshed and invigorated, instead of wearing out himself and his dogs, by slaving after partridges under a broiling sun in September. The evenings begin to close, and he then enjoys his party and his fireside, after a day's shooting of just sufficient duration to brace his nerves, and make every thing agreeable.

Penalty for killing game out of season to be not less than 5*l.* nor more than 50*l.*, at the option of the magistrates.

One regular penalty is not fair. There should rest with the magistrates the power of making a very great distinction between one, who could prove that he had killed a head of game for a *longing lady*, or a sick person, and another, who wantonly destroyed it in open violation of the law.

The Act for refusing to give names;

The periods for killing game, with the mere alteration of deferring partridge-shooting till October;

And a proper *time fixed* for killing *hares,* which has *never yet been done!*

The Act for killing pigeons;

The duty on dogs, &c.; may remain as they now stand;

Except that these, and what few other laws it may be necessary to extract from the old statutes, should be taken from the chaos in which they are at present immured, made as clear as possible, and ADDED TO THIS ONE ACT in the present reign. And let all the contradictory nonsense about Henry, James, Anne, &c., be thrown into the fire, as being so complex as often to confuse even lawyers themselves, and therefore calculated only to ensnare the unwary, and be a subject of ridicule to every man of common sense.

Game laws, or any other laws, admitting them to be the best measures ever adopted, may, for want of being consistently arranged, and justly modified, be completely changed in their features, and laid fairly open, not only to the tap-diverting sarcasms of travesty patriots, but to the just criticism of respectable people. Yet, however judgmatically the game laws might be arranged, it becomes highly necessary that these laws, as well as every concern, if rendered of a serious nature, should be supported by such gentlemen as are an ornament to a most honourable profession, and who are always the first to open for their clients the doors of reconciliation. But with regard to the *frivolous* points that are repeatedly contending, how sincerely is it to be regretted, that so many expensive law-suits should be for ever taking place, and particularly about the *game?* How easily, in many cases, might they be avoided, to the greatest *interest* of *both* parties! For instance, if any little difference occurred, why not have it decided by a *certain number* of gentlemen chosen by each party? To the *decision of other persons* it *must* come *at last:* though most likely before a less competent tribunal!—for it stands to reason, that a promiscuously assembled jury cannot be made such perfect masters of every circumstance, as persons selected, who are ably *versed in the subject* of dispute; and especially as the final decision, in a court of justice, may be liable to depend on the judgment of a dozen poor men, who can scarcely read or write, or even understand a single point of an argument.

If, therefore, people, who have the honesty to require no more than what is just and fair, would also have the good sense to withhold going to law *on every trumpery altercation*, there would be much more happiness among mankind; and there could accrue but one evil, and this of a minor consideration; which is, that a certain proportion (I mean the dross only) of hireling dons, instead of being arrayed like demigods, with their notes of discord, would be obliged to resign the lion's skin for the more certain revenue of a methodist preacher, or a strolling player; and such of those blue-bag satellites, as are scouted by all honourable branches of the law, might be reduced to the appointment of carrying parcels for a coach-office, or wheeling gravel on a turnpike road.

PENALTY ON OFFICERS KILLING GAME, &c.

[*Extracted from the Articles of War, or Mutiny Act, of the present Reign: dated* 1831.]

"Sec. 67. And for the better Preservation of Game and Fish, in or near such Places, where any Officers shall, at any time, be quartered, be it enacted, That every Officer who shall, without leave, in writing, FROM THE PERSONS ENTITLED TO GRANT SUCH LEAVE *, take, kill, or destroy any Game or Fish, within the United Kingdom of *Great Britain* and *Ireland*, and, upon complaint thereof, shall be, upon Oath of one or more credible Witnesses, convicted before any Justice, shall, for every such Offence, forfeit the Sum of *5l.*"

* No longer "*the Lord of the Manor*," as was once the error here.

NEW GAME ACT.

Dated 5th of October, 1831.

Since the publication of the Sixth Edition of "INSTRUCTIONS TO YOUNG SPORTSMEN," the Act of 1 and 2 W. 4, c. 32, has been passed with relation to the Game Laws, an Abstract of which is as follows:—

The first Section REPEALS ALL the *following Statutes.*

13 Ric. 2, st. 1, c. 13.	7 Jac. 1, c. 11.	2 Geo. 3, c. 19.
22 Edw. 4, c. 6.	22 & 23 Car. 2, c. 25.	13 Geo. 3. c. 55.
11 Hen. 7, c. 17.	4 W. & M. c. 23.	13 Geo. 3, c. 80.
19 Hen. 7, c. 11.	5 Ann. c. 14.	39 Geo. 3, c. 34.
14 & 15 Hen. 8, c. 10.	9 Ann. c. 25.	43 Geo. 3, c. 112.
25 Hen. 8, c. 11.	8 Geo. 1, c. 19.	48 Geo. 3, c. 93.
33 Hen. 8, c. 6.	10 Geo. 2, c. 32.	50 Geo. 3, c. 67.
23 Eliz. c. 10.	26 Geo. 2, c. 2.	58 Geo. 3, c. 75.
2 Jac. 1, c. 27.	28 Geo. 2, c. 12.	59 Geo. 3, c. 102.

SHORT EPITOME OF OLD NONSENSICAL STATUTES REPEALED.

13 Rich. 2, Stat. 1, c. 13. Prohibits Artificer, &c., not having Lands, &c., to the value of 40*s.* a Year, or Priest, not having 10*l.* a Year, from keeping any Greyhound, &c., or using Ferrets, &c., or taking or destroying Hares, or Conies, or other Gentlemen's Game.

22 Edw. 4, c. 6. Prohibits Persons, not having Freehold Lands of the value of Five Marks a Year, from "having any Mark, or Game of Swans."

11 Hen. 7, c. 17. Prohibits any Person from bearing any Hawk, of the Breed of England, or taking any Hawks in their Warrens or Woods, or driving them from their Coverts, or taking any Pheasants or Partridges by Net, Snares, or other Engines, out of his own Warren; or the taking of the Eggs of any Falcon, Gosshawk, Laner, or Swan.

19 Hen. 7, c. 11. Prohibits the taking of any Herons, unless with Hawking or Long Bows, or taking young Herons out of the Nest, or destroying their Eggs.

14 & 15 Hen. 8, c. 10. Prohibits any Person from tracing and killing any Hare in the Snow, under a Penalty of 6*s.* 8*d.*

25 Hen. 8, c. 11. Prohibits the destroying Eggs of Wild Fowl, from 31 March to 30 June.

33 Hen. 8, c. 6. Prohibits the use of Crossbows and Handguns, unless by Persons having 100*l.* a Year in Lands, Annuities, or Offices; or who shall be licensed by the King.

23 Eliz. c. 10. Prohibits hawking in another Man's Corn, after it is eared, and before it is shocked, under a Penalty of 40*s.*; and killing any Pheasant or Partridge in the Night time, under a Penalty of 20*s.* for the former, and 10*s.* for the latter.

2 James 1, c. 27. Prohibits shooting, or destroying, any Pheasant, Partridge, Pigeon, "Hearn," Mallard, Duck, Teal, Widgeon, Grouse, Heath-cock, Moor-game, or Hare, or taking the Eggs of any Pheasant, Partridge, or Swan, or destroying the same in the Nest; or tracing any Hares in the Snow, or destroying them with Hare-pipes, Cords, &c. Also, the keeping of any Greyhound, for coursing, or any Setting Dog, or Nets, to take Pheasants, or Partridges (except Persons having Lands of Inheritance of 10*l.* a Year; or for Life or Lives, of the value of 30*l.* a Year, or Goods and Chattels to the value of 200*l.*; or being the Son of a Knight, or a Baron of Parliament, or of some Person of higher degree, or the Son and Heir of any Esquire).

Also the selling, or buying to sell again, any Deer, Hare, Partridge, or Pheasant.

7 James 1, c. 11. Prohibits the destroying, or killing, any Pheasant, or Partridge, with Hawk, or Dog, between 1st July and the 31st August, under a Penalty of 40*s.*; and 20*s.* for every such Pheasant, or Partridge, taken or killed.

22 & 23 Car. 2, c. 25. Prohibits setting or using of Snares, &c., under a Penalty not exceeding 10*s.*, and making Compensation to the Party injured; and this Act also prohibits the killing of Conies in Warrens *.

4 Will. & Mary, c. 23. Prohibits the burning, between 2d of February and 24th of June, any Grig, Ling, Heath, Furze, Goss, or Fern, on any Mountains, Hills, &c. And the

5 Ann. c. 14. Gives particular directions concerning the burning of Ling, &c., in Sherwood Forest, and other Places in Nottinghamshire; and subjects Higglers, Carriers, Innkeepers, Victuallers, and Alehouse-keepers, having in their Custody any Hare, Pheasant, Partridge, &c., to penalties.

9 Ann. c. 25. Prohibits the killing of any Hares, Pheasants, Partridges, Moor- (or Heath-) Game, or Grouse, in the Night time, under a Penalty of 5*l.*; and enacts, that no Lord of a Manor shall make more than one Gamekeeper within one Manor with power to kill Game.

8 Geo. 1, c. 19. Directs that when any Person shall be liable to any pecuniary Penalty for Offences against the Game Laws, any other Person may recover the Penalty by Information, before a Justice, or sue for the same.

10 Geo. 2, c. 32. So far as regards the *Game* Laws, Prohibits the taking of Wild Fowl, in Nets, between the 1st of July and the 1st of September.

26 Geo. 2, c. 2. Directs that Suits for pecuniary Penalties, under the Game Laws, may be brought before the End of the second Term, after the Offence committed.

28 Geo. 2, c. 12. Directs that Persons selling or exposing for Sale any Game, shall be liable to the Penalties of the 5th of Anne against Higglers, &c.

---

* And by the 3d section, "every person, not having Lands and Tenements, or some other estate of inheritance, in his own or his Wife's right, of the *clear* yearly value of 100*l.* per Annum, or for term of life, or having a Lease or Leases of Ninety-nine Years, or for any longer term, or of the clear yearly value of 150*l.* (other than the Son and Heir apparent of an Esquire, or *other Person* of higher degree, and the Owners and Keepers of Forests, Parks, Chases, or Warrens), is prohibited from having, keeping, or using any Guns, Bows, Greyhounds, Setting Dogs, Ferrets, Coney Dogs, Lurchers, Hays, Nets, Lowbels, Hare-pipes, Guns, Snares, or other Engines aforesaid."

2 Geo. 3, c. 19. Prohibits the killing, selling, buying, or possessing, of any Partridge, between the 22d of February (altered by 36 Geo. 3, c. 39, to the 12th of February, and by the 39 Geo. 3, c. 34, to the 1st of February) and the 1st of September, subject to a Penalty of *5l.* for every such Fowl.

13 Geo. 3, c. 55. The time for killing *Black* Game from August 20 (afterwards altered, by 43 Geo. 3, c. 112, to 1st September), to December 10.
Grouse, commonly called *Red* Game, between 12th August and 10th December; and Bustards between 1st of May and 1st of September.

13 Geo. 3, c. 80. Prohibits the killing, taking, or destroying, or using of any Gun, Dog, Snare, Net, or other Engine, with intent to kill, &c., any Hare, Pheasant, or Partridge, Moor Game, or Heath Game, in the Night, or in the Day time, upon a Sunday or Christmas Day, under a Penalty, for the first Offence, not exceeding *20l.*, nor less than *10l.*; and for the second, not exceeding *30l.*, nor less than *20l.*

39 Geo. 3, c. 34. [See 2 Geo. 3, c. 19, *ante*.]

43 Geo. 3, c. 112. [See 13 Geo. 3, c. 55, *ante*]

48 Geo. 3, c. 93. Lords of Manors may appoint Gamekeepers, whether qualified or not.

50 Geo. 3, c. 67. Prohibits the taking Black Game in Somersetshire and Devonshire, between December 10 and September 1.

58 Geo. 3, c. 75. Prohibits the buying or selling of Game.

59 Geo. 3, c. 102. Is for the further regulating the Appointment of Gamekeepers in Wales.

N.B. THE NEW ACT COMMENCED, AND TOOK EFFECT, ON THE 1st OF NOVEMBER, 1831.

SKETCH OF THE OLD STATUTES WHICH STILL REMAIN IN FORCE, ETC.

N. B. The old laws, which are *not* repealed (as heretofore abridged in the "Instructions") are those which relate to

Shooting TAME PIGEONS:—

Duties on Dogs:—

Stealing Dogs, or Tame Birds:—

Forms of Deputations, and Notices:—

ACTION for Trespass;

And "*Persons found at night, armed with intent to kill game,*" *&c. &c.* An epitome of which will hereafter follow that of the New Act.

There is no limitation of time for *killing hares!* Now, as the certificate does not expire till the 5th of April, hares may be lawfully killed at improper times of the year! This surely must have been overlooked in framing the new Act! It will be observed, by the following Abstract, that the Act for *Game Certificates* is the same as before, with the *addition of the new penalty to the old one;* and that EVERY ONE who takes out a CERTIFICATE is NOW QUALIFIED TO SHOOT, provided he has leave, or is not objected to, by the proprietors of the land or of the game.

*** The want of classification, or proper order under each head, proceeds from the Act itself, and not from the compiler's abridgement of it.

The several NEW Enactments are as follow :—

Sec. 2. The word "GAME" to include *Hares, Partridges, Grouse, Heath- (or Moor-) Game, Black-Game,* and *Bustards.*

PENALTY FOR SHOOTING ON SUNDAY, OR CHRISTMAS DAY.

Sec. 3. Any person who shall kill, or take, any Game, or use a Dog, Gun, Net, or other Engine, for that purpose, on a Sunday, or Christmas Day, is subject, on conviction by Two Justices, to a Penalty not exceeding 5*l.*, with Costs.

TIME PROHIBITED FOR KILLING GAME.

Any Person who shall kill or take any *Partridge* between the 1st of February and the 1st of September;

Or any *Pheasant* between the 1st of February and the 1st of October;

Or any *Black Game* between the 10th of December and the 20th of August, (or in Somersetshire, Devonshire, or the New Forest, between the 10th of December and the 1st of September);

Or any *Grouse,* called *Red Game,* between the 10th of December and the 12th of August;

Or any *Bustard,* between the 1st of March and 1st of September —is subject, on Conviction by Two Justices, to a Penalty not exceeding 1*l.* for every Head of Game so killed or taken, with Costs.

PENALTY FOR POISONING GAME.

Any Person laying Poison to kill Game, is made liable to a Penalty not exceeding 10*l.*, with Costs.

PENALTY FOR HAVING GAME AT A PROHIBITED TIME.

Sec. 4. Persons licensed to deal in Game (as after mentioned), who shall buy, or sell, or have in their Possession, any Bird of Game, after Ten Days (one inclusive and the other exclusive) from the Days limited; and Persons, not licensed, who shall buy or sell any Bird of Game after such Ten Days, or shall have, in their Possession, any Bird of Game (except such as are kept in a Mew or Breeding Place) after Forty Days, shall be subject, on Conviction before Two Justices, to a Penalty not exceeding 1*l.* for every such Head of Game.

GAME CERTIFICATES.

Sec. 5. *The Act not to affect the existing Laws respecting Game Certificates.*

GENERAL QUALIFICATION FOR EVERY ONE.

Sec. 6. Every Person *who shall have an annual Game Certificate,* shall be *authorized to kill Game (subject to* an *Action* for any *Trespass* committed by him); but no Certificate, on which a less Duty than 3*l.* 13*s.* 6*d.* is chargeable, shall authorize any Gamekeeper to kill or take Game; or use any Dog, Gun, Net, or other Engine, except within the Limits of his Appointment.

GAME, THE EXCLUSIVE PROPERTY OF THE LANDLORD.

Sec. 7. Under existing Leases, or Agreements, made previous to the passing of this Act, the Landlord shall be entitled to enter, or authorize any other Person or Persons, having an annual Game Certificate, to enter, upon such Land, for the purpose of killing or taking Game; and no Tenant, under such Lease or Agreement, shall have the right to kill or take the Game, on such Land, unless such right is expressly granted, or allowed to him, by his Lease or Agreement; or except he shall have paid a Fine on the granting or renewal of such Lease or Agreement; or the same shall have been made for more than Twenty-one Years.

Sec. 8, 9, 10. This Act not to affect any existing or future Agreements respecting Game; nor any Rights of Manor, Forest, Chase, or Warren; or any of his Majesty's Forest-Rights, or any Cattle-Gates, or Right of Common. The *Lord of the Manor*, therefore, is still to have the *Game* on the *Wastes;* and also the Right of *giving leave* to *Sport* on the *same*, to all Persons who *have Game Certificates.*

INCREASED PRIVILEGE OF LANDLORDS.

Sec. 11. Landlords having reserved to themselves the Right of killing the Game upon the Land, may authorize ANY other Person or Persons to Shoot, *who have obtained* an annual *Game Certificate.*

PENALTY FOR TENANT ALLOWING PEOPLE TO SHOOT.

Sec. 12. Where the Landlord has the Right to the Game, the Tenant shall not pursue, kill, or take the same; or *give Permission to any other Person so to do*, under a *Penalty*, on Conviction before Two Justices, not exceeding 2*l.*; AND, for EVERY HEAD of Game, not exceeding 1*l.*, with Costs!!

GAMEKEEPERS AND DEPUTATIONS.

Sec. 13, 14. Lords of Manors may appoint a Gamekeeper, or Gamekeepers, and authorize them to seize all Dogs, &c., used within the Manor by *uncertificated* Persons *.

Lords of Manors may grant Deputations.

EXCLUSIVE PRIVILEGE FOR WALES.

Sec. 15. Persons seised in fee, or for Life, of Lands, *in* WALES, of the clear annual Value of 500*l.*, and not within any Manor, Lordship, or Royalty, or enfranchised or alienated therefrom, are authorized to appoint a Gamekeeper or Gamekeepers, &c.

* [By this Statute, and by the repeal of the 9th of Anne, c. 25, it appears that we are now allowed *any number* of *keepers* on *one manor*. It is presumed, however, that all of them must have a Three Guinea and Half License, except the One who holds the deputation.]

REGISTER OF GAMEKEEPERS.

Sec. 16. No Appointments of Gamekeepers to be valid until registered with the Clerk of the Peace.

LIBERTY TO SELL GAME.

Sec. 17. *Certificated* Persons *may sell Game* to *licensed Dealers;* but no Game Certificate, with a less Duty than 3*l.* 13*s.* 6*d.*, shall authorize any *Gamekeeper* to *sell Game, except* on account of his *Master.*

PERSONS ADMISSIBLE AS GAMEDEALERS.

Sec. 18. The Justices of the Peace of every County, &c., shall hold a Special Session, in the present Year, between the 15th and 30th of October, and in every succeeding Year in July, for granting Licenses to deal in Game; and the Majority, not being less than Two, are authorized to grant to any Householder, or Keeper of a Shop, or Stall (NOT *being an Innkeeper, or Victualler, or licensed to sell Beer by Retail; or the Owner, Guard, or Driver, of any Mail Coach, Stage Coach, Stage Waggon, Van, or other public Conveyance; or a Carrier, or Higgler, or in the employment of any such person)* a License to buy Game of any Person who may *lawfully* sell it; and also to sell it, at One House, Shop, or Stall, kept by him, and who shall affix, to the Front of the House, Shop, or Stall, a Board, with the Christian and Surname, together with the words, "LICENSED TO DEAL IN GAME;" and every such License, granted in the present Year, shall be in force from the 1st of November till the 15th of July next; and all future Licenses shall be in force for One Year from the granting thereof.

RESTRICTIONS ON, AND DIRECTIONS TO, GAMEDEALERS.

Sec. 19. Every Person who shall have obtained a License, shall ALSO obtain a CERTIFICATE on Payment of 2*l.* DUTY, in the same manner as Game Certificates; and no Person obtaining a License shall deal in Game before he shall have obtained such Certificate, under a Penalty of 20*l.*

Sec. 20. *Collectors* of *Assessed Taxes* to make out a List of Persons who have obtained Licenses to deal in Game.

Sec. 21. *In case of* two or more PARTNERS in the same Shop or Stall, *only* ONE LICENSE *is necessary.*

Sec. 22. Licensed Persons, on being convicted of any Offence against this Act, to forfeit their License.

ADDITIONAL PENALTY FOR SHOOTING WITHOUT A CERTIFICATE.

Sec. 23. Persons killing or taking any Game, or using any Dog, Gun, &c., for the purpose of searching for, or killing, or taking Game, without having a Game Certificate, subject to a Penalty not exceeding 5*l.*, AS WELL AS TO THE PENALTY UNDER THE GAME CERTIFICATE ACT.

PENALTY FOR TAKING EGGS.

Sec. 24. Persons who, not having the Right of killing the Game upon any Land, nor having permission of the Person who has such Right, shall wilfully take out of, or destroy in, the Nest, upon such Land, the Eggs of any Bird of Game, or of any Swan, Wild Duck, Teal, or Widgeon, or shall knowingly have in his possession any such Eggs so taken, shall, on Conviction by Two Justices, pay a Sum not exceeding 5*s.* for every Egg, with Costs.

PARTS OF THE ACT FURTHER RELATING TO LICENSED DEALERS, &c.

Sec. 25. Persons not having a Game Certificate, or not licensed to deal in Game, who shall sell, or offer for sale, any Game, or, having a Game Certificate, shall sell, or offer for sale, any Game to any Person, *except* a *Person licensed to deal in Game,* to forfeit, on Conviction by Two Justices, a Sum not exceeding 2*l.* for every Head of Game so sold, or offered for sale.

Sec. 26. Proviso authorizing Inn or Tavernkeepers to sell Game for *Consumption in their own Houses, without a License,* such Game having been *procured* from some *Person licensed to deal in Game.*

Sec. 27. Persons not licensed to deal in Game, who shall BUY it from any UNLICENSED Person, to be subject to a *Penalty,* on Conviction before Two Justices, not exceeding 5*l*, with Costs.

Sec. 28. Licensed Dealers *buying Game* from any Person *not* having a *Game Certificate,* or a *License to deal* in Game, or selling, or offering for Sale, any Game at his House, Shop, or Stall, *without* having such *Board affixed,* or who shall affix such Board to one House, or more Houses, &c., or shall sell any Game at any place other than his House, &c.; or if any unlicensed Person shall pretend, by affixing such Board, or by exhibiting any Certificate, or by any other Device or Pretence, to be a licensed Person, to be subject, on Conviction by Two Justices, to a Penalty not exceeding 10*l.*, with Costs.

Sec. 29. The *Servants of licensed Dealers* may *sell Game for* their *Masters,* and *one licensed Dealer* may *sell* on account of *another.*

PENALTY FOR TRESPASS.

Sec. 30. Persons *trespassing on any Land,* in the day time, in search or pursuit of Game, Woodcocks, Snipes, Quails, Landrails, or Conies*, on Conviction, by One Justice, subject to a Penalty not exceeding 2*l.*, with Costs; and Persons to the number of Five, or more, so trespassing, subject to a Penalty not exceeding 5*l.* for *each person,* with Costs; and the leave or license of the Occupier of the Land (if not entitled to the Game) shall not be a sufficient defence against the Landlord.

ARREST OF TRESPASSERS.

Sec. 31. Trespassers, in search or pursuit of Game, may be required to quit the Land, and to tell their Names, and Abodes; and, in case of *refusal,* may be *arrested,* and, on Conviction before one Justice, shall be subject to a Penalty not exceeding 5*l.*: Proviso that the Party arrested must be discharged, unless brought before a Justice within Twelve Hours: but he may, nevertheless, be proceeded against by Summons or Warrant.

INCREASED PENALTY FOR TRESPASSERS, WHEN FIVE OR MORE ARE CONCERNED.

Sec. 32—34. Where Five or more Persons shall be found with a Gun on any Land, or any of His Majesty's Forests, &c., in the day time (viz. between the beginning of the last Hour before Sunrise, and the Expiration of the first Hour after Sunset) in pursuit of Game, Woodcocks, &c., and shall, by violence or menace,

* Why not "*Rabbits?*" as "Coney" means *either Rabbit* or *Simpleton!*

endeavour to prevent any authorized Person from approaching, for the purpose of requiring them to quit the land, or to tell their Names, or Places of Abode, *each person* shall be subject, on Conviction before Two Justices, to a Penalty not exceeding *5l.*, with Costs.

PENALTY FOR TRESPASSING ON HIS MAJESTY'S FORESTS, ETC.

Sec. 33. Penalty for Trespassing on His Majesty's Forests, Parks, Chases, or Warrens, in the Day-time, on Conviction before One Justice, not exceeding 2*l.*

EXEMPTION FROM PENALTY FOR TRESPASS, TO HUNTERS, LORDS OF MANORS, ETC.

Sec. 35. The Provisions as to *Trespassers not* to apply to Persons *hunting* or *coursing* with *Hounds* or *Greyhounds,* and being in fresh *pursuit* of any Deer, Hare, or Fox, *already started ;* nor to any Person exercising any Right, or reputed Right, of Free Warren, or Free Chase ; nor to any Gamekeeper within the Limits of a Free Warren or Free Chase ; nor the *Lord,* or Steward of the Crown, of *any Manor,* or *reputed Manor.*

GAME MAY BE TAKEN FROM TRESPASSERS.

Sec. 36. Game may be taken from trespassers, who shall not deliver up the same when demanded.

MODE OF PAYMENT FOR PENALTIES.

Sec. 37. Penalty to be paid to some one of the Overseers of the Parish, or Place, where the Offence shall be committed, for the use of the general Rate of the County.

IMPRISONMENT IN FAILURE OF PAYMENT.

Sec. 38. Penalties to be paid immediately on Conviction ; or within such period as the Justice, or Justices, shall think fit ; and, in default, the Person convicted shall be imprisoned (with or without hard labour) for a Term not exceeding *Two* Calendar Months, where the Penalty, exclusive of Costs, shall NOT *amount to 5l.* ; and *not exceeding Three* Calendar Months in *any other* case.

Sec. 39. The Thirty-Ninth Clause contains the Form of Conviction as follows :—

' } BE it remembered, That on the Day of
' to wit. } in the Year of our Lord at in the
' County of [*or* Riding, Division, Franchise, Liberty, City, &c. *as*
' *the Case may be*], *A. O.* is convicted before me *J. P.* One [*or* us *J. P.* and
' *J. J. P.* Two, *as the Case may require*,] of His Majesty's Justices of the Peace
' for the said County [*or* Riding, *&c.*], for that he the said *A. O.* did, on
' at kill [*or* take] Game, [*or* did use a Dog, *&c.* for
' the Purpose of killing Game], he the said *A. O.* not being authorized so to
' do for Want of a Game Certificate, contrary to the Statute in such Case made
' and provided [*or* did, *here specify any other Offence, and the Time and Place*
' *when and where the same was committed, as the Case may be*] ; and I [*or* we] do
' adjudge that the said *A. O.* shall for the said Offence, forfeit the Sum of
' [*or* we do adjudge that the said *A. O.* shall for the said Offence forfeit
' the Sum of being after the Rate of for every Head
' of Game so, &c. or for every Egg so, &c.], and shall forthwith pay the said
' Sum, together with the Sum of for Costs ; and that in default of
' immediate Payment of the said Sums, he the said *A. O.* shall be imprisoned
' [*or* imprisoned and kept to hard Labour] in the of
' for the Space of unless the said Sums shall be sooner paid ; [*or*
' and I] [*or* we] order that the said Sums shall be paid by the said *A. O.* on or
' before the Day of and in default of Payment on or
' before that Day, I [*or* we] adjudge the said *A. O.* to be imprisoned [*or* im-
' prisoned and kept to hard Labour] in the of for
' the Space of unless the said Sums shall be sooner paid] ; and I
' [*or* we] direct that the said Sum of (*i. e.* the Penalty) shall be
' paid to being one of the Overseers of the Poor of, &c. to be by
' him applied according to the Directions of the Statute in such Case made and
' provided ; and I [*or* we] order that the said Sum of for Costs
' shall be paid to (the Complainant). Given under my Hand
' [*or* our Hands] the Day and Year first above mentioned.

' *J. P.*
' [*or J. P.* and *J. J. P.*]'

Sec. 40. The Justices to have power to summon Witnesses ; and Persons refusing to attend, or to be examined, to forfeit a Sum not exceeding 5*l*.

TIME FOR PROSECUTIONS, FOR PENALTIES, &c.

Sec. 41. Prosecutions to be commenced within Three Calendar Months after commission of the Offence.

Sec. 42. The Prosecutor is not obliged to negative, by evidence, any Certificate, License, &c.; but the Party seeking to avail himself of such Defence to be bound to prove it.

Sec. 43, 44. Convictions to be returned to the Sessions, to which Persons convicted are entitled to Appeal.

NO EVASION, FOR WANT OF FORM, TO BE ALLOWED.

Sec. 45. No summary Conviction, or Adjudication, or Appeal, shall be quashed for *want* of *form*, or removed by Certiorari, or otherwise; and no Warrant of Commitment shall be held void for any defect, provided it be alleged that it is founded on a Conviction, and there shall be a good and valid Conviction to sustain it.

OPTION FOR PROSECUTOR TO PROCEED BY THE OLD ACTION, OR THE NEW PENALTY, FOR TRESPASS.

Sec. 46. *This Act not* to *preclude Actions* for *Trespass*; but NO ACTION, at Law, shall be maintained for the SAME TRESPASS, by any Person, at whose Instance, or with whose Concurrence, or Assent, Proceedings shall have been instituted under THIS ACT.

ACTIONS AGAINST MAGISTRATES, AND OTHERS, FOR ANY THING DONE IN PURSUANCE OF THIS ACT*.

Sec. 47. All Actions for any thing done in Pursuance of this Act, shall be laid and tried in the County where the Fact was committed, and shall be commenced within Six Calendar Months, after the Fact committed; and One Calendar Month's Notice in Writing, given to the Defendant of such Action, and the Cause thereof; and the Defendant may plead the General Issue, and give this Act and the special Matter in Evidence; and no Plaintiff shall recover in such Action, if Tender of sufficient Amends shall be made before the Action be brought, or a sufficient Sum be paid into Court after such Action is brought.

Sec. 48. THIS ACT NOT TO EXTEND TO SCOTLAND OR IRELAND.

* This clause relates to *actions* brought *against* magistrates, and other persons, for any thing done by them which exceeds their power.

SCHEDULE (A.)

FORM OF LICENSE.

At a Special Session of the Justices of the Peace of the County of [*or* Riding, &c., *as the Case may be*] acting for the Division of [or *otherwise, as the Case may be*] in the said County, holden at in the said on the Day of in the Year We being Justices acting for the said assembled at the said Special Session, do hereby authorize and empower *A. B.* of [*here insert the Name, Description, and Place of Residence, and, if more than One in Partnership, say, C. D.* of, &c. and *E. F.* of, &c. being Partners,] being a Householder [*or* Householders], [*or* Keeper (*or* Keepers) of a Shop or Stall, *as the Case may be*], to buy Game from any Person authorized to sell Game by virtue of an Act passed in the Second Year of the Reign of King William the Fourth, intituled "An Act to amend the Laws in England relative to Game;" and we do also authorize and empower the said *A. B.* [*or C. D.* and *E. F.* being Partners] to sell at his [*or* their] House [Shop *or* Stall] any Game so bought, provided that the said *A. B.* [*or C. D.* and *E. F.* being Partners] shall affix to some Part of the Outside of the Front of his [*or* their] House [Shop *or* Stall], and shall there keep, a Board, having thereon in clear and legible Characters his Christian Name and Surname, [*or* their Christian Names and Surnames,] together with the following Words, "Licensed to deal in Game."

This License will expire on

(Signed) Justice of the Peace.
Justice of the Peace.

SCHEDULE (B.)

Form of Certificate to be issued by Clerks of Commissioners of Assessed Taxes to every Person licensed to deal in Game.

Received from *A. B.* [*or C. D.* and *E. F.* being Partners], residing at [Parish, Township, *or* Place] in the County of (in exchange for this Certificate), a Receipt under the Hand of *G. H.* one of the Collectors of Assessed Taxes for the said [Parish, *&c.*] for the Sum of being the Duty chargeable on the said *A. B.* [*or C. D.* and *E. F.* being Partners] in respect of his [*or* their] License to deal in Game.

Certified this Day of in the Year in pursuance of an Act passed in the Second Year of the Reign of King William the Fourth, intituled "An Act to amend the Laws in England relative to Game."

This Certificate will expire on

(Signed)

Clerk to the Commissioners of Assessed Taxes
for the Division of
in the County of

OLD GAME LAWS NOT REPEALED.

SHOOTING CERTIFICATE.

(*Act* 48 *Geo.* 3. *Cap.* 55.)

PENALTY for shooting without, 20*l.*

To be taken out annually, in the parish or place where your assessed taxes are paid; costs 3*l.* 13*s.* 6*d.* and 1*s.* fee to the collector.

For menial servants, hired as gamekeepers, costs 1*l.* 5*s.*, and the 1*s.* fee to the collector.

When demanded by any assessor, collector, land owner, commissioner, inspector, surveyor, occupier of land; also *gamekeeper,* or *other person;* provided the *two latter* produce *their certificates,* previously to requiring yours. Penalty for refusing, 20*l.*

If you have not your certificate to produce, your name, and place of abode, may be asked.—See penalty for refusing.

A certificate is not only required for killing *game;* but also for SHOOTING *Woodcocks, Snipes, Quails, Landrails,* or *Rabbits,* though, for the latter, open to certain exceptions.

As the clause is so short, I will quote from it precisely—" Every person using any dog, gun, net, or other engine, for the purpose of taking, or killing, game; or any woodcock, snipe, quail, landrail, or any conies, in Great Britain," &c.

With two exceptions only—

" 1st, the taking woodcocks and snipes with nets and springes; and, 2dly, the taking or destroying" (meaning *shooting,* or any other mode of destruction, it is presumed) " conies in warrens or in any inclosed ground; or by any person on land in his occupation, either by himself, or by his directions."

All certificates expire on the 5th of April in each year*.

---

* A conviction, under the game laws, once took place at Godalming, on the following curious grounds:—An information was lodged against a qualified gentleman, for having shot at and killed, *after the 5th of April,* a *snipe,* not having a license; and, according to the literal construction of the act, the commissioners of taxes were compelled to fine him in the penalty of twenty pounds, although it appeared he had regularly applied for a license, and had been in the habit of sporting with a license for some years previous. The inference to be drawn from this conviction, therefore, is, that no man can shoot *even snipes,* upon his own estate or elsewhere, between

Be careful, therefore, to *receive* your next certificate before you recommence killing game; in order to defy all pettifogging informers.

GAMEKEEPERS

With only 25*s.* certificates are subject to the full penalties of unlicensed persons; and, with even a 3½ guinea certificate, are subject to *either* the *new penalty or old action* for *trespass*, if they *outstep the bounds of the manor*, for which they are appointed.

DEPUTATION OF A GAMEKEEPER.

The deputation granted to a gamekeeper must be registered with the clerk of the peace, within twenty days after it is granted, and a certificate taken of the same, under penalty of 20*l.* The *deputation* for one keeper holds good till another is appointed. If a new gamekeeper is appointed within the year, the *game certificate* of the former keeper *may be transferred to him* for the remainder of the year; and this must be done, *free of all expense,* by the clerk to the commissioners of the district.

FORM OF A GAMEKEEPER'S DEPUTATION.

(To be written on a 1*l.* 15*s.* *stamp.*)

Know all men, by these presents, that I , of , in the county of , esq. lord of the manor of , in the same county, have nominated, deputed, and appointed, and by these presents do nominate, depute, and appoint , of , yeoman, to be gamekeeper of and within my said manor of , with full power, license, and authority to pursue, take, and kill any hare, pheasant, partridge, or other game whatsoever, in and upon my said manor of , for my sole and immediate use and benefit; and also to take and seize all such guns, bows, greyhounds, setting dogs, lurchers, ferrets, trammels, lowbells, hays, or other nets, hare-pipes, snares, or other engines for the pursuing, taking, or killing of hares, rabbits, pheasants, partridges, or other game, as shall be used within the precincts of my said manor, by any person or persons, who by law are prohibited to keep or use the same. In witness whereof I have hereunto set my hand and seal, this day of , 1830.

(Signature, and seal.)

Sealed and delivered in presence of *(the signature of* ONE *witness, specifying his place of abode, is sufficient.)*

---

the 5th of April and the 20th of July (the earliest day, as it appears, on which licenses are issued), without subjecting himself to a similar penalty.—*Star newspaper.*

REFUSING TO GIVE NAMES.

If you have *not* a *certificate* to *produce, at the time it is called for, your Christian and surnames, and place of abode,* may be demanded, by any assessor, &c. &c. (as before mentioned); and penalty for *refusing them, or giving a false name,* is 20*l.*

TAME PIGEONS, OR HOUSE DOVES.

Unless they are your own property, or you are desired by the lawful owner to kill them, the penalty for shooting them is 20*s.* for *each pigeon.*—(Under statute of 1 Jac. I.)

For *shooting at* pigeons, with *intent to kill,* the penalty would (by 2 Geo. II.) be the same as for killing *one* pigeon, *viz.* 20*s.* Informations for these offences must be commenced within two months.

"But" (says a treatise on the game laws), "notwithstanding the provisions of the above acts, it has been determined, that the owner of land may kill such pigeons as he shall find thereon devastating his corn." But, after having killed the pigeons, he must not take them away.

DOGS.

[*Annual duties on, from the* 5*th of April,* 1832, *to the* 5*th of April,* 1833.]

All *sporting* dogs* (*including lurchers* and *terriers,* or *other* dogs, *where two or more are kept*), 14*s.*

For *other* dogs, where *only one* is kept, 8*s.*

The duties on *dogs* are *not* increased, in proportion to the number kept.

* *Except greyhounds,* for which the duty is 1*l.* for each dog; and a pack of hounds *compounded* for, the duty on which is 36*l.*

DOGS EXEMPTED FROM DUTY.

Whelps, which are not six months old, at the time of returning your list for taxes.

Dogs belonging to any of the royal family, who are exempt from all duties on sporting.

Poor persons, who are not assessed for dwelling-houses, *may keep one* dog, provided it be not a *sporting* dog.

PENALTY FOR STEALING DOGS *.

By 7 and 8 Geo. IV. c. 29, the offender, on conviction, before a justice of peace, to forfeit, for the first offence (over and above the value of the dog), a sum not exceeding 20*l.* For the second offence, to be imprisoned (with hard labour), not exceeding twelve calendar months, and whipped, at the discretion of the justice. Sect. 31.

Persons found in possession of a stolen dog, or the skin thereof (knowing them to be stolen), are liable to the same penalties. Sect. 32.

Such is here the inefficiency of the law, that dog-stealing in London has now become the regular trade of men calling themselves "the *Fancy*;" and of whom there are, at least, fifty leading characters, besides their spies and outposts. These fellows, by way of a blind to avoid suspicion, either assume the character of plasterers, carpenters, &c. &c., and carry the very tools in their hands; or hawk about oranges, hardwares, and other little articles for sale. They have dens in the

* N. B. This law holds good also for (as the act says) "ANY BEAST *or* BIRD *ordinarily kept in a state of confinement*," &c.: and, in sect. 32, it says, "*That if any such dog, or any such* BEAST, *or the skin thereof; or any such* BIRD, *or any of the* PLUMAGE THEREOF, *shall be found in the possession, or on the premises, of any person; and the person shall know the same to have been stolen*," &c. &c.—"*liable to the same penalties.*"

neighbourhood of Whitechapel, Shoreditch, Tottenham-court Road, and Westminster; outposts about Greenwich, Ball's Pond (a noted place on the right of the North Road), Lisson Grove, and Paddington; and a rendezvous, in Long-acre, for drinking and business. I have been told that their chief consul is an old stager above forty years' standing, who is nearly blind, and worn out; but of this I cannot answer for the truth.

Their system is brought to such perfection, that if your dog only turns round a corner, out of your sight, he is liable to be instantly enticed away, at a rapid pace, by the never-failing means of ———. Their plan is to take the dog off to one of the most distant of the dens, from where the robbery is committed, and there keep him, in safe and close confinement, till the "customer," as they term it, shall advertise a reward amounting to what they think rather more than half the value; or, to use their own words, "*chanted*" at a price that will "*fetch*" him. On this being offered, you will generally recover your dog; because their agent of the district, who is always on the look-out for "*chants*," will either go or send to you with the joyful tidings of your favourite; pretending, at the same time, with an oily tongue and pious face, that he gets nothing by it, "except *vot* your honour will be pleased to give" him "for" his "trouble," in addition to the advertised reward. But the man who actually steals the dog never appears in the business; by which he avoids all risk of being "had up." The club find that this plan answers much better, and is less liable to detection, than offering the dogs for sale; particularly as they frequently get possession of the same dog several times. There have been instances of their being paid fifteen guineas, in successive rewards, for one lady's lap-dog that was perhaps not worth ten shillings. If a dog is not "*chanted*," before he becomes all but starved, they kill him, and sell the skin; unless it should so happen that they have orders from "gentlemen"!! for dogs—an opportunity of starting him for Scotland, Ireland, &c.—or can find an immediate purchaser, who will give a few shillings more than the skin would produce. If "hard up" for "blunt," however, some of them will go and sell the dogs in the streets, as soon as possible after they have caught them: but, *of course*, in a diametrically *opposite part of the town* from *where they found them.* Here they sometimes cheat their own society: but of this they think nothing, and will even rob one another. "Dog rob dog," is their slang, and standing motto.

All thieves have the knack of instantly quieting even the fiercest watch dogs, by throwing them a kind of narcotic ball. This they call "*puddening*" them. By means of which recipe, some of the "Fancy" go journeys, to execute particular orders at a long distance from London. Be very cautious, therefore, before whom you boast about the goodness of your dogs; or what you feel a pride in, may be the very means of your losing them; because when "fancy men," in any line of "business," have orders to execute, they will assume all trades and disguises, and thus ingratiate themselves with the very servants of your household, in order to "suck" them for information. The following circumstance is a specimen of their town manœuvres:

In the month of May, 1830, Mr. Lang (of the celebrated shooting gallery and excellent gun repository in the Haymarket) lost a favourite setter. He posted handbills, offering two guineas reward; on hearing of which a man came and told him the reward was not enough; but that, if he would make it *four* guineas, he could find his dog; and the amount must be deposited in the hands of a landlord, who would procure him a ticket-card. He should then be met, to his appointment, in some private field, where he would receive his dog; on condition that no questions should be asked. Mr. Lang sent his shopman, about *half past ten at night*, to White Conduit Fields, to meet the parties, who, on receiving the ticket, delivered up the dog. But there was great hesitation in transacting *this* affair, in consequence of the dog having on a *lock* to a steel chain collar, with Mr. Lang's name; and which therefore induced them to proceed with extreme caution, through fear, as they supposed, of detection for *felony*. The whole amount, paid for recovering this setter, was 4*l*. 17*s*.—2*l*. 10*s*. of which went to the man who had him. The rest was divided among others of the "Fancy." The same person who gave Mr. Lang the information said that, if ever he lost a dog and applied to him, he could undertake to get him back again within thirty-six hours, provided he would make it worth his while to do so; because all dogs taken by the "Fancy" are brought to their office, and regularly booked by the secretary. But if a word is said about *law*, the dog is immediately put to death; and either buried skin and all, or sent to the bottom of a pond.

As an instance of this—

A gentleman who had lost a dog offered *twenty guineas* to recover him; and *twenty guineas more* for the *apprehension* of the thief, or even the name of any one concerned in the robbery. In consequence of the *latter* part of the advertisement, the dog was instantly *destroyed*. Whereas, had nothing but the first clause been placarded, the dog would have been restored without loss of time. On destroying this dog one of the "Fancy" observed to his associates, "Vot 's the wally of twenty pound compared to a man's life? !"

(under an idea, it is presumed, that the theft was aggravated by some very strong case.)

If any one of the society was known to be untrue to his comrades, or, as they call it, not "blue" to his trade, he would be marked; and, if he was discovered in getting any of them apprehended, they would, sooner or later, "settle his hash."

It is somewhat extraordinary, among so many opulent people who have been thus robbed, that no one should have ever set a trap for some of these worthies. Because nothing could be more easily done, by risking a few useless dogs, and expending a little money, without which, of course, no business can be executed in a workmanlike manner. A quarto volume might be filled with anecdotes, specimens of the "march of intellect"—the fruits of "a little learning"—under this head. But, having now relieved our attention from the dry subject of the *law*, by a momentary glance at the manœuvres of the *lawless* (and I trust a sufficient one to make young sportsmen look sharp after their dogs), I will proceed with my other gleanings from the chaos of technical jargon.

TRESPASS.

We have still the old action for trespass against one who goes on land, &c. after notice; or even if the judge shall certify, on the back of the record, that the trespass was *wilful* and malicious.

An unlicensed person may accompany a licensed sportsman, *provided he has neither gun nor dogs of his own;* and a servant may assist by beating bushes, &c. for his master.

EXEMPTIONS FROM TRESPASS BEFORE AND AFTER NOTICE.

A person, *even after notice,* may go on the land of another, to serve a subpœna, legal writ, or, in short, for any lawful purpose.

It was formerly supposed, that any one might go over the land of another *(not doing any real damage)* while hunting a *wild* fox, as a "noxious animal;" but, upon late trials, it has appeared, that *following fox hounds will in no way justify a trespass.*

The defendant therefore stands about the same chance

of escaping the verdict by following foxhounds, as the plaintiff *(in a case not aggravated)* would have of being pitied by sportsmen, if ducked in a horse-pond for bringing such an action of trespass!

NOTICES

[N. B. While (as at present) we have a *summary penalty* for trespassing in *pursuit of game,* it may be thought useless to reprint any thing relative to *notices.* But, as there may be some persons who prefer the old mode of proceeding, I shall let the matter stand, as before, for their information.]

May be personally served, or left at the place of abode of the party.

Verbal notices are quite sufficient, if accurately proved.

All notices to come from *the tenant,* and *not* from the *landlord,* who cannot support an action of trespass upon the land, of which *he is not the occupier.* [*Sed quere?* since the new act.]

Gamekeepers, *or other persons,* may be deputed *to serve* either verbal or written notices, by lords of manors, occupiers of land, &c.

SPECIFIC INSTRUCTIONS HOW TO WARN OFF A TRESPASSER.

FORM OF A PROPER NOTICE TO BE SENT TO, OR SERVED ON, ANY PERSON IN PARTICULAR.

To *(name the person's Christian and surnames)* of *(name his residence.)*

I hereby give you notice, not to enter or come into or upon any of the lands, woods, underwoods, shaws, or coverts [or into or upon any of the rivers, ponds, pools, waters, or watercourses] in my occupation, in the parish of *(name the parish; or, if the lands lie in more than one, the several parishes),* in the county of *(name the county or counties),* as, in case of your doing so, I shall proceed against you as a wilful trespasser.—Witness my hand this *(name the day of the month)* day of *(name month)* 1833.

(Sign your name.)

The sentence, within the crotchet, relative to "waters," may, of course, be adopted or not, as required.

In a case of joint occupation, the notice must, of

course, be given in the first person plural, with both signatures.

This written or printed notice had better be served by delivery of a *duplicate* than of a mere copy; and would be still more unquestionable, if the person serving it was able to prove the *signatures to each duplicate*, and the identity of the person served.

In case of warning off a trespasser, a second person, for a witness, is sometimes desirable, though *not absolutely necessary*, unless it may become so by death. This, *or any other* notice, in a *newspaper*, is of no avail unless it can be *proved*, that the defendant *had read* it.

Suppose, then, a trespasser comes on the land, when the occupier cannot be found to sign a notice, what is to be done?

The occupier, to be guarded against this, should previously and *bona fide* have given directions to any person, who is actually his servant, to forbid all trespassers; by which that person, in his absence, may *say*:—

> "Sir; by order of my master, Mr.   , who is the occupier of this land, I am directed to forbid all persons from trespassing on it; and I accordingly *forbid you* from trespassing on it."

To prevent the possibility of mistake, let every servant be taught to say the above as regularly as a catholic would repeat his breviary; and not, as many thickheaded clodpolls do, by saying, "*Zur, I've a got measter's arders to farbed ivery body*," by which nothing personal is implied.

In case of a verbal notice, a witness, in addition to

the one serving it, would be desirable, particularly if this *witness also* was quite perfect in the *preamble.* By this means he may, on being cross-questioned, candidly own, that he had learnt it by heart; and, if not terrified, or browbeaten into a blunder in the repetition of it, by the *modesty* or ingenuity of a cross examination, he would very soon *prove* the *legality* of the *verbal notice* he had given.

With less pains taken to warn persons off than what is prescribed in the foregoing notices, there is little doubt but there would be ground for an action of wilful trespass. From my very humble knowledge in such matters, however, I have thought it best to dictate with extreme, and therefore, possibly, with unnecessary caution.

FORM OF A GENERAL NOTICE,

Which, after all, may be the *best* to answer *every* purpose.

The following printed notice, signed by yourself and all your tenants, will save much trouble, and be found extremely useful; as it may be read, or even shown by any common labourer. By this means, therefore, your carters, your shepherds, or the most humble person in *or out* of your service, may at all times be empowered to warn off immediately any stranger, whom they might find trespassing on your estate.

Let the person (while merely *showing* the notice) say:—

Sir; here is my authority, and I accordingly forbid *you* from trespassing on this estate.

FORM OF THE NOTICE.

We, the undersigned, do hereby authorise
, the bearer of this notice, to warn off all persons whom he may find shooting, or otherwise trespassing, on any of the lands [or waters] in our respective occupations, situate in the parish [or parishes] of
, in the county [or counties] of
and we do declare, that we will prosecute, as a wilful trespasser, any person whomsoever continuing or coming upon our lands after having been enjoined to quit by the said , pursuant to this our notice.

Signed by us, this day of , 18

Here follow the signatures of the *landholder* and *all* his *tenants*.

The foregoing directions, with respect to *notices*, are, I trust, all that can be required either for landlords, tenants, keepers, or their printers.

DOGS, TRESPASS OF.

An unqualified person cannot *use* dogs for sporting, although they may be *bona fide* the property of one who is qualified.

If an unlicensed person *keeps* a dog for sporting, he is liable to the penalty of 5*l.* and also to have his dog *seized*, as becoming the property of the lord of the manor. But it would, perhaps, be prudent for the lord, or his keeper, first to *seize* the dog, *before* he ventured to shoot or destroy him.

It is a common trick among low farmers and poachers, who keep a wirehaired greyhound, or a lurcher, to cut his tail, and *pass him off for a sheep-dog*. The most effectual way to prosecute an offender of this description is, *first*, to lodge an information against him for *keeping such a dog*; and, *after that is paid*, for the lord of the manor, or his keeper, to *lay hands on the dog*, after which he becomes the property of the lord, and may then, by him or his keeper, be safely taken, shot, or otherwise destroyed, in *any place within the limits of that lord's manor.*

In case, however, that doubts should exist as to the dog being of the description specified in the act ("greyhound, setting dog, or lurcher,") it has been suggested, that it would be advisable, in lodging the information, to use the word *setting dog* as a kind of general term. This point I must leave to the more experienced to judge; but, was an unqualified person actually *seen using any dog* in the *destruction of game, I* should then, if he had *no certificate,* put him in the hands of the *tax-gatherers;* where he would find himself in a sort of *hornets' nest,* from which there would be *very little hope of escape.*

By the 52 Geo. III. cap. xciii. s. 8. (the act relating to *certificates)* " *hound, pointer, spaniel,* or *other dog*" is added.

For farther information on this, *vide* under " Time within which Actions must be brought."

One who is warned off a ground, and *sends* his dog thereon, *is* as much *liable to an action of trespass,* as if he went there himself.

WASTE LAND,

Sporting on, the exclusive right of the lord of a manor.

It has been given as an opinion, that, although a person may, by *common rights,* have the liberty of *going, sending* or *keeping his cattle,* on the *waste land,* yet he has no right to go *there,* in pursuit of *game,* without leave from the lord of the manor.

FREE WARRENS AND DECOYS.

The game, in a *free warren,* is considered as *private property,* as are also the wildfowl, &c. within a decoy; and, consequently, a person sporting on either, would be subject to an action *accordingly* (with costs), and without receiving any previous notice.

The exercise of a *free warren*, however, is, in most cases, now difficult to be proved.

WILDFOWL.

Any one may shoot *them on the coast, from a public path, &c. &c.*

Where a person, with neither permission from the lord of the manor nor licence, has a right to carry a gun, provided he does not use it for the destruction of *game.*

The shooting of *wildfowl,* therefore (according to the best professional opinions I have collected), is such a use as cannot be deemed an illegal one.

It is said, that a lord of a manor, or his keeper, cannot seize the gun of *any person whatever,* unless it has been used, by the person carrying it, in destroying, or with an intent to destroy *game.* *(Sed quere?)*

TIME WITHIN WHICH ACTIONS MUST BE BROUGHT.

The time prescribed for bringing an action of *trespass,* affecting land (which is called an action *quare clausum fregit*), for the recovery of *damages,* is SIX YEARS.

With regard to cases where the possibility of bringing an action, within the limited time, might be precluded by the *absence* of *either party,* I have thought it advisable to put the following questions to two gentlemen who are eminent in the profession, for the purpose of here giving brief directions as to what should be done.

Question. Supposing A should trespass on the lands of B, while B is beyond the sea, can B sue for the trespass after his return?

Answer. He can, provided he commences his action against A within the time limited (*by the* 21 *Jac.* 1., *cap.* 16) after his return, which is six years, and which would run from the time of his return.

Question. Again, supposing A and B both be in the kingdom, and A, after having committed a trespass on the lands of B, should leave the kingdom, or withdraw himself to a distant part of it, and there secrete himself, until the period, within which an action may be commenced, is expired, can B afterwards sue him for the trespass?

Answer. No, he cannot, as his right of action will be barred by the statute, *unless* he sue out a writ within the limited period, and, if A's residence be unknown, and he cannot be met with, to be served with it, or he should continue out of the kingdom, the action may be kept on foot, by proper continuances, regularly filed, till A *can* be met with; and THEN B, if he can get him served, may proceed with his action after the expiration of such period, the same as if A had been served within it.

LORDS OF MANORS.

Since the several inclosure acts, doubts have been entertained, whether lords of manors have a right to sport over the freehold of any other person, within the manor, after notice; or whether a deputation to a gamekeeper will justify his going on any grounds, except the lord's own soil?—CLEARLY NOT.

A *lord of a manor*, or his *gamekeeper* (unless in a *free warren*, or by an *especial right reserved*, in letting or selling property), *cannot* sport on the land of another, without being *liable to the same action as any other trespasser;* neither can *he* prevent those, who are qualified, from sporting *(on the grounds not his own)* within the manor. But the lord of a manor, or even a *reputed* manor (and his keeper too, it is here presumed), is *not liable* to the NEW PENALTY *for trespass, while within the bounds of the said manor.*

ACT

PASSED SINCE THE FIFTH EDITION.

PERSONS FOUND AT NIGHT ARMED WITH INTENT TO KILL GAME.

By 9 Geo. IV. c. 69, it is enacted that persons taking or destroying game by night, viz. from the first hour after sunset till the first hour before sunrise, should be committed for the first offence for three months, and second offence for six months, and in both cases kept to hard labour and find sureties, and for the third offence be liable to be transported.

Owners or occupiers of land, lords of manors, or their servants, may apprehend offenders, who, if they offer violence, are deemed guilty of misdemeanour, and liable to be transported for seven years, or imprisoned for two years. Limitation of time for proceeding under this Act, one year.

Three persons entering land *armed* by night, for the purpose of taking game, &c., a misdemeanour punishable by transportation or imprisonment. Game within this Act deemed to include hares, pheasants, partridges, grouse, heath- or moor-game, black game, and bustards.

The preceding abstracts may perhaps be useful as a little directory to the principal game laws, in which most persons are liable to be concerned, and many of which are necessary to protect the rights and liberties of the people. But we could not have chosen a more insipid subject for the climax of a book, than any thing relating to *Law*. My reason, however, for having left this till the last article, of the present edition, is to reserve the power of entering any alteration that may hereafter take place in the Game Laws, without deranging the pages of my humble " Instructions to Young Sportsmen."

THE END.